FOOD & DRINK TOURISM

SAGE was founded in 1965 by Sara Miller McCune to support the dissemination of usable knowledge by publishing innovative and high-quality research and teaching content. Today, we publish over 900 journals, including those of more than 400 learned societies, more than 800 new books per year, and a growing range of library products including archives, data, case studies, reports, and video. SAGE remains majority-owned by our founder, and after Sara's lifetime will become owned by a charitable trust that secures our continued independence.

Los Angeles | London | New Delhi | Singapore | Washington DC | Melbourne

Sally Everett

FOOD & DRINK TOURISM

Principles and Practice

Los Angeles | London | New Delhi
Singapore | Washington DC | Melbourne

Los Angeles | London | New Delhi
Singapore | Washington DC | Melbourne

SAGE Publications Ltd
1 Oliver's Yard
55 City Road
London EC1Y 1SP

SAGE Publications Inc.
2455 Teller Road
Thousand Oaks, California 91320

SAGE Publications India Pvt Ltd
B 1/I 1 Mohan Cooperative Industrial Area
Mathura Road
New Delhi 110 044

SAGE Publications Asia-Pacific Pte Ltd
3 Church Street
#10-04 Samsung Hub
Singapore 049483

Editor: Matthew Waters
Editorial assistant: Lyndsay Aitken
Production editor: Sarah Cooke
Copyeditor: Mary Dalton
Proofreader: Katie Forsythe
Indexer: Jess Farr-Cox
Marketing manager: Alison Borg
Cover design: Francis Kenney
Typeset by: C&M Digitals (P) Ltd, Chennai, India
Printed and bound by CPI Group (UK) Ltd,
Croydon, CR0 4YY

Library of Congress Control Number: 2015952317

British Library Cataloguing in Publication data

A catalogue record for this book is available from
the British Library

ISBN 978-1-4462-6772-1
ISBN 978-1-4462-6773-8 (pbk)

To my parents and Em – my love of food and drink stems
from happy memories travelling the world with you.

CONTENTS

ABOUT THE AUTHOR

Dr Sally Everett is Deputy Dean (Quality and Student Experience) at the Lord Ashcroft International Business School, Anglia Ruskin University and is a Principal Fellow of the Higher Education Academy. Dr Everett was Senior Lecturer in Tourism at the University of Bedfordshire, before becoming its Head of Tourism, Leisure and Sport Management, and then the Head of Marketing, Tourism and Hospitality. In 2013 she became a Deputy Dean at Anglia Ruskin University.

Her research interests include business education pedagogies, food tourism, and rural tourism development and visitor management. She has published widely in the subject area of food tourism, with many papers in peer-reviewed international tourism journals. Sally loves to travel the world and takes every opportunity to eat and drink the local food on offer wherever she may be.

ACKNOWLEDGEMENTS

I am most grateful to my friends, family and colleagues who have supported this project and provided me with many wonderful photographs and accounts of their food and drink tourism experiences. I am blessed to have such well-travelled and adventurous 'foodie' friends. I travel a lot, but I am yet to see many of the amazing places they have seen, and tasted. My thanks must also go to everyone who allowed me to take their photo during my trips with them (work and leisure). In particular, I would like to thank my dear friend Julie Pottinger who is happiest when she is exploring the world – her photos of coffee tourism in Bali, whisky in Laos and cookery schools in Thailand have been gratefully received. Thanks must also go to my colleagues Sandra for the Oktoberfest images, Amanda for the Milan Expo, and Nadith and Denham for helping me obtain tea tourism images in Sri Lanka. I have many friends who supported this project from day one, but I owe much to Hele and Julie who have listened to me talking about food and travel for over 20 years now!

I am very fortunate as the Deputy Dean of the Lord Ashcroft International Business School at Anglia Ruskin University to have the opportunity to travel to our numerous international partners. A large number of the photos were taken during those visits and so I am very grateful to the senior management team for establishing so many wonderful franchise arrangements around the world. The extent and variety of our international partnerships is a real blessing.

I would like to acknowledge the kindness and interest in my work shown by a number of organisations, owners and managers who have provided me with images, quotes and ideas. I must thank Heribert Gaksch, Marketing Director at PB Valley Khao Yai Winery in Thailand; Halpe Tea, UHE Exports (pvt) Ltd in Sri Lanka; 98 Acres Resort Sri Lanka; Regency Teas in Colombo, Sri Lanka; Christina at the Eko Mosaik project in Bosnia Herzegovina; Sally Lynch of Taste Trekkers; Karisma Kreatif; Visit Penang; Trip Advisor Ozlem Warren; Red Tractor Assurance Scheme, and all the many companies used as case studies within these chapters. I also want to thank the publishers of food and drink tourism articles who have given me permission to reproduce data and figures in this book: Taylor & Francis, SAGE Publishing, and Elsevier, and my co-authors of previously published papers on this subject, Cara Aitchison and Susan Slocum.

A special thanks must go to my good friend Jess who was my professional proofreader extraordinaire! Despite having an extremely busy schedule, she was able to turn around my draft chapters within hours – expert, professional and efficient (www.thefilthycomma.co.uk/). Her jokes and observations in the margins of my manuscript were a very welcome distraction!

I must also thank Matt, Molly, Lyndsay and Sarah at SAGE Publishing. They have been very patient with me, especially when I got a new job in the middle of writing the manuscript which meant I had to renegotiate my original deadlines. Your guidance and interest in my book has been very much appreciated.

My heartfelt thanks to my loving parents for introducing me to wonderful parts of the world during family holidays. Their love of food and drink has certainly manifested itself in my academic work and writings. From childhood holidays in the wild islands of Scotland to the intense flavours of my mother's homeland in Malaysia, I developed a keen palate and deep love of exotic and identity-infused food from a very early age.

Finally, I must thank my soulmate and fellow food-loving travelling partner, Em. I would not have managed to complete this book without you (and our darling dog Obi). I owe you so very much (especially when I force you to pose in photos and visit food festivals!). Thank you for your patience, understanding and love – especially in the final few months when we should have been having a summer holiday and organising our wedding! You have believed in me from the beginning, and this book would have remained incomplete without your encouragement, love and cooking that keep me fed and watered during those long writing sessions!

Writing this book has been a truly wonderful experience, and it has opened my taste buds and senses to many amazing places. I hope you enjoy this book as much as I enjoyed writing it. Taste and savour the world – it's the only way to truly appreciate and know it!

INTRODUCTION (AN APPETISER)

THE AIMS OF THIS BOOK

Whether it is tasting local cheese at a family-run dairy in Holland, sampling bread at a market in France, learning to prepare spicy dishes in Thailand, drinking tea in a Sri Lankan plantation, or working on an organic farm in South America, travelling for food and drink experiences has become a popular tourist activity and this book is dedicated to this growing field of interest and culinary engagement. Food and drink are central to the touristic experience. This textbook aims to provide a comprehensive and engaging reference resource on food and drink tourism and food-motivated travel and leisure. It offers a multi-disciplinary approach to the subject and has been written to support any course that looks at food and drink related travel. It aims to provide an accessible text that acknowledges that this subject area must be informed by many academic fields within the social sciences and business education. It embraces theories and examples from numerous subject disciplines, including tourist studies, tourism management, cultural studies, business, sociology, marketing, politics, geography, business, event management and hospitality. By offering a multi-disciplinary perspective, it aims to provide a student-focused, research-informed, and relevant book for anyone interested in food and drink tourism.

This text feeds a growing interest in the area of food and drink travel and tourism as new courses and modules continue to develop around issues of rural regeneration, economic renewal, sustainability, production, consumption, destination promotion, special interest tourism, agri-tourism, research-informed policy and various health and well-being agendas. This book not only acknowledges the business and economic value of food, but also seeks to raise awareness of its cultural value and contribution to society through discussion and analysis. Food is one of the central commodities of economic commercial exchange in the world, and is one of the few goods that is physically internalised and consumed for basic human survival and pleasure. Studies of food in the social sciences have traditionally pursued analyses of cultural engagement and identity, but in combination with tourism, this 'food/drink' and 'tourism' partnership also provides a focus of study for anyone interested in some of the major challenges facing the world today, such as climate change, sustainability, poverty alleviation and rural deprivation (illustrated by case studies from around the world).

This book provides a research-informed approach that considers a multiplicity of academic fields, whilst integrating issues relating to current policy and practice in an interactive, informative and student-friendly format. It draws together many of the current key texts and models used to support university courses into one central resource. It also seeks to stimulate and support the growth of higher education provision in all areas that look at food tourism, niche tourism, cultural tourism, events, rural development, agricultural policy and diversification. This text uses different pedagogic approaches, perspectives and examples to illustrate many of the diverse and international dimensions of food and drink tourism. It is supported by research, critical theory reflections, real-life case studies, student exercises, diagrams, policy documents, media excerpts and activities, and discusses some of the most recent examples of food and drink tourism from around the globe. Furthermore, as part of these discussions, the book supports an employability agenda and gives an overview of many potential employment and career opportunities in this exciting sector of tourism (see the 'Working with Food and Drink Tourism' boxes).

This text consists of 22 stand-alone chapters so that each can be read on its own if you are particularly interested in a specific topic, or you can use it to support a full course or module and read it from start to finish, completing the exercises as you progress through the chapters. It has been written to support both undergraduate and postgraduate studies and suggests Further Reading if you wish to explore any of the areas in more detail. The book is structured into three main thematic parts: the growth and development of food and drink tourism (Part One), the promotion and branding of food and drink tourism (Part Two), and food and drink attractions and events (Part Three). In the first part, the chapters start by asking 'what is food tourism?' and the food tourist, before looking at the history of culinary exploration, its development as a niche form of tourism, its links to globalisation and localisation, its relationship to agricultural policy and how the topic areas have developed from parent subject fields such as wine tourism (Chapter 7), which has informed much of the work on food tourism. The second part is dedicated to issues of marketing, and the chapters address branding, product design, regional marketing organisation and agencies, and interpretation at food tourism sites. Finally, the third part seeks to bring the concepts and ideas alive in a series of chapters looking at how food and drink tourism has manifested itself in a number of global contexts. These chapters cover a wide range of specific events and international initiatives, including farmers' markets, food festivals, trails, niche drink tourism experiences, museums, sustainable development projects, visitor attractions and supply chain interventions, and concludes with a chapter looking at the future of food and drink tourism. As the Case Study of Skibbereen in Ireland illustrates, food and drink tourism can bring significant rewards to a locality and a community, but often starts from very humble beginnings (for further information see www.atasteofwestcork.com).

Small beginnings for the Taste of West Cork Food Festival,
Skibbereen, Ireland

FIGURE 0.1   *Skibbereen Food Festival visitor, West Ireland. Photo by author*

FIGURE 0.2   *Skibbereen Food Festival sign, West Ireland. Photo by author*

West Cork in Ireland is at the vanguard of Ireland's culinary revolution. Irish food had a poor reputation until the 1970s, when the food renaissance emerged most significantly in West Cork – a revival attributed to a young Dublin couple who migrated to the area to make cheese. It has been suggested that it is the high levels of in-migration to the area that accounts for its more advanced status of speciality food production. Today, the area has Ireland's greatest concentration of artisan food producers where artisans have 'won the moral victory for real food over the last fifteen years' (McKenna and McKenna 2010: 2). It is rapidly establishing itself as the food tourism centre of Ireland, with its local food producers inspiring substantial work on local food initiatives and networks. The successful development of the Fuchsia Brand, especially its 'Taste of West Cork' food tourism initiative, is further evidence of the commitment to promoting quality food with a local provenance and distinctive identity. West Cork is a clear example of a place with an 'emerging gastronomic identity', a region where 'gastro speak' is commonplace, and the heart of this is Skibbereen, which hosts the annual food and drink festival.

The hugely successful and popular Skibbereen Food Festival in West Cork, Ireland started from humble beginnings. In an interview with a local fish-smoker at the market, she recalls,

> 'There were six of us who started the market in Skibbereen; it was a grey area, not sure if we would get arrested! As even though the land we were on had been covenanted to the town twice before 1900, cattle, sheep, food had been traded there before. But a group that sold all this then sold it, I don't understand how they could sell something that wasn't theirs. It was all tied up in legal red tape. We thought the Fairfield was covenanted so we traded there. It was really good socialising because when you work and you are small, you tend to get lost in your own little world and problems arise and its get to bounce things off somebody ... that group of people now share the market.' (Everett 2007: 197)

Further information:

A Taste of West Cork, details available from: www.fuchsiabrands.com/home.

McKenna, J. and McKenna, S. (2010) *The Bridgestone Irish Food Guide* (The Bridgestone Guides). Cork: Estragon Press.

This brief introduction is aimed at 'whetting your appetite' for future chapters in this book as well as providing you with an outline of its key features and pedagogic approaches. So before you progress to the first chapter, which looks at 'what is food and drink tourism?', and 'who is the food tourist?' and assesses the value and contribution of food tourism to key global agendas such as poverty alleviation and environmental sustainability, it is important to introduce some of these key features. One of these elements is the use of international case studies like that featured above for West Cork in Ireland. These have been provided to give real-life context to the discussions and should help you link theory to practice. Secondly, the textbook provides 'Critical Reflections' boxes, so watch out for these! These aim to provide additional information and should be especially helpful for final year projects or postgraduate study of the subject. These boxes encourage you to consider and explore more complex issues, theories and perspectives. They are especially useful if you are looking to study a particular aspect of food and drink tourism in greater detail, because they will introduce you to additional theoretical perspectives, conceptual frameworks and critical theory in relation to food and drink tourism. Examples of some of these perspectives include Marxism, post-structuralism, postmodernism, thinking from the Frankfurt School, theories of Fordism/neo Fordism, (post)colonialism, Foucauldian approaches, and critical tourism perspectives.

Another key feature of this textbook is the 'Working with food and drink tourism' box. This is an innovative addition to many new textbooks and it is aimed at promoting an employability agenda and guiding you in your career choices.

Working with food and drink tourism

Once you have read the first few chapters, you will realise that food and drink tourism is a rapidly growing sector. This has meant employment opportunities are emerging all the time around the world. Look out for the 'Working with food and drink tourism' boxes, as this book will give you some employment ideas and information at the end of each chapter about working in the various sectors which draw from, and contribute to, food and drink tourism. You might be interested in a job and career in food tourism policy development, or wish to work in the hospitality industry in hotels or restaurants, or manage a food/drink tourism visitor attraction, or become a food event organiser, or an interpretation and education officer. You might be surprised by the number of opportunities that are open to you in this vast and eclectic field of tourism.

END OF CHAPTER POINTS

In addition to an introduction and key objectives at the start of each chapter, you will also find a set of key learning points at the end of each chapter. These 'End of Chapter Points' are aimed at providing a brief summary of the chapter you have just read and to help you revise and revisit some of the most important issues, themes and points relating to food tourism.

FURTHER READING

Finally, a section on 'Further Reading' is provided at the end of each chapter to encourage you to learn more about the different topics and undertake your own investigations beyond the boundaries of this textbook. Many of the sections will provide references to key books, journal articles, policy documents and websites. The 'Further Reading' section will list the most relevant sources used in the chapter to enable you to delve more deeply into some of the key issues and concepts. *Bon Appétit!*

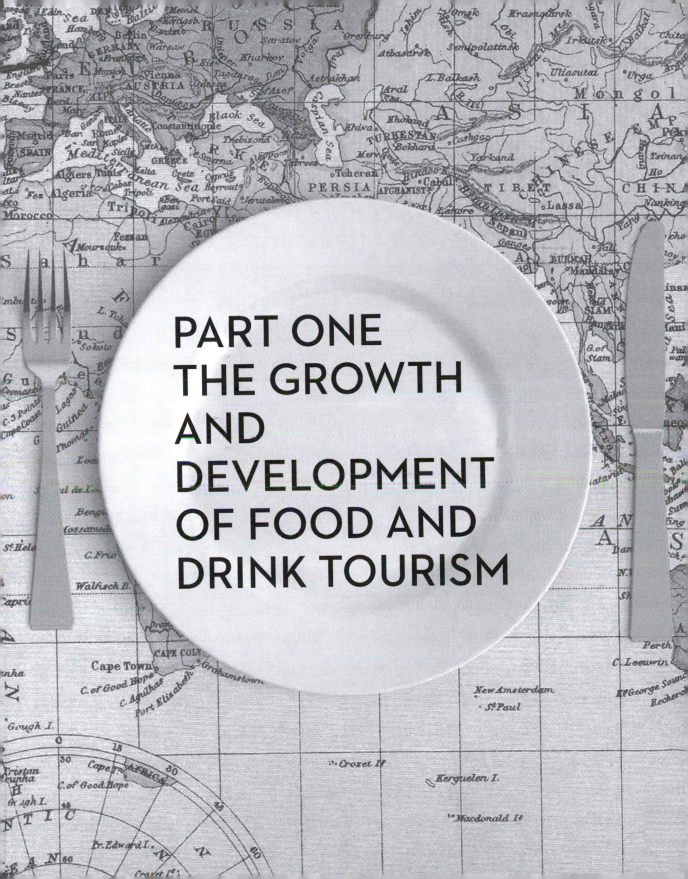

PART ONE
THE GROWTH AND DEVELOPMENT OF FOOD AND DRINK TOURISM

1

WHAT IS FOOD AND DRINK TOURISM?

CHAPTER OBJECTIVES

- To provide some definitions of food and drink tourism and related terms
- To introduce different typologies and models of food and drink tourists
- To illustrate the breadth and variety of the food and drink tourism on offer
- To assess the value and contribution of food and drink tourism to local communities, economies, and the environment
- To provide an introductory reading list covering topics throughout this book

CHAPTER SUMMARY

This first chapter introduces the concept of food and drink tourism. It provides definitions and models, and discusses the different typologies of the (food) tourist that have been used and adopted. It draws recent work together to provide an overview of the sector and its various components. In offering an outline of the different types of food and drink tourism (food tourism, gastronomic tourism, culinary tourism, special interest tourism, cultural tourism) and linking them with key aspects (such as events, festivals, trails, cookery, shops, museums, vineyards, breweries, restaurants), this chapter gives you a real 'taste' of what is covered in the rest of the book. The chapter briefly discusses the various components of food-motivated travel and outlines the size and scale of the industry.

Importantly, countries around the world are using food as a means to extend their tourist season, alleviate poverty, diversify their offer, and regenerate areas of deprivation (e.g. Rwanda, Malaysia, Mauritius and Croatia) and examples are provided to highlight the role and extensive reach of food tourism. It also provides a brief commentary on the emerging food and sustainability agenda, and outlines issues affecting global food and drink production and consumption today.

WHAT IS FOOD AND DRINK TOURISM?

There are numerous definitions of food and drink tourism and it is unlikely that we will ever agree upon one. It is probably best that one single definition is not established because it would undermine and overly simplify the very nature of this ever-changing, multi-faceted and complex activity. Similarly, as scholars have struggled to define 'tourism' due its multi-dimensional and contested nature, it would be misleading and unhelpful to frame 'food and drink tourism' within rigid conceptual boundaries. One of the main issues is what to even call the activity, because there are many terms and categories that cover slightly different aspects of food and drink tourism (and significantly overlap), which are summarised below (with wider forms of tourism acting as unifying terms) (Figure 1.1).

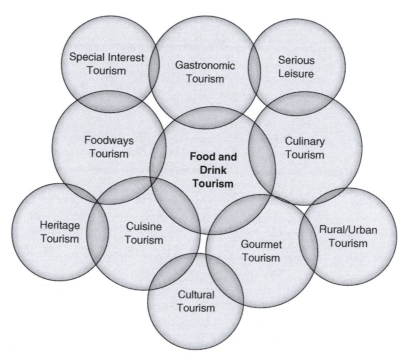

FIGURE 1.1 *Different types and categories of food and drink tourism*

Perhaps one of the broadest definitions given for food tourism is provided by the World Food Travel Association (WFTA, 2015) (previously known as the International Culinary Tourism Association), as 'something every visitor does' (see http://worldfoodtravel.org). This is certainly testament to its centrality in the tourism experience, although perhaps its vagueness makes this term rather meaningless. Academic scholars have also offered definitions of 'food tourism', which vary over whether food should be the primary motivation, or merely part of the overall touristic experience. The most cited definition to date is Hall and Mitchell (2001: 308), which is the 'visitation to primary and secondary food producers, food festivals, restaurants and specific locations for which food tasting and/or experiencing the attributes of specialist food production regions are the primary motivating factor for travel'. It is the desire to experience a particular type of food or the produce of a specific region. Certainly Hall and his fellow authors (Hall et al., 2003) regarded it as a form of 'serious leisure' (Stebbins, 2007). Another useful definition of food/culinary tourism was provided by Long (2004: 7):

> Culinary tourism is any tourism experience in which one learns about, appreciates, or consumes branded local culinary resources. In other words, culinary tourism is an intentional and reflective encounter with any culture, including one's own through culinary resources. Culinary tourism encompasses travel specifically motivated by culinary interests as well as travel in which culinary experiences occur but are not the primary motivation for the trip.

Perhaps it could simply be defined as 'food and drink motivated travel', which reflects any level of desire to engage in an experience involving food and drink away from home (primary or secondary motivation). Other types and sectors of tourism also include elements of food and drink tourism, such as cultural tourism (attractions and local cuisines), festival and event tourism (food and drink festivals and events), and heritage tourism (museums and places of production). It is its embedded nature that makes it difficult to define and pin down, but simultaneously ensures it should be at the forefront of any curriculum looking at tourism.

However, this book primarily focuses on activities undertaken by those who make a conscious effort to visit specific food/drink tourism sites (premeditated (primary) or decision once in the location (secondary)) and those who consciously produce and deliver these experiences, rather than an exploration of the more generic hospitality sector in tourism (although this is briefly discussed in the context of the supply chain in Chapter 20). Food and drink tourism is certainly an eclectic term, if not a phenomenon, and covers myriad different aspects of the touristic experience. An indicative typology of culinary tourism is provided below, adapted from Smith and Xiao (2008: 290). It highlights the multiplicity of experiences that can be associated with this area of tourism, illustrating the diverse characteristics and elements of this sphere of tourism activity.

TABLE 1.1 *Food and Drink Tourism types, Smith and Xiao 2008: 290*

Facilities	Events	Activities	Organisations
Building/structures	Consumer shows	Consumption	
Food processing facilities	Food and drink shows	Dining at restaurants	Restaurant classifications or certification systems
Wineries/Breweries	Cooking equipment (kitchen shows)	Picnics utilising locally-grown products	Food/wine classification systems (organic, etc.)
Farmers' markets	Product launches	Purchasing retail food/beverages	Associations (e.g. Slow Food)
Food stores	Festivals	Pick your own operations	
Food-related museums	Food festivals	Touring	
Restaurants	Wine festivals	Wine regions	
Land uses	Harvest festival	Agricultural regions	
Farms		City food districts	
Orchards		Educational observation	
Vineyards		Cooking schools	
Urban restaurant districts		Wine tasting/ education	
Routes		Visiting wineries	
Wine routes		Observing chef competitions	
Food routes		Reading food, beverage	
Gourmet trails		Magazines and books	

WHO IS THE FOOD TOURIST?

Lacy and Douglass (2002: 8) claim that 'every tourist is a voyeuring gourmand' and indeed all tourists eat and drink; however, this may be a little simplistic when we wish to look more closely at the market. Rather, the food and drink 'tourist' should be conceptualised on a spectrum from someone with very high interest where the primary motivation is to engage in food and drink related activities in line with the 'food tourist' or 'gastronome' to low and no interest (no interest in food and drink and likely to avoid local food establishments, equating to the 'laggard'). The seminal tourist typology by Cohen (1979) was taken by

Everett and Aitchison (2008) to examine the correlation between interest and food tourism type. A revised version is provided here to give an overview of the relationship between tourist 'type' and the level of spend, activity and market size (Figure 1.2). These aspects will be discussed further in Part 2.

Typologies			Propensity to pay more for local food	Food related activity (restaurant, farmers markets, local sales)	Cultural transmission and education	Number of tourists
Cohen (1979)	Mitchell and Hall (2003)	Enteleca Research (2001)				
Existential	Gastronome	Food tourists	High	High	High	High
Experimental		Interested purchasers				
	Indigenous foodies					
Experiential		Un-reached				
Diversionary	'Tourist' foodies					
		Unengaged				
Recreational	Familiar foods					
		Laggard				
			Low	Low	Low	Low

FIGURE 1.2   *The correlation between tourist type and food tourism engagement. (Source: Everett and Aitchison 2008, permission granted by publisher)*

There is clearly a growing general interest in trying local foods, visiting local markets and engaging with gastronomic establishments when on holiday. The Visit Scotland Visitor Survey (Visit Scotland, 2011) highlights the significant level of interest in trying local food, with its survey reporting that 52% of visitors wanted to try local foods (Table 1.2 presents data from this survey with food-related activity in bold).

It has been found that food and beverage constitute up to one-third of total tourist expenditure (Kim et al., 2009a; Meler and Cerović, 2003) and has become a distinct sector in the travel and tourism industry, rather than an inconsequential holiday necessity. The World Food Travel Association estimated that food tourism is worth nearly $8 billion each year in the United Kingdom (ICTA, 2012), which is testament to its contribution to the rapid growth of new forms of special interest and niche tourism. Although the spend per head on food and drink varies across locations and according to tourist markets, recent reports suggest tourists to the UK and USA spend 36% of their total expenditure on food and drink (ICTA, 2012), 21% or £700m/year in Scotland (Visit Scotland, 2011), and 33% in Northern Ireland (Northern Ireland Tourist Board, 2012). In Jamaica, the daily expenditure on food by the tourist is five times greater than that of the average

TABLE 1.2 *The value of food and drink tourism, data taken from the Visit Scotland Visitor Survey (2011)*

Activity	% visitors asked
Sightseeing by car/coach/foot	52
Trying local food	**52**
Visited historic house/stately home	47
Visited cities	47
Shopping	47
Short walk	45
Centre based walking	40
Visited cathedral/church/abbey	38
Visited museum/art gallery	38
Visited a country park/garden	36
Night out visiting pubs	**32**
Beach	29
Historic railway	21
Visited whisky distillery	**20**
Went on a guided tour	20
Had a picnic/BBQ	**20**
Watched wildlife	16

Jamaican, which highlights its important economic contribution. Research has found that among all possible areas of expenditures while travelling, tourists are least likely to make cuts in their food budget. Consequently, there are significant opportunities to work and get involved in this growing industry sector.

Working with food and drink tourism: a growing industry

Tourism is a fast growing global industry and in many parts of the world, employment in this sector is the largest sector in the country. Figures are mainly taken from the World Travel and Tourism Council (WTTC) which produces tourism reports of the economic and employment impact of 184 countries and 25 geographic or economic regions in the world.

Global picture

International tourist arrivals grew by 4.3 % in 2014 to 1.133 billion in 2015. In 2014, international tourism generated US$ 1.5 trillion in export earnings and contributed

10% of global GDP, and accounted for 1 in 11 jobs (UN World Tourism Organisation (WTO) 2015). The World Travel & Tourism Council (WTTC) anticipates that tourism will have a global value of US$ 10.8 trillion by 2018, almost double its present worth in 2015. The UN's World Tourism Organisation claims that by 2020, the number of travelling tourists will approach 1.6 billion. By 2022, it is anticipated that tourism will support 328 million jobs, or one in every ten jobs, and half will be in the food, hospitality and hotel sector. For example, by 2018, tourism is projected by the WTTC to be worth 80% of the GDP of Antigua and Barbuda, with 95% of all jobs there expected to be related in some way to tourism, which is the highest dependency on the planet (WTTC, 2015).

European Union

In the EU, the direct contribution of tourism to GDP was US$ 669.9bn (3.6% of total GDP) in 2014, and is forecast to rise by 3.0% in 2015, and to rise by 2.7% p.a. from 2015–2025, to US$ 898.7bn (4.0% of total GDP) in 2025 (WTTC, 2015). In 2014 tourism directly supported 11,062,000 jobs (5.0% of total employment). This is expected to rise by 2.3% in 2015 and by 1.5% p.a. to 13,123,000 jobs (5.7% of total employment) in 2025. In 2014, indirect jobs in the EU supported by the industry were 11.1% of total employment (24,694,000 jobs). This is expected to rise by 2.1% in 2015 to 25,206,500 jobs and by 1.2% p.a. to 28,367,000 jobs in 2025 (12.3% of total). By 2025, tourism and the Horeca (this term refers to hotel, restaurant and catering companies covering **H**otel/**R**estaurant/**C**afé) sector will account for 13,123,000 jobs directly, an increase of 1.5% p.a. over the next ten years.

United Kingdom

Based on the WTTC Travel & Tourism Economic Impact study (WTTC, 2015) the direct contribution of travel and tourism to GDP was GBP 61.9bn (3.5% of total GDP) in 2014, and is forecast to rise by 3.7% in 2015, and by 3.2% p.a., from 2015–2025, to GBP 88.2bn (3.7% of total GDP) in 2025. The total contribution of travel and tourism to GDP was GBP 187.7bn (10.5% of GDP) in 2014, and is forecast to rise by 4.0% in 2015, and by 3.1% p.a. to GBP 263.9bn (11.2% of GDP) in 2025. Travel and tourism generated 1,892,500 jobs directly in 2014 (5.7% of total employment) and this is forecast to grow by 2.1% in 2015 to 1,932,500 (5.7% of total employment). This includes employment by hotels, travel agents, airlines and other passenger transportation services (excluding commuter services). It also includes, for example, the activities of the restaurant and leisure industries directly supported by tourists. By 2025, tourism will account for 2,280,000 jobs directly, an increase of 1.7% p.a. over the next ten years. There are 249,000 tourism businesses in the UK (10% of the total number of businesses). Over 80% of tourism and hospitality industry businesses employ fewer than ten people. Turnover rates in the sector have declined significantly to 23% and 80% of people working in the sector are British (People 1st, 2011).

Source: WTTC 2015, Economic Impact Analysis. Available from: www.wttc.org/research/economic-research/economic-impact-analysis/regional-reports

Travelling to destinations in order to sample, taste and experience the food or drink of a particular region or culture is certainly not a new phenomenon; the human desire to experience place through the palette has a long and traceable history (as discussed in Chapter 2). However, there has been a significant rise in forms of tourism consumption that intimately engage with the gastronomic landscape (Hjalajer and Richards, 2002). As part of a rise in new consumption patterns and niche tourism activities (discussed in Chapter 4), food- and drink-motivated travel is gathering momentum. Within the past 20 years, food and drink have become significant 'pull' factors in their own right (Okumus et al., 2007), and provide a touristic framework on which to construct a destination's overall marketing strategy (discussed further in Part II on branding and marketing).

The World Travel Market spokesperson, Fiona Jeffery, exclaimed that 'food tourism is on the boil like never before, holiday makers are choosing where they go by what they can put into their stomachs… food tourism today is where ecotourism was 20 years ago' (World Travel Market 2008). This textbook has emerged from this gastronomic climate and seeks to engage with food tourism as a way of helping you explore and understand 'undigested' areas of tourism, culture, economic development and hospitality. By embracing different disciplinary theoretical and empirical 'ingredients', the book aims to provide you with a comprehensive and useful text that you can use to support your studies.

THE ROLE OF FOOD TOURISM IN ADDRESSING GLOBAL NEEDS

Food and drink tourism has a global role to play. Many countries are now using food as a way to extend their tourism season, alleviate poverty and regenerate deprived areas (Hall and Gössling, 2013). Rather than just focusing on the consumer and types of food tourism, this textbook is also concerned with providing an ethically aware analysis of food and drink tourism by considering the topics and issues within the wider sustainability agenda. This discussion is developed throughout the main chapters, but this introductory first chapter provides a brief commentary on the wider food and sustainability agenda and current issues affecting global food and drink production and engagement today.

As previously stated, food and drink tourism is not only about high-end gastronomic experiences, but encapsulates a growing interest in purchasing local produce, eating street food, meeting producers and enjoying culturally distinctive cuisines. Some of the fortuitous consequences of this increasingly popular culinary touristic activity include the prolonged circulation of tourism spend in the local economy and the reduced reliance on air-flown raw materials and emission-heavy mechanised production. These are all central components in seeking to deliver on sustainability goals and preserving communities and resources.

To give an example from a social and justice perspective, a shocking story reported in *Democracy Now* claimed that 'Every 30 Minutes: Crushed by Debt and Neoliberal Reforms, Indian Farmers Commit Suicide at Staggering Rate'

(*Democracy Now*, 2011). It elaborated on this shocking statement, which highlights the links between food, producers and poverty:

> A quarter of a million Indian farmers have committed suicide in the last 16 years – an average of one suicide every 30 minutes. The crisis has ballooned with economic liberalization that has removed agricultural subsidies and opened Indian agriculture to the global market. Small farmers are often trapped in a cycle of insurmountable debt, leading many to take their lives out of sheer desperation.

Although this book cannot discuss in detail the significant issues facing the developing world, this kind of scenario emphasises the poignant (and often fragile) link between food and the livelihoods of people. Although restaurant menus have benefited from the absorption of global techniques and ingredients, a real concern over the standardising impact of multi-national food operators such as supermarkets and fast food chains on small, local producers and businesses is now very apparent. Food and drink tourism has an ethical role to play. Certainly, there is a sense that aggressive commercial food activity and the increased standardisation of food threatens the inherent economic and environmental qualities of local food and their producers. Academics such as Everett and Aitchison (2008) and Sims (2009) are now arguing for the support and promotion of regional cuisines through tourism, even if it is as simple as supporting and lifting restrictions on local roadside sellers on tourist routes, as shown in Figure 1.3.

FIGURE 1.3   *A roadside coconut seller talks to a tourist in Mauritius. Photo by author*

For example, in Croatia, Renko et al. (2010) have found that food presents an effective instrument for enhancing rural tourism development in a country emerging from war and transitioning from central economic planning to a market economy. A clear link has been found between food tourism and helping regions move out of the vicious circle of poverty. Research has found that there is a more rapid economic development of Croatian islands where tourism and gastronomy are united. Certainly food tourism is increasingly being recognised as a powerful vehicle in sustaining rural businesses and communities, and many countries have witnessed a significant rise in food tourism destinations, trails and festivals. Many places have transformed previously deprived rural regions with food tourism-induced prosperity (Sharples, 2003b). Furthermore, governments have also realised the potential of food tourism's ability to enhance the sustainability of tourism development, and many are creating policy agendas that support agriculture and tourism partnerships. The result is that food is increasingly becoming part of the sustainability agenda for many communities and emphasis has been placed on food and drink tourism to supplement the agricultural sector and broaden the scope of regional development schemes in deprived rural areas. However, it should also be noted that communities are not always able to respond easily to need, and development has not always been strategic and beneficial to local communities.

CASE STUDY

Poverty alleviation in Rwanda

A study by the Overseas Development Institute (Ashley, 2007) on tourism in Rwanda found that there were significant opportunities for local people to be involved in, and benefit from, tourism. The research looked at local participation in the tourism economy and identified areas where income could be increased. A flow of 17,000 upmarket business tourists in Kigali was found to generate US$ 1.5 million per year in income for 'poorish' households: semi-skilled and unskilled workers, food producers, and artisans. Income from hotel employment and food sales was found to be roughly equal. They also found that around 13,000 tourists

visited the Parc National des Volcans and Musanze area, which generated around US$ 1 million per year in income for a wide range of poor workers and food producers. A number of recommendations were made to help increase poor people's incomes, which included many food-based initiatives that could be linked to selling food and drink to tourists. Recommendations to support local people included:

- Work on the food supply chain to hotels, lodges and restaurants to boost product quality and volume, and help poor farmers access this market;
- Assist poor households to access training, employment and promotion in hospitality;

- Pilot practical initiatives to help businesses enhance their own 'inclusive business' models, and create webs of business linkages in key destinations;
- Partner with domestic and international tour operators, lodges and hotels, conference organisers, artisans and farmers to make a range of cultural experiences, shopping opportunities and handicraft products an integral part of a Rwandan visit;
- Help poor farmers to sell to hotels: tourists consume food worth a few million dollars a year. Much of this is sourced in Rwanda, but action is needed to help local producers increase the quality, range, and seasonality of their production, so they can boost sales to hotels; and ensure smaller poor farmers, particularly women farmers, can access this important market. This will involve partnership with agriculturalists, chefs, and government, plus a more detailed analysis of the current food supply chain. (Source: www.odi.org.uk 2011)

These findings are not just relevant to Rwanda. It is clear that food and drink tourism can provide sources of economic diversification in rural areas where traditional sources of income such as agriculture are no longer sufficient. There is a need to build linkages from the local economy to tourism supply chains and in this way, industries related to tourism can grow, become more competitive and contribute to a more equitable and healthier economy. Projects that have promoted local food to tourists have been found to help support local economies, sustain skills, raise employment, keep young people in the community and ensure the tourist spend circulates for longer in the local economy. For example, the Scottish government (through its 'Scotland Food and Drink' campaign) plans to create an industry worth £10 billion by 2017 to support new jobs and raise income. Another example is the state of Ipoh in Malaysia, which spent RM22,000 (Malaysia dollars) on the publication of a new food guide to support Malaysia's plan to generate RM30 billion from tourism by 2020 (Yeoh, 2013). The success of similar projects is certainly testament to the impact of tourists when they chose to support local producers. These consumer habits are driven by a belief that local produces quality, but also that it helps local people. Eating has almost become a political action.

In regard to environmental ethics and issues, Fernandez-Armesto exclaims (2001: 252), 'Fussiness and "foodism" are methods of self-protection for society against the deleterious effects of the industrial era: the glut of the cheap, the degradation of the environment, the wreckage of taste'. Food tourism has been found to offer a way of harnessing consumer reaction to standardised cheap food by offering a tastier, local and unique experience. Certainly many traditional industries, such as farming, are facing new challenges with increasingly globalised supply chains and price-competitive marketing strategies employed by food service providers. Food tourism is argued by many to have a fundamental role to play in stemming the tide of perceived globalisation and social homogenisation (Reynolds, 1993) (these issues are addressed and discussed further in Chapter 5).

Recent work has also highlighted the link between food tourism and environmental sustainability (Everett and Atchison, 2008; Sims, 2009), finding that food tourism has led to an increase in environmental awareness and sustainability, providing a means of enhancing and extending the tourist spend without overly compromising the environmental, social or cultural fabric of a region. Sims (2009: 334) has added that 'the appeal of local food lies in its ability to encompass everything from a concern for environmental and social sustainability, through to consumer demands for foods that are safe, distinctive and traceable' and 'tourist consumption of local foods creates a market opportunity that can encourage the development of sustainable agriculture, help conserve traditional farming landscapes and assist the local economy'. This is perhaps best illustrated in the work of the Slow Food movement (see the Case Study on the Slow Food movement, Chapter 11).

Before you move onto the more specific areas of food and drink tourism in this book, it is a good idea to ensure you understand what food and drink tourism actually is and how it can be defined (or not!). Have a go at this next Activity which will help you research and explore definitions of food and drink tourism.

ACTIVITY   **DEFINITIONS FOR FOOD AND DRINK TOURISM**

Try to find another three definitions of food tourism from academic books, journals and websites. Assess their strengths and weaknesses. Do you think they provide a comprehensive definition of food and drink tourism? What are the key elements required in a definition?

Now try and devise your own definition of 'food and drink tourism'.

If you feel confident with the concept and characteristics of food and drink tourism and feel you have a good understanding of what it is now, you may like to read and consider 'food tourism as a postmodern consumption' in the Critical Reflections box below. Think about whether you think food tourism is the ultimate form of postmodern consumption, or not.

Critical Reflections: food tourism as postmodern consumption?

The study of food tourism can contribute to our understanding of the dimensions and complexity of postmodern forms of consumptive activity, offering a useful lens through which to investigate and explore 'new' and 'old' forms of tourism. It has been suggested that following the post-war upheavals of the 1940s there has been a rise in the complexity of consumption away from homogenised, regulated and standardised producer-dominated Fordist modes towards an increased density of signs, images and non-material forms of production and consumption (Jamal and Kim, 2005). These ideas are further explored in Chapter 4.

As you will read in this book, there is an argument that eating exotic and global foodstuffs has become part of a new postmodern culture, characterised by pluralised and aestheticised experiences that have fostered new patterns of tourism consumption and the development of new individualised identities. Food and drink tourism characterises these 'new' tourism experiences (Armesto López and Martin, 2006; Poon, 1993), symptomatic of a move from large-scale packaging of standardised leisure to new consumer imperatives that have led to the development of new patterns and a rise in the number of consumers actively engaged in new forms of tourism experience.

CHAPTER SUMMARY

At this point, you should have a sense of the significance and importance of food and drink in the tourism industry and its value as a subject of academic study. You should be able to identify some of the many ways in which it can contribute to tourism development and how it has the potential to deliver many of the key priorities and policy objectives of various countries and regions. If you want to know more, then locate some of the sources listed in the Further Reading list below. As with each chapter, key learning points are listed that should summarise what has been covered.

END OF CHAPTER POINTS

- Food and drink tourism is an eclectic and difficult-to-define term that must be studied with a multi-disciplinary approach to fully understand its complexities, breadth and contribution.
- Food and beverages constitute up to one-third of total tourist expenditure.
- There is no one 'food tourist' type; rather a spectrum of food tourists ranging from low to high interest, and from inactive to active.
- Food and drink tourism is being used as an effective way to extend the tourism season, alleviate poverty and regenerate deprived areas (especially in developing countries).
- Environmental sustainability goals can be met through the active promotion of local and regional food and drink to tourists and their related purchases.
- Food and drink tourism can generate a significant level of employment in the coming years.

FURTHER READING

Everett, S. (2009) 'Beyond the visual gaze? The pursuit of an embodied experience through food tourism', *Tourist Studies*, 8,(3): 337–58.

Everett, S. and Aitchison, C. (2008) 'The role of food tourism in sustaining regional identity: a case study of Cornwall, South West England', *Journal of Sustainable Tourism* 16 (2): 150–67.

Getz, D., Robinson, R.N., Andersson, T.D. and Vujicic, S. (2015) *Foodies and Food Tourism*. Oxford: Goodfellows.

Hall, C.M. and Mitchell, R. (2000) 'We are what we eat: food, tourism and globalization', *Tourism Culture and Communication*. 2: 29–37.

Hall, C.M., Sharples, E., Mitchell, R., Macionis, N. and Cambourne, B. (eds) (2003) *Food Tourism Around the World. Development, Management and Markets*. Oxford: Butterworth Heinemann.

Hjalager, A. and Richards, G. (eds) (2002) *Tourism and Gastronomy*. London: Routledge.

Long, L. (ed.) (2004) *Culinary Tourism*. Lexington, KY: University Press of Kentucky.

Sims, R. (2009) 'Food, place and authenticity: local food and the sustainable tourism experience', *Journal of Sustainable Tourism*, 17 (3): 321–36.

2

A HISTORY OF CULINARY EXPLORATION AND FOOD TOURISM

CHAPTER OBJECTIVES

- To provide an historical context for the changing nature of food and drink exploration and tourism
- To provide a brief chronology of the discovery and exchange of exotic and foreign foods by early explorers and merchants
- To outline the historical relationship between food and the slave trade
- To introduce some of the first food tourists and explore their early writings
- To link the history of food exploration with current thinking on food tourism

CHAPTER SUMMARY

Travelling in search of food for sustenance goes back to the dawn of humankind when hunting and gathering from nearby lands was commonplace. Evidence indicates that agricultural development and farming goes back going back more than 20,000 years in some parts of the world (although Harris (1996) claims it is closer to 10,000 years). In terms of food tourism, food may well have represented more than a bodily requirement and need for sustenance very early on in the evolution of humankind; the search for food as a leisure activity enjoys its own distinctive history. This chapter will trace food-related travel back to the discovery of new lands and exploration (including exploitation through the slave trade) in the fifteenth century and discuss the early European explorers who sailed in search of valuable commodities (namely gold and spices) and new lands to conquer as the first 'food tourists'.

The chapter includes a timeline that traces the replacement of the Mongols by the Ottoman Turks, to the explorers who brought spices back to their homelands. It sets the scene with Christopher Columbus reaching the Bahamas, moving on to John Cabot and cod fishing in Newfoundland in 1496, to Vasco de Gama successfully locating the Indies in 1498, to the sixteenth-century voyages of Sir Francis Drake, in which he is famously reported to have returned to England with the potato in 1586. The early explorers opened the way for a new breed of traveller by the seventeenth century, namely writers such as Defoe who were keen to explore, and then the Grand Tour of Europe in the eighteenth century, before extensive exploration of Australia and Africa in the nineteenth century.

This chapter draws on historic travellers' diaries to provide excerpts of their travel writings and adventures with food, for example seventeenth- and eighteenth-century writers (including those on the Grand Tour) such as the Scottish-born Tobias Smollett who wrote *Travels through France and Italy* (1766), and figures such as William Thomas Beckford, Elizabeth Craven and Captain Philip Thicknesse.

HUMANKIND'S EARLY RELATIONSHIP WITH FOOD

> Food, moreover, has a good claim to be considered the world's most important subject. It is what matters most to most people for most of the time.
>
> (Fernández-Arnesto, 2001: xiii).

Food historians have made numerous guesses about when and how food practices have developed, and by whom. For instance, on the most basic question of whether to eat something or not, cultural anthropologists suggest people selected or rejected food based on observation (i.e. if plants were avoided by the other animals in the area) along with basic trial and error (unfortunately leading to death or sickness in some cases). It has been suggested that agricultural practices date back almost 20,000 years in some parts of the world, although much research suggests it was closer to 10,000 (Harris, 1996; Pringle, 1998) when a Neolithic Revolution replaced pre-agricultural methods of collecting, hunting and fishing. However, Pringle (1998) claims evidence indicates that hunter-gatherers in the Near East first cultivated rye fields as early as 13,000 years ago. The domestication of food plants and animals certainly began to constitute the main source of human food. One interesting story in Greek legend is that humans owe the ability to cultivate crops to the generosity of the goddess Demeter, goddess of the harvest, who gave wheat seeds to a priest who then travelled across the Earth in a dragon-drawn chariot, sowing the dual blessings of agriculture and civilization – certainly one form of food-inspired travel! This fascinating relationship between food, myth, and cultural identity will be explored in future chapters.

It is generally believed that the Egyptian civilisation began around 3100 BC and this was a time when hunter-gatherers settled in agricultural villages, and animals and people migrated into the region from western Asia. The population supported itself first by hunting the many wild species that lived in and around the Nile, and people began to establish agricultural communities; this is the time when wild pigs and cattle began to be domesticated. Alcock (2005) found that hunting became a sport for the wealthy rather than a means for obtaining food, although poorer people continued to hunt game and wild fowl, and to snare fish, to diversify their diet.

Flandrin (1999) suggests that the first recipe dates from Mesopotamia in around 2000 BC, but this does not necessarily imply that the Mesopotamians invented cooking. They simply had reasons to write down their recipes and were the first (along with the Egyptians) to develop writing and a way of recording actions and things of note. However, the absence of written recipes does not mean that there was not an interest in gastronomic matters, because traces of Egyptian cooking methods have been found in tombs dating from as early as the fourth millennium. It is the fourth-century Roman figure Apicius who is credited as the author of the first cookbook, which contained details of several Roman dishes. Once Rome and the Italian peninsula were conquered by northern tribes, the dishes became very simple, made from staples like roasted meats and crops harvested nearby. In the south, notably Sicily, things were different because Arab conquests introduced spices and techniques from North Africa and the Middle East. Certainly, their influence is present today as almonds and citrus fruits form a key part of the island's offering.

Food and drink have always been intrinsically entwined with the social habits and way of life of people. For example, the 'holy days' of the agricultural year have a direct link with the 'holidays' we still now enjoy. Medieval celebrations revolved around feast days, and these were originally based on ancient agricultural celebrations that marked when certain crops were planted or harvested. Likewise, in the Jewish calendar, the festival of Shavuot has been transformed from a purely agricultural harvest day into an historical and religious holiday. Originally mentioned in the Torah as a harvest festival, Shavuot has become another pilgrimage festival based on marking a time of sadness before a time of explicit joy, and the mystical idea of marriage between God and Israel. Certainly, the consumption of food and drink has directly influenced and informed the world's cultural history.

THE GLOBAL SEARCH FOR EXOTIC COMMODITIES AND FOOD

A hunger for spices, new foods and exotic flavours drove explorers to the corners of the earth and inspired extensive global exploration and the undertaking of far-flung journeys. Commonly known as the 'spice trade', the movement of goods around the world was complex and riddled with power struggles. It is believed that people from the Neolithic period traded in spices and other high-value materials as early as the tenth millennium BC, but it is the Egyptians in around 3000 BC who first mention trading spices around the area of Somalia, Djibouti, Eritrea and the Red Sea coast of Sudan (Nabhan, 2014; Najovits, 2003). By 500 BC Arab tribes had taken control over the land-trade of spices from South Arabia to the Mediterranean Sea and routes around Petra to Gaza. By this time, the Indians and the Arabs had control over the sea-trade with India, but by the late second century BC, the Greeks had taken control of the sea after they had learnt the routes. From around the fifth century, the Romans extended the spice trade, and from the eighth until the fifteenth century, the Republic of Venice held the monopoly of European trade with the Middle East. The silk and spice trade brought tremendous wealth as spices were among the most expensive and in-demand products of the Middle Ages. By 1453 the Ottomans took Constantinople and the Byzantine (Roman) Empire was no more, and by the fifteenth century, the Ottoman Turks were dominant in the spice trade (Turner, 2008).

ACTIVITY   **THE SPICE TRADE ROUTES**

Download or locate a simple map of the world; research the movements of the spice trade; then draw a clear coloured line to illustrate the spice trade routes around the different countries and continents. For an extra challenge, add the dates and the names of key individuals. Discuss any patterns that emerge. Why might this be?

It was the Italian explorer Christopher Columbus who reached what he thought were the Indies in 1492, but he had actually landed at Haiti and the Bahamas. As his crew searched for gold and spices, they came across a vast array of new and unfamiliar foodstuffs, from sweet potatoes to beans, birds, fish, crab and maize. He made three more voyages and during those trips; Columbus visited the Greater and Lesser Antilles, the Caribbean coast of Venezuela and Central America. All these places were claimed for the Crown of Castile (Spain) and initiated the Spanish colonisation of the New World. However, it is the Portuguese explorer, Vasco de Gama, who was arguably more successful in reaching the Indies (in 1498), where new spices and fortunes were found (his voyage is depicted in Figure 2.1). This Portuguese stranglehold on spices would remain until the mid-sixteenth century, when 80 London merchants established the East India Company (Royal Charter in 1600).

Certainly there were food-related surprises as explorers circumnavigated the globe. For example, it is clearly noted that the Spaniards took a dislike to Aztec civilisation due to their ceremonial cannibalism. However, other foodstuffs sparked their interest and it was the Conquistadors who acknowledged the usefulness of the potato. For the English, it was famously Sir Frances Drake who, on his way to Virginia in 1586, stopped in Cartagena in the Caribbean, came across the potato and brought it back to England. A summary of some of these explorers and their findings are outlined in Table 2.1.

FIGURE 2.1 *Vasco da Gama lands at Calicut, 20 May 1498 (painted 1880)*

TABLE 2.1 *Brief chronology of global food exploration and travel*

Period	Explorers and their food discoveries
C13 and C14	Rapid expansion of the Mongol Empire which covered an area of 33,000,000 km2 (22% of the Earth's total land area) and saw Genghis Khan rule from 1206. This led to dramatic movements of foodstuffs. Food movement generally followed the Silk Route, one of the main trade routes in the central part of Asia, facilitating the exchange of goods and barter trade in Asia, Africa and some parts of Europe.
Early C15	Ottoman Turks replace the Mongols as dominant players in the spice trade. Explorers begin to seek out new riches and bring spices back to their homelands. For example, the Portuguese Prince Henry the Navigator sailed down the African coastline to find riches in Africa (mainly gold), with limited success.
1453	The conquest of Constantinople by Mehmed II in 1453 means the Ottoman state became an empire. It reached its peak in 1590, covering vast parts of Asia, Europe and Africa. During the sixteenth and seventeenth centuries, in particular at the height of its power under the reign of Suleiman the Magnificent, the Ottoman Empire became one of the most powerful states in the world.

(Continued)

TABLE 2.1 *(Continued)*

Period	Explorers and their food discoveries
1492–1503	Christopher Columbus (born Republic of Genoa, now Italy) completed four voyages across the Atlantic Ocean to facilitate the Spanish colonization of the New World by establishing trade routes and colonies. Columbus had hoped to reach the East Indies by sailing westward with support of the Spanish crown to ensure they beat rival powers in the lucrative spice trade with Asia. During his first voyage in 1492, Columbus landed in the Bahamas at a locale he named San Salvador. He also visited the Greater and Lesser Antilles, as well as the Caribbean coast of Venezuela and Central America, claiming them for the Spanish Empire.
1497	John Cabot (Italian explorer) landed in North America and discovered a plentiful level of cod fishing in Newfoundland, reporting "the sea there is full of fish that can be taken not only with nets but with fishing-baskets".
1498	Vasco de Gama (Portuguese explorer 1469–1524) successfully located the Indies. Landed in Calicut on 20th May 1498. Reaching the legendary Indian spice routes unopposed helped the Portuguese Empire improve its economy. The first spices were pepper and cinnamon but soon included other new products, which lead to a commercial monopoly for several decades.
1586	Voyages of Sir Francis Drake (English explorer, 1540-27th January 1596). Famously brought back the potato in 1586, although it did not become widely popular in Europe until the eighteenth century.
1600	East India Company received Royal Charter. Traded mainly in cotton, silk, indigo dye, salt, saltpetre, tea and opium. The company gained a monopoly on trade with all countries east of the Cape of Good Hope and west of the Straits of Magellan. The company struggled in the spice trade due to competition from the Dutch East India Company. Imports of pepper from Java were an important part of the Company's trade for twenty years.
C17	By the seventeenth century, exploration and discovery of foods was less about developing trade routes, conquest and Empire, and more about exploration and discovery. Writers such as Daniel Defoe began to explore the word and write novels of adventure. His works on foreign travel and trade include *A General History of Discoveries and Improvements* (1727) and *Atlas Maritimus and Commercialis* (1728). His 'A tour thro' the whole island of Great Britain (1724–27)' provided a panoramic survey of British trade.
C17th and C18th	Called the 'Gastronomic Grand Tour' by Tannahill (1998), this is a time of exploration by the rich and middle-classes and a time where new and exotic foodstuffs were being found and enjoyed for pleasure and interest. Numerous writers (e.g. Tobias Smollett) wrote about travel (e.g. Smollett's *Travels through France and Italy* (1766)) which provides detailed narratives of the food and drink being enjoyed by such enthusiastic early tourists.
C19	Explosion of exploration, particularly of Australia and Africa. Rather than food tourism, lots of explorers seem to be dying of starvation at this time. Examples include Edward John Eyre (1815–1901), the first European to walk across southern Australia from east to west, who survived on morning dew and kangaroos; Robert O'Hara Burke (1820–1861) and William John Wills (1834–1861) were the first Europeans to cross Australia from south to north, but died from exhaustion and hunger. Sir John Franklin (1786–1847) proved the existence of a Northwest Passage. In 1845 his ship became trapped in ice, and the desperate, freezing and starving survivors resorted to cannibalism; the survivors then got lead poisoning from poorly-canned food. Famously, David Livingstone (1813–1873) was a British missionary and explorer who explored the interior of Africa and searched for the source of the Nile River.

By the late nineteenth century, food and drink from all over the world was available to a wider population of people as a result of early explorers and conquests. For example, in Constantinople (now known as Istanbul), Ottoman cuisine was a

THE GROWTH AND DEVELOPMENT OF FOOD AND DRINK TOURISM

product of exploration and cultural conquest and offered a diverse and varied new diet. It was an example of a globally informed culinary offer, and bustling scenes of street-cooking shown in Figure 2.2 (Rue de Stamboul, Constantinople, Turkey, 1890s) were commonplace.

FIGURE 2.2   *Cook in the Rue de Stamboul, Constantinople, Turkey, 1890s*

Through food, the world became closer to the masses and ports bustled with market and trading activity, as shown in Figure 2.3, which depicts frantic trading in Constantinople in Turkey 1895.

FIGURE 2.3   *Bazaar and selling goods, Constantinople, Turkey 1895*

However, there was a price attached to this endless desire for food and ever-increasingly array of commodities: the barbaric use of slaves. This harsh period in history and the stories of the plantations where the slaves worked is an intrinsic part of the history of the movement and trading of food.

THE SLAVE TRADE: THE DARKER SIDE OF FOOD EXPLORATION AND CONSUMPTION

Although it seems a far cry from current food consumption and culinary tourism, the historic trade and acquisition of exotic foodstuffs was directly supported by the transatlantic slave trade from the sixteenth through to the nineteenth centuries. Thomas (1997) is one of many scholars to suggest that the first European slave traders were from Portugal and it was the Portuguese who built the first European fort (Fort Elmina) in Africa in 1481. However, the potential riches and advantages from engaging with slavery did not go unnoticed by other European rivals and soon Spain became one of biggest slave-trading nations and used slaves on their plantations in the Caribbean and South America. Thornton (1998: 31) has suggested that 'the actual motivation for European expansion and for navigational breakthroughs was little more than to exploit the opportunity for immediate profits made by raiding and the seizure or purchase of trade commodities'.

The vast majority of slaves transported to the New World were Africans from the central and western parts of the continent, sold (by Africans) to European slave traders who then transported them to the colonies in North and South America. This process became known as the 'triangular' trade, where the first side of the triangle was the export of goods from Europe to Africa. Many African rulers took part in the trading of enslaved people and for each captive, the African rulers would receive goods from Europe. The second leg of the triangle shipped Africans across the Atlantic to the Americas and the Caribbean. The final part of the triangle was the return of goods and the products of slave-labour plantations to Europe from the Americas; these goods were often foodstuffs such as sugar and molasses. The map in Figure 2.4 shows this 'triangular' movement.

England was one of the last countries to engage with the slave trade, but it soon became one of the most lucrative enterprises of the seventeenth century (Morgan, 2000). To support trade with Africa, King James I set up the first monopoly in 1618; then the formation of the Royal African Company in 1672 allowed English colonies in America to buy slaves from English traders. As plantations grew, the slave trade increased exponentially. Britain acquired colonies in America and the Caribbean and demand for slaves to work tobacco, rice, sugar and other crops on plantations grew and was fuelled by a growing desire for foodstuffs from distant lands 'discovered' by the early explorers. The plantation economies of the New World were built on slave labour, and people's desire for sugar, coffee, cotton and

FIGURE 2.4   *The triangular trade*

tobacco fuelled this trade. The Trinidadian scholar Eric Williams (1994) argues that profits from slavery 'fertilised' many branches of the metropolitan economy and set the scene for England's industrial revolution. Williams makes explicit the link between the money made from slavery on the one hand, and the financing of British capitalist development on the other.

When the monopoly on trade with Africa was abolished in 1698, merchants from other ports in Britain such as Bristol and Liverpool quickly profited from the slave trade. One of the many examples is John Pinney (1740–1818), who earned his fortune in Bristol from his sugar plantations in Nevis in the Caribbean (see the Case Study on John Pinney). Certainly, slave-owning merchants who dealt in slaves and slave produce were the most affluent people in eighteenth-century Britain. As more people could afford new commodities such as tobacco and sugar, merchants met this new demand by setting up slave plantations in Virginia and the Caribbean. While there was a growing taste for exotic stimulants and luxuries, consumers had little idea of the human cost involved in these products reaching their tables. The merchants certainly did, as they continued to enslave more and more people. Philip Curtin (1969) calculated that about ten million slaves were taken from Africa to fuel these enterprises.

John Pinney

John Pinney was a rich sugar plantation owner in Nevis (Caribbean) and a slave owner from Bristol, UK. He became extremely rich as he regularly offered loans to other plantation owners and received significant income from his own plantations. He often wrote about his views on his slaves and in one letter written to a friend in the 1760s he does express some uneasiness about keeping slaves, but managed to reconcile it with his religious beliefs: 'I can assure you I was shock'd at the first appearance of human flesh exposed for sale. But surely God ordained' em for the use and benefit of us: otherwise his Divine Will would have been made manifest by some particular sign or token'. (The Georgian House, Bristol. Details from: https://www.bristolmuseums.org.uk/georgian-house-museum)

After much protest and high-profile debate, the United States Congress passed the Slave Trade Act of 1794, which prohibited the building or outfitting of ships in the United States for use in the slave trade, followed by Congress outlawing the import of slaves in 1807, beginning on 1 January 1808. In Britain around the 1780s, the Quakers, under Granville Sharp, began to publicly campaign against slavery and by 1807, the Slave Trade Act banned the slave trade in Britain, although it was not against the law to own slaves until 1834. By 1869 Portugal also abolished slavery in the African colonies. Yet, even today, although it is officially illegal in all nations, slavery continues in many countries and work continues to eradicate the practice completely.

EARLY CULINARY TRAVEL ADVENTURES

Food exploration was not all about slavery, of course: there was a taste for adventure as well as an appetite for profits by the eighteenth century. Tannahill (1988) offers a useful and detailed discussion on culinary engagement and food as part of the 'Gastronomic Grand Tour' from the eighteenth century. Certainly by this point, nations were beginning to offer food with nationalistic identity and Tannahill's narrative takes the reader around different countries (including France, the Iberian peninsula, Russia, Australia, China and India) and outlines what the intrepid traveller may have seen, drunk and tasted. However, despite the explosion of interested travellers and people seeking to explore new lands for fun rather than conquest, Tannahill suggests their descriptions of foreign food were often very funny, defamatory, and influential. Clearly, Italy was establishing a strong culinary cuisine on the foundation of the spice trade and despite some lively debate over the origins of pasta (the Chinese or the Italians?), macaroni was a firmly established culinary offer to those engaging on the Grand Tour, where middle-class tourists even attracted the nickname of 'Macaronis'. This link between travellers and the food they enjoyed is certainly testament to the growing profile of food and drink tourism.

The food offered in different countries in the eighteenth century was a reflection and direct outcome of trade activities and conquest: from Spain and Portugal, where barbarians had introduced mutton, to the Arab introduction of rice and citrus fruits, to the outcomes of Spain's victories overseas which brought back tomatoes, peppers and cacao (chocolate). In contrast, it is clear from records of the time that the northern fringes of Europe (areas around Scandinavia) were struggling to provide enough food to avoid famine. Viking food influences remained (e.g. gravlax, cured salmon) as to keep going through the winter much food had to be preserved (smoked, dried or salted).

However, rather than trace food around each country, this chapter now turns to those early food and drink tourists and explores the subject through their writing and their eyes. One of these writers was Tobias Smollett.

Tobias Smollett (1721–1771)

Smollett was a Scottish-born poet and author. Known for a number of different literary works, his travelogue *Travels through France and Italy* was published in 1766. In April 1763, he travelled with his wife across France to Nice, visiting Genoa, Rome, Florence and other towns of Italy. After staying in Nice for the winter he returned to London by June 1765. His account of that journey is written in colourful detail and reads like many travelogues a tourist might write today. Smollett looked at the people all around him, the history of each place, the social interactions and morals, and of course the food of all the places he visited. Smollett's work indicates he was a man of great curiosity and certainly an early food tourist. On 2 September 1764, Smollett wrote some wonderful descriptions of the food he saw around him during the trip:

The markets at Nice are tolerably well supplied. Their beef, which comes from Piedmont, is pretty good, and we have it all the year. In the winter we have likewise excellent pork, and delicate lamb; but the mutton is indifferent. Piedmont, also, affords us delicious capons, fed with maize; and this country produces excellent turkeys, but very few geese. Chickens and pullets are extremely meagre. ... Autumn and winter are the seasons for game; hares, partridges, quails, wild-pigeons, woodcocks, snipes, thrushes, beccaficas, and ortolans. Wild boar is sometimes found in the mountains: it has a delicious taste, not unlike that of the wild hog in Jamaica; and would make an excellent barbecue.

Other prominent travel diaries and letters (which invariably included detailed narratives on food and drink) from the Grand Tour period included those by William Thomas Beckford, Elizabeth Craven and Captain Philip Thicknesse. William Beckford (1760–1844) was an art collector, politician and travel writer. His book *'Dreams, Waking Thoughts, and Incidents'; in a Series of Letters from Various Parts of Europe* (1783) is an enthralling romantic account of the people and places he encounters, with much finding its way into *Sketches of Spain and Portugal* (1834). Again, his writings suggest that food and drink were an intrinsic part of the touristic adventure around Europe:

> Looking out, I beheld the grand canal so entirely covered with fruits and vegetables, on rafts and in barges, that I could scarcely distinguish a wave. Loads of grapes, peaches and melons arrived, and disappeared in an instant, for every vessel was in motion; and the crowds of purchasers hurrying from boat to boat, formed one of the liveliest pictures imaginable. (William Beckford, Venice, Letter XIII, August 3)

Perhaps more unusual were the narratives from female travel writers of the day. One such woman was Elizabeth Craven, the third child of the fourth Earl of Berkley (1750–1828), well known for her travelogues. Travel writings included *Letters from the Right Honourable Lady Craven, to His Serene Highness the Margrave of Anspach, during Her Travels through France, Germany, and Russia in 1785 and 1786* (1814) and *A Journey through the Crimea to Constantinople* (1789) in which she recalls (in Letter LX11 from 1786 from Constantinople), 'nothing can look more dry and unlike food than these fish'.

Finally, another prolific writer who wrote extensively about food on his travels was Captain Philip Thicknesse (1719–1792) who, after the premature death of two wives, travelled extensively with his third wife, Anne Ford, and wrote about their travels. One such travel journal was *A Year's Journey through France and Part of Spain* (1777) in which he writes enthusiastically about his engagement with food and drink:

> I need not tell you that this is the province which produces the most delicious wine in the world; but I will assure you, that I should have drank it with more pleasure, had you been here to have partook of it. In the cellars of one wine-merchant, I was conducted through long passages more like streets than caves; on each side of which, bottled Champagne was piled up some feet higher than my head, and at least twelve deep. I bought two bottles to taste, of that which the merchant assured me was each of the best sort he had. (Thicknesse, 1777, Rheims in France, Letter X)

> The dessert (in a country where fruit is so fine and so plenty) was only a large dish of the seeds of pomegranates, which they eat with wine and sugar. In truth, Sir, an Englishman who has been in the least accustomed to eat at genteel tables, is, of all other men, least qualified to travel into either kingdoms, and particularly into Spain. (Thicknesse, 1777, Spain, Letter XXXI)

THE GROWTH AND DEVELOPMENT OF FOOD AND DRINK TOURISM

If you are interested in researching the origins of food, or wonder who found which spice and from where, you could become a culinary anthropologist (or food historian). Food history is an interdisciplinary field that examines the history of food, and the cultural, economic, environmental and sociological impacts of food. Food history is different from the field of culinary history, which focuses on the origin and recreation of specific recipes. Although a rather niche career area, it is one that would allow you to research world cuisines and explore identities, places and foods. Culinary anthropology will take you around the world and can open up opportunities in the media, or working on major history or culinary projects. Any major history project needs someone who can serve as the voice of authority on what the people or culture involved ate. The possibilities for a food historian are truly limitless.

Food historians look at food as one of the most important elements of a culture, reflecting the social and economic structure of society. Food history is a new discipline, considered until recently a fringe discipline. The first journal in the field, *Petits Propos Culinaires*, began in 1979 and the first conference was the 1981 Oxford Food Symposium.

If you are interested in food history you will need to usually pursue a master's degree or higher with a concentration in culinary arts, food studies or gastronomy. A useful site for further information about getting a career in food history is: www.rachellaudan.com/culinary-history/getting-started-in-food-history.

TODAY'S CULINARY TOURIST AND EXPLORER

Travel writers during the Grand Tour left a legacy that has continued and the genre of travel writing has become one of the most lucrative areas of writing (more on the travel media and current writing in Chapter 9). The apparent rapid growth and interest in food and drink around the world is certainly not new, but in today's world we are bombarded by food-themed promotion in tourism marketing and development strategies from across the globe.

Some of the issues discussed above are still very relevant today. We still exist in a world where the desire for the new and exotic, the flavoursome and spicy often has a social, as well as economic, price.

ACTIVITY   THE GRAND TOUR FOOD TOURISTS

Try to locate and briefly research the food- and drink-inspired writings of another Grand Tour writer not mentioned in this chapter.

What are their first impressions of the food they find in one of the new destinations? Do they regard it with abhorrence, or do they embrace the food of the 'Other'? What would your reaction be to this food experience?

CHAPTER SUMMARY

It is difficult to condense the entire history of food and drink travel and exploration into one chapter; however, you should now have realised that travelling to experience food and drink is not a new preoccupation or recent human activity. Although early explorers sought riches, prestige and colonial gain (often at the brutal expense of other nations and peoples), it is clear that people have travelled for over 20,000 years to find new tastes, flavours and experiences. It is clear that food became culturally embedded and underpinned the way people lived (for example the 'holy days' of the agricultural year soon became enjoyed as 'holidays'). By the sixteenth century, new foods were no longer being discovered by romantic colonial-sponsored explorers such as Columbus and Vasco de Gama, but new places, people and flavours were being enjoyed and written about by middle-class tourists of the Grand Tour.

END OF CHAPTER POINTS

- Agricultural development dates back almost 20,000 years, although the search for food (hunting and fishing) dates back to the dawn of humankind.
- The search for and consumption of food and drink has directly influenced and informed the history of the world and the cultural and social identity of nations.
- Evidence suggests that the Egyptians were the first to trade spices on a significant scale.
- By 1453 the Ottomans took Constantinople (now Istanbul) and it played a key role in the spice trade.
- The explorer Vasco de Gama led the Portuguese stranglehold on spices until the mid-sixteenth century before London merchants established the East India Company.
- The trade of exotic foodstuffs was reliant on the 'triangular' transatlantic slave trade from the sixteenth through to the nineteenth centuries.
- The Grand Tour of the seventeenth and eighteenth century was the first time people travelled and enjoyed new food and drink for enjoyment and leisure. Grand tourists such as Tobias Smollett, William Thomas Beckford, Elizabeth Craven and Captain Philip Thicknesse wrote some of the earliest forms of modern travel (food) writing.

FURTHER READING

Alcock, J. (2005) *Food in the Ancient World*. Westport, CT: Greenwood Press.

Curtin, P. (1969) *The Atlantic Slave Trade: A Census*. Wisconsin: University of Wisconsin Press.

Fernandez Arnesto, F. (2001) *Food. A History*. London: Macmillan.

Flandrin, J. and Massimo, M. (1999) *Food: A Culinary History*. New York: Columbia University Press.

Najovits, S. (2004) *Egypt, the Trunk of the Tree*, Volume II: *A Modern Survey of an Ancient Land*. New York: Agora Publishing.

Tannahill, R. (1988) *Food in History*. London: Penguin.

Thomas, H. (1997) *The Slave Trade: The Story of the Atlantic Slave Trade, 1440–1870*. London: Simon & Schuster.

Thornton, J. (1998) *Africa and Africans in the Making of the Atlantic World, 1400–1800*, 2nd edn. Cambridge: Cambridge University Press.

Turner, J. (2008) *Spice: The History of a Temptation*. London: Vintage.

Williams, E. (1994) *Capitalism and Slavery*. Chapel Hill, NC: University of North Carolina Press.

Useful website: www.foodtimeline.org.

3

IDENTITY DEVELOPMENT AND THE CULTURAL DIMENSION OF FOOD AND DRINK

CHAPTER OBJECTIVES

- To explore the links between food, drink and identity development
- To provide a multi-disciplinary overview of key literature on food and identity
- To highlight the cultural and social role of food and drink in the touristic experience
- To examine the role of food and drink as markers of identity
- To explore food and drink tourism as embodied and performed practice

CHAPTER SUMMARY

This chapter looks at how food links to identity creation and discusses the sociological and cultural dimensions of food tourism. In 1825, the French gastronome Brillat-Savarin (1825, republished 2009) famously stated, 'Tell me what you eat and I'll tell you who you are', and it is this sentiment which infuses research dealing with food and identity development. This chapter introduces food and tourism from a variety of subject and disciplinary perspectives, including sociology, cultural studies, anthropology and geography.

The chapter links together different subject areas and highlights the cultural and social role of food and drink in the touristic experience and in developing a sense of place. For example, Caplan (2013) draws on the sociological ideas of Sidney Mintz, who, in *Tasting Food, Tasting Freedom* is keen to express the power of food and its different meanings within different societies, calling food 'vehicles of deep emotion' (1996: 69). Other ideas discussed in relation to food and consumption include Cook and Crang's (1996) geographical approach to food; Howes (1996) and MacClancy's (1992) research on cultural consumption; Bell and Valentine's (1997) *Consuming Geographies: We Are Where We Eat*; and tourism texts such as Urry's (1995) *Consuming Places*. Issues of identity, culture, nationalism and history are intrinsically bound up with issues of food; after all, many of us eat (and travel) to taste the 'Other'. Lastly, this chapter draws on recent research to look at the idea of food and drink tourism as embodied, multi-sensual and performed experiences which are intrinsically bound up with how we experience place and understand ourselves.

FOOD IN IDENTITY FORMATION

This chapter looks at some sociological and anthropological approaches that have been used to explore how food has an intangible relationship with human life, suggesting it is the ultimate emblem of identity formation. Food should be regarded as not simply an expression of producer and consumer connections, but central in reproducing and constructing identities. As Mintz (1996) argues, eating particular foods (aside from nourishment) is a way of making a statement about who we are, what we believe, and what we can do. Mintz's anthropological work specifically uses sugar to illustrate how people invest social meaning into basic foodstuffs (see the discussion of slavery and sugar in Chapter 2), and more recently Jolliffe (2012) has traced sugar heritage through the lens of tourism. It is within such work that food is ascribed power to act and where it is regarded as a root of identity formation. Eating makes a personal declaration, and thus consumption is simultaneously a form of self-identification and communication.

In crossing social, cultural and historical contexts, food is central to society. People construct meaning and identity around food and its role as an identity marker. Therefore, it is important to situate culture, food and identity in the context of place and regional identity. For example, Bell and Valentine's (1997) cultural geographical approach intertwines sociological analysis of food within geographies of place, with specific emphasis on the formation of personal and collective identities. They explore the role of food in constructing a 'sense of place' and how it might in turn influence the consumption of place, where 'every meal can tell us something about ourselves' (1997: 3). This kind of geographical analysis of 'we are where we eat' brings the concept of food as a social construction to the forefront of identity development. Food is a cultural artefact: a vehicle for developing our own identity whilst simultaneously experiencing the 'Other' (Howes, 1996).

For example, you can travel around India and it will be very clear that different regions across the country offer different dishes associated with that specific province or area; for example, Nagaland boasts of its rice beer, whereas over in the west, Goa may offer its own specialist local dishes (commonly fish-based). Like many countries, India's cuisine is a consequence of its turbulent and colourful history where it has been invaded and occupied by other cultures, each leaving its own mark on the food offering. For example, Aryan influences brought body-enhancing properties; Persian and Arab influences led to the Mughal style of cooking with the use of dry fruits; the British developed a successful tea industry; and the Portuguese left their mark on regions with influences seen today in dishes like the curry, Vindaloo.

ACTIVITY   FOOD AND YOUR IDENTITY

Think about what food or drink best represents your personal identity. Why have you chosen that particular foodstuff or beverage? Discuss the reasons behind your choice. Are the reasons historical, cultural, social and/or personal?

   Now think about what food or drink item best symbolises your hometown or place of birth. What is it about the food or drink that links it to the place and to its people?

This concept of experiencing the 'Other' within tourism can be traced to Edward Said (1978). Said's anthropological 'Orientalism' thesis offers a theoretical framework with which to understand the construction of identity in regard to an 'Other' (what is seen as inferior or alien from the West's perspective), although it is worth noting that his work has been accused of being overly simplistic and its binary-focus of colonised/coloniser offers little scope for agency on the part of the 'colonised'. For a less dualistic approach to the concept of the 'Other' in tourism, you might wish to read Sheller's (2003) study of the Caribbean. Tourism geographers are increasingly employing relational concepts of identity, in which identities are constructed within different contexts and through different means such as food.

PLACE-IDENTITY AND HERITAGE DEVELOPMENT THROUGH FOOD

Places are in a continuous state of 'becoming' through heritage processes in which identity symbols are produced and exchanged. There are complex interwoven processes between outside powers creating commodified landscapes of consumption and the destruction of place by tourists. For example, Gold and Gold (1995) found that the image of Scotland has been based on a largely inaccurate historic picture at odds with modern images of Scotland. The symbols of pre-modernity are often in contrast with those more objective features of new architecture, vibrant culture and industry. This tension between the promotion of a socially constructed image of 'escape' whilst building an identity of place has been tentatively discussed with reference to food and drink tourism. There are indications that people who fear they are losing the connection with the past are travelling to the margins to try and resist processes of delocalisation through food consumption (Boniface, 2003).

Another example is Haukeland and Jacobsen's (2001) study on food tourism in Norway, which is indicative of a rising awareness of the role of food as a heritage ingredient in tourism. They claim that 'peripheral areas may offer opportunities in terms of imagery based on what is perceived as traditional and authentic food' (2001: 10). Food tourism should be regarded as having the ability to stimulate and regenerate rural and peripheral areas and thus sustain and preserve cultural methods and practices (Everett and Aitchison, 2008). It is the link between the spatial, social, cultural and temporal which the study of food and tourism can understand. After all, 'it is the memory and recreation of such unremarkable things as a herring with onions that puts together a history of people and a place' (Jochnowitz (2004: 112).

CASE STUDY

Tartan food and the Celtic Scottish identity

FIGURE 3.1   *Tartan-clad food products on display in Scotland. Photo by author*

It is not uncommon to find food products and packaging linked to a region's history and heritage, as shown in the image of tartan-covered products in this shop in Scotland (Figure 3.1). Early travel writing was characterised by historical reproduction of the 'Celtic fringe' as being lost in the 'mists of time', alluring and romantic. Such a 'sense of oldness' continues to pervade the marketed tourism offer in many countries. Kneafsey (1998) suggests that tourism offers a way of regenerating crumbling senses of place-identity through engagement with an historic 'Celtic' other. Certainly tartan-wrapped food products for tourists highlight one of the ways in which 'identities' have become central discourses and overly commodified in the tourism offer. Place-identity is often used as a label to sell products saturated in symbols that contribute to the development of a presentable heritage. Time has become a dominant discourse in tourism marketing literature and ideas of a pre-modern life are being developed through constructed assemblages of traditional practices and images. Identities may become destabilised through the commodification and creation of hybrid Celtic identities where Celtic art, music and food have experienced such a proliferation that their historical value is weakened.

As outlined in the Case Study example of 'Celtic' imagery above, 'Celtic' food history is being reconstructed, marketed, repackaged and reinvented for the twenty-first century consumer.[1] Burnett and Danson (2004) argue that the conception of Scotland (also Ireland and Cornwall) is dominated by an iconography drawn from concepts of tradition and rurality. The current offer is a far cry from the unappetising food offer of offal and porridge discussed in historical texts about Scotland. Today it is celebrated and Van Westering expresses delight when 'trips to Ireland lure [tourists] to the Giant's Causeway, not forgetting the mussels and oysters; trips to the Highlands and Islands of Scotland touch on the delights of wild salmon and a plethora of game' (1999: 75).

Carter et al. (2007) argue that 'sense of place' is where powerful discourses of landscape influence people to the point where an identity becomes equated with a particular locale through a projection, process or performance. The concept draws attention to the emotional side of the affective bond between a place and the individual, particularly when a complex identity such as 'Celtic' transcends regional and political boundaries (especially as there is no actual territory called 'Celtia'). It is a concept that encapsulates the meanings of the social and natural landscape to individuals and groups. The history and images of the 'Celtic' periphery and landscape have no doubt become embedded in portrayals of the region and in its food offer. In suggesting that place is the actual sensual experience, it is implied that the whole environment is claimed by feelings and it is a perception held by individuals (not a tangible part of the place itself).

---

[1] 'Celtic' refers to those ancient peoples and civilisations around the Atlantic periphery, now closely associated with the peoples of Scotland, Ireland, Brittany, Wales and Galicia.

It is useful when looking at food tourism that food biographies and movements are considered, as it is important to grasp the complexity of the food system and to understand the meanings that are socially invested in food; for example, the religious symbolism of bread and wine at Communion, and the historic links to cannibalism as the literal destruction of enemies, or the Mooncake festival in the Chinese calendar to celebrate the full moon (a festival often regarded as intangible cultural heritage). As social anthropological analyses have revealed, food is part of a physiological, social and symbolic environment.

FOOD AS A SYMBOL AND SOUVENIR

The consumption process is not merely the buying and consuming of artefacts, but, through their active incorporation into people's lives, identities are formulated. Cultural objects need to be seen as socially constructed, not only in their meaning, but also in the material processes by which they are produced, distributed and ultimately consumed. One useful concept that has been employed in tourism research is the idea of 'interpellation' where objects enter life and have a social effect. It is the idea that material objects are embedded in specific cultural contexts as people use things to objectify social relationships. This approach is attributed to Appadurai (1986), who ascribes commodities with a 'social life', and traces the life histories of objects with a particular focus on the dynamics of cultural change and transfer of knowledge. This work has had particular influence on studies examining the touristic souvenir, where material goods can evoke melancholic remembrance and evoke allegorical intentions (Goss et al., 2005; Morgan and Pritchard, 2005).

Turning more specifically to foodstuffs and their stories, sociological studies give food/drink a central role in the symbolic system, granting it the ability to convey meanings as well as to nourish and sustain. A food repertoire is representative of a society. Conceptualised as a set of cultural artefacts that can be harnessed to grasp an understanding of wider systems (Cook and Crang, 1996), food is not just an everyday object without meaning, but may represent a symbol and marker of identity, and is an allegorical artefact with traces of human intention and action beyond its most obvious context.

Food and drink are impregnated with meanings and represent the consumption of myriad emotions, places and identities. They are integral in forming webs of social relations and meanings, where food is often at the centre of the strongest cultural rituals. Bessière claims that 'like a venerated, sanctified object, the gastronomic souvenir shared and eaten among friends can also prolong the act of social distinction and differentiation' (2001: 117). It is clear that food and drink are often the objectification and direct crystallisation of the physical and symbolic landscape, providing a link between place and its identity. For example, this is particularly true of the tea tourism plantations in Sri Lanka shown in Figure 3.2, where tourists spend time with the local pickers amongst the tea bushes – there is a complete immersion into the geography of place through engagement with the producers (www.halpetea.com). Tea tourism is further discussed in Chapter 17.

FIGURE 3.2   *Tourists enjoy a tea tourism experience in Sri Lanka.*
Permission given and credit for photo: Halpe Tea, UHE Exports (pvt) Ltd

Lévi-Strauss (1970 [1964]) was a leading structural anthropologist and presented a dualistic view of food and society where he perceived 'nature/raw' as 'uncivilised' as opposed to 'culture/cooked' as symbols of civilised society. However, what you will notice throughout this book is that food and drink tourism activities provide an antithesis to these ideas. There is a growing myth of the natural in reaction to processed foodstuffs that is challenging the nature/culture dichotomy put forward by Lévi-Strauss. Such conceptualisations now seem untenable with the evolution of touristic activities that dilute these differences, such as sourcing vegetables in a local market, buying direct from the growers at the place of production, or enjoying fresh fruit at a 'pick your own' site. These sites seem to offer something more 'civilised' for today's discerning consumer in search of something different in the places they visit.

FOOD AND THE 'NOSTALGIC' EXPERIENCE OF PLACE

Tourism engagement with food can bestow many powerful feelings of yesteryear, nostalgia and identity. Bessière (1998) suggested that locally produced food in rural regions encapsulates a lost and idealised past, providing a tangible object that represents liberation from a 'stressed society'. By transcending time and space, such food is attributed and embedded with imagined qualities of representing a kind of 'Eden uncontaminated' (Boniface, 2003). Food and drink are often presented as objects capable of re-establishing severed connections to nature and times past. Certainly, discourses of 'purity' and 'naturalness' are often presented when discussing local food and drink. For example, a policy initiative by the UK Countryside Agency (2002) called 'Eat the View Scheme 2001' encouraged reconnection with nature and rural life through food, promoting a myth of returning to 'nature'. Recent years have certainly seen a rising popularity of 'natural' products, building on the concept of the fresh in a processed environment and 'handmade in a plastic world' (Graburn, 2006), perhaps offering urbanites a chance to return to rural roots in a post-industrial environment.

Reconnection with nature is linked with concepts of nostalgia and a yearning for 'yesteryear'. Being deeply embedded in systems of meaning, food should be recognised as a poignant reminder of cultural identity and tradition, with a capacity to conjure the sense of a purer place, but also hold time and memory in an era of hyper-mobility. Lowenthal (1985) claims that there is no better term than 'nostalgia' to express the sense of modern malaise in an increasingly globalised world and it is through material symbols and relics that we engage with a socially constructed version of the past. Food is being purposely embedded in these intangible constellations of the past to evoke a sense of a place temporally and spatially apart. Nostalgic resurrection is often generated by familiar feelings, emotions and sensory recollection of the past.

CASE STUDY

Nostalgia and food: the Virginia Food Heritage Project, USA

The Virginia Food Heritage Project in the USA asks you, 'Do you remember ever eating an Albemarle Pippin or Buckingham apple picked fresh from a tree? What about a Power's Heirloom tomato, or Turkey Craw Cornfield beans? These are a few of the fruits, vegetables and other farm products that generations of central Virginians once grew, but that are now disappearing. Some are gone already.'

The project is an example of the many collaborative, community-based projects that seek to develop a greater understanding and documentation of a region's food heritage. It seeks to ensure that the region's identity is retained and supported through food projects. VFHP seeks to build knowledge about heritage place-based foods, and to create future opportunities for economic development and community-building. The project is a collaboration of growers, gardeners, community planners, historians, conservationists, and scholars who are gathering local knowledge about local agriculture and food heritage, and plan to use this knowledge to inform decision-making that will shape the landscape and lives. The project is housed within the Institute of Environmental Negotiation at the University of Virginia.

Source: http://vafoodheritage.com

FOOD AND DRINK AS MULTI-SENSORY ENGAGEMENT

Urry's seminal *The Tourist Gaze* (1990b) examines the tourism experience and demonstrates how it is characterised by different visual signs from those present in everyday life. Drawing directly on Foucault's conception of 'gaze', the ocular-centric approach (particularly in the original edition) shows how tourism experiences are socially organised and systematised through the visual appropriation of place. Although the work has often been taken too literally in suggesting that the visual sense is the central organising sense for tourists, it is a useful starting point in considering how food affects us through all the senses and emotions. It could be suggested that tourism research has been overly dominated by concepts of visualism and it is through food that we might be able to show how the object and viewer are connected to more sensual, embodied experiences with more active bodily involvement (physical, intellectual, cognitive and the gaze). Even Urry stated later that 'I think there is a multiplicity, and the way to approach the analysis of these multiplicities of tourist gaze is, among other things, to think about the taste-scapes, smell-scapes, sound-scapes, touch-scapes' (Urry interviewed in Franklin, 2001).

It is important to recognise and consider the poly-sensual nature of tourism and move beyond a unilateral ocular view. For example, olfactory (smell) sensations can play a central role in experiencing place (Dann and Jacobsen, 2003). Certainly, looking at the multi-sensual experience of place helps us to see how food and drink might be studied in a way that goes beyond the prioritisation of the visual in conceptualising the touristic experience. Everett (2008) argues that food offers one of the ultimate sensual tourism experiences which engages all of the senses and involves an immersive physical internalising of a culture, as opposed to a distanced, passive 'gaze'. Food provides an arena of total immersion, where objects are internalised and the wider practice often encompasses entry into places that are submerged in images, signs, languages, costumes, people and entertainment. Being 'the only product that can be experienced using all the human senses, therefore deepening the tourism experience' (du Rand and Heath, 2006: 210), it surely demands attention.

Many tourism textbooks will now argue that tourism is an integral expression of everyday life, not a distinctive escape from it. This is one conceptual area where food and drink tourism research can make a contribution; where the analysis of food-motivated travel can explore and contribute to new conceptualisations of tourism consumption (many of which are outlined in this book). Not only is food one of the few essential 'ingredients' required in our everyday lives, it is one of the most popular items that we purchase on holiday as a souvenir in order to re-live or remember past experiences (Morgan and Pritchard, 2005). Food tourism research can help further explore Franklin's (2003: 2) contention that tourism activity 'is a central component of modern social identity formation and engagement … that is infused into the everyday'.

Cheese making behind the window, Arran, Scotland

Glass viewing windows have become a popular and 'safe' way to demonstrate food production to tourists, but, rather than promoting food as a way of engaging with multi-sensual forms of tourism, some visitor attractions offer a 'sanitised gaze' and controlled tourist space. For example, the Torrylinn Creamery on the Isle of Arran in Scotland (Figure 3.3) is one of many food attractions where viewing windows create encapsulated arenas without smell or social interaction (due to hygiene, health and safety requirements).

FIGURE 3.3 *The Torrylinn Creamery, Isle of Arran, Scotland. Photo by author*

The viewing window is a sheet of glass, but the promotion of a sensuous experience is constrained. Such sites dilute the experience through the controlled physical separation of the tourist from the producer where food is not smelt, tasted or touched – merely viewed (Everett, 2008). This concept and approach is further explored in Chapter 10.

Place can be experienced with the body. Consequently there is value in conceptualising the process as an iterative circuit where the body is taken to the place, and in turn, the place is experienced by embedding aspects of it into the body through tastes, smells, sounds. Body and space are mutually defining; a two-way interface. This situation is described by Calvino (1981) in van Westerling (1999: 81):

> The true journey implies a complete change of nutrition, a digesting of the visited country – its fauna and flora and its culture (not only the different culinary practices and condiments but the different implements used) …This is the only kind of travel that has meaning nowadays, when everything else visible you can see on television without rising from your easy chair.

Food tourism involves cognitive and bodily engagement in order to experience space. Tourists seek to experience the environment and this can be undertaken through culinary bodily engagement. This chapter seeks to make explicit the link between embodiment, food and place. Furthermore, through touristic spatial encounters the everyday is said to become blurred and unsettled as places are encountered by the body. This concept of embodiment also permeates work on 'emotional geographies' (Davidson and Milligan, 2004). Certainly food consumption is directly linked to emotional responses, provoking both positive and negative emotions in different people.

PERFORMATIVITY: FOOD TOURISM AS A 'REPERTOIRE OF SYMBOLIC STAGES'

Not only can place be experienced through food, but embodied practices can also inscribe places with identity. Tourists enact and inscribe space with their own stories and create their own sense of place. This is referred to as 'performativity', which is a dimension of active bodily involvement and a concept discussed widely in recent tourism research. It has been theorised as a way of making sense of self and the world. Pursuing a concept of a 'performance' (as opposed to a gaze) widens the focus to consider the more multi-faceted, multi-sensory experiences that make up tourism, such as adventure (Cloke and Perkins, 1998), sex tourism (Clift and Carter, 2000) and food tourism (Everett, 2008).

Edensor (2001) argues that tourists create their own performance maps and play out identities to (re)produce tourist spaces in which they are able to redefine their own landscape. As part of a 'performance turn' it has been argued that we are no longer trapped in a representational world, but look at what tourists actually do. In placing specific emphasis on 'things' (e.g. food) and their importance in tourism performance in the way they enhance the physicality of the body, such work stresses the inescapable hybridity of human and non-human worlds, the material and the non-material. Performativity is about how the body engages with the natural world and is certainly a useful concept in terms of looking at food and drink consumption. Thrift's (1997) non-representational theory also links with performativity as it encourages us to move away from representations and focus on non-representational forms of engagement, such as dance. Pioneered by Goffman (1959), the idea of drama in the everyday is pervasive, fuelling work on tourism places as regulated performance spaces. For instance, Haldrup and Larssen (2006) claim that tourism performances are often subtly choreographed, both by tourists themselves and the tourism industry.

Working with food and drink tourism: volunteering as a researcher on food and drink projects (an example from Pompeii, Italy)

If you want to get involved with food and drink you could volunteer on a range of research projects. One example is the Pompeii Food and Drink Project, which offers people a chance to study the ancient Roman city of Pompeii, Italy through the vehicle of food and drink in an ongoing research project. In AD 79 the volcano Mount Vesuvius erupted and buried the Roman city of Pompeii with volcanic ash, leaving little time for people to escape from disaster. The city has been preserved by the ash and is now a popular World Heritage site. This 157-acre tourist attraction contains houses, shops, temples, baths and streets. Researchers have documented plant-life, bakeries and aspects of manufacture and trade. This unusual 'tourism' research package attracts volunteers to analyse the patterns of daily life by a study of the structures associated with food and drink. This kind of experience directly builds on the link between heritage, place and tourism, and, like most volunteering projects, would help you gain valuable skills, as well as provide an overseas experience.

Further details can be found at: http://pompeii-food-and-drink.org.

Experiences are socially and spatially managed, where touristic things can be taken and used as active agents in the production of tourism landscapes. Although food tourism sites are promoted as places offering authentic, embodied, multi-sensual experiences of local food, they are increasingly becoming 'themed' spaces undergoing perpetual re-imagining and manipulation. One of the themes in this book is the role of 'food tourism providers' in reinforcing, re-encoding enactive norms and stereotypes of identity and food. Through concepts such as performativity and embodiment it is suggested that food tourism can contribute insightful perspectives in the reconfiguration of relationships, places and identities.

Critical Reflections: food, place identity and the 'cultural turn'

Although conceptualised as a plurality of 'turns', the concept of a 'cultural turn' can be traced back to the 1960s. It shifted thinking towards 'meanings' rather than objective and quantifiable political or economic 'explanations', placing culture in the spotlight and focusing attention on ideas of identity, belonging, justice and power. This 'turn' in thinking hailed the development of a massive theoretical phenomenon that saw the emergence of a new era of social thought and academic theorisation, drawing on work emerging from cultural studies, particularly from the Birmingham Centre for Contemporary Cultural Studies (CCCS). Culture became a productive intellectual resource to rewrite understandings of life in the modern world. It fostered the emergence of theoretical fluidity informed by postmodern and post-structural thinking which challenged and unmasked traditional realist perspectives.

In geography, the 'cultural turn' meant embedding the cultural into the economic and vice versa, and placed emphasis on the complexities involved in the interaction of the economic and cultural practices that were shaping and influencing people's lives. Places became seen as more than social containers and constructs of political contestation. This approach had particular resonance with the discourses of 'new' cultural geographies on place construction where 'all landscapes are symbolic' (Cosgrove, 1989: 125). The cultural turn questioned the idea that identity was immutably fixed and stable. Identities began to be actualised in numerous ways, fuelled by a move towards deconstruction and consideration of the micro-scale, and the emergence of theoretical fluidity informed by postmodern and post-structural thinking.

Cresswell (2004) argued that the landscape must be conceptualised as both 'what is seen' and 'the way it is seen', thus conjoining the material and the symbolic. In line with post-structuralist work that questioned whether identities could be mapped, conceptualised and represented at all, Stuart Hall (1996) challenged the idea that identity was measurable. He suggested that there had been an impasse in identity theory and asked 'who needs identity?' It was clear that when geographical discourses shifted in the cultural turn, conceptualisations of identity were also significantly redefined. Identity began to be approached as plural and contradictory. Rather than fixed categories, regional identity became regarded as complex, with vague meanings combined in a meaningful socio-political space where unrelated elements were grouped together in what Sayer (1992) labelled 'chaotic conceptions' (after Marx). The call to 'deconstruct' place-identity specifically problematised links between regions and identity.

CHAPTER SUMMARY

This chapter has drawn on a number of disciplines to show how studies of food and drink tourism must look beyond disciplinary borders and recognise potential contributions from beyond tourism literature and theories. Tracing the evolution and impact of the cultural turn (see Critical Reflections box) in other subject fields may help develop food tourism as a subject in its own right, whilst also contributing to the wider theoretical development of tourism studies. The gradual turn to cultural aspects is evidenced by the blurring of the production/consumption relationship and the increasing attention being paid to identity, nostalgia, power and adoption of qualitative case study methodologies. It is, however, acknowledged that contemporary food tourism research is openly engaging with issues of society and culture, although scholars have by no means fully investigated the key cultural aspects of food tourism. As a consequence, it may provide a vehicle for retaining something of the social and material in touristic experiences.

Food tourism can make a positive contribution to the recent wave of work in tourism studies on embodiment and performativity. These trends indicate a theoretical shift towards more critical accounts of production/consumption which engage with concepts of power, agency and non-representational theory in food research that are becoming ever more prevalent in cultural geographical discourses. It suggests that food is a polysemic artefact that is able to characterise place and identity; consequently it can be utilised to theorise the complex nature of postmodern production and consumption. It can be harnessed in the cultural examination of place and can contribute knowledge to the growing body of work examining embodiment and the poly-sensual nature of 'new' forms of tourism. In furthering the concept of the 'taste-scape', we can broaden tourism discourses beyond the ocular-centrism of the tourist 'gaze' discourse. Further work is required to analyse this aspect of tourism activity and the value in engaging with non-representable forms of this 'new' tourism. More sensuous tourism geographies should be promoted as a way to generate new knowledge about the tourism experience.

END OF CHAPTER POINTS

- Food can (re)produce and construct national, regional and individual identities.
- The concept of experiencing the 'Other' within tourism can be traced back to Edward Said's (1978) 'Orientalism' thesis and can be associated with tasting the food of the 'Other'.
- Food tourism can regenerate rural and peripheral areas and consequently sustain and preserve cultural methods, heritages and practices.
- Food and drink should be regarded as part of a physiological, social and symbolic environment.
- Food and drink are impregnated with meanings and represent the consumption of myriad emotions, places and identities.
- Food and drink experiences and offerings are capable of re-establishing severed connections to nature and times past.
- Experiences are socially and spatially managed, where touristic things such as food can be taken and used as active agents in the production of regulated tourism landscapes and social imaginaries.

FURTHER READING

Appadurai, A. (ed.) (1986) *The Social Life of Things: Commodities in Cultural Perspective.* Cambridge: Cambridge University Press.

Bell, D. and Valentine, G. (1997) *Consuming Geographies: We Are Where We Eat.* London: Routledge.

Boniface, P. (2003) *Tasting Tourism: Travelling for Food and Drink.* Aldershot: Ashgate.

Caplan, P. (1997) *Food, Health and Identity.* London: Routledge.

Cook, I. and Crang, P. (1996) 'The world on a plate: culinary culture, displacement and geographical knowledges', *Journal of Material Culture,* 1 (2): 131–53.

Edensor, T. (2001) 'Performing tourism, staging tourism: (re)producing tourist space and practice', *Tourist Studies,* 1 (1): 59–82.

Everett, S. (2009) 'Beyond the visual gaze? The pursuit of an embodied experience through food tourism', *Tourist Studies,* 8 (3): 337–58.

Howes, D. (ed.) (1996) *Cross-cultural Consumption. Global Markets, Local Realities.* London: Routledge.

Mintz, S. (1996) *Tasting Food, Tasting Freedom: Excursions into Eating, Culture and the Past.* Boston: Beacon Press.

Molz, J. (2004) 'Tasting an imagined Thailand: authenticity and culinary tourism in Thai restaurants', in L. Long (ed.), *Culinary Tourism.* Lexington, KY: University Press of Kentucky, pp. 53–75.

Said, E. (1978) *Orientalism: Western Representations of the Orient.* New York: Pantheon.

Urry, J. (1995) *Consuming Places.* London: Psychology Press.

Urry, J. (1990) *The Tourist Gaze: Leisure and Travel in Contemporary Societies, Theory, Culture & Society.* London: Sage.

THE GROWTH AND DEVELOPMENT OF FOOD AND DRINK TOURISM

4

NICHE TOURISM AND THE GROWTH OF FOOD-INSPIRED TRAVEL

CHAPTER OBJECTIVES

- To illustrate how food and drink tourism sits within the wider spectrum of special interest (niche) tourism
- To explore different interpretations and forms of special interest and niche tourism
- To outline how special interest tourism (especially food and drink) is being adopted in niche marketing strategies
- To introduce specific niche forms of food and drink tourism (such as coffee tourism, beer tourism, whisky tourism and cookery schools) that will feature in later chapters

CHAPTER SUMMARY

This chapter situates food and drink tourism within the category of 'special' interest tourism (SIT) (also known as 'niche tourism' or 'alternative tourism'). This is an increasingly popular area for tourism studies and this chapter will place food and drink leisure pursuits within the wider growth of postmodern and more individualised forms of tourism. Moreover, food tourism will be presented as a significant contributor to the rapid growth of new forms of special interest and niche tourism (Douglas et al., 2001; Novelli, 2005; Weiler and Hall, 1992).

This chapter outlines the development of food and drink tourism and maps it onto other forms of niche tourism, such as music, art, dance, folklore, wildlife and sport tourism. It outlines what these areas have in common and why these new forms of consumption have emerged. Certainly, there has been a significant rise in forms of tourism consumption that intimately engage with the gastronomic landscape (Brunori and Rossi, 2000; Richards, 2002). As part of a rise in new consumption patterns, food-motivated travel is gathering momentum. It has become a significant 'pull' factor in its own right and provides a touristic 'keystone' with which to construct a destination's overall marketing strategy.

This chapter also introduces more specific special interest areas within food and drink tourism such as cookery schools, and also coffee, tea, whisky and beer trails (addressed in more detail in Chapter 17). Although outlined here in the context of special interest areas, these niche sectors are discussed in more depth in Part III.

THE GROWTH OF SPECIAL INTEREST TOURISM

This chapter discusses food and drink tourism within the context of growing interest in 'new' forms of tourism experience, which has been fuelled by reconfigured consumption patterns and a desire for less packaged, niche, more individual and less formalised modes of tourism consumption. It should be noted that 'niche' does not necessarily equate to 'small' because so-called niche markets can often generate large numbers of tourists (for example, ecotourism and sport tourism). Many organisations are now offering a wide range of touristic activities beyond the traditional mass beach holiday that respond to market needs for more tailored products, small groups and a more discerning offer. For example, you only need to search the internet to uncover a wide and diverse range of opportunities to join wildlife tours, bird- or whale-watching trips, watercolour trips, festival tourism, salsa tourism, and other more bizarre and unusual forms of tourism or leisure interest such as bog snorkelling or shark tourism. It seems almost any activity can become a prefix for the word 'tourism' now, such as *dance* tourism, *art* tourism, *eco*-tourism, *film* tourism, *medical* tourism, *hunting* tourism, '*dark tourism*', and even *hip-hop music* tourism (see Xie et al., 2007). Beynon and Dunkerly (2000: 26) suggest that there has been an 'indigenisation of music, art, architecture, film and food' and certainly a desire for 'tasting the world' has become a popular pursuit. Although Chapter 2 outlined the very early beginnings of food exploration, there has certainly been a rise in food-motivated travel over the last 20 years.

Some useful books and articles that look at a wide range of these special and niche forms of tourism activity include: Douglas et al. (2001); Novelli (2005); Trauer (2006); and Weiler and Hall (1992). Although such interests are not new in themselves, the term refers to non-commercialised, individualised activity which can relate to an activity type (some listed above), geographical area (perhaps a remote destination or inhospitable area such as Arctic tourism or mountain tourism), or social group (such as holidays for those aged over 60, trips for single travellers or the gay market). There is no one clear definition of special interest tourism; Hall and Weiler (1992: 5) suggested it was when the 'traveller's motivation and decision-making are primarily determined by a particular special interest with a focus either on activity/ies and/or destinations and settings'. Later on Swarbrook and Horner (1999: 38) proposed that the special interest tourist is motivated by a desire to indulge in an existing interest or develop a new interest in a novel or familiar location. Novelli (2005) chooses to refer to 'niche tourism', a term adopted from 'niche marketing' that effectively describes providing a specific product to satisfy a particular market. It has become regarded as the antithesis to mass tourism and the product of 'new tourism' (discussed below).

It has been suggested that special interest tourism was originally associated with 'serious leisure' participants (Stebbins, 1982; Weiler and Hall, 1992), but it has now become a significant market segment and increasingly 'novice' and 'soft' leisure participants are consumers of special interest areas. Certainly tourism consumption patterns reflect an increasingly diverse spectrum of interests in late-modern leisure society. Trauer (2006) suggests that special interest tourism should be viewed as an interdisciplinary system, which comprises the overall environment (local to global), the tourist demand system, and the tourism industry supply system with the media as a major influence on tourism today. Figure 4.1 shows the merging of all these components in this interactive system.

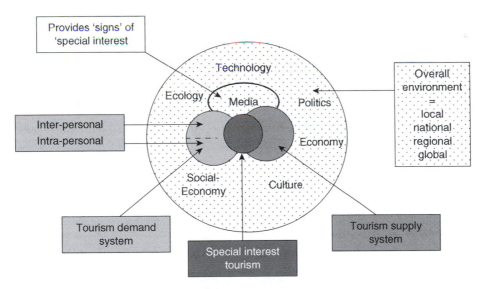

FIGURE 4.1 *Special interest tourism as an interactive system (Trauer 2006, SIT as interactive system, reproduced with permission)*

NEW MODES OF CONSUMPTION

The growing attractiveness of niche forms of tourism reflects a changing world
that is increasingly more pluralised, aestheticised and heterogeneous. Although
not wholly uncontested as a theory, it has been suggested that advances in transport, capital, labour and migratory patterns have led to an increasingly fluid
Western society (Harvey 1989). Following the upheavals of the 1940s, the post-
war Western world underwent a degree of cultural transformation, reflected in
the increase in hybrid and diasporic communities, rising complexity of the modes
and nature of consumption and increased density of signs and images (e.g. television and advertising). Jamal and Kim (2005) point to a growing era of mobile,
disorganised capitalism that involves the dominance of non-material forms of
production, particularly facilitated by rising levels of media and internet activity.
This postmodern cultural transformation and societal restructuring is certainly
reflected in the character and nature of tourism.

This change in the way society is structured has often been conceptualised in
terms of a shift from homogenised Fordist modes of consumption (standardisation
and uniformity) towards something post-Fordist (different, varied and personalised)
in nature (see the Critical Reflections box on Fordism below). Studies such
as Gale's (2005) work on the decline of British seaside resorts employed this
theoretical perspective to explain the shifts in tourism behaviour patterns. This
apparent restructuring has often been attributed to the end of Fordist modes
of production and consumption (the standardised and mechanised methods
employed by Henry Ford to produce production line cars) that characterised the
earlier part of the twentieth century. With the increased methods and styles of
production in what has become called a 'post-Fordist' era, it has been suggested
that tourism is no longer characterised by large numbers of tourists resembling

a kind of mass production line with a high degree of standardisation, familiarity and homogeneity. Rather, in an age of post-Fordist tourism (effectively 'beyond' or 'after' Fordism), we see the creation and development of specialised, individual and niche markets marked by flexibility and choice; a market where food- and drink-motivated tourism has a very obvious role to play as an alternative activity that resists mass production and more regulated consumptive patterns.

Critical Reflections: Fordist to post-Fordist to neo-Fordist modes of consumption

As mentioned above and in Chapter 1, Fordism is a term associated with Henry Ford and the very standardised and mechanised way that cars were produced by the end of the nineteenth century. The term has generally been adopted by Western Marxist thinkers, although it was first introduced by Antonio Gramsci in 1934 in his essay on *Americanism and Fordism* and has become a central theory in understanding society and socio-economic phenomena. As society has become more fluid, terms such as 'post-Fordism' and even a return to some standardisation through 'neo-Fordism' have been adopted to reflect modern changing consumption patterns.

Shaw and Williams (2004) argue that many tourists are in a very weak position to negotiate new forms of consumption. For many marginal economic groups, acts of tourism consumption are restricted and often centre on elements of Fordist patterns of consumption. Therefore, rather than pursuing activities in line with the flexibility and individualism associated with a post-Fordist pattern, scholars contest the simplistic theoretical approaches by suggesting there has been an apparent development of 'neo-Fordist' patterns of consumption characterised by the success of Disney and similar theme parks. There is an argument that some of the elements of standardisation and predictability that characterised old forms of Fordist consumption still coexist with new forms of tourism consumption, with cheap, inclusive and standardised packages as popular as ever.

Urry (1990b) argues that some tourists are 'post-tourists': they are aware of the artificiality and inauthenticity of postmodern touristic spaces (such as Disneyworld), yet seem content to gaze playfully upon the lives of others. The 'post-tourist' is apparently happy with a multitude of choices, characteristic of an eclectic mix of the visual, material, hyperreal and symbolic, as long as it constitutes an 'experience'. The concept goes some way in reconciling the seeming paradox where tourists are apparently searching for a 'natural' experience in an overly processed world, yet their self-ironic attitude means they are content to pursue activities within overtly constructed and inauthentic settings (Rojek, 1995).

There has been research on the apparent co-existence of different forms of tourism consumption by examining the types of tourists engaged in different activities. Poon (1993) has attempted to distinguish between 'new' and 'old' tourism experiences and tourists. In essence, it could be claimed that mass tourism, characterised by large-scale packaging of standardised leisure, has come under pressure from global forces shaping tourism (transport, environmental limits and new consumer imperatives), leading to the development of new tourism patterns and of a 'new tourist'. It is this concept of a 'new tourist' (or someone who could be considered a postmodern tourist) that seeks to explain the rise of the middle class as producers and consumers of new forms of travel as they react or respond to a rapidly globalising world. Food tourism certainly forms part of this rapid growth in new forms of 'special interest' tourism and can be conceptualised as a reaction to the perceived 'massification' of tourism.

Featherstone (1991) suggests that tourists also engage in an 'endless quest for new experiences' to enhance their own cultural capital (see Critical Reflections: Bourdieu's concept of cultural capital, below). This desire for cultural ascend- ancy amongst a growing market of critical consumer tourists has been examined in regard to environmentally-sound holidays (e.g. Krippendorf, 1986). Although often explained with theories of ethical decision-making and political expres- sion, the desire for cultural capital accumulation is reflected in the growth of food tourism, which is providing a way to develop personal distinction. There are many motivations behind the growth of special interest tourism. For example, in addition to finding avenues with which to alleviate a sense of loss of individual- ism, other motivations might include creativity, health, new experiences, human relations and personal growth. Cultural capital should be recognised as a means of developing personal distinction and, as Munt (1994) has suggested, might be more about 'ego' than 'eco'.

Critical Reflections: Bourdieu's concept of cultural capital

The concept of cultural capital is most closely associated with the work of the French sociologist, Pierre Bourdieu (1984). Although consumptive practices have been pre- sented as one aspect of cultural resistance, they were originally theorised as a means with which to construct individual identity and distinction. Generally categorised as forms of economic, cultural and social capital, 'capital' is Bourdieu's unifying theme. It is both inscribed into the objectivity of things and something that can be personally accumulated. Consequently, tourism research has often utilised the concept to explain how qualities are expressed to mark oneself (or a place) as distinctive from others.

Although originally developed by Bourdieu to explain the educational sys- tem, his theories enjoy a wide resonance and are used to understand the development of new forms of tourism. Bourdieu suggests it may be pertinent to reflect on the extent to which producers of tourism also engage in activities as a way of formulating 'distinction'. Bourdieu has helped fuse cultural studies and sociology in examining the development of new cultures and the rise of new cultural intermediaries (food tourism brokers) as bearers of new forms of cultural capital. Certainly Bourdieu argues there is a need to look beyond economic theory to take account of the social world, urging a theorisation of the complicated nature of social status and class and how taste is expressed in its various guises. These ideas build on the Critical Reflections box in Chapter 3 on the 'cultural turn'.

In a review of special interest tourism and relevant typologies, Brotherton and Himmetoglu (1997) suggested a simple 'Tourism Interest Continuum', proposing that a transition from safe to more adventurous kinds of travel and holidays occurs in a form of tourism cycle, with the tourist 'trading up' and purchasing social prestige, cultural capital and ego-enhancement. They put forward a basic, three-part decision-making process (adapted into Figure 4.2). It shows the key decision-making steps outlined by Brotherton and Himmetoglu (1997).

This process shows the difference in deciding where to go, but more specifically the introduction of 'what' can be done. There is significant overlap across the different categories, but they display similar motivational approaches to many other models of special interest tourism, which include Hall et al.'s (2003) on primary/secondary and subsidiary interest; 'passive/active participation' (Gammon and Robinson, 2003); and wine tourism (Charters and Ali-Knight, 2002). A useful figure is provided by Trauer (2006), reproduced in Figure 4.3, which takes a number of different research findings and maps special interest tourism onto tourist interests and motivations.

General Interest Tourism
- Where would I like to go?

Mixed Interest Tourism
- Where do I want to go and what activities can I pursue there?

Special Interest Tourism
- What interest/activity do I want to pursue, and where can I do it?

FIGURE 4.2   *Three SIT questions based on Brotherton and Himmetoglu (1997)*

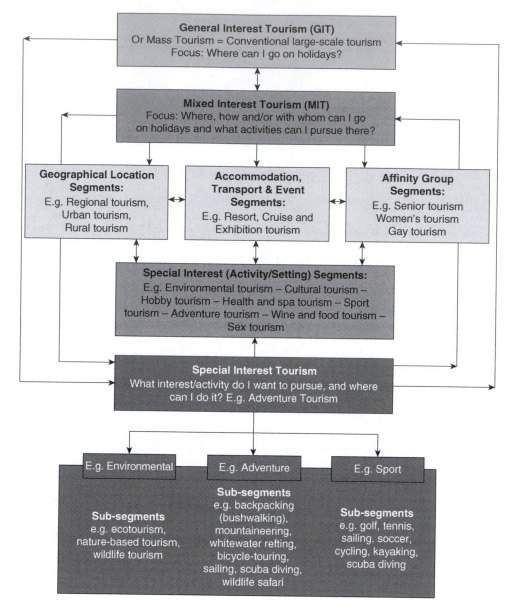

FIGURE 4.3 *A special interest tourism cycle (Trauer, 2006). (Permission given)*

MARKETING SPECIAL INTEREST TOURISM

Trauer (2006) has suggested that, in promoting SIT, such purchases produce a kind of 'cult' status where 'like-minded' activists recognise and adopt symbols. It is through such signs and symbols that they can demonstrate an interest or level of commitment to that activity, or mode of consumption. The media have a significant role to play in promoting such images and use associations with such niche areas to present a sense of individuality: something special and something with cultural capital. Trauer claims that it generates a possible cognitive and affective response and builds both knowledge and familiarity with the activity and also the places within which it occurs. This emotive response often features as a central objective to destination marketing strategies. As Ryan (2003) reiterates, the tourist comes to the tourism location with pre-conceived images within which they have allocated themselves a role.

Novelli (2005) suggests the term 'niche tourism' is directly influenced by the more established concept of 'niche marketing'. Certainly there is a belief that special interest tourists are more discerning, are prepared to pay for the experience (rather than a cheap mass tourism holiday) and seek a sense of elitism or prestige. Niche tourism offers a highly sophisticated approach to marketing which allows for segmentation and the opportunity to build a more intimate relationship with the consumer, capitalising on people's desire to express their personal identities through their activities and consumption patterns. This relationship builds on pre-conceived images and expectations and rests on the promotion of symbols of individualism and uniqueness. Niche tourism approaches are becoming central to regional destination marketing approaches that seek to galvanise the cumulative attractiveness of certain places. For example, Thailand has traditionally been associated with sun, sea and sand holidays, offering young people a hedonistic, mass tourism experience (Aktas, 2011). However, more recently it has been promoting a new identity through luxury and special interest tourism, primarily culinary tourism. The Case Study of Baipai Cooking School (below) is an example of the new businesses opening in Thailand which aim to attract the more discerning, older traveller to Thailand.

This 'niche' tourism offer based on cookery schools is being reported regularly through international news channels and is helping to establish a new reputation for Thailand. For example, in 2012, the BBC World News reported that a woman called Saiyuud Diwong, who had lived in the Bangkok slums all her life, was now offering something new:

> Five years ago she was encouraged by a friend to start a cookery school. After working on her English language skills she set up her business in the middle of the slum and started teaching foreign tourists how to cook traditional Thai food – simple, spicy and fresh, with ingredients from the local market. She is now the main breadwinner in her household and earns about $800 (£505) per month. (Diwong quoted in BBC World News, 24 August 2012)

CASE STUDY

Baipai Thai Cooking School, Thailand

'Whether Thai food is your favourite one, or cooking is your hobby, or may be just curiosity. There is no better way to learn Thai cooking than once you are in Thailand and taking a Thai cooking course, taught by qualified Thai professional' (Baipai Thai Cooking School, 2015).

▶

Established in April 2002, the Baipai School is an example of one of many new cookery schools meeting a growing interest in culinary tourism. Accredited by the Ministry of Education of Thailand and located just outside Bangkok in a small house, it has been developed to meet a special interest need in cookery holidays. They offer half-day and full-day courses to tourists and locals keen to engage in this specialised touristic activity (as shown in Figure 4.4). A more detailed discussion about tourists as producers, and cookery schools as food tourism is included in Chapter 19.

FIGURE 4.4 *A tourist enjoys a Thai cookery school, Thailand. Credit photo: Julie Pottinger*
Source: www.baipai.com

A quick internet search for 'cooking in Thailand' uncovers an impressive list of businesses, trips and activities. It seems Thailand is successfully rebranding itself as a culinary destination.

In more generic marketing literature there are clear examples of how companies are moving away from traditional mass marketing techniques towards more niche marketing approaches (e.g. Dalgic and Leeuw, 1994; Kotler, 1989; Richards, 2011a). Dalgic and Leeuw (1994) suggest that through the application of company specialisation, product differentiation, relationship marketing and customer focus, niche firms can focus their marketing activities on a limited part of the market with relatively few competitors. Certainly for destinations, targeting niche tourism segments is believed to encourage repeat visits as it allows destination marketing organisations to focus on tourist needs, which leads to more effective product positioning. To achieve this destination positioning, it is necessary to identify the attributes that the visitor regards as important, and those that are unique, to ensure it stands out from other destinations (Lew, 2008; Morgan et al., 2002). As mentioned, the adoption and development of niche-based tourism products can act as a destinational pull and lead to growth of market share.

To ensure the successful positioning of a destination it is important to promote both a consistent image and spectrum of activities to satisfy the desires of the consumer. Certainly, Tarlow (2003) claims that niche marketing appeals to tourism officials as they target their product towards consumers who have the highest propensity to travel and then who speak highly of it. Research indicates that SIT tourists are higher-yield than other tourists: they stay longer, spend more and participate in more activities (Keefe, 2002). It is this strategic segmentation that is central to a successful strategy. Huh and Singh (2007) suggest there are four key criteria by which these markets are segmented: socioeconomic/demographic; geographical; psychographical; and psychological/behavioural.

Promoting niche tourism as part of a destination marketing approach is a competitive strategy. In an ever-changing and competitive global market place, special interest tourism promotion provides a way of standing out from the market and generating increased profits from higher-earning, more discerning and more committed consumers. For example, there are several destinations that have successfully focused development around the expansion of one or two niche sectors. Examples include the government-backed golf strategy in Scotland in 2000, now worth over £100m to the economy (plus wider benefits), or the success of film-induced tourism in New Zealand following a high-profile campaign promoting the landscapes featured in the Lord of the Rings trilogy (Beeton, 2010). Another example is the gay and lesbian travel market, which has led to significant growth in tourism numbers in the USA where popular 'Pride' festivals are now held across the world in destinations such as Sydney, Australia which hosts the *Mardi Gras* festival, alongside similar parades run in many cities across the UK.

CASE STUDY

New culinary destinations – Peru, South America

One country that has embraced niche tourism marketing using food and culinary promotion

is Peru. Although this South American country may not be considered a traditional gastronomic country like France or Italy, it has been aggressively promoting its gastronomic offer through the Peru Tourism Bureau. It is certainly regarded as a food tourism destination, with Frommer's Peru guide stating that 'Peruvian Cuisine is among the finest and most diverse cuisines found in Latin America and indeed the World' (Schlecht, 201: 24), and the Organization of American States (OAS) names Peruvian gastronomy as the 'cultural heritage' of the Americas (*El Comercio* 23 March 2011). Certainly Peru is promoting this identity through the media, magazine articles such as *Gourmet* and *TIME*, and travel guide books: 'street carts to haute cuisine, restaurants offering exquisite interpretations of Peru's unique fusion culture' (*Lonely Planet*, Peru 2013:10).

Further information: http://visitperu.com/peru gourmet_ing/bestcuisine.html

Godfrey and Clarke (2000) claim that although destination development often begins with new ideas and initiatives, it is as much to do with attractions and services as it is about marketing and promotion. Although destinations are gradually exploring new sectors, Morgan et al. (2002) have suggested that very few destination marketing organisations (DMOs) have really considered or explored the markets for their various niche products. One theory that has been used to highlight the behaviour of economic sectors by providing products in low volume, but in greater variety, is the 'long tail' theory (Lew, 2008). This emphasises the shift in some places from mass tourism and 'short head' theory, where profit is based on a narrower product range sold in high volume. The long tail destination is highly individualised, providing specialised products and services that are demanded by niche consumers. It comes down to perceptions of value rather than volume.

NICHE FORMS OF FOOD AND DRINK TOURISM

The category of food and drink tourism could be categorised as a 'macro niche' area of cultural tourism, rural tourism, heritage tourism and even event tourism. The category of food and drink can be further segmented into a number of 'micro niche' areas. Figure 4.5 provides a simplistic illustration of how malt whisky tourism in Scotland can feature as the fifth level of segmentation from special interest tourism, which is presented as the top level category.

Whisky tourism is a very popular sub-category of drink tourism. More than one million people visit whisky centres and distilleries in Scotland each year, spending around £27 million in total. The Scotch Whisky Association (SWA) claims that distilleries and visitor centres directly boost the economy, the job market and the tourism industry. Another popular sub-category of drink tourism that has attracted academic interest is beer tourism. Both are discussed in more detail in Chapter 17. However, for the purposes of illustration here, one of the most visited beer festivals is Oktoberfest in Munich, Germany (see the following Case Study). Whole destination marketing strategies have been known to centre on beer tourism; for example, Belgium has become known as a beer (and chocolate) destination, and one of the most visited and promoted attractions in Dublin, Ireland is the Guinness factory.

FIGURE 4.5 *Example of how malt-whisky tourism can be segmented within a special interest tourism categorisation*

CASE STUDY

Oktoberfest, Munich, Germany

FIGURE 4.6 *Enjoying the Oktoberfest, Munich in Germany. Photo given with permission. Credit Sandra Selmanovic*

Oktoberfest is a 16-day beer festival held every September in Munich, Bavaria, Germany. Although beer tourism is considered 'niche', this festival is the world's largest and attracts around 6 million people every year. It has gained global status as the ultimate food and drink event. Oktoberfest was first held as a party to celebrate the wedding of the Bavarian crown prince Ludwig to Princess Therese from Saxony-Hildburghausen on 12 October 1810. Oktoberfest is now firmly embedded into the culture of the region. Other places such as London and Texas (USA) now hold similar Oktoberfest celebrations based on the Munich event. It is the ultimate beer tourism event!

The most researched sub-category of drink tourism is undoubtedly wine tourism. Many would argue research into wine tourism pre-dates research on food tourism. The resources and findings available on wine tourism are extensive, which is why it is discussed separately in Chapter 7. However, it should be considered a sub-category of drink tourism and it is appropriate to include it in this chapter as a 'niche' form of tourism.

Other beverages discussed in academic tourism literature are tea and coffee, also discussed in more detail in Chapter 17. In particular, Lee Jolliffe has championed research on this sector of drink tourism. In drawing tea tourism examples from a wide variety of places including India, Canada, Sri Lanka, China, England and Japan, she argues that tea tourism offers the authentic experiences sought by discerning tourists (e.g. tea tours, tea attractions and tea houses). Turning to coffee tourism, Jolliffe (2010) discusses the numerous touristic activities that involve purposeful visits to see coffee production and coffee-providing destinations and attractions. Jolliffe provides an extensive overview of how these kinds of niche tourism touch upon almost every corner of the globe. There are even opportunities to gain valuable work experience in tourism by joining coffee projects (as featured in the 'Working with food and drink tourism' box below).

Working with food and drink tourism: Coffee Works, Ecuador

Volunteering is a great way to obtain valuable skills and work experience (see Chapter 19 too). Volunteers are welcomed to the small village of El Airo in the southern part of Ecuador's Loja province. Known for growing the best coffee in Ecuador, the 'Coffee Works' project is one of many examples of a work-based community project that attracts people to work alongside local people to help sustain skills, build relationships and help local farmers with the coffee harvest. As stated, 'During this time you will learn every step of the coffee process including harvesting, de-pulping, fermenting, washing, drying, sorting, toasting, grinding, packaging and marketing'.

Source: www.volunteerecuadorcoffeeworks.com/coffee-dreams-coffee-tourism.php
See the discussions and examples presented for coffee tourism in Chapter 17.

Such beverage-motivated travel should be regarded as an integral part of food and drink tourism. Furthermore, these kinds of 'niche' tourism are directly associated with a more sustainable and greener form of tourism that can often utilise the skills and knowledge of tourists to support community development and the economic growth of developing nations. This aspect of tourism development is addressed at the end of Chapter 17.

ACTIVITY   RESEARCHING NICHE TOURISM

Use an online database or your online library to locate and read an academic, peer-reviewed journal article on a niche form of food or drink tourism (e.g. coffee, tea, beer, wine, cheese, cider, sake, whisky, etc.). You may need to put key food tourism words into your search engine to locate this specific type of article (e.g. 'tourism' and 'beer').

TABLE 4.1 *How special interest tourism can be mapped against tourism models and typologies*

Model /typology	Subject, discipline or focus of model	'Special interest' tendencies/category	'Mass' tourist tendencies/ category
De Gracia (1964)	Leisure studies	Contemplation	Recreation
John R. Kelly (1983)	Leisure studies – *Leisure identities and interactions*	High levels of personal identity, social identity, presentation and role identity	Lower levels of personal identity, social identity, presentation and role identity
Iso-Ahola (1983)	Leisure studies		
Cohen (1972)	Tourism	Non-institutionalised, e.g. 'explorer' and 'drifter'	Institutionalised, e.g. 'individual' and 'organised' mass tourist

(Continued)

(Continued)

Model /typology	Subject, discipline or focus of model	'Special interest' tendencies/category	'Mass' tourist tendencies/ category
Plog (1974)	Tourism	Allocentric	Psychocentric
Dann (1977)	Tourism	Pull (towards interest)	Push (away from mass tourism)
Poon (1993)	Tourism	New tourist	Old tourist
Feifer (1985)	Tourism	Post tourist	Mass Tourist
Gray (1979)	Tourism	Wanderlust	Sunlust

Special interest typologies

Gammon and Robinson (2003)	Sport tourism	Active	Passive
Hall (2003)	Health spa tourism	Primary	Secondary
Richards (1996); Craik (1997)	Cultural tourism		
Arsenault (1998) and (2001)	Educational tourism	Formal	Informal
Morpeth (2001)	Bicycle tourism		
Charters and Ali-Knight (2002)	Wine tourism		
McKercher, Ho and du Cros, (2002)	Cultural tourism	Culturally motivated tourists	Culturally attracted
Acott, La Trobe and Howard (1998)	Eco Tourism	Deep	Shallow

(Reproduced with details from: Brotherton, B. and Himmetoglu, B., 'Beyond destinations – special interest tourism', *Anatolian International Journal of Tourism and Hospitality Research*, 8 (3) (1997), pp. 11–30)

1. Outline the type of tourist involved (use Table 4.1 to help you) and find out what is said about their motivations i.e. why do people get involved with this type of activity?
2. According to the article, how is it marketed and where?
3. What can be learnt about niche forms of food and drink tourism from this article?

It would be useful to discuss your article with others to build up your knowledge of different forms of food and drink tourism.

CHAPTER SUMMARY

This chapter has introduced and discussed the concept of 'special interest tourism', also known as 'niche tourism'. It has presented a number of definitions and has encouraged you to think about the vast array of activities and touristic interests that could be considered 'special interest', such as art tourism, dance tourism, sport tourism and event tourism. It has situated food and drink tourism within the spectrum of these alternative forms of tourism, but has also illustrated how food and drink tourism can be further segmented into 'micro' niche types such as cookery schools, beer tourism, tea tourism, coffee tourism and whisky tourism.

This chapter has also introduced the concept and theories of 'new' forms of tourism that have been used to explain the growth of special interest tourism. It has outlined how changes in society have been conceptualised in terms of a shift from standardised and homogenised Fordist modes of consumption towards post-Fordist (different, varied and personalised) modes. It has also suggested that some activities can be considered 'neo-Fordist' where new modes of tourism are not always individual and uniquely personalised.

The nature and use of niche marketing strategies was also discussed. It has been suggested that many destinations are targeting niche tourism segments to attract new markets and encourage repeat visitation. Some traditional 'mass' destinations are now reinventing themselves (e.g. Thailand with culinary tourism, or Scotland with golf tourism) and their destination marketing strategies are shifting to focus on tourist needs, which leads to more effective product positioning and new identities.

Finally, the chapter looked at the 'micro' niches of food tourism and discussed the many food and drink tourism interests and pursuits that can be categorised under the more macro 'food and drink tourism' umbrella term. By outlining the different special interests within the category such as whisky tourism, beer tourism, tea and coffee tourism it has shown how 'food and drink tourism' has its own special interest tourism category and can be broken down into a plethora of different modes and activities. In drawing on a variety of international case studies and examples, this chapter has sought to show you the wide-ranging and varied nature of food and drink tourism.

END OF CHAPTER POINTS

- There is no agreed definition for special interest tourism, or 'niche tourism'. It is the pursuit of a specific tourism activity to satisfy a particular market or interest.

- Tourism consumption patterns reflect the diverse spectrum of interests in late-modern leisure society, in which niche forms of tourism reflect a changing world that is more pluralised and heterogeneous.

- Post-Fordist tourism ('after' Fordism), is a theory that explains the development of specialised, individual and niche markets characterised by flexibility and choice.

- Niche marketing aims to build a relationship with the consumer, capitalising on people's desire to express their personal identities through their activities and consumption patterns.

- Special interest tourism often (although not always) seeks to attract higher-earning, more discerning and more committed consumers.

- Food and drink tourism can be segmented into a number of 'micro niche' areas, such as tea, coffee, cookery school, beer and whisky tourism.

FURTHER READING

Bourdieu, P. (1984) *Distinction: A Social Critique of the Judgement of Taste*. Cambridge, MA: Harvard University Press.

Douglas, N., Douglas, N. and Derret, R. (eds) (2001) *Special Interest Tourism*. Milton, Queensland: John Wiley and Sons Australia, Ltd.

Jolliffe, L. (2007) *Tea and Tourism. Tourists, Traditions and Transformations*. Clevedon: Channel View Publications.

Jolliffe, L. (2010) *Coffee Culture, Destinations and Tourism*. Clevedon: Channel View Publications.

Morgan, N., Pritchard, A. and Pride, R. (eds.) (2002) *Destination Branding: Creating the Unique Destination Proposition*. Oxford: Butterworth-Heinemann.

Novelli, M. (2005) *Niche Tourism: Contemporary Issues, Trends and Cases*. Oxford: Butterworth-Heinemann.

Plummer, R., Telfer, D., Hashimoto, A. and Summers, R. (2005) 'Beer tourism in Canada along the Waterloo–Wellington ale trail', *Tourism Management*, 26 (3): 447–458.

Trauer, B. (2006) 'Conceptualizing special interest tourism: frameworks for analysis', *Tourism Management,* 27(2): 183–200.

Weiler, B. and Hall, C.M. (1992) *Special Interest Tourism*. New York: Bellhaven Press.

5

THE GLOBALISATION AND LOCALISATION OF FOOD AND DRINK

CHAPTER OBJECTIVES

- To introduce and critically discuss the concepts of 'globalisation' and 'localisation'
- To outline the relationship between food and globalisation
- To discuss how food and drink tourism has contributed to processes of globalisation and localisation
- To present Ritzer's 'McDonaldisation' thesis in the context of food tourism
- To offer a case for globalisation in the context of feeding the world's growing population

CHAPTER SUMMARY

This chapter introduces ideas of global/local food and discusses the concepts and theories of globalisation and localisation in the context of political and economic regulation. It introduces seminal research such as Ritzer's (1993) 'McDonaldisation' thesis, Wu and Cheung's (2002) work on the globalisation of Chinese food and Nützenadel and Trentmann's (2008) work on food and globalisation. After some brief definitions, the chapter explores the work of Ritzer, who looked at growing fears of homogenisation and expressed concern about the destruction of place identities through rationalised and standardised practices. It will briefly highlight and critique the relevance of his thesis in regard to new forms of consumption where the fast-food restaurant, especially the pioneering and still dominant chain of McDonald's restaurants, is presented as the ultimate example of the rationalisation process.

The chapter also looks at the globalisation and localisation of food, for example adaptation to local tastes, such as the McDonald's McAloo and McTikka burgers offered in India, and Starbucks offering coffees with local flavours, or how the 'local' is now present all over the world in the case of the 'Irish Pub' (see the Case Study on pp. 80–1). It explores the reaction to fast food and draws links to the power and influence of the mass produced food industry. The growth of ethical consumerism is also discussed in the context of how a homogenised food offer seems to remain defiant in the midst of growing concern about its negative health implications. The economic injustice of the system of global food distribution is also discussed.

Furthermore, this chapter looks at the application of science to the production, manufacture and distribution of food, which means for many people that food is plentiful, convenient and there is widespread choice. In assessing issues of starvation around the world, the chapter looks at ways of producing food efficiently through science and technology. This chapter seeks to challenge some orthodox views and uses the lens of food and drink to take a broad view of globalisation and its complex political and economic dimensions.

WHAT IS GLOBALISATION?

The term 'globalisation' is much debated and contested and there is no agreed definition. It was first used in the 1960s to describe the changing nature of society and the influences on a worldwide scale (Waters, 1995). It is a concept that has been adopted by a number of different disciplines and uses many different perspectives from economics, technology, culture, politics, and environmental studies. The Oxford Dictionary defines it as 'the process by which businesses or other organisations develop international influence or start operating on an international scale'. Two further definitions offered by sociologists are the 'spatio-temporal processes of change which underpin a transformation in the organisation of human affairs by linking together and expanding human activity across regions and continents' (Held et al., 1999: 14), and 'interconnectedness of the world as a whole and the concomitant increase in reflexive, global consciousness' (Robertson, 2001: 461).

Some argue that there is a clear economic link to the process of globalisation that is fostered through transnational organisations; however, many, such as Robertson (2001), suggest there is no single driving force to globalisation. Different forces, such as religion, culture and technology, are also key causal forces in the evolving process of globalisation. Therefore, globalisation should not be regarded as a monolithic concept, but as a multi-dimensional and complex mixture of homogenisation (similarity) and heterogenisation (difference). Globalisation should therefore never be regarded in simplistic terms as either a civilising or destructive force. Its impacts across countries and time should be approached and studied in ways that acknowledge its haphazard, discontinuous and sometimes contradictory nature.

FOOD AND GLOBALISATION

It is perhaps unsurprising that one of the most prominently discussed discourses within the food tourism literature is 'globalisation'. Although the concept of globalisation is far wider than the growth of food companies, a significant body of work has been looking at the close connections between the two. Consequently, specific attention is paid in agro-food research to the growing spectre of global fast food giants and the reactive development (and retention) of locally identifiable culinary products (Tregear, 2003). Boniface (2003) draws attention to the idea of active 'disenchantment' having occurred as a result of the perceived rationalisation of society and homogenisation of foodstuffs. It is suggested that food and drink tourism provides a means through which distinctiveness can be reasserted and offers a mechanism with which individuals can consciously resist gastronomic blandness. Likewise, in his book on food history (introduced in Chapter 2), Fernandez-Arnesto expresses his belief that, 'Fussiness and "foodism" are methods of self-protection for society against the deleterious effects of the industrial era: the glut of the cheap, the degradation of the environment, the wreckage of taste' (2001: 252). It is this concept of counteracting an apparent dilution of culinary distinctiveness that lies at the centre of many arguments for the promotion of local and distinctive food and drink, and this apparent reaction of individualism to culinary standardisation and the domination of global multi-national food corporations is addressed in this chapter. One example of local resistance against an apparent destruction of local identity and community has been an ongoing campaign against the opening of supermarkets and large food stores. In the UK, one particularly prominent national campaign has been against a supermarket giant Tesco (see the campaign website at http://tescopoly.org). The sign on a fishing shed in the coastal town of Aldeburgh in the UK illustrates this depth of feeling (Figure 5.1 Aldeburgh against Tesco.plc).

Under the theme of 'Chinese Foodways in the 21st Century: Prospects of Globalization of Chinese Food and Cuisine', a number of scholars including Sidney Mintz came together to discuss the impact of Chinese food on the world in 1997. The outcome was an edited book (Wu and Cheung, 2002) encompassing a variety of issues and approaches to globalisation, using Chinese food as the main conceptual vehicle. Three main parts of the book ('Sources of the Globe', 'Chinese Food and Food for Chinese', and 'Globalization: Cuisine, Lifeways and Social Tastes') highlight how this one culture's food has spread across the globe. The book traces how it has evolved and changed the societies and cultures it has entered. In tackling issues such as immigration, identity, diasporic communities, colonisation and human transformation, it outlines the global reach and power of one nation's food. These different aspects of globalisation help illustrate many of the themes within the work of Nützenadel and Trentmann (2008), which provides an historical overview of the relationship between food and globalisation by bringing together numerous aspects of global history with food studies.

FIGURE 5.1 *Aldeburgh campaign against Tesco.plc. Photo by author*

If you think the product is globally mass-produced and distributed put in under 'global'. If you think the product can only be purchased from one location or one retailer/producer, then write the name in the 'local' column. For some items you might feel they are both local in nature but have a global market, so write these in the central column (for example, a regional speciality that is mass produced). Figure 5.2 is an example to help guide you.

When you have completed your table, discuss the following in your groups:

1. How easy did you find this exercise? Give reasons for your answer.
2. What kinds of products were difficult to categorise?
3. What conclusions can you draw from this exercise about the food and drink we buy and consume?

GLOBALISATION AND 'MCDONALDISATION'

There is perhaps no better food-related conceptual dimension of globalisation than Ritzer's (1993) aptly named 'McDonaldisation' thesis. Since this, there have been subsequent and related concepts, such as 'Coca-colonisation' (Kuisel, 1993). Ritzer describes McDonaldisation as 'the process by which the principles of the fast-food restaurant are coming to dominate more and more sectors of American society as well as the rest of the world' where Western society has become placed in an 'iron cage of rationality' (a term adopted from Max Weber – see the Critical Reflections box on p. 77).

Leslie (1995: 113) highlights concern about food standardisation:

> But if the food production process erased much of the material substance of traditional life in rural areas, the food distribution process eroded the culinary heritage of regions. The drive to rationalise and standardise combined with the global sourcing of ingredients, has muted the effects of climate and seasonality and internationalised the cuisine of western societies.

CASE STUDY

Local residents against McDonald's and the 'McLibel' case

Numerous organisations have reacted to the perceived negative effects of fast food chains, and particularly McDonald's. One of these organisations is the 'Local residents Against McDonald's' group. A long list of campaigns from around the world against McDonald's is published on their website:

▶

www.mcspotlight.org. Campaigners argue that McDonald's threatens local businesses in communities and leads to increased levels of litter and traffic, claiming 'people are increasingly also raising objections to McDonald's targeting local children, and to the spread of low wage jobs. Many proposed new stores are opposed and many local campaigns have been successful, despite the company trying to use their resources and influence to override the wishes of local people.

Linked to this campaign is what came to be known as the 'McLibel' trial, which lasted more than ten years: the longest running case in English history. The case McDonald's Corporation v. Steel & Morris [1997] was filed by McDonald's Corporation against environmental activists Helen Steel and David Morris (often referred to as 'The McLibel Two') over a pamphlet critical of the company. After appeals, they won the case and the full story (from their perspective) can be read at: www.mcspotlight.org.

LOCALISATION

Research points to a growing resistance to an apparent homogenisation of foodstuffs in an industrialised food systems structure, where 'localisation' becomes adopted as a panacea to the process of globalisation and a perceived sense of 'placelessness'. In a study of local food systems, Feagan argues that such practices pose increasingly visible structures of resistance and counter-pressure to global food systems and draw attention to the renewed concern and search for a 'sense of place', conceived as an attempt to 'recapture spatio-cultural identity in an era of identity-confusion under globalisation' (2007: 32). Although local/global dichotomies are frequently deconstructed to favour a merger of the local and global (Robertson, 1994; Waters, 1995), the concept of 'globalisation' remains prevalent and is a useful focus of reference in socio-cultural geographical food research (see Collins, 2008).

Hjalager and Richards (2002: 3) argued that 'far from producing a homogenised gastronomic landscape, the tension between globalisation and localisation is said to be producing ever more variation'. Similarly, in a positive approach to the food globalisation debate, Hall, Mitchell, Hjalager and Richards (2002:71) offer a perspective that enables this contested concept to be tackled, placing the complex development of food tourism in the context of this 'emergent, evolutionary phenomenon'. In essence, they suggest that, even with the undeniably heightened movement of people and foodstuffs across the globe (especially through tourism) and the growing concern that local and regional foods are being rationalised and standardised in a kind of 'McDonaldisation' process, there is potential for food tourism to promote individualism, strengthen distinctive identities and rekindle local food traditions. Food tourism is said to provide a kind of reaction, but there is little research on how this actually manifests itself.

WHEN THE GLOBAL IS LOCAL AND THE LOCAL IS GLOBAL: GLOCALISATION

As mentioned in the Activity box, there are foods that could be referred to as 'glocal'; a term encapsulating the tension between the global and the local. There are numerous examples of societies and cultures either incorporating elements of the global to suit local needs and priorities, or adopting local elements to meet global needs. This halfway house has been termed 'glocalisation' by economists and sociologists and there is evidence to suggest this approach helps to strengthen and increase a sense of local belonging and identity. What is interesting is how relatively few products are sold in a globally standardised form; rather, most products are given a 'local flavour' and modified to suit the local culture, values and tastes. For example, Chinese tastes including rice and noodle dishes are accommodated in the McDonald's branch in Yangshuo near the Li River in China, as shown in Figure 5.3.

Globalisation is impossible to conceptualise without the concept of localisation; such is the nature of dichotomous conceptualisations. Rather than being destructive, where globalisation invades local contexts, it can be argued that new forms of local cultural identity and self-expression can be intertwined with wider processes. This dichotomy can be become blurred when global foods are embraced in the locale and localised foods become global, thereby undermining

FIGURE 5.3 *McDonalds at Yangshuo, China. Photo by author*

many of the assumptions that lie behind some more rigid globalisation perspectives. For example, the Cornish pasty is associated with one county in England, but they are widely distributed by global manufacturers and are now being sold stuffed with Indian curry or French cheese.

The concepts of localisation and globalisation of food and drink are particularly important to consider when looking at the relationship between producer and consumer. It can be argued that food and drink tourism seeks to overcome a possible disconnection from increasingly globalised and depersonalised food systems. There is a strong sense that aggressive food firms and the increased standardisation of food threatens the inherent cultural and environmental qualities of local foods, and a strengthening of regional cuisines is needed (Ilbery and Kneafsey, 1998). This kind of thinking about food localisation has become a powerful focus for agro-food research because it seems to dilute the common concept that globalisation is ineluctable. Hines (2000: 4) describes it as 'the ever increasing integration of national economies into the global economy through trade and investment rules and privatisation, aided by technological advances', where 'localisation is a process which reverses the trend of globalisation by discriminating in favour of the local'. However, this dichotomy should be questioned. Often such social forces are not merely a direct reaction or simply a negative 'anti-globalisation' protest, but may work with and alongside the system to bring change (Mak et al., 2012). Tregear (2003) has suggested that although global processes have been ongoing since early industrialisation and led to a rural exodus, delocalisation and loss of inherited knowledge and skills, they have been manifested most strikingly with the growth of large food producers.

Bové and Dufour – The world is not for sale!

Often the concepts of food globalisation and identity are closely associated with the destruction of local cultural identities and the encroachment of Westernised consumer culture. One of most dramatic acts of resistance to the perceived impact of global corporate forces was the actions of two farmers, Bové and Dufour, who dismantled a McDonald's in Millau, Aveyron in France in 1999 as an act of protest against commercial powers. In 2002, they were sentenced to three months in prison. Bové was imprisoned for 44 days and later ran for the French Presidential Election in 2007; although defeated, on 7 June 2009, he was elected to the European Parliament as a member of Europe Écologie, a coalition of French environmentalist political parties.

Further information available from: Bové, J. and Dufour, F. (2001) *The World is Not For Sale: Farmers Against Junk Food*. London: Verso.

One critique of Ritzer's (1993) pessimistic portrayal of the identity-diluting power of McDonaldisation is the apparent growth of post-Fordist 'mass customisation' (discussed in Chapter 3) and the dramatic restructuring in the fast food system, which has had to incorporate postmodern demands and local customs and tastes. It is possible to question the supposed omnipotence of global corporations in bringing about culinary homogeneity. Although it still retains significant uniformity, rather than a standardised and calculable 'McWorld', subtle changes have made begun to make McDonald's part of local cultures. Ritzer (2009) is very aware that McDonald's has to work hard at negotiating regional tastes and customs. Examples include the introduction of salmon burgers in Norway, Teriyaki burgers in Japan and the withdrawal of cheese to meet Halal demands in many Islamic countries. This is one of the paradoxes of globalisation: the local is not weakened where global processes are able to reinstate local traditions.

Simultaneously, local foods are evolving to meet global demands, bringing a series of changes to the nature of many localised 'traditional' foods. This process is twofold: firstly, local foods have been modified to meet the demands of a global tourism market, including removing guinea pig from menus in Peru and dog meat from Korean restaurants. Secondly, local food- and drink-based products are extending into the global market, epitomised by the Irish-themed pub where local food and drink become mass produced, consumed and rationalised (McGovern, 2003). Interestingly, the global Irish brand Guinness even finds itself being offered as a flavour of ice-cream miles away from Ireland, on the beach in Trinidad, as shown in Figure 5.4.

FIGURE 5.4 *Guinness-flavoured ice cream being sold to tourists at Maracas Beach in Trinidad. Photo by author*

In a study of food tourism and globalisation, Mak et al. (2012) suggests the common perception and attitude towards globalisation is as a threat to local gastronomic identities, but their research and conceptual model suggests globalisation actually offers an impetus to reconstruct and reinvent local gastronomic traditions, cultures and processes. They suggest it leads to reinvention, emergent cultures and the conservation of food heritages. They claim:

> From the world culture perspective, food identities and cultures do not necessarily suffer but instead benefit from the dialectical relationship between globalisation and localisation. Destination marketers and culinary suppliers should harness the positive effects of globalisation by reviving and reconstructing local traditions and particularities for the tourism market. (2012: 192)

CASE STUDY

The global 'local' Irish pub

It seems you cannot go to any city in the world without coming across an Irish-themed pub. From the USA to Beijing to Sydney to Tel Aviv, the Irish pub is a global phenomenon and an example of how 'local' has become global. Becoming a site of cultural tourism

(McGovern, 2003), the Irish pub is a local place provided on a global scale. Cronin (2003) looks at how the Irish pub both acts as a marketing tool in promoting tourism to Ireland, but also provides a place of home and familiarity for the Irish (and others) when abroad. One online tourism blogger writes, 'Why then must their pubs dot the globe in a diaspora of leprechauns and black and tans?' (Long, 2011). Certainly, one argument is that this very 'local' symbol promotes an oasis of camaraderie and friendship when you find yourself in unfamiliar countries and places. Ireland has over more than 10,000 pubs, which have a global reputation for creating a welcoming atmosphere; the Irish bar is now a recognised global extension of that hospitality.

Although the McDonaldisation thesis could be criticised for its failure to acknowledge these processes of 'glocalisation', one of the main points to acknowledge is the need to recognise the implications of an increasingly standardised process and growing detachment of food production from its natural origins, and the location of its production a long way from its eventual consumption. This sense of detachment from nature has fuelled shifts to reassert nature and perhaps in direct contradiction to the structural principles behind Lévi-Strauss's 'culinary triangle' (see the Critical Reflections box below).

Critical Reflections: Lévi-Strauss's 'culinary triangle'

A significant body of food tourism research shares many epistemological traits with the structural explorations of food characterised by anthropological and sociological approaches of the 1960s. These approaches were particularly prevalent in the anthropological research of Claude Lévi-Strauss (1970 [1964]), whose studies have transfixed those working on the subject. Approaching food as a 'cultural system', Strauss epitomises early interpretations that concur with Roland Barthes's view that the entire social world is signified by food.

It is perhaps Lévi-Strauss's seminal 'culinary triangle' (1966) shown in Figure 5.5 that best illustrates this structural approach of binary thinking, placing concepts within a rigid framework of two polarities: nature/culture – elaborated/unelaborated, arranged around the three points of the raw, cooked and rotten. Essentially, Lévi-Strauss believed that there was no culture without the existence of food preparation through cooking and heating, thus differentiating civilised (culture) from the uncivilised (nature) in a strict dichotomy.

(Continued)

(Continued)

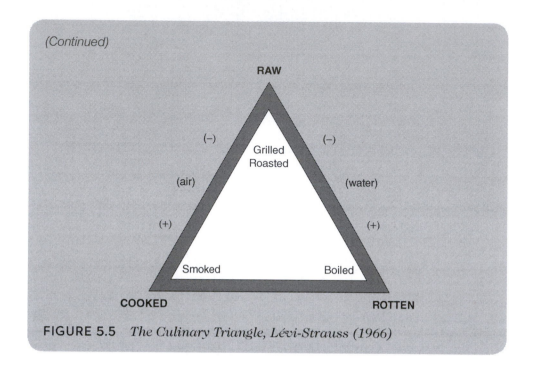

FIGURE 5.5 *The Culinary Triangle, Lévi-Strauss (1966)*

In resisting the standardisation of industrial food production and associated food scares, Murdoch and Miele (1999: 481) suggest that 'modern consumers are acting like the mediaeval citizens of Florence ... in attempting to flee modern plagues'. Therefore, it could be argued that one way to draw together these aspects of food consumption is to look at them from a food and drink tourism perspective and examine how buying local products on holiday might challenge and resist the structures of regulation, rationalisation and commercialisation. The rapid growth of food festivals, culinary events and producer-led initiatives certainly indicates that there is a renewal of interest in local produce, which may be a reaction to a perceived dilution of regional identities and local cultures.

ACTIVITY   MAKING YOUR 'LOCAL' FOOD GLOBAL

Think of a food or drink product from your home town or local region. Try to think of something not easily found elsewhere. Now, think about how you might sell, market and promote this product in the following countries and markets:

1. Japan
2. Botswana
3. Switzerland

FEEDING THE WORLD – THE NEED FOR COMMERCIALLY PRODUCED FOOD?

The arguments for localisation and the problems associated with globalisation have been outlined, but it should be stated that the widespread and global reach of ideas, people and industry should not be regarded only as a destructive and negative process. It is important to look at the application of science to the production, manufacturing and distribution of food. It is through such means that food is made available for people around the world, giving both much-needed sustenance, but also increased convenience and choice. Globalisation could be regarded as a saviour rather than a destroyer of livelihoods and it could be argued that changing patterns of food distribution are important in feeding the world. In producing food efficiently through science and technology (see the Case Study below on Syngenta), there are some obvious benefits (Laudan, 2010).

It has been suggested that food processing and mechanisation can ensure foods are safer by removing toxins, and factory processes allow for longer preservation, which supports wider distribution to countries that may be unable to grow or produce certain important foodstuffs (Friedrich et al., 2009). Processed foods are usually less susceptible to early spoilage than fresh foods and are better suited for long-distance transportation from the source to the consumer. Furthermore, it increases yearly availability of many foods, thus potentially alleviating food shortages and improving the overall nutrition of populations. For further information, read Rachel Laudan's (2010) 'In praise of fast food' in Goldstein's (2010) *Gastronomica Reader*.

CASE STUDY

Feeding and fuelling the world through seed technology – Syngenta

As one of *The Times* 100 Business Case Studies, the US company Syngenta is providing food for the world through industrial methods and upskilling farmers. It is suggested that global demand for cereals is likely to increase by a further 40% and global demand for meat by 60% in the next 40 years. Food production

▶

from existing agricultural land will need to double by 2050 to meet this demand and avoid starvation. Syngenta is the world's third largest seed producer. It employs around 29,340 people (Annual Report, 2014). It works in over 90 countries. They have 8 million large farms worldwide with over 100 hectares as well as the 450 million small farms with two hectares or less. The need for food is growing at a rapid rate. Syngenta adopts technology to create more supply and claims it does this without damaging the environment. It develops products that lead to better crop yields and new and better seeds.

Syngenta's work supports three major themes: (i) Food security: the UN defines this as when all people have access to enough safe food to meet their needs; (ii) Energy security: countries want to be less dependent on others for fuel, and Syngenta helps by investing in and supporting biofuel technology; and (iii) Climate change: using biofuels helps to reduce greenhouse gas.

This is one example of a global company which seeks to have a positive local impact. For more details, see their website: www.syngenta.com. Go to the full case study example: *The Times 100 Edition* at www.thetimes100. co.uk) and try to answer the student questions listed there:

1. What factors have led to the increased demand for food and fuel in recent years? Use facts and figures from the case study.

2. Describe one social, legal, economic, political and technological change that Syngenta has had to consider in developing new products.

Of course, there is more than one interpretation of the impact of mass global production. Others argue that this approach to food production fails to take into account the many hidden costs, including environmental damage, excessive resource usage, declining rural economies and farmer livelihoods, and public health consequences in an illusion of control (Stuart, 2008). Unlike the situation projected by the Case Study business (Syngenta), some argue industrial production has led to a culture of over-consumption in Western countries, particularly in the United States, where there is an obesity epidemic and large amounts of food are simply thrown away (Schlosser, 2012).

CHAPTER SUMMARY

This chapter has presented 'globalisation' as a debated and contested term that has been adopted to explain and encapsulate a changing world and the influences affecting global society, culture and development. It is a multi-disciplinary term that must be considered and approached from many different perspectives and contexts. It has been argued that it is unhelpful to conceptualise it in terms of negative and positive impacts, but it must be considered as an evolving process that draws on (and influences) a number of different forces such as religion, culture, society and technology. Globalisation has been examined through activities and case studies as a multi-dimensional and complex mixture of homogenisation and heterogenisation.

In terms of food and drink tourism, it has been suggested that a growth in interest in local food and producers may be the consequence of a reaction to the increasingly standardised and rationalised production and consumption of food. If the world is becoming increasingly homogenised, then food tourism may present a way of counteracting the dilution of culinary distinctiveness (e.g. shopping at a local farmers' market). In particular, this chapter has presented the 'McDonaldisation' thesis, first coined by George Ritzer to explain the impacts of the perceived domination of global multi-national food corporations. By presenting a Case Study of McDonald's, it is hoped you have been able to consider how food can be globally pervasive, but you are also encouraged to be critical in terms of identifying local elements and processes within what might seem overly standardised processes lacking any differentiation.

Perhaps in contrast, the concept of 'localisation' has also been presented as a reaction to (and consequence of) globalisation. It is argued that there is potential for food tourism to strengthen distinctive identities and support local food traditions; certainly the desire to avoid standardised and homogenised food has benefited local producers. However, the chapter also suggests it should not be about dichotomies and the concept of 'glocal' can go some way in describing the merging of the local and the global in constructive and mutually informing ways. The way global brands and products (such as Starbucks and McDonald's) have adapted to local markets and cultures demonstrates this phenomenon most clearly. It has also been suggested (through a Case Study of the Irish pub) that local traditions are becoming more international and globally recognised.

Finally, it is suggested that globalisation and increased industrialisation and mass production can be forces for positive change, ensuring some of the most deprived countries and poorest nations have access to food. Industrialised and mechanised production has ensured that food can be produced cheaply and makes it more affordable for those in need – although this stance is sometimes hard to justify when you look at the food waste produced by the USA and UK, and contrast this with the high levels of starvation in many African countries.

END OF CHAPTER POINTS

- Globalisation should not be regarded as either a civilizing or a destructive force; it is far more complex than this.
- Food and drink tourism has been regarded as a reaction to concerns that the world is becoming increasingly globalised and standardised.
- The concept and term 'McDonaldisation' was originally coined by American sociologist George Ritzer.
- Reactions to homogenised food offerings have included protests against large food companies such as McDonalds (the McLibel trail) or 'The world is not for sale'.

- Globalisation is difficult to conceptualise without the accompanying concept of localisation.

- 'Glocalisation' is a term coined to explain the merging of the local and global; this is demonstrated by local foods being internationally available, or global brands adapting to local culture and tastes.

- Lévi-Strauss developed a 'culinary triangle' (1966) which links nature (the uncivilised) and culture (the civilised) to the three food points of raw, cooked and rotten.

FURTHER READING

Goldstein, D. (2010) *The Gastronomica Reader*. California: The University of California Press.

Lévi-Strauss, C. (1970 [1964]) *The Raw and the Cooked: Introduction to a Science of Mythology*, trans. John and Doreen Weightman. London: Jonathan Cape.

McGovern, M. (2003) 'The cracked pint glass and the servant: the Irish pub, Irish identity and the tourist eye', in M. Cronin and B. O'Connor (eds), *Irish Tourism: Image, Culture and Identity*. Clevedon: Channel View, pp. 83–103.

Molz, G. (2005) 'Guilty pleasures of the golden arches: mapping McDonald's in narratives of round-the-world travel', in J. Davidson, L. Bondi and M. Smith (eds), *Emotional Geographies*. Aldershot: Ashgate, pp. 63–83.

Nützenadel, A. and Trentmann, F. (2008) *Food and Globalization: Consumption, Markets and Politics in the Modern World*. Oxford: Berg.

Ritzer, G. (1993) *The McDonaldization of Society: An Investigation into the Changing Character of Contemporary Social Life*. Thousand Oaks, CA: Pine Forge Press.

Wu, D. and Cheung, S. (2002) *The Globalization of Chinese Food*. London: Routledge.

6

FOOD, TOURISM AND AGRICULTURAL POLICY

CHAPTER OBJECTIVES

- To outline the relationship between food and drink tourism, agriculture and fisheries policies
- To examine the tensions and issues involved in combining tourism and agriculture policies and industries through food and drink tourism initiatives
- To critically present and discuss the literature on food and agriculture
- To evaluate the rationale and success of agricultural policies in relation to tourism
- To consider the impact of agricultural crises on (food and drink) tourism

CHAPTER SUMMARY

Food tourism and agriculture are intimately linked and this chapter introduces this important relationship. In looking at the policies and the issues surrounding rural diversification strategies, producer pressures and supply chains, this chapter makes links to some earlier issues discussed in Chapter 5 around homogenisation and standardisation. This chapter outlines the context of the relationship between food and drink tourism and agriculture, but also looks at the challenges and possible solutions, and then looks forward with a discussion of the links between food and drink tourism in relation to agricultural production, growing global populations and the aspirations that will drive food production policy in the future.

The link between food culture, agriculture and farming is as old as humankind itself. Wherever you go in the world, you are likely to come across markets where farmers are selling their produce to local people, but also increasingly to tourists and visitors. For example, this might include the close and direct connection with locals and tourists visiting markets in North Cyprus as shown in Figure 6.1, or more formalised initiatives, as demonstrated by the manager of a social enterprise explaining crop growth to tourists at the Eko Mosaik project in Bosnia Herzegovina as shown in Figure 6.2 (provides a Case Study in Chapter 18).

This chapter looks at work on food, tourism and agricultural policy and uses examples from across the globe to illustrate how farming and fishing is explicitly linked to tourism. It outlines the economic context for agricultural production which is often derived from state intervention and agricultural policies, and establishes the links between these policies, the development of tourism, and food and drink provision. After all, Hjalager and Corigliano (2000: 281) state that 'the development and standards of food for tourists are not determined uniformly by tourism policies, but more significantly by national economic, agricultural and food policies'.

The chapter assesses different global agricultural policies and diversification strategies. These initiatives are primarily developed to increase the competitiveness of small farms, and create jobs in an effort to ease rural-to-urban migration patterns and build sustainable rural economies (Sims, 2009). It looks at the impact of agricultural crises such as foot and mouth disease, and discusses the creation of

FIGURE 6.1 *Tourists and locals enjoy buying produce from farmers in a market in North Cyprus. Photo by author*

FIGURE 6.2 *Project director at the Eko Mosaik project, Bosnia Herzegovina where tourists visit a social enterprise farm. Photo by author*

various policies aimed at creating a sustainable, competitive and diverse farming and food sector, contributing to a thriving and sustainable rural economy (through food tourism strategies). One example of this was the United Kingdom's Policy Commission on the Future of Farming and Food and related government White Papers in 2001/2 (Department for Environment, Food and Rural Affairs (DEFRA) 2002). This chapter also looks at fisheries policies and some of the bodies involved in protecting marine life and coastal economies (such as the Marine Management Organisation and the Marine Stewardship Council) and discusses the debates on fisheries policy, coastal communities and the links to coastal tourism.

To support the discussion, policy excerpts, photos and international examples (including Bermuda, South Africa, China, the USA and Bosnia) are included alongside stories from farmers and producers. Successful projects are used to illustrate key points and offer ideas about employment in this key area of policy development and agricultural strategy.

AGRICULTURAL CHALLENGES AND PARADOXES OF SHORTAGE AND DIVERSIFICATION

When images of starvation are projected on our television screens, you may think that the world does not produce enough food to feed everyone, but world agriculture produces 17% more calories per person today than it did 30 years ago (Lang, 2010). Despite a 70% population increase, this is enough to provide enough food per person per day for the whole world. Yet the United Nations Food and

Agriculture Organization estimates almost one in eight people in the world (870 million people) were suffering from chronic undernourishment in 2010–2012. The main problem is inequality in distribution and that many people in the world do not have the land to grow, or income to purchase enough food. As Pretty et al. (2010: 219) states:

> Despite a significant growth in food production over the past half-century, one of the most important challenges facing society today is how to feed an expected population of some nine billion by the middle of the [21st] century. To meet the expected demand for food without significant increases in prices, it has been estimated that we need to produce 70–100 per cent more food, in light of the growing impacts of climate change, concerns over energy security, regional dietary shifts and the Millennium Development target of halving world poverty and hunger by 2015. The goal for the agricultural sector is no longer simply to maximize productivity, but to optimize across a far more complex landscape of production, rural development, environmental, social justice and food consumption outcomes.

There are clear challenges in policy development which support population growth, the need for sustainable forms of land use and efficient agricultural production. Food security and shortages are global issues. Increasing prices for basic foods such as lentils, flour and oil (and in Asian countries, a shortage of rice) are having a detrimental impact on populations (in places such as India, China and the Horn of Africa).

There is a clear economic tension, as the world struggles to feed itself and agricultural developments seek to feed the world through mechanised production, genetically modified food, artificial heat and light. The demand for mass-production in food is growing (as seen in Chapter 5) as governments seek to feed their people. However, you may argue that the push for local food and drink tourism purchasing seems to encourage people to reject genetically modified industrial products (Nunkoo and Ramkissoon, 2011) and move away from imports from developing countries, which often provide valuable income to such countries. It is a complex situation when advocates of food tourism promote the consumption of naturally grown produce from its origin, and yet it can be argued that food tourism promotion also offers a way to help people become aware of the bigger world issues affecting food and its quality. Bové and Dufour (2001: 146) have stated that providing food for the planet is not about increasing numbers of multi-nationals, but supporting local producers: 'As far as world leaders are concerned, the entire planet should submit to market laws. Our struggle is based on resistance to this development.' In particular, the perceived influence of large companies over the development of regulation and infrastructure is regarded as a significant obstacle to developing a local food offer that could support people in local areas. Bové and Dufour (2001) insist there is a worldwide dictatorship governed by multi-nationals. The tension between production and supply is clear: you must have distribution to feed the world, and distribution is controlled by multi-nationals that make homogenised food products.

In parts of Africa, there is an interesting emerging picture where tourism supports food production. For example, the 'pro-poor' economic report for Rwanda in 2007 showed that strategic approaches were being used in tourism to alleviate starvation and poverty (Ashley, 2007: 1). It is clear there is a place for food and local purchasing to increase poor people's incomes, aside from the overall growth of the sector. The report suggests measures such as, 'work on the food supply chain to hotels, lodges and restaurants to boost product quality and volume', and increasing help so that poor farmers can access this market; practical initiatives to help businesses enhance their own 'inclusive business' models; and 'partnerships with tour operators, lodges and hotels, conference organisers, artisans and farmers to make a range of cultural experiences … an integral part of a Rwandan visit' (Ashley, 2007: 1). Tourism may not reach the poorest of the poor, but it offers opportunities for the economically active, and can provide a livelihood that keeps families just above the poverty line. The Rwandan tourism value chain appears not to benefit the very poor, who rely on macro-economic impacts such as foreign exchange, but farmers are encouraged to produce more through diversification strategies and increased financial options gained through tourism. Similar findings on pro-poor tourism and its link with agriculture can be found across the developing world; for example, the situation in Mexico is discussed in Torres and Momsen (2004: 294), who found the need for 'explicit creation of tourism and agriculture linkages to achieve pro-poor tourism objectives'.

It is increasingly apparent that legislation and regulation of agricultural production and distribution have supported sustainability goals for many rural economies and communities. It is important to be aware of the relationship between policy directives, tourism and agriculture, and how these sectors work together (or not) to deliver key development agendas. For example, agricultural production in the UK derives from post-1980 state agricultural policies, which focused on three dimensions of change: from 'intensification' to 'extensification'; from concentration to dispersion; and from specialisation to diversification (Ilbery and Bowler, 1998). Pretty (2002) has argued that policy integration (agricultural policy and consideration of tourism and vice versa) is vital and success rests on how policy-makers effectively integrate tourism policy into agricultural practices. The success of this kind of full integration is subject to some doubt, as many policies seek other environmentally sensitive management practices and frameworks to support agriculture, rather than tourism. Where tourism has provided a useful avenue for promoting sustainability and food production, this has happened when farmers directly meet with consumers and highlight the importance of their consumption choices (Everett and Aitchison, 2008). For example, farmers' markets (as discussed in Chapter 13) promote this level of integration and it is through this diversification of the market that food and drink tourism can support agriculture.

Rural tourism is regarded as a way of boosting a struggling agricultural industry and sustaining a rich and diverse rural landscape (Lane, 1994), where tourism is a key earner in rural areas, and a healthy, attractive and diverse farmed landscape is the foundation for its future. Diversification strategies have become a key component of agricultural policy in many smaller countries within Europe, underpinned by a clear desire to increase the competitiveness of small farms, create jobs, ease rural-to-urban migration patterns and build sustainable rural economies. Tourism has become a primary diversification strategy. For example, in the UK, the creation of the Policy Commission on the Future of Farming and Food (PCFFF) in 2001 demonstrated how a government aimed to create a thriving and sustainable rural economy through supporting a sustainable, competitive and diverse farming and food sector. Food tourism was clearly recognised as a means of achieving sustainable farming through diversification and the reconnection of consumers to the environment, reflecting increasing concern that social, cultural and environmental sustainability is achieved when food and tourism work together, although the relationship of these two sectors can still be highly problematic (Everett and Slocum, 2013).

In terms of the European Community, opportunities to develop multi-functional rural enterprises and initiatives are influenced by the European Commission's (EC) Common Agricultural Policy (CAP). Their proposals for 2014–2020 recognise the value in bolstering social capital to achieve 'sustainable management of natural resources and climate action' (EC, 2013: 3). In seeking to develop a European Innovation Partnership for agricultural productivity to help strengthen the link between research and the agricultural sector, it is timely to look at these relationships. In considering its objective 'to improve the rural economy and promote diversification to enable local actors to unlock their potential and to optimize the use of additional local resources' (EC, 2013: 7), research must be undertaken on how this might be achieved and resourced. The UK government's response to the European Commission's findings acknowledged the need to diversify outside traditional farming boundaries and advocated building on the public's enthusiasm for locally produced food, reconnecting the consumer to the farmer (DEFRA, 2002). In expressing the importance of promoting speciality and regional foods to tourists as well as the need for farms to diversify their business by running tourist-focused enterprise, such policies set a new agenda for many rural enterprises.

ACTIVITY   **ANALYSING NATIONAL AGRICULTURAL AND FOOD POLICIES**

Use the internet to find a current national government policy relating to agriculture and food. It could be one from your own country, or any country of your choice. Numerous policies exist in the public domain and can be found with a straightforward search (for example, Nigeria, India, Peru, China and Switzerland). An example of Food 2030 from the UK is included in the Case Study. Write some brief notes on the following for your case:

- What are its key themes and messages?
- What, if anything, is said about promoting food and drink to visitors and tourists?
- If you were to add a brief section or paragraph to this policy to help establish this link with tourism, what elements and actions would you include?

Food 2030, DEFRA, UK

When the UK government launched its food strategy Food 2030 (DEFRA, 2010), it sought to provide one of the most ambitious policy documents for food and agriculture. The strategy highlights the importance of social capital, where consumers' demand is 'met by profitable, competitive, highly skilled and resilient farming, fishing and food businesses, supported by first class research and development', where 'achieving a sustainable and secure food system for 2030 depends on everyone in the food system working together' (2010: 5). In underlining the desire to encourage tourism, the document clearly recognises that the agricultural sector provides jobs, supports the economy, and builds the character of the countryside, 'which in turn attracts tourism trade, adding further to the sustainability of rural economies' (DEFRA, 2010: 21).

Further information from: DEFRA main website, available from: www.gov.uk/government/organisations/department-for-environment-food-rural-affairs

If we move beyond the UK and Europe to China, a similar approach is apparent. It has been suggested by Yuan (2013) that a 'tourism-agriculture' partnership in China has a direct positive impact on both sides. Yuan has found this coupling stimulates interaction between the rural tourism industry and big agriculture, which shapes new products, extends rural tourism and agricultural industrial chains, and fosters closer coordination. This helps the industry by adding value through the extension of agricultural techniques to specific agricultural brands. The coupling of tourism and agriculture has also been found to provide a new space to stimulate tourist consumption desire and increase their time available for travel; promoting service industries in rural areas, and providing new opportunities for farmers to increase their income by catering to tourists, even on a small scale. For example, producers are now taking advantage of increased tourist interest, as shown in Figure 6.3, which shows a small rural food seller in China where tourists pass by.

Over in Australia, in a study of farm diversification near Sydney, a similar story can be found, with farms looking to develop marketing and new service provision. The Hawkesbury Harvest Farm Gate Trail example offered by Knowd (2006) makes explicit links between tourism, food and sustainable development. With farming under threat from urban population growth through housing demand and mining, farmers have faced significant competition and crisis. In seeking to ensure the value and significance of agriculture, this is a project that brought the community together to provide local produce to visitors through a trail, and rural tourism would be used as a tool for rural development (Bramwell and Lane, 2000; Chambers, 2014). The trails include small producers, artisan sites, and farm gate locations. Such successes

FIGURE 6.3   *Street food seller, Yangshuo in China. Photo by author*

attracting tourism have meant many farmers have expanded their offer and more lucrative avenues, including gourmet food industries, have emerged: 'tourism is an integrating force. ...[it] sets the scene for establishing new relationships between agriculture and other industries' (Knowd 2006: 39).

Even in the small island of Barbados we see a similar quest for sustainable development where farming and tourism have been closely aligned, with a focus on improving the innovation and technology of farming. Working with the Inter-American Institute for Cooperation on Agriculture (IICA), projects such as improving the production of sheep, but also engagement in farm based activities, food festivals and community projects such as rum shop tours have helped bolster the economy. As discussed, the focus on building capacity in agro-tourism is a common approach in the government policy of most countries with a rural and agricultural base. However, in a country like Barbados, the linkages between food production sector and tourism are reported to be as low as 10–30%. The Promotion of Regional Opportunities for Produce through Enterprise and Linkages (PROPEL) project is seeking to help small farmers increase the quality and quantity of fresh, regionally grown fruits and vegetables. The Canadian High Commissioner Richard Hanley stated, 'it will help those farmers build links to steadily expanding regional Caribbean food markets, thereby increasing economic growth. So the grower of fruit might one day supply a cruise ship in port with fresh produce' (IICA, www.iicacan.org, 2015).

Clearly, the issues are global and internationally relevant, and the move towards food tourism is widespread, illustrated by the Economic Commission for Latin America and the Caribbean. A report stated that:

food tourism has the potential to strengthen and expand the linkage between tourism and agriculture in Caribbean countries. The question which needs to be asked, though, is how the benefits from increased tourist expenditure would be distributed among the various stakeholders especially farmers and small scale food processors. (McBain, 2007: 29)

It is of course difficult to provide examples from every country here, but those included should give you an idea of the significance of coupling food and tourism in pursuing global objectives. Certainly, it has become commonplace to raise awareness of agriculture and some of the challenges faced by farmers through tourism initiatives. For example the challenges faced by the Caribbean sugar farmer make up a tourism exhibit at the Eden Project, Cornwall. This display is shown in Figure 6.4.

FIGURE 6.4 *Sugar Farmer Exhibit, Eden Project, UK. Photo by author*

FOOD, TOURISM AND AGRICULTURAL POLICY: THE ACADEMIC LITERATURE

Before we look at specific tourism literature, it is worth highlighting some of the work and theory surrounding food policy and governance. Work by Lang (2003, 2010) has been particularly informative in outlining the radical changes that have taken place in terms of food production and process:

> The twentieth century witnessed a revolution in the nature of the food supply chain, the implications of which are only now being worked through at policy and institutional levels. The period was characterised by unprecedented changes in how food is produced, distributed, consumed and controlled. (Lang, 2003: 555)

Lang's work has concentrated on looking at the many technical and social transformations in agriculture and how this restructuring has been led by, or led to, policy changes. Overall agricultural restructuring has changed due to the way food is grown and reared, biotechnology, sourcing (local to regional to global), processing methods, work patterns and labour, marketing, logistics and distribution, the role of retailers and changing consumer tastes: so much so that a 'new human geography of food emerged' (Lang, 2003: 556). It is argued that such changes have meant government action has become less fragmented and higher-profile. One much-cited example of government intervention is the Farm Bill in the USA, outlined in the following Case Study.

CASE STUDY

The Farm Bill (2013), United States of America

First created during the Great Depression in the 1920s to support struggling farmers, the Farm Bill is the main agricultural and farming policy of the federal US government. It established the policies and federal funding levels for agriculture, agricultural research, nutrition programmes, and rural economic development programme. The last Farm Bill was passed in 2008 and expired September of 2012. In offering perspectives on the development of the 2013 Farm Bill, Roger Johnson (President of the National Farmers Union (USA)) felt that the National Farmers Union (NFU) sees the federal government's role in farm policy as providing a safety net to help in these two circumstances: when disasters strike, and when markets collapse. It is also important that these farm programmes are structured to only provide assistance when needed, not make payments when times are good. Seen as a necessary policy to support farmers, there is a need to push for help in diversification which may include local selling and tourism. For example, the farm bill incentivises disadvantaged people to purchase food from local specialty crop growers to help bridge their nutritional gap while simultaneously providing a market for these farmers and supporting the local economy.

Essays on the latest Farm Bill can be found at the Farm Foundation website: www.farm foundation.org.

A lot of tourism literature suggests food tourism is an effective vehicle for regional development, which strengthens local production through backward linkages in tourism supply-chain partnerships in South Korea (Choo and Jamal, 2009); Telfer and Wall (1996) in Indonesia; Montanari and Staniscia (2009) in the Apennines of central and southern Italy; and Renko et al. (2010) in Croatia. Food tourism is recognised as an important vehicle in delivering policy objectives, supporting agriculture and bolstering rural economies. In rural areas where food production constitutes a large percentage of the economic output, research has looked at how food and drink tourism are perceived to offer new opportunities to promote and distribute local produce while supporting an agricultural economy. This is shown in small rural communities in Ireland, where produce such as local apple juice is sold to tourists in Galway (Figure 6.5). While Fleischer and Tchetchik (2005) question whether rural tourism can benefit from agriculture, many governments have promoted tourism's sustainability credentials through the consumption of local food products (du Rand and Heath, 2006).

With increasing fears of global food homogenisation (addressed in Chapter 5) and the need to support regional regeneration, food tourism has traditionally been approached from two distinct sectors: agriculture and tourism. The coupling discussed above is not always fully utilised. Everett and Slocum (2013) suggest agricultural producers are facing pressures to diversify their offerings and distribution networks in an attempt to secure a viable future in the globalised food chain. Simultaneously, tourism providers struggle to find the regional distinctiveness

FIGURE 6.5 *Irish apple juice, Galway, Republic of Ireland. Photo by author*

FOOD, TOURISM AND AGRICULTURAL POLICY

97

necessary to differentiate themselves (Bramwell and Lane, 2000). Montanari and Staniscia (2009: 1482) suggest that 'food and tourism are part of a systemic network of production; tourism alone is not able to increase the value of quality food'.

Certainly tourism literature has highlighted the link between food, tourism and the environment. Everett and Atchison's (2008) study of Cornwall found food tourism led to an enhancement of environmental awareness. Buller and Morris (2004) and later Sims (2009: 334) add similar sentiments: 'the appeal of local food lies in its ability to encompass everything from a concern for environmental and social sustainability, through to consumer demands for foods which are safe, distinctive and traceable' and 'tourist consumption of local foods creates a market opportunity which can encourage the development of sustainable agriculture, help conserve traditional farming landscapes and assist the local economy'. Clearly, tourism events and attractions do raise awareness and can promote agriculture, as shown in Figure 6.6, which shows an outside exhibition promoting sustainable farmed products in Geneva, Switzerland.

Boniface's work (2003) refers to a 'turning point' in the use of the British countryside and reflects on the growing concern regarding the quality of food and the increasing market for local produce. She argues that traditional industries, such as farming, are facing new challenges with increasingly globalised supply chains and price-competitive marketing strategies employed by food service providers. This sentiment stretches beyond Britain; Bessière (2001: 118) claimed that rural

FIGURE 6.6   *Promoting sustainable farmed products, Geneva, Switzerland.*
Photo by author

THE GROWTH AND DEVELOPMENT OF FOOD AND DRINK TOURISM

areas and food tourism have a fundamental role to play in stemming the tide of perceived globalisation and social homogenisation:

> ultimately, it is the erosion and standardisation of traditional culinary practices that allows us to understand the resurgence of rural gastronomy ... rural areas are thus seeing themselves becoming spaces of reconciliation, welcome and affirmation of culinary heritages.

Local and regional government agricultural and tourism policy is often presented as a product of interrelated, interdependent and often competing interests and is woven from geographical, cultural, and historical differences at national and regional levels (Church et al., 2000). Approaches to policy, such as DEFRA's (2007) Rural Development Programme for England (2007–2013) often pursue contradictory policy instruments, despite working towards comparable results and similar goals. In the UK, policy relating to food tourism has been primarily developed and influenced by the agricultural sector through DEFRA and many commissions have been implemented by the food and drink sector in Scotland, Wales and Northern Ireland. Agriculture and its various components are certainly attractive to tourists, and increasingly privately owned, hidden agricultural enterprises are opening up their doors as doing so continues to offer a greater financial reward than actually growing or selling the produce. One example is Figure 6.7, a small olive producer in Crete that has opened its doors to tourists.

FIGURE 6.7   *Tourists can visit an old olive producing farm, Crete. Photo by author*

A lot of academic literature has focused on agricultural diversification strategies from a corporate or large-scale production approach (Reinsch and Lynn, 1990), but when you look at small-scale, family-run farms, there are significant differences behind the strategies for diversifying, the mode of entry into new businesses, and the financial, organisational, and strategic effects of diversifying (Sharpley and Vass, 2006). For example, in a study of wineries in the Southern United States (Alonso, 2011), the collaboration of small/family-owned operations for exchanging ideas about tourism initiatives has helped build the recognition and success of wineries producing muscadine wine. Furthermore, Van der Ploeg and Renting (2004) identified three reasons why small farms diversify: 'broadening', the introduction of new productive activities (this includes agri-tourism and nature management); 'deepening', which refers to differentiations of supply networks or niche production (including organic products, specific character products, short food supply chains); and 'regrounding' which refers to the mobilisation of the households' resources (such as pluri-activity and new forms of cost reduction).

Clearly, farmers and agricultural production have become more closely aligned with tourism policy and tourism research. Hopefully you can now appreciate the close (sometimes tense) relationship between these policy perspectives and areas. Perhaps one area often forgotten in terms of food production is fish and seafood. It is therefore worth turning briefly to fisheries policies, as these can be the most controversial of all.

FISHERIES AND MARINE POLICIES

It is important to consider fisheries policies because they can have a significant impact on food supplies and tourism. Links between fisheries policies, communities and coastal tourism are increasingly close. Most coastal countries have a fisheries policy, from Australia to the Arctic (including the North Pacific Fishery Management Council, which set up a new Fishery Management Plan for fish resources in the Arctic in 2009) and many have focused primarily on sustainability, environmental consciousness and economic profit. For example, the fisheries policy of Uganda stated:

> The national vision for Uganda's fisheries sector is an ensured sustainable exploitation of the fishery resources at the highest possible levels, thereby maintaining fish availability for both present and future generations without degrading the environment. (National Fisheries Policy for Uganda (NFP), 2002)

Although many fisheries policies have not traditionally concentrated on tourism, increasingly tourism is being used as a reason and vehicle to ensure fish stocks are healthy and to raise awareness of the importance of fish and seafood (a subtle protest by a fisherman against the EU can be seen in Figure 6.8).

FIGURE 6.8 *A small fishing boat in Cornwall shows their opinion of fish quotas, UK. Photo by author*

The European Union (EU)'s controversial Common Fisheries Policy (CFP) sets the quotas for Member States in terms of how many they are allowed to catch of each type of fish. It sets the common principles for EU management, under which each Member State can use different management approaches, such as licences, limited entry or individual fishing quotas. Catches and landings must be recorded and areas may be closed to fishing to allow stocks to recover. It also provides market interventions to support the fishing industry. This policy has been heavily criticised by fishermen, who state that it is a direct threat to their livelihoods. Created to manage fish stock for the EU as a whole, Article 38 of the 1957 Treaty of Rome stated that there should be a common policy for fisheries (the EU Policy can be found at: http://ec.europa.eu/fisheries). To monitor such developments, countries have established organisations to support sustainable development in the marine area and to promote clean, healthy, safe, productive and biologically diverse oceans and seas. The Marine Management Organisation (MMO) for the UK (found at www.gov.uk/government/organisations/marine-management-organisation) is one of many bodies looking after coastal communities, ensuring healthy marine provision and supporting coastal economies.

Some have stated the CFP has had disastrous consequences on the environment, although evidence indicates that fishing stocks have been in decline for some time. However, areas have been over-farmed and the absence of property rights in the waters has led to overfishing and price rises. Around the North Sea, many varieties of fish are in decline, such as cod. One of the most controversial elements of the quotas is that a huge number of fish are thrown overboard after being caught; however, as these fish are dead, this does not alleviate the problem as intended and keeps the price high. The policy has stirred up much hatred, as can be seen from the boat featured in Figure 6.8 and the Case Study below on the 'Fish Fight'.

CASE STUDY

Resistance against the CFP: the 'Fish Fight'

Heightened media coverage by television personalities (such as the UK's celebrity chef Hugh Fearnley-Whittingstall's 'Fish Fight') has raised awareness of the impact of aggressive policies on fish stocks and marine protected areas, such as the CFP. There is a powerful political story being told through television programmes, YouTube clips and videos. The campaign is asking for:

1. Consultation on 127 Marine Conservation Zones (MCZs) along with other Marine Protected Areas (MPAs) to achieve an Ecologically Coherent Network.

2. Sustainable fishing that does not damage the sea floor, such as sustainable levels of potting, static gear, angling and pelagic trawling.
3. Bottom trawling, dredging and other destructive industries such as aggregate dredging and port development need to be stopped to ensure fish are spawning and that nursery, breeding and feeding habitats are maintained or recover.
4. Support for some Marine Reserves, areas where no extractive or damaging activities are permitted to help ecosystem recovery.

Read more at: www.fishfight.net

Many organisations are working to ensure fish stocks are protected. For example, the Marine Stewardship Council (MSC) focuses on fishery certification programmes and seeks to reward sustainable fishing practices, thereby influencing the choices people make when buying seafood, and working with others to transform the seafood market on a sustainable basis. This work has been central in supporting and collaborating with fishermen, retailers, processors, consumers and others to drive change forward and work towards supporting the fishing industry with recognised and credible seafood ecolabels. Obviously, such work goes beyond just supporting and helping develop food tourism, but it highlights the links.

Another example is South Africa, which has a coastline over 3,000 km long and an Exclusive Economic Zone (EEZ) of 200 nautical miles. The fishing industry is worth R1.7 billion (0.5% of South Africa's GNP and 1.5% of the GRP of the Western Cape Province). Tourism and leisure use a lot of these marine resources, for example whale-watching, seal- and seabird-watching and recreational diving are economically significant (Nielsen and Martin, 1996). Certainly there is a large potential for developing eco-tourism and, linked to this, appropriate food tourism through sustainable and locally sourced produce.

Critical Reflections: Agricultural Change Theory

Agricultural change happens all the time as farmers across the world decide what, where, and how to cultivate. This goes well beyond how much food is produced, how much money is made, and how the environment is affected. In thinking about agriculture, it is relevant to consider Agricultural Change Theory and the two seminal writers on the relationship between farming and population, Malthus and Boserup. Thomas Malthus (1959 [1798]: 5) argued for an intrinsic imbalance between population increase and food production, finding it was the fate of human numbers to be checked by 'misery and vice', generally in the form of starvation and war, stating that 'the power of population is indifitely greater than the power in the earth to produce subsistence for man ... Population, when unchecked, increases in a geometrical ratio.' However, the Danish agricultural economist Ester Boserup challenged the assumption by Malthus, stating that agricultural methods determine population (via the food supply). Rather than technological change determining population (via food supply), Boserup (1965: 41) claimed that population determined agricultural methods and 'necessity is the mother of invention', which countered Malthus's assumption that agricultural systems tended to produce at the maximal level allowed by available technology.

In looking at the role of political economy, it is suggested that agricultural change is shaped by external economic systems, and farmers have to contend with economic factors that affect the cost of inputs and value of output beyond local energetics. Market incentives can induce farmers to intensify in the absence of land shortage. Political economy theorists would state that few small farmers grow crops exclusively for subsistence or sale now; most do both, and often favour crops that can be used for food or sale. Market involvement does not totally negate Boserup's model, but it clearly introduces variables that can override the effects of local population and energetics.

Working with food and drink tourism: government bodies

Have you thought about working for the government? This might include leading policy development, undertaking research or managing data analysis projects. Government bodies are regularly advising jobs and often run graduate schemes.

(Continued)

(Continued)

If you are interested in policy development and the civil service, you might like to consider the departments responsible for agriculture, food, fisheries and farming. In the UK this is currently the Department for Environment, Food and Rural Affairs (DEFRA), or in Australia the Department of Agriculture, Fisheries and Forestry (DAFF), or in Norway the Ministry of Agriculture and Food. Recruitment methods vary, but a wealth of jobs are offered across departments and linked organisations. The civil service helps the government of the day to develop and deliver its policies as effectively as possible. It incorporates three types of organisations: departments, agencies, and non-departmental government bodies that work in a wide range of areas, touching on everyone's day-to-day lives, such as education, health and policing. Civil servants work in a huge variety of roles and the roles can be an enormously rewarding. Fast-track routes for promising graduates and experienced professionals are often offered, and professional entry routes encourage people with skills developed in the private sector to transfer into the civil service at the right level.

THE IMPACT AND LEGACY OF AGRICULTURAL CRISES

Agricultural crises can be devastating for people and places. One of the most damaging in recent years has been bovine spongiform encephalopathy (BSE), commonly known as mad cow disease. BSE is a fatal neurodegenerative disease in cattle that causes brain and spinal degeneration. The country most recently affected by it was the UK and it led to over 180,000 cattle being infected, and consequently over 4.4 million cattle being slaughtered during an eradication programme in the 1980s. The first case was reported in 1986, and by November 1987 the British government accepted that BSE was endemic. The first reported case in North America was in December 1993 from Alberta, Canada with the first US occurrence following in the same month. By 8 December 2012, the Japanese government issued a ban on imports of raw beef from Brazil, based on reports that a cow had died in 2010 in southern Brazil carrying diseased proteins. The Brazilian Ministry of Agriculture maintained that its beef was free of BSE. With 36 confirmed cases, Japan experienced one of the largest number of cases of BSE outside Europe. It was the only country outside Europe and the Americas to report non-imported cases. Suffice to say, millions of people stopped eating beef.

Even as recently as August 2013, an English newspaper reported that 'Muddled American and Japanese tourists are cancelling trips to Britain in tens of thousands because they mistakenly believe they could catch mad cow disease from the foot-and-mouth epidemic, travel chiefs said today' (Mail Online, 20 August 2013). It is certainly clear that agriculture and tourism are interconnected, especially in a crisis. It can be a devastating or productive marriage. However, in 2012 the UK was also hit by a horse meat crisis when traces of horse meat were found in many processed 'beef' products; this actually led to more people visiting farmers' markets and local food producers. Consumers go to the local farmers for meat as they know the provenance and can meet the producer. The relationship can clearly work both ways.

In 2001, the UK experienced a devastating outbreak of food and mouth disease (FMD), which impacted heavily on agriculture, tourism and leisure. The loss of tourism revenue was around £5 billion and led to the direct loss of 150,000 jobs. A study by Williams and Ferguson (2005) in the Lake District in Cumbria highlighted the often tragic links between agriculture and tourism. They also highlight the misunderstandings that surround the role of tourism in supporting and creating rural landscapes and lives. This was evidenced when the government decided to 'close' the countryside, leading to a fall in expenditure of £198 million in the Lake District area alone, with 20,000 job losses and a quarter of tourism businesses shut. There seemed to be a misunderstanding by the government of the impact, as they prioritised farmers (with help such as subsidies), but offered limited help to the tourism industry. Certainly, although the right thing was to reduce the spread of the disease, the images of slaughter and burning of animals projected across the world put off potential visitors. The panic response not only killed animals, but destroyed tourism for several years.

Lang (2010) has suggested that the crisis was a shock to political elites, but in some respects the situation was normal; food policies are failing to respond adequately. He suggests that 2005–8 reinforced how the dominant twentieth-century productionist policy paradigm is fading, and producing more food does not always resolve social problems. The crisis did eventually help the government see the importance of tourism to the rural economy and it recognised that plans for managing animal diseases in the future needed to be considered in a much wider context. A positive consequence was the prompt to diversify income and spread risk. One of many examples of diversification in the wake of the crisis is Layhead Farm Cottages, in the Yorkshire Dales. Rosemary and Tim Hyslop had over 400 sheep on their 220-acre farm in the Yorkshire Dales and lost them all in a cull of livestock in one day in July 2001. Thankfully, they had already turned to tourism by building cottages in 1994, and the crisis prompted them to convert more farm buildings to offer tourist accommodation along the walking trail. They are now optimistic about the future.

Hall (2010a) has looked at how crises affect tourism and discusses the issues caused by pandemics and perceptions of food security at destinations. Food shortage and limited agricultural production is clearly another side to the agriculture-tourism relationship. For example, in 2012, it was reported in global newspapers that Greece was struggling to provide food for tourists during its Eurozone crisis. Dr Andreas Andreadis, president of the Association of Greek Tourism Enterprises, tried to reassure potential tourists: 'We want to encourage international tourism and assure potential tourists that there has never been a better time to come to our country.' Unfortunately the Greek debt Eurozone crisis in 2015 has certainly exacerbated this situation.

The Caribbean has also reported concerns over food security which has highlighted their dependence on foreign food imports. For example, Jamaica announced a new $150 million, 2,000-acre rice cultivation project in April 2012. The need to support agriculture is key but must provide opportunity for the region's most vulnerable people, as well maximising resources. Bloggers and writers urged that 'governments must be stronger when dealing with the tourist industry and mandate that they must buy local first, then secure imports after' (Kevin Edmonds http://nacla.org/blog/other-side-paradise). Supporting the agricultural sector will free up a great deal of revenue for health and education projects, currently spent on food imports. Similarly, in Africa, half of all Kenyans are living below the poverty line and there is increasing desertification; many are reliant on outside aid for food and water. Following poor rainfall, many subsistence farmers are forced to eat the grain for next year's harvest. There have been reports of conflict breaking out over access to grazing lands with a water supply.

CHAPTER SUMMARY

It would be misleading to claim that food and drink tourism was the panacea to the world's agricultural crises and food woes, but equally the relationship must be recognised and acknowledged. It remains a time of unease about food distribution and economic inequality and this chapter has sought to illustrate the intrinsic links between agriculture, food policy and tourism. By drawing on examples from across the globe (including the UK, USA, Australia, China, and Jamaica), this chapter has tried to provide a global context. A report from Rwanda (Ashley, 2007: 7) summarises the relationship that we should strive to develop between food and agriculture:

Help poor farmers to sell to hotels: tourists consume food worth a few million dollars a year. Much of this is sourced in Rwanda, but action is needed to: help local producers increase the quality, range, and seasonality of their production, so they can boost sales to hotels; and ensure smaller poor farmers, particularly women farmers, can access this important market. This will involve partnership with agriculturalists, chefs, and government, plus a more detailed analysis of the current food supply chain.

As outlined here, these arguments are not relevant just to Rwanda, but are internationally relevant. For example, a number of countries mentioned could benefit from developing food tourism: not just high-end experiences, but promoting local both to rejuvenate rural economies, and to ensure the environment and food demand work together. It has been argued that food tourism offers sources of economic diversification in rural areas where traditional sources of income such as agriculture are no longer sufficient (Hall et al., 2003), but work on the benefits of food tourism remains relatively piecemeal, with an emphasis on economic analyses and supply chain work.

In brief, this chapter states that there is value in building linkages from the local economy to tourism supply chains and in this way, industries related to tourism can grow, become more competitive and contribute to a more equitable and healthier economy. Promoting local food through food and tourism policy can help in supporting local economies, sustaining skills, raising employment, and providing lifelines for producers. Food tourism promotions are delivering tangible economic gains, as indicated in the Scotland baseline GDP figures. The government-led 'Scotland Food and Drink' plans to create an industry worth £10 billion by 2017 to support new jobs and raise income, and this is certainly testament that tourists are also choosing to support local producers. These consumer habits are driven by a belief that local produces quality and there is safety in the food.

END OF CHAPTER POINTS

- Policy development for farming and fishing must be considered within the context of tourism.
- There is enough food to feed the world, but problems lie in uneven distribution and unequal access to land to grow food, or income to purchase enough.
- There is an apparent (but unwarranted) tension between the strategy of using mass production to feed a growing global population and the promotion of local food and food tourism.
- Tourism can offer an opportunity for the economically active, and can provide a livelihood for families.
- Food tourism can support sustainable farming through diversification and the reconnection of consumers to the environment. The relationship of these two sectors can still be highly problematic.
- A focus on building capacity in agro-tourism is a common approach in the government policy of most countries with an agricultural base (e.g. China), where farmers can become part of the tourist 'product' (see Figure 6.9).

FIGURE 6.9   *Farmers in the River Li in China*

- Food tourism has been presented as an effective vehicle for regional development which strengthens local production through backward linkages in tourism supply-chain partnerships.
- Food and agricultural crises can have a devastating impact on food tourism or offer a blessing in disguise (where need to know the food's provenance bolsters arguments for local food consumption).

FURTHER READING

Everett, S. and Slocum, S. (2013) 'Food and tourism: an effective partnership? A UK-based review', *Journal of Sustainable Tourism*, 21 (6): 789–809.

Fleischer, A. and Tchetchik, A. (2005) 'Does rural tourism benefit from agriculture?', *Tourism Management*, 26 (4): 493–501.

Hall, C.M., and Gössling, S. (2013) *Sustainable Culinary Systems: Local Foods, Innovation, and Tourism & Hospitality*. London: Routledge.

Lang, T. (2010) 'Crisis? What crisis? The normality of the current food crisis', *Journal of Agrarian Change*, 10 (1): 87–97.

Torres, R. and Momesen, J. (2004) 'Challenges and potential for linking tourism and agriculture to achieve pro-poor tourism objectives', *Progress in Development Studies*, 4 (4): 294–318.

Yuan, Z. (2013) 'Dynamic effects and development tendency of coupling between rural tourism industry and big agriculture (English)', *Tourism Tribune*, 28 (5): 80–8.

7

WINE TOURISM AND THE DEVELOPMENT OF 'WINESCAPES'

CHAPTER OBJECTIVES

- To trace the origins and development of wine tourism as a tourist activity and experience
- To discuss and present different forms and aspects of wine tourism
- To outline the key academic literature and research on wine tourism
- To examine the characteristics of the wine tourist and offer a few different typologies and categorisations from the literature
- To explore wine tourism as a powerful marketing tool and creator of place identity
- To illustrate some key points of wine tourism development with case studies, activities and examples

CHAPTER SUMMARY

This chapter looks at the development of wine tourism and draws on examples of wineries, vineyards and restaurants from around the globe that offer unique vintages, wine tours, wine festivals and other speciality wine-based events. It looks at the 'Old World' producers (such as France, Italy, Spain and Portugal), but also the 'New World' wine regions (including Australia, Canada and the USA), where wine tourism plays an important role in boosting tourism. For example, the National Wine Centre of Australia showcases the Australian wine industry; visitors from around the world visit Northern California's Wine Country; and

Argentina now has a booming wine tourism economy. *Wine Business Monthly* (Thach, 2007: 1) reported that:

> When a Rioja winery decided to invest millions in the construction of the celebrated Frank Gehry Hotel de Marques de Riscal, many were amazed at the amount of money that was poured into the project. Yet this is just one example of the growth that is being seen around the world in wine tourism.

This chapter looks at this rapid growth, the reasons behind it, how wine tourism literature has underpinned work on food tourism, and why regions have embraced wine tourism. An example is Thailand, and a wine-tasting tour is shown in Figure 7.1. These ideas will be further developed in Chapter 17, on drink and beverage tourism.

A definition of wine tourism offered by Geißler (2007: 29) is as follows:

> Wine tourism embraces and includes a wide range of experiences built around tourist visitation to wineries, wine regions or wine-related events and shows – including wine tasting, wine and food, the enjoyment of the regional environs, day trips or longer term recreation, and the experience of a range of cultural and lifestyle activities.

Quite simply, wine links to many sectors of tourism and is surprisingly far-reaching, with supply links to restaurants, hospitality, transport, accommodation and events such as festivals, celebrations and shows. Consequently, this chapter suggests that

FIGURE 7.1 *Wine Tasting Tour, Thailand (permission obtained, PB Winery)*

THE GROWTH AND DEVELOPMENT OF FOOD AND DRINK TOURISM

anywhere can become what Peters (1997) calls a 'winescape'. Increasingly it is not always the countries and areas that can produce and grow the vines: wine is used to generate tourism in urban, non-producing areas in the form of festivals or events. Like food tourism, areas are recognising that wine tourism offers a way to support rural areas, sustain cultural heritage and improve the economy. Robinson (1994: 980) suggests that:

> Wine-related tourism has become increasingly important. For many centuries not even wine merchants travelled, but today many members of the general public deliberately make forays to explore a wine region or regions. This is partly a reflection of the increased interest in both wine and foreign travel generally, but also because most wine regions and many producers' premises are attractive places ... and then there is the possibility of tasting, and buying wines direct from the source, which may involve keen prices and/or acquiring rarities.

THE HISTORY OF WINE TOURISM

Wine tourism has a long and colourful history. We know that vineyard tourism has been enjoyed since the days of the Grand Tour (Chapter 2), and even as far back as ancient Rome and Greece. However, it is perhaps only since the nineteenth century that wine became the specific focus and centre of a touristic activity (Hall et al., 2000: 2). This was particularly the case with the development of the 1855 Classification of Wine, when Napoleon III organised the Universal Exposition in Paris. This event, in the Gironde region of France, was a grand fair which presented the best wine and produce of France to the rest of the world and led to wine producers and traders writing a list of the best wine estates. The list ranked the châteaux into five main categories, in descending quality from '1st Growth' to '5th Growth', formalising existing knowledge and informal classifications. For the first time, this classification gave wine-producing regions identity and marketable differentiation.

Johnson (1989) in *Vintage: The Story of Wine* reported that half the world grows grapes and produces wine, with the top producing nations being France, Italy, Spain and the USA. Despite the production levels, it is interesting to note that France was relatively reluctant to engage with wine tourism development; this may be down to pride, feeling little need to promote it, or simply a different focus on how wine can be used to promote a destination. Consequently, wine tourism literature has tended to be geographically concentrated in the areas of Australia, Canada, New Zealand, the USA and UK, and much literature has concentrated on these markets. However, in the last ten years there has been a clear growth in other non-traditional locations, including South America, Eastern Europe and even the Middle East (Israel). New countries include Hungary, Moldova and Portugal, which are all developing routes and trails.

There are a number of reasons wine tourism is promoted and developed. These include raising brands, increasing profit, market intelligence and feedback, increasing customers and raising awareness with potential new markets and customers, education, and destination identity. Peters's (1997) concept of the 'winescape' was one of the first studies to really look at how places have been shaped by wine tourism activity. In brief, Peters felt that 'winescapes' must have three elements: vineyards, wine-making activities, and wineries where wine is produced and stored. However, increasingly this definition is redundant as wine tourism attractions do not always have the physical vineyards or production sites: they can simply be 'themed' with wine tourism (places include museums, events, festivals and trails, and even churches, as can be seen in Sarajevo in Bosnia in Figure 7.2).

FIGURE 7.2 *Wine shop attracting tourists in a church, Sarajevo, Bosnia Herzegovina. Photo by author*

National Wine Centre of Australia, telling the history of wine

The National Wine Centre of Australia is located on the edge of Adelaide's Botanic Gardens. It operates as a conference centre and offers an innovative and engaging wine tourism experience. Visitors to the centre experience the wine-making process from the vine up through an interactive Wine Discovery Journey. As part of their experience, visitors are encouraged to taste Australian wines and these are served with meals in the restaurant. Clearly aimed at raising awareness of Australian wine, it offers an impressive shop window for wine and caters for all tourists from the 'novice to the wine connoisseur'. The open cellar is one of the largest in the southern hemisphere, with the capacity to store up to 38,000 bottles, with approximately 12,000 bottles of Australian wine cellared year round (similar to the cellar shown in Figure 7.3). The award-winning, multi-media exhibition helps visitors to understand the role wine has played in history, recognise the position of Australian wine in today's international market and appreciate the relationship between food and wine.

FIGURE 7.3 *Wine barrels in the cellar (Permission obtained, PB Valley Khao Yai Winery)*

Source: www.wineaustralia.com.au

ACADEMIC APPROACHES TO WINE TOURISM RESEARCH

Given the breadth of this subject area and the industry, it is difficult to encapsulate all components within one chapter, so we will return to aspects of wine tourism in subsequent chapters relating to marketing, destination development, tourist types and food and drink events. Wine tourism literature covers everything from visiting vineyards to cellar door sales to wine festivals and trails. The link between wine and nature and the early knowledge and academic focus of writing that has subsequently informed work on food tourism seems to warrant a dedicated chapter. Current thinking and research on wine tourism is evolving rapidly. This is perhaps best showcased in the regular International Wine Tourism Conference (the 2016 conference will be held in Barcelona; details from www.iwinetc.com) and the first conference was held in 1998. Wine tourism also attracts extensive coverage in numerous academic texts and papers, such as Bruwer (2003), Charters and Ali-Knight (2002), Carmichael (2005), Getz and Brown (2006), Telfer (2001), and papers within such journals as the *International Journal of Wine Marketing*.

The wealth of literature and studies on wine tourism alone is testament to the growth and size of the industry. This is certainly illustrated by the edited collection of work from Hall et al. (2000), *Wine Tourism Around the World*, with its 'introductory tasting' of wine tourism. Their definition of wine tourism has been used as a template for numerous subsequent definitions of wine, and food, tourism. Hall and Macionis (1998: 197) define wine tourism as 'visitation to vineyards, wineries, wine festivals and wine shows for which grape wine tasting and/or experiencing the attributes of a grape wine region are the prime motivating factors for visitors'. However, this is clearly from the consumer perspective and increasingly work has begun to look at the producer and destination (Gómez and Molina, 2012).

Some of the earliest academic work on wine tourism emerged in the 1990s but was generally rather descriptive and lacked critical analysis and theory. As wine tourism has developed and people have become more active in pursuing wine-related activities, research has begun to focus on wine in business and promotion (Williams, 2001), wine events and visits (Hall and Macionis, 1998), and the wine tourist (Charters and Ali-Knight, 2002). In a more recent study of wine tourism in Spain and brand image, Gómez and Molina (2012) have presented a useful framework of the literature comprising four quadrants. They argue that wine tourism literature has focused on: supply, demand, supply and demand, and 'other' studies, which include brands, wine routes and comparative differences. Getz and Brown (2006) suggest that critical features of wine tourism experiences for consumers include three core dimensions, which they present as 'core wine product', 'core destination appeal', and 'the cultural product'.

As with many tourism studies and offerings, a life-cycle model has also been adopted for wine tourism. Macionis (1996) introduced a four-stage development life-cycle model for the wine tourism product in Australia that can be summarised as: incipient, developing, mature, declining. This model has been taken forward in a number of countries (Dodd and Beverland, 2001). Examples include Slovenia, where the life-cycle of the wine tourism product and growth of wine tourism providers have been analysed in the case of the Goriška Brda wine tourist district by Jurinčič and Bojnec (2006). Gazulla et al. (2010) also take the life-cycle model and look at the wine tourism industry in the Rioja region in Spain. In identifying the critical life-cycle stages of the wine from the point of view of the associated environmental impacts and comparing its environmental performance with other wines and beers, it analyses the 'bottlenecks' in development, and assesses the key stages to achieve economic return on environmental investment. The offer can be lucrative and attractive, as shown in Figure 7.4.

FIGURE 7.4 *Fortified wines being offered in the Algarve, Portugal (Photo by author)*

THE WINE TOURIST

Wine has become part of people's lifestyles (especially in the West) and people seek out wine for leisure and pleasure. A number of studies have attempted to classify the wine tourist and their personal characteristics and interests. This research has focused on a number of destinations across the world, including Australia (Charters and Ali-Knight, 2002), New Zealand (Alonso et al., 2008; Mitchell and Hall, 2001), Italy (Presenza et al., 2010), and Spain (Gazulla et al., 2010; Gil and Sánchez, 1997). In their wine tourism articles, Charters and Ali-Knight (2002) looked at Western Australia and found that wine tourism is often part of an overall 'bundle of attractions' for a tourist, and most visitors described as 'wine tourists' in much of the literature would be unlikely to associate themselves with that label. Their classification comprised four groups, although more recent work has added factors such as brand loyalty and wider contextual factors into the categorisation (Marzo-Navarro and Pedraja-Iglesias, 2012).

Research suggests people travel specifically to find, enjoy and taste wine. Getz (2000) and Getz et al. (2014) argue that wine tourism is initiated by consumers. In their study of New Zealand, Alonso et al. (2008) offer research on these consumers and their key characteristics. This kind of consumer segmentation approach is often used for identifying consumers and includes behavioural, psychographic, geographic and demographic features, along with benefits sought (Wedel and Kamakura, 2002). These aspects have been adopted in wine tourism research exploring the wine tourist (Charters and Ali-Knight, 2002; Mitchell et al., 2000).

Much wine tourism literature has concentrated on visitors' behaviour, and has tried to classify it in terms of motivation. Macionis and Cambourne (1998: 42) described some wine tourists as 'the passing tourist trade who thinks a "winery crawl" is just a good holiday'.Furthermore, Hall and Macionis (1998) presented a useful tripartite typology of winery visitors: 'wine lovers' (those for whom a winery visit is a central motivation for their tourist activity); the 'wine interested' (wine is a pastime rather than a passion, and motivated by a number of additional factors); and the 'curious tourists' (those who are largely unaware of wines and wine drinking, and view the winery visit as a novel experience). A simple typology of the wine tourist is in Figure 7.5.

The wine tourist			
The wine lover (highly interested)	The wine interested (the interested)	The wine novice (limited interest)	'Hangers on' (part of a group, no interest)

FIGURE 7.5   *A simple typology of the wine tourist based on wine tourist labels from Charters and Ali-Knight (2002)*

CASE STUDY

PB Valley Khao Yai Winery, Thailand

Several destinations have recently become wine tourism destinations and it might surprise you to know that Thailand is one of these.

Thailand has a small domestic wine industry, gradually becoming better-known throughout the world. Much of the wine comes from 150 kilometres north-east of Bangkok in a region known as Khao Yai. Thailand has very few wine tourism locations (PB Valley Winery and Siam Winery) and to date only has produced wine for the purpose of wine tourism.

The first winery to open in Khao Yai in 1997 was PB Valley Khao Yai Winery. Thailand is much further south than you may expect for wine (normally between latitudes of 30 to 50°), but located at 14.3° north on a plateau north of the Khao Yai National Park, the dry cool weather during the winter creates a microclimate that makes grape-growing possible.

In 1989, Dr Piya Bhirombhakdi (an entrepreneur) decided to produce wine with a world-class taste for the people of Thailand. The first vineyard was 20 hectares and planted with Shiraz for red wine and Chenin Blanc for white, featuring French rootstock, and Tempranillo from Spain. With the harvest of 1998, PB Valley Khao Yai Winery celebrated its first milestone. The 1999 vintage proved that quality wine could be successfully produced in Thailand. They now provide at least 2,000 jobs in the local communities, and offer an attraction that welcomed 115,000 visitors in 2013.

In an effort to build on these earlier studies with new and emerging destinations, Batra (2008) undertook a study of wine tourism and tourists at the PB Valley Khao Yai Winery and found that the flavour and the depth of wine were the most important factors in the respondents' wine selections, but perhaps this is almost secondary to the original motivation.

FIGURE 7.6 *PB Valley Khao Yai Winery (With thanks to Heribert Gaksch, Marketing Director, for the data and images)*

Getz and Brown (2006) claim much research on the wine tourist has focused on consumers at the cellar door, and there are many studies of wine consumers' preferences around the world (Getz, 1998; Hall, 1996). For example, Gil and Sánchez (1997) looked at Spanish wine-purchasing behaviour and found that the origin of the wine was most important in the purchasing behaviour of buyers of local wine. Spanish consumers also considered the price and grape vintage. Some other studies have identified that product, packaging, promotion, purchase and situational factors are central parts of the wine selection process (Hall et al., 2000; Lockshin et al., 2001).

VINEYARDS: THE BUILDING BLOCK OF WINE TOURISM

The wine market is extremely competitive and wine producers often look for new distribution channels; direct cellar door sale to visitors is becoming increasingly popular (McDonnell and Hall, 2008). Pine and Gilmore (1999: 11) have suggested that attractions 'intentionally use services as the stage and goods as props, to engage individual customers in a way that creates a memorable event', which suggests that producers need to be creative in developing attractive wine tourism activities. Celebrity vineyards are even now becoming very popular

FIGURE 7.7   *Advert for a day trip to the Cliff Richard vineyard, The Algarve, Portugal. Photo by author*

wine attractions, including the singer Sir Cliff Richard's vineyard in Portugal, which hosts tours and visits for tourists visiting the Algarve (Figure 7.7 shows an advert for this trip).

Wine tourism has a number of different components, but from a destination point of view, wine-related attractions are the main focus. Central to their success are visitors' motivations and attitudes that allow and encourage wine producers to educate their customers and sell them their wine directly (Getz, 2000). Vineyards and wineries are the main attractions, although not all wineries want or need to develop a tourism orientation (Getz and Brown, 2006). As discussed earlier, tourism offers an attractive way of providing diversification from agricultural production to the provision of value-added services and experiences (Macionis, 1998). Tourism can offer a secondary focus for wine-makers that supports the main industry of wine production.

Selling direct at the 'cellar door' certainly provides greater profit for smaller producers and is therefore attractive to wine producers (Charters and O'Neill, 2001); however, the start-up costs to offer an experience to the visitor must be considered. By attracting visitors to the place of production, such producer–consumer interaction is certainly supporting education about wine, wine products and wine regions, including local cultures and 'winescapes' (Fraser and Alonso, 2006). Small vineyards are most reliant on this kind of close interaction and selling, whereas large producers do not need it to sustain their business, and it can detract from the core business and use up management time (Dodd, 1995). Wine producers have therefore developed vineyard experiences to provide cellar-door tasting and sales, vineyard and cellar tours, wine festivals, conference facilities, cafés and restaurants, and 'experience days': all ways to raise awareness and increase sales (as promoted in wine shops such as Figure 7.8, the wine shop at PB Winery in Thailand). It also creates brand and product loyalty in the longer term and should lead to the future repurchase of the brand.

FIGURE 7.8   *The wine shop at PB Winery in Thailand (permission obtained from PB Valley Khao Yai Winery, Thailand)*

Ram Winery in Golan Heights, Israel

Another newcomer to wine tourism is Israel. The Ram Winery is perhaps a surprising recent addition to the growing list of global wine locations, which is why it provides a fascinating case study. Located in the picturesque Golan Heights of Israel on the border with Syria, this family-run winery was established in 2000 and produces approximately 6,000 bottles annually. Despite its precarious and politically strategic location between the two countries, it has led the way in Israel's wine tourism production.

The wine it produces is from Cabernet Sauvignon, Shiraz and Merlot varieties. The winery is open to the public and boasts that it can cater for up to 15 participants. This is obviously modest, but still provides an interesting attraction. As part of the touristic experience, it includes an explanation of the various stages of the vine's growth and wine production from the grape harvest, aging the wine in barrels, and up to the bottle, as well as sessions of wine tasting.

Further information available from: www.golan wines.co.il/english

WINE ROUTES AND TRAILS

The wider development of routes and trails is discussed in Chapter 15, but for this chapter, it is useful to concentrate on wine routes as visitor attractions. Frochot (2000: 73) suggests that a wine route is a:

> [d]esignated itinerary (or several) through the wine region which is thematically signposted as well as being interpreted via a free leaflet and map, which notes the different vineyards and winemakers and provides information on sites of historical and other interest.

A wine route is a tourist route which connects several wine attractions such as estates, vineyards and wineries together in a clear and logical order. Often these sites have physical attractions (facilities such as wineries on wine estates), vineyards, and roads and markers (signposts) directing the tourist to the individual wine route estate enterprises. Wine routes are usually characterised by a bounded space in the form of an often officially demarcated wine region or geographical indication (Bruwer, 2003).

The first wine roads can be traced back to the Weinstraße (wine road) in Germany, established in 1935 to connect the various vintners' villages to promote and boost wine sales. The German Wine Route hosts numerous wine festivals, which makes it a major tourist attraction. The largest wine festival worldwide with more than 600,000 visitors each year is the Wurstmarkt, which is held in front of the world's largest wine barrel in Bad Dürkheim in September. Such routes have since developed all over the world. The first wine route in South Africa was opened in Stellenbosch in 1971 and its success led to the proliferation of other routes across the country. Preston-Whyte (2000) reported that there were 14 routes in the south-west Cape and although challenged by regulation and disease of the vines, wine routes offer a powerful vehicle to promote South African wines. As wine routes are also regional they have a clear set of attributes and therefore the Cape route has sought to project a distinctive trademark and unique identity.

Moving north-east towards Canada there is the North-west Wine Route. This was created in the 1990s and connected seven Canadian wine regions, from Windsor to New York State (Telfer, 2000). The wine route (proposed by Donald Ziraldo) aimed to raise the profile of wine producers and offered tourists cross-border experiences. As interest has grown, facilities have developed to meet demand, including spas, restaurants, and festivals. Eighty percent of the grapes grown in Canada come from the Niagara Peninsula, the heart of Canada's wine-making due to its microclimate, created between the two Great Lakes of Erie and Ontario. The wine roads of Niagara in Canada are well-established, with clear branding and publicised attractions. Telfer's (2001) study of 25 wineries in the Ontario region found wineries take an aggressive approach to tourism including in their marketing strategies, and those who have benefited most have used additional on-site wine and related merchandise sales. Others also take advantage of passing traffic and ensure they are well signposted.

Wine routes are the roadways to the core attractions, the wine production sites. However, it is interesting to acknowledge how other less traditional countries are using the 'route' and road concept to create regional identity and provide a more sustained experience for tourists. One example is Chile, which is using wine tourism as a secondary interest to diversify its touristic offer (Sharples, 2002), or Slovenia, which now has 14 wine-growing districts offering at least one established wine road. Another example is Hungary and the Villány-Siklós Wine Route which is presented in the following Case Study.

CASE STUDY

Hungary's first wine region, Villány-Siklós Wine Road

The Villány-Siklós Wine Route is the first stronghold of Hungarian wine tourism and was established in 1995. It was the first such to be developed in Hungary. It connects 11 towns and villages in a protected wine-growing area. The wine culture of this region is promoted heavily throughout the road, but also in a dedicated Wine Museum. Furthermore, the October Red Wine Festival

▶

is held once every two years and introduces the popular Villány wines: Blue Port, Merlot, Kékfrankos and Cabernet.

It is in the southernmost wine region of Hungary, one of the sunniest wine districts of the country. In the sub-Mediterranean climate of Villány the grapes (such as Cabernet Sauvignon, Cabernet Franc and Merlot) grow well. The area is primarily known for its red wines, which are reminiscent of the Médoc wine style. In Siklós mainly white wine is produced. The wines of the Villány wine region are considered excellent quality and a commercial success by experts and consumers and the Hungarian wine market. The first full origin protection system of Hungary was developed there. The wine producers of Villány are frequently among the most successful participants in wine contests and exhibitions. So far, wine producers or wine cellars of Villány have been awarded Wine Producer of the Year or Wine Cellar of the Year six times.

Further information: http://villanyiborvidek.hu/en

ACTIVITY   DEVELOPING A WINE TOURISM OFFER

Choose and research one of the countries listed below which has some (but very limited) wine production and develop a brief wine tourism strategy for development. Consider who your market is going to be. What will be the focus for your strategy (exhibitions, cellar door sales, festival and events, wine road/trails)? What will the experience be like? A good list of wine-producing countries can be found through the Wine Institute website (www.wineinstitute.org). Countries you could choose from include Luxembourg, Venezuela, Jordan, Taiwan, Libya, Bolivia, Tanzania and Kyrgyzstan.

WINE FESTIVALS AND EVENTS

Hall and Sharples (2008) argue that food and wine events are different to other events and festivals that primarily focus on marketing and securing brand dominance. Rather, food and wine events are about external promotion, but link closely to the maintenance and sustainability of communities and therefore ways of life, cultural and social identities and lifestyles. Of course, food and drink events are the focus for Chapter 14 and this section will only briefly outline the role of festivals and events in the wine tourism offer. This part is therefore best read in conjunction with the longer chapter on food events.

There is a rapidly increasing number of food and wine festivals taking place around the world and many new festivals and events are now being developed as a deliberate part of a regional or national tourism strategy. Festivals and events allow 'winescapes' to be created away from vineyards and wine production sites, offering transitory and temporary places of wine tourism. For many wineries and wine regions an annual wine festival is a strategic tool for encouraging cellar door visitation and brand awareness. Wine festivals offer the opportunity to socialise, possibly with friends and family, whilst learning about and enjoying a natural, agricultural setting and product. Revenue and recognition is generated for the participating wineries, and awareness of the area and its resources is enhanced.

CASE STUDY

Fête des Vignerons, Switzerland

The Fête des Vignerons (Vevey Winegrowers Festival) is the event of the Brotherhood of Winegrowers. In the seventeenth century, the Brotherhood of Winegrowers (Agricultural Association or Abbaye of St Urban) organised a yearly pageant that processed through Vevey on Lake Geneva. At a time when the Protestant Reformation was extremely strict and tolerated few expressions of community rejoicing or revelry, the Brotherhood of Winegrowers' pageant attracted increasing numbers of spectators. It focused on improving wine-growing techniques and rewarding good performance in vineyard workers. From then on, when finances and economic and political circumstances allowed, the best workers were rewarded and crowned.

The success of each new Winegrowers Festival and the organisers' ambition to constantly improve the celebration meant increasing financial investment, so it became very difficult to organise more than five festivals per century. In this small city, often unaware of the reality of the winegrowers' and farmers' lives, the once-a-generation Winegrowers Festival is a festival of remembering and of identity. It brings together ancestral traditions and contemporary preoccupations, taking the spectators back to their past, whilst celebrating the present lives of working men and women. The Winegrowers Festival is regarded as a true celebration of the cycle of life. The next festival will take place in 2019, which will be 20 years after the preceding one (1999) – there is a lot of time to prepare!

Source: www.fetedesvignerons.ch/en

MARKETING WINE TOURISM AND THE WINE TOURIST

Wine tourism marketing is not just about increasing sales at the door: it has the power to create and develop a region's identity, raise awareness and increase distribution channels. It has been recognised as a powerful marketing tool and place identifier. In particular, one of the drivers has been to create brand loyalty for small producers in an increasingly competitive market. Certainly, competitive positioning of wine tourism regions has become an important strategic issue as the volume of wine tourism and activities associated with it has increased. Many regions are now aggressively marketing to attract high-yield wine tourists (Getz and Brown, 2006), including a number of small villages and rural areas. For example, when Tomljenović and Razović (2009) asked why Croatian vineyards promoted wine tourism, the most important goal was the development of the brand awareness of Croatian wines. Wine-makers felt it was a way to penetrate international markets and expose Croatian wines to international visitors already in the country to build awareness, recognition and perhaps, they hope, international demand.

ACTIVITY **DEVELOPMENT PLAN FOR A SMALL FAMILY VINEYARD LOOKING TO BECOME A TOURIST ATTRACTION IN FIVE YEARS**

Imagine you have been approached by a small family-owned vineyard called Rock Hill Wines to set up a new tourist attraction. Their vineyard is a 20-acre site of free-draining flinty soil and overlaying chalk, situated on a south-west-facing slope to maximise the sunshine available during the summer months. The first vines were planted in 1976, so they are established in their wine production, but wish to offer more. The vine varieties grown include Müller-Thurgau, Ortega, Schönburger, Reichensteiner, Rondo, and Pinot Noir, which are intense and allow for good early cropping. Ideas include offering cellar door sales, wine tours, an event space, and a small café. However, they also want to offer something unique that makes them stand out from the crowd.

Research other similar sites around the world and then develop a brief strategy to present this to the family. Try to be as innovative as you can, whilst also ensuring you provide estimates of their return on investment. You may also offer ideas about marketing methods and branding.

Certainly, wine tourism is a form of consumer behaviour and this behaviour must be understood to inform a clear strategy that destinations adopt to develop and market wine-related attractions and imagery. It needs to ensure there is an effective marketing opportunity for wineries to educate, and to sell their products, directly to consumers. In the late 1990s, Western Australia engaged enthusiastically in developing wine-marketing strategies (Carlsen and Dowling, 2001). The success showed how central marketing is to developing and promoting destinations and the region's identity. For example, other well-known wine locations have developed strong regional identities, such as Burgundy in France (known for its food as well as wine); Bordeaux, which links its wine profile to its French chateaux heritage; and California with its sunshine and young, vibrant culture (and thus wines).

Getz and Brown (2006) asked how wine regions emulate the appeal and tourism success of established sites. It is important to figure out what wine tourists look for when a trip is planned. There are numerous studies of how tourists are attracted to wine regions. Williams (2001) used the images in the *Wine Spectator* magazine and found a shift through the decade of the 1990s, from a focus on production to more visual and aesthetic elements. Bruwer (2003) suggested that wine regions needed to offer a 'difference of place', which must be branded clearly and attractively.

Working with food and drink tourism

Wine tourism is becoming a key sector when talking about job opportunities. One example is Spain, which claims that 50,000 jobs could be created in the next few years. The internet is full of adverts for wine tourism-related jobs, perhaps more so than food tourism. One says:

> Interested in working with a dynamic, creative and innovative team? Want to travel the world in search of the best wineries and grapes? Determined to thrive in a unique, in-demand niche market with like-minded experienced travel experts? Wine Tours of the World may be the right place for you! (see www.winetoursoftheworld.com)

Some recently advertised jobs include 'Freelance Wine Guides' with a focus on those who love to travel, be with people and have a reasonable command of one foreign language. 'They need to combine a vibrant warm personality with tact, and be organised. They need to be able to work well in a team with an expert guide and sometimes other Tour Managers, both giving and taking instructions.' Other related jobs include Programme Administrators, who also take tours but work in the office and need 'to be very organised and capable of working at speed and at times under pressure. They will have good written foreign languages, and (as well as a deep love of travel, food and wine), computer skills.'

These may seem like dream jobs, but the key is to be able to demonstrate these transferable skills such as being organised, languages and working under pressure *before* you are asked anything about wine itself!

CHAPTER SUMMARY

This chapter has suggested that wine tourism is a subject area and focus of research in its own right. Above all other types of food and drink, wine tourism preceded much of the research and work on food tourism. There is now a wealth of wine tourism literature based on work on Australia, Canada, New Zealand, the USA and UK, as well as research focusing on non-traditional locations such as South America, Eastern Europe and Asia. Some of the most comprehensive work includes Hall et al. (2000) and Getz (2000), who presented the academic community with the earliest textbooks on wine tourism. Studies by Charters and

Ali-Knight (2002), Getz and Brown (2006), and Mitchell and Hall (2001) have also become seminal texts for this subject area.

It is since the nineteenth century that wine really became the specific focus and centre of touristic activity. The development of activities and opportunities has led to what Peters (1997) called the 'winescape', which describes places that have shaped wine tourism activity (vineyards, events, cellar doors and trails). Vineyards and wineries are the main attractions, although not all wineries need to develop a tourism orientation (Getz and Brown, 2006); sometimes tourism can be a secondary focus for wine-makers, which supports the main industry of wine production.

By attracting visitors to the place of production, this wine-focused producer–consumer interaction is promoting education about wine, raising awareness of wine products and putting wine regions and local cultures on the world map. Wine tourism is more than visiting vineyards; it has the power to create and develop a region's identity and increase distribution channels. It has been recognised as a powerful marketing tool and place identifier. There are also more and more food and wine festivals popping up around the world and many new festivals and events are now being developed as a deliberate part of a regional or national tourism strategy.

END OF CHAPTER POINTS

- There is a significant body of literature on wine tourism that is testament to the growth and size of the industry and appetite for academic research and insights about this phenomenon.

- There is no agreed definition of the 'wine tourist': consumer segmentation approaches are often used for identifying consumers, which include behavioural, psychographic, geographic and demographic details, along with benefits sought.

- The first wine roads can be traced back to the Weinstraße in Germany (1935).

- Small vineyards are most reliant on cellar door sales, whereas large producers are less reliant on visitors, as they can detract from the core business of production.

- Wine tourism is a powerful marketing tool and place identifier. It offers a way to support rural areas, sustain cultural heritage and improve the economy.

FURTHER READING

Charters, S. and Ali-Knight J. (2000) 'Wine tourism – a thirst for knowledge?', *International Journal of Wine Marketing*, 12,(3): 70–80.
Charters, S. and Ali-Knight, J. (2002) 'Who is the wine tourist?', *Tourism Management* 23 (3): 311–19.

Dodd, T.H. (1995) 'Opportunities and pitfalls of tourism in a developing wine industry', *International Journal of Wine Marketing*, 7 (1): 5–16.

Getz, D. (2000) *Explore Wine Tourism. Management Development and Destinations*. New York: Free Press.

Getz, D. and Brown, G. (2006) 'Critical success factors for wine tourism regions: a demand analysis', *Tourism Management*, 27 (1): 146–58.

Hall, C.M., Sharples, L., Cambourne, B. and Macionis, N. (2000) *Wine Tourism around the World: Development, Management and Markets.* Oxford: Butterworth-Heinemann.

Houghton, M. (2001) 'The propensity of wine festivals to encourage subsequent winery visitation', *International Journal of Wine Marketing*, 13 (3): 32–41.

Marzo-Navarro, M. and Pedraja-Iglesias, M. (2012) 'Critical factors of wine tourism: incentives and barriers from the potential tourist's perspective', *International Journal of Contemporary Hospitality Management*, 24 (2): 312–34.

Mitchell, R., and Hall, C.M. (2006) 'Wine tourism research: the state of play', *Tourism Review International*, 9 (4): 307–32.

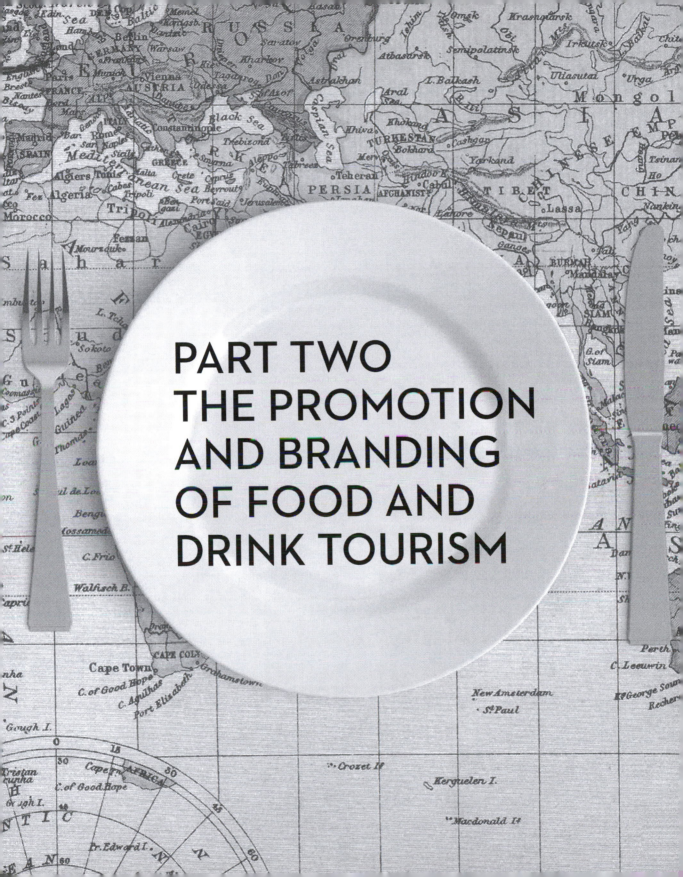

PART TWO
THE PROMOTION
AND BRANDING
OF FOOD AND
DRINK TOURISM

8

MARKETING AND BRANDING FOOD AND DRINK TOURISM

CHAPTER OBJECTIVES

- To discuss marketing frameworks and the 'marketing mix' in relation to food and drink tourism
- To present different marketing activities used to promote food and drink tourism
- To discuss how food is used to promote place and how place is used to promote food
- To explore marketing frameworks and approaches based on tourist typologies and categorisations
- To examine branding and the power of advertising to promote place through image and visual vehicles
- To discuss the relevance and impact of externally-approved designations and accreditations and how these support destination marketing

CHAPTER SUMMARY

This chapter introduces the next main section, Part II, which focuses on marketing, promotion and the development of an attractive and enticing food and drink tourism offer. It provides case studies on how national and regional agencies are adopting food tourism to attract tourists and regenerate places, and examines how destination marketing strategies are using food and drink to promote and grow tourism. Aspects of destination branding and marketing frameworks are introduced in this chapter, and reference is made to online marketing, advertising and labelling. Marketing is not just advertising, but a complex set of approaches and tools that build relationships and generate loyalty. The most effective marketing methods are often the more subtle ones, as opposed to more expensive, multi-million-pound advertising campaigns adopted by global brands and international food companies.

Drawing on seminal marketing ideas such as the 4Ps marketing mix framework and extended approaches to the services marketing mix, which embraces the less tangible elements of a destination, it looks at marketing activities and how they relate to different market segmentations of the food and drink tourism market. In regard to offering helpful critical content, the chapter includes a Critical Reflections summary box which looks at destination image theory and how this has been pursued within the tourism literature when discussing destination marketing and cumulative attractiveness.

This chapter builds on discussions about marketing food and drink tourism to look at issues of selling and branding – from principles of branding an entire region or country to branding to sell a single product. Recent market reports indicate food packaging is at least a $15 billion business, so it will look at approaches to branding products that appeal to certain markets and interests, such as 'heritage branding' (aspects include the traditional, rustic, local, and homemade). It also looks at how people sell products, as opposed to people actually buying because of the product, that is the decision-making behind the packaging, images and names (and how this influences choice). In looking at some food brands that could be classed as iconic, it explores the nature of the relationships consumers have with mainstream food and drink brands and how this drives the 'touristic'. This chapter will also briefly look at the relevance and impact of externally approved designations used as marketing tools, such as the EU Protection of Geographical Indications and Designations of Origin, and examines how these support and add value to destination marketing campaigns.

FOOD AT THE CENTRE OF MARKETING CAMPAIGNS

Tikkanen (2007) has suggested that governments and agencies have begun to use food and culinary products in destination promotion relatively recently, and to put the development of food experiences at the centre of product offerings. Therefore, it is worth looking at a tourism campaign that illustrates how food and drink are being put at the very heart of destination marketing campaigns. The Case Study below is about Malaysia in South-East Asia. Karim et al. (2009) claim that Malaysian food is renowned for its multiple combinations of flavours and variety, and in order to strengthen Malaysia's position as a world-class food tourism destination, it has invested heavily to stimulate the inward flow of food-interested tourists. They find a positive food image is crucial in promoting Malaysian food in tourists' minds, and image is a key factor in the selection of a destination (Baloglu and McCleary, 1999; Beerli and Martin, 2004).

Malaysia

Malaysia is a federal constitutional monarchy in South-East Asia, of 13 states and three federal territories. It is 127,350 sq. miles in size, split by the South China Sea into two similarly sized regions: Peninsular Malaysia and East Malaysia (Malaysian Borneo). Malaysia is a multi-ethnic, multi-cultural and multilingual society. The population is made up of indigenous tribes and Malays, with inward migration from Chinese and Indian cultures due to foreign trade. Malaysia's cuisine reflects the multi-ethnic makeup of its population, with influence from the Malay, Chinese, Indian, Thai, Javanese and Sumatran cultures. Malaysia promotes itself as 'Truly Asia', and is a wonderful example of how food is used to market a country and its people. The food of this diverse country is one of its main selling points and it certainly capitalises on this at every opportunity.

Malaysia attracted 27.4 million visitors by the end of December 2014 and this number continues to increase year on year (http://corporate.tourism.gov.my), driven by extensive food-related campaigns, including targeted regional promotions such as Penang (see Figure 8.1) and more general promotion as a culinary destination, which is shown in the marketing literature (Figure 8.1).

FIGURE 8.1 *Penang street food leaflet promoting street food and hawker stalls. Credit: Karisma Kreatif*

MARKETING LITERATURE ON FOOD AND DRINK PROMOTION

There is no shortage of marketing theory and academic writing on the subject of destination promotion and marketing (Buhalis, 2000; Echtner and Prasad, 2003; Faulkner, 1997; Gretzel et al., 2000; Hudson and Miller, 2005). However, before you look into specific literature, it is useful to consult more generic marketing literature to grasp the wider context and underpinning theory relating to marketing and destination promotion. Firstly, there is value in exploring the seminal approach to marketing by scholars who present the '4Ps' of marketing in what is commonly known as the 'marketing mix' (summarised in Figure 8.2). The 'marketing mix' is a seminal term describing the different choices organisations have to make in the process of bringing a product or service to market. The 4Ps were first developed in 1960 by E.J. McCarthy, and further developed since by scholars in terms of tourism and hospitality (most notably by Philip Kotler).

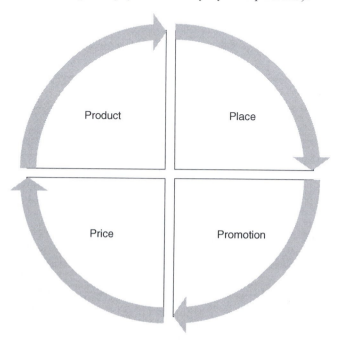

FIGURE 8.2   *The 4Ps Marketing Mix*

However, there are now extended mixes, such as the 'services marketing mix', which encapsulates intangibles such as the tourism experience (Kotler et al., 2006). In addition to the basic marketing mix (Product, Price, Place and Promotion), it includes People, Process and Physical Evidence. Furthermore, there is the 'e-marketing mix', developed to reflect extensive reliance on, and use of, the internet in marketing; and the 'environmental marketing mix', which reflects increasing demand for environmentally friendly products and services. This adopts new terminology, such as 'carbon footprint' and 'offsetting'. Certainly it could be argued that food and drink tourism marketing can be approached and discussed with any of these 'mixes' given its sustainable character, intangible nature and adoption of digital marketing.

One way to think about this from a food and drink tourism perspective is shown in Table 8.1, which illustrates a completed table using the example of a distillery (see also Chapter 17).

THE PROMOTION AND BRANDING OF FOOD AND DRINK TOURISM

TABLE 8.1 *The Services Marketing Mix for food and drink tourism, Dewar Whisky*

The Services Marketing Mix	Brief definition in terms of food/drink tourism	Case study: Dewar's World of Whisky, Scotland
Product	Food tourism is intangible and tangible (measurable). Tourism is seen as intangible, but food is tangible so both need to be considered. It can include the benefits to tourists, the design, the size, the experiences, etc.	'World of Whisky' guided tour of distillery, shop and bottles of whisky. Unique whisky only distilled in this site. Heritage symbolism and history relayed with each bottle *'Travel back in time on a journey of discovery which includes film shows, interactive challenges and period recreations'*
Price	This is tricky in a complex package such as tourism. Pricing involves taking into consideration material, labour, overhead costs	Various tours and offerings mean they can target a wide audience. Basic tour: Adult £7.50, Concession £6, Children £4, but also £25 connoisseur tour and a private tour for £99 plus whisky purchases (information correct in March 2015)
Place	Generally where the service is located, but could be destination or even placing of the promotion	Physical place is Aberfeldy in Perthshire, but also place includes website and imagery featured on their website, www.dewars.com
Promotion	Numerous ways that food/place are promoted. Includes advertising, websites, packaging of food, leaflets	Very effective and dramatic website, accompanied with leaflets, through tourism offices, posters, and wide range of social media vehicles (Facebook, Twitter, Pinterest, Google+)
People	All human actors involved in service delivery, e.g. staff, the customer, and other customers	Distillers, shop staff, managers, marketing, guides – *'our knowledgeable and friendly guides share the art and enchantment of whisky making'* (leaflet; 2014)
Process	Customer interface between the business and consumer – delivery and operating systems	Messages conveyed through website and pre-visit marketing, but also complete onsite experience including tour, coffee shop, brand store and grounds (see Chapter on onsite marketing)
Physical Evidence	The material part of a service, e.g. buildings, equipment, signs and logos, brochures, your website	Distillery, shop, website, bottles of whisky

---

ACTIVITY   **AN EXAMPLE TO ILLUSTRATE THE 4PS OF MARKETING**

Research and complete a table of your own like Table 8.1, considering the services marketing mix above for a destination or food/drink attraction of your choice. Provide an analysis under each heading from a chosen case study as in the table above.

Food is said to be the fourth-most important attribute in how tourists perceive a destination (Hu and Ritchie, 1993) after climate, accommodation and scenery. However, although there is a lot of work on destination promotion, the amount of literature on the use of food and drink in destination promotion remains relatively scarce (Okumus et al., 2007; Stanley and Stanley, 2015). Despite this, in looking at the growth of the food tourism literature, several approaches have been adopted to great effect, so it is advisable to explore some of the more frequently discussed approaches to tourism and food tourism marketing studies (Du Rand and Heath, 2006; Hall et al., 2003; McKercher et al., 2008).

In looking at destination marketing literature, it is clear that differentiation is key to attract people to destinations, and the focus has to be on identifying and promoting unique tangible and intangible products and services. It is this kind of differentiation that induces visitation. Boyne et al. (2003) claim that adopting a marketing philosophy approach to developing food-related tourism is highly challenging, as we lack sufficient understanding of the food-buying behaviour of tourists, and possess limited data on the needs and interests of the food tourist. Du Rand and Heath (2006) also note that food has been a relatively underdeveloped part of tourism studies; these explore the marketing mix or strategy of a region alone, despite research showing that food and drink are key tangible and intangible goods and services within a destination's portfolio (Boyne and Hall, 2004; Okumus et al., 2007). Certainly, there is debate on approaches to food images and how they can be used effectively in destination promotion. Other under-researched areas include the intersection between heritage and food marketing, largely ignored by marketing and branding academics (Otnes and Maclaren, 2007), although this is being addressed in a collection of chapters on heritage cuisines in Timothy (2015).

DESTINATION MARKETING STRATEGIES AND PLACE PROMOTION

It is now increasingly rare to find promotional and marketing materials for a destination without reference to its food and drink offer (Fields, 2002; Getz et al., 2014; Kim et al., 2009b). Organisations such as the Australian Tourist Commission, Canadian Tourism Commission, and Hong Kong Tourism Board are dedicated to the promotion of place through food and food-related marketing strategies (Ignatov and Smith, 2006; Okumus et al., 2007; Plummer et al., 2005). Food is as diverse as the peoples and cultures of the world. Given the incredible range of destinations open to tourists, destinations need to stand out and, increasingly, Unique Selling Points (USPs) are being developed (or created) in food and drink. Food's intrinsic link to regional and national identity make it one of the most powerful weapons in the marketing armoury of a destination. Using food in destination marketing attracts tourists to a place (Enright and Newton, 2005) where destination marketing strategies offer differentiation (Horng and Tsai, 2010; Jones and Jenkins, 2002). An example of national investment in dedicated marketing campaigns is shown in Figure 8.3, which promotes Switzerland as a gourmet destination, promising 'There is no such thing as a single Swiss cuisine. As you travel through Switzerland you'll find Berner Rosti, buttery home-fried potatoes in Bern; Malakoff cheese fritters in Canton Vaud...'

FIGURE 8.3   *Front page of the Gourmet Travel Switzerland Magazine. Permission from Regis*

There are an increasing number of creative approaches to culinary attraction development and promoting gourmet unique selling points, with countries creating food offers from a limited base, or sometimes no historic foundations at all. One such example is the beautiful east coast historic town of Hoi An in Vietnam, where one just has to walk through its pedestrianised areas to see rows of new cookery schools (Figure 8.4 and see Chapter 19), a backdrop to tourists enjoying its colourful and busy market. Certainly visitors enjoy culinary offerings to rival any top culinary destination (Figure 8.5).

Cohen and Avieli (2004) suggest that Hoi An has purposely invented its culinary heritage in the context of modern tourism, but finds this strategy has not always been recognised by the local people, who have struggled to identify with this reinvented image. Another example is Singapore; studies by Henderson (2014) critically assess how marketers and governments are using marketing approaches to build a national cuisine.

Despite the numerous ways in which national governments and agencies are employing attractive narratives of food, we need to acknowledge how they relate to different market segmentations within food/drink tourism. Certainly food can be the driving force that motivates people to visit a destination, and we see this in destinations such as Italy and France, but now less established destinations such as Australia, Switzerland (as Figure 8.3 shows above), and Costa Rica (Case Study below) are now

FIGURE 8.4   *A cookery school promotes itself in Hoi An, Vietnam. Photo by author*

FIGURE 8.5   *Market sellers in Hoi An, Vietnam. Photo by author*

responding, and spend on marketing and promoting is increasing. Destinations are creating new narratives and through this are inventing cultures, whilst developing stories and traditions to capitalise on the demand for special interest tourism. Developing an iconic cuisine can be regarded less as a reflection of reality (or history), than a marketing exercise in creativity, imagination and ingenuity. Increasingly, local and regional foods are part of a packaged commodity, a vehicle of identity development and recognition that draws on concepts of identity, linked with notions of a 'sense of place' through emotional attachment.

CASE STUDY

An emerging food tourism destination: Costa Rica

With a headline like 'Costa Rica hopes to attract adventurous eaters with new decree', it is clear that destinations are turning to food for tourism promotion. March 2015 saw Costa Rica's Vice President Ana Helena Chacón state that the country should be as well-known for its cuisine as it is for its beaches and sloths, with the article asking, 'But will foodies add Costa Rica to a Latin American circuit alongside culinary destinations like Mexico and Peru?'

Chacón has now presented a decree from Casa Presidencial naming Costa Rican cuisine a matter of public interest. 'The National Plan for Sustainable and Healthy Costa Rican Gastronomy acknowledges food as a cultural expression of the peoples here, and aims to protect and promote the country's national dishes and produce. Part of the goal of the decree is to position Costa Rica as a destination of agricultural and food tourism.'

Source: www.ticotimes.net/2015/03/21/costa-rica-hopes-to-attract-adventurous-eaters-with-new-decree-2. [Accessed: 22/3/15.]

FOOD TOURIST MARKET SEGMENT MODELS AND CATEGORISATIONS

In Chapter 1, the typology of the food tourist was discussed. It is therefore a natural step from this categorisation to look at how the marketing approach must meet the needs of these different groups and target markets appropriately. Different tourists respond to different marketing approaches and therefore there is a need to differentiate ways of communicating food and drink messages (Horng and Tsai, 2010; Ignatov and Smith, 2006). In looking at the types of approach needed, Boyne et al. (2003) offer a useful way to divide consumers into four types, which focuses on the importance they place on food when considering a destination. Table 8.2 shows a version of this framework overlaid with the typologies outlined in Chapter 1 from Boyne et al. (2003) and Mitchell and Hall (2003).

TABLE 8.2 *Different food tourist marketing approaches (based on Boyne et al. (2003) and Mitchell and Hall (2003))*

Type	1	2	3	4
Approach to marketing as outlined by Boyne et al. (2003)	Food is central in the experience, and tourists actively search for information about local gastronomy, featured food, and high-quality cuisine.	Food is important, but tourists do not actively search for relevant information but do respond to messages about culinary tourism, but information must be received in advance.	Tourists do not consider food to be a significant element of their trip, but may join in food-related activities if they experience delicious meals along the way	Tourists are not interested in good food and drink or food tourism activities, even when they are exposed to marketing information about excellent food and drink
Tourist Type (Mitchell and Hall, 2003)	Gastronome	Indigenous Foodies	Tourist Foodies	Familiar Foodies

Table 8.2 indicates that tourists falling into types one, two, and three should be presented with information about local food products because this ties into their interests. Information that closely matches the needs of type three tourists should be provided, and this information should be placed in clearly marked locations other than websites, because tourists of this type do not actively search for information about food on tour websites.

There is also opportunity to market food through other tourist segments and markets, and this is increasingly the case with special interest groups: for example, religious tourists in Israel, where Ron and Timothy (2013) found that Biblical food has been reinvented as a heritage cuisine for religious tourists in the Holy Land in Jerusalem, or Buddhist Temple Food (Son and Xu, 2013). Similarly, we find adventure tourists seek 'scary food' experiences (Gyimóthy and Mykletun, 2009), discussed in more detail in Chapter 14.

ADVERTISING AND DIGITAL MARKETING

Advertising is perhaps the most visible dimension of the marketing mix, with estimates claiming $545.40 billion was paid in 2014 (eMarketer, 2014). Advertising images are key to visitation (Lin et al., 2011), with the USA food and beverage market spending $12.06 million on outdoor advertising in the USA, and total expenditure of $136.53 million. Although prepared food advertising topped $1.68 billion (Statista, 2014), it is worth noting that the food marketing system is the largest direct and indirect non-government employer in the USA.

In terms of destination advertising, it is increasingly common to see explicit adverts focusing on attracting people to a place through food, rather than just trying to sell food. The stereotypes of food, meals and traditions often find their way into advertising that distils a wide variety of regional difference in ingredients, style and approach into a digestible simplified package of symbols and images: a brand. For example, newspapers regularly contain adverts to places linked with food.

It is widely agreed that striking images of food are the central aspect in effective advertising and certainly food photography is an art form and specialist skill. Good photographs can add significantly to promotional materials, while poor images can have an equally negative impact. Food photography is a specialised area with photographers being in demand.

In terms of strong global brand and labelling to generate tourism, one such example is the apparently omnipresent brand of Guinness. Haven-Tang and Jones (2006) suggest thatGuinness has boosted Ireland's international image, while the Scottish food brand has virtually built on unique products such as haggis. As suggested by Urde et al. (2007: 4), 'a heritage brand is recognisable from the following characteristics: a track record, longevity, core values, history, and the use of symbols' and Guinness has arguably developed an established heritage that speaks to consumers through a plethora of symbols, graphics, nostalgia, packaging and advertising. Taking an historical perspective, heritage identities such as Guinness acquire new identities over the passage of time and take on board new meanings, becoming intimately associated with places, cultures and with time frames (Everett, 2015). The clever creation of a brand history linked to a sense of cultural continuity and communal tradition provides a sense of ubiquitous presence (Beasley and Danesi, 2002; Timothy 2015). The almost ubiquitous brand is on display outside a restaurant in Lagos, Portugal (Figure 8.6)

Another example is Bacardi Rum's New Marketing Campaign which celebrates 'Rich Cuban Heritage', drawing on its origins and its founder Don Facundo Bacardí Massó, and his dramatic historical narrative about bringing change to the rum industry (Bacardi, 2014). These approaches illustrate how image and labels are used to promote the place of origin and production to tourists: 'if you enjoyed this, then visit its birthplace', much like film tourism: 'you have seen the film, why not visit the set?' (Kim, 2012).

By far the most powerful advertising campaigns use the internet and adopt digital marketing technologies; website advertising and online promotion are key. No product or destination will survive without positive and impactful web presence and continuous investment. The internet has great potential for promoting regional tourism, and is relatively inexpensive compared with other promotion and advertising media (Standing and Vasudavan, 2000). An effective website can reach global audiences: it is accessible all day from anywhere in the world. It is difficult for tourists to form a clear image of a destination without the actual experience, and therefore the multi-media interactive nature of the Web is now

FIGURE 8.6   *Guinness sign outside restaurant, Lagos, Portugal. Photo by author*

fundamental as it adds a new dimension to destination marketing. The content of a website is thus very important, and must be updated regularly in the field of tourism marketing, as in any other field (Lin and Huang, 2006). Kim et al. (2009b) claim that limited research has examined food tourism marketing on the internet and their study of West Texas helpfully looks at the effective use of web marketing by destination marketing organisations in food tourism and how this affects tourists' destination decisions.

Horng and Tsai (2010) further suggest travellers search for information on tourism websites and the content of these websites is one of the main factors contributing to repeated visits (Rosen and Purinton, 2004, discussed in the next chapter). The more interactive designs are more effective, allowing tourism organisations to encourage participation and engagement,and thereby increasing the likelihood they might consider a return visit.

THE PROMOTION AND BRANDING OF FOOD AND DRINK TOURISM

BRANDING FOOD AND DRINK TOURISM

> A brand for a company is like a reputation for a person. You earn reputation by trying to do hard things well. (Jeff Bezos, CEO Amazon.com cited by Bloomberg Business 2004)

> Authentic brands don't emerge from marketing cubicles or advertising agencies. They emanate from everything the company does. (Howard Schultz, CEO Starbucks cited in Schultz and Jones Yang (1997).

Brand is a key component of effective advertising and a good brand is a powerful marketing tool, though one which requires a massive investment in time and effort. Successful food and drink brands that generate visits are an accretion of various identities, linked to institutions, places, cultures, and to time frames. Branding is considered a major tool to market a product, and can be 'a name, term, sign, symbol, or design, or a combination of them intended to identify the goods and services of one seller or group of sellers and to differentiate them from those of competition' (Gertner and Kotler, 2002: 249). There is little doubt that differentiation to competitors is in the focus of branding.

One significant growth area in food tourism branding is the concept of heritage branding. Although Balmer et al. (2011) claim that heritage has been the focus of attention in marketing and management in the fields of heritage marketing, heritage tourism and the nascent area of corporate heritage brands for some time, this has not always been in the case for food and drink. Balmer's corporate heritage identity framework is useful to adopt in our context as it places the heritage identity construct *vis-à-vis* other related constructs such as nostalgia, tradition and custom. In outlining the concept of relative invariance which seeks to explain the seemingly contradictory position of how heritage identities remain the same by adapting to change, there is the message that 'corporate heritage identities and brands are invested with special qualities in that they are a melding of identity continuity, identity change and are also invested with the identities of time (times past, present and future)' (Balmer et al., 2011: 1380). This approach is discussed in more depth by Everett (2015) and Timothy (2015).

As the association between place, promotion and food becomes ever more potent in the minds of consumers and in the marketing armoury of those responsible for destination promotion, we increasingly see heritage images used for destination promotion, where foods are explicitly linked to their place of origin, or associated with an image that conveys an appropriate feel or message. Marketing campaigns are increasingly adopting messages that relay this nostalgic rhetoric and hark back to small-scale, cottage and rural production. One example is Nordic cuisine in Copenhagen and its ambition to become the gastronomic capital of Scandinavia, positioning itself as a global culinary leader (Askegaard and Kjeldgaard, 2007).

To attract the discerning consumer, destinations are pursuing strategies that exploit stories and traditions behind regional and local food. Food in the right packaging of cultural and social heritage narrative has the potential to attract tourists and lead to the continuing production of such images to sustain tourist numbers (Cohen and Avieli, 2004; Hashimoto and Telfer, 2006). Such concepts should be considered when discussing culinary heritage and the continuation of traditional foods within regions (Everett and Aitchison, 2008).

One of the most popular and effective approaches to creating a strong brand is to provide a sense of historic origins and messages that conjure images relating to nostalgia and tradition. Capitalising on links to the production history of food in a destination is often effective, particularly manufacturing approaches where product packaging increasingly features farmers, historic backgrounds and faded images to give a sense of the 'homemade' and the rustic. There is extensive adoption of rustic-looking wrapping such as paper bags or old newspapers, old-fashioned typefaces that appeal to tourists searching for something different to their homeland, and souvenirs that play to stereotypes, and which might include country cottage cooking, desert Bedouin camps or tribal myths and ancient stories. Foodstuffs are used in tourism marketing, representing culturally embedded symbols where identity is enshrined in food items and heritage identities. Items have multiple institutional role identities, utilised in various contexts and for a variety of purposes to sustain and strengthen the image of an attraction or improve the image of a food offering (Hjalager and Corigliano, 2000). As well as providing sensory pleasure, food is the anchor for narratives of cultural expression and visitor attraction. In the quest for sustainability, branding is adopted as a way to support the sustainable social, cultural and environmental development of rural regions with a rich natural or cultural heritage.

THE POWER OF LABELS AND ASSOCIATIONS

Labelling and packaging are key to developing a strong brand, providing visual mechanisms to sell product, advertise and attract consumers. The message, 'you've tasted it, now come and visit where it was made' is pervasive. For instance, wine offers a fascinating example of how past and current narratives are employed to promote visitation of places. Wine labelling increasingly draws on the concept of 'terroir' and heritage, which serve to forge a 'vintage' identity, often masking the youth of some wine regions (Harvey et al., 2014). In well-known wine regions such as Bordeaux, La Rioja and Piedmont, vines have been an iconic part of the landscape for centuries and time integrates vines into regions' culture and tradition, progressively becoming place references (Banks et al., 2007), where the iconic nature of some wines helps identify the wine-producing region.

Alonso and Northcote (2009) ask how new wines overcome the absence of established traditions that lend themselves to regional branding for old world heritage. They explore this and the strategies adopted by regions lacking a traditional background in wine-making. A lack of heritage offers challenges, but heritage can be created and winery operators in emerging wine-producing regions are using alternative means for 'origin branding' which emphasise heritage and landscape characteristics and centre on the wider concept of a 'rural idyll'. For example, in California the heavy Italian influence is used to build an identity based on the 'Old World' Italian vineyards to foster a theme, now dubbed 'Cal-Ital landscapes'.

Wine is a good example of how branding can promote place and through its promotion and marketing, attract people to visit a destination. There is a recognised lack of a traditional heritage of wine making in New World wine destinations such as California, New Zealand and Australia. Barossa Valley in Australia is an example of wine, food, and the region's German heritage contributing to its growing popularity as a tourist destination: the heritage of wine plays a fundamental role in the region's tourism strategy. Alonso and Northcote (2009: 1249) find that 'wineries are acting as ambassadors in their regions, educating visitors, helping create a wine culture which "connects" their region with the outside world, advertising and marketing their region in the process'. In the absence of 'Old World' wine heritages, producers are constructing new heritages that link wine-making with other vintage industries and rural landscapes, forging a new local identity which has importance as a cultural marker, not just a marketing device.

Critical Reflections: destination image theory using Echtner and Ritchie (2003)

Food has a role to play in developing a destination's attractiveness, as it creates strong associations with place and tourist. Destination image theories seek to explain what influences tourist choice and how image informs touristic attitudes towards a certain destination. It explains how images create strong or weak cognitive attachments between tourists and destinations. Echtner and Ritchie (2003) offer a seminal theory using a three-continuum model based on three dimensions: (1) attribute-holistic, (2) functional-psychological and (3) common-unique. First, 'attribute-holistic' is how a customer understands a product through individual attributes making holistic impressions. The tourist assesses a destination in parts using different attributes and activities. Second, 'functional-psychological' describes both the functional characteristics (physical attributes such as activities and nature that are directly measurable, e.g. price) and psychological characteristics, which are more abstract (e.g. restaurant atmosphere) and difficult to measure. Images are holistic buildings and attributes, which can be influenced by overall feelings or impressions. There is no clear line dividing functional and psychological characteristics, but the separation of functional and psychological as well as holistic and attributes is used to show the diversity of the destination image. Third, 'common-unique' components can consist of psychological or functional traits. Common functional attributes include elements such as the infrastructure or accommodation of a destination, and psychological attributes describe the quality of service or friendliness of residents. An example of a unique functional image is the Taj Mahal in India.

The customer cannot know everything about a product, so they construct their own image of reality based on what they have seen or heard. Knowledge about a destination is gained by previous experiences or external sources, like the mass media and the views of others. For destination marketing organisations it is important to draw on these to influence the destination image. Further study of the various sources of information and how important they are in forming the destination image can be found in Gunn (1988), who developed a model of seven phases to better understand the travel experience, which starts from early mental images from the media or news to the final phase, which is a modified image based on the experience of the destination (or food).

THE ROLE OF DESIGNATIONS AND ACCREDITATIONS IN MARKETING

Chapter 10 will focus on the importance and role of food agencies, which include the European Union and through this, the EU Protection of Geographical Indications and Designations of Origin schemes. However, in terms of marketing, these designations are incredibly powerful – so much so that political tensions are created to ensure countries protect their methods of differentiation. There is a sense that food is becoming increasingly globalised through universal conformity and standardisation, although globalisation should not be regarded as the destroyer of all, as there are opportunities for co-existence and conjugation (Mak et al., 2012). It appears that the forces driving globalisation can act to strengthen specific food cultures.

One initiative to secure such histories is the growth of externally approved designations such as the EU Protection of Geographical Indications and Designations of Origin, which support destination marketing campaigns by focusing on protecting foods produced, processed and prepared in a given geographical area using recognised know-how and food linked to the geographical area. Gellynck et al.'s (2012) study of European Union traditional food products illustrates this powerful link and allure when food is formally recognised and linked to particular geographic areas. Such designations take on a significant role in the market and are increasingly requested by consumers seeking 'a return to traditions'. Spilková and Fialová (2013) argue that food can form the focus of the potential rural tourism packages in remote areas, acknowledging that the EU has recognised the potential of food as an important factor in regional development by protecting regional and traditional food, with designations able to stimulate endogenous economic development in areas that lack any other kind of distinctive attractiveness or specific potential. The Protected Designation of Origin (PDO) and Protected Geographical Indication (PGI) recognise products with a strong association with regional development, as many products come from the less favoured areas, thereby helping regionally distinctive products to give an alternative development strategy for rural regions.

Working with food and drink tourism: marketing, advertising and branding

An online search for marketing and advertising jobs in the food industry will generate numerous links to a plethora of marketing and advertising positions. A simple search in a job site for 'marketing' and 'food' (without tourism) will return thousands of opportunities around the world. Marketing food is big business and is a growing sector. Websites dedicated to careers in their sector are being developed quickly (e.g. yourfoodjob.com).

Opportunities in the food tourism marketing sector include a wide range of roles such as: food festival marketing and promotional teams, product marketing managers, brand managers, public relations for tourism agencies, creative content directors and account managers. More specialised opportunities in recent years include positions like Semiotics and Cultural Insight Manager, or Digital Content Officer (food). An interesting practical guide for those involved in the marketing and promotion of food tourism is Stanley and Stanley (2015) and is a useful place to go for industry insights into this sector.

CHAPTER SUMMARY

Marketing is the very complex and multi-faceted mechanism by which consumer expectations are managed and constructed. Increasingly food and drink are becoming central components and actors in the promotion of place and people. Food and drink attract visitors to a place and can be attractions themselves. Marketing approaches make explicit verbal and visual links between an area's history, cultural heritage and food offering. Regional products, dishes and culinary stories are now providing destinations with powerful virtual and iconographic narratives of the culture of a place and its history.

Place promotion poses the challenge of increasing visitor numbers whilst ensuring destinations retain their original attractiveness and character, and it is clear from the literature and recent campaigns that destinations and countries are employing food and drink in ever more creative and innovative ways. We are also seeing the emergence of elaborate marketing campaigns from countries that previously underplayed their culinary and gastronomic offerings, including Singapore, Vietnam, Costa Rica and Switzerland. Places are now realising the benefits of food tourism attraction development and spend on marketing and promoting is increasing.

This chapter has suggested that marketing approaches using food often make explicit reference to discourses of purity and authenticity, and use the language of heritage and tradition. These approaches seek to encapsulate the idea of locally embedded symbols and sense of place from agricultural nostalgia. Messages and narratives are increasingly about sustaining cultures and ways of life, and this chapter suggests that iconic food can be used to shed light on the history of the country, its geography and character, as well as offering a powerful link to its political and economic systems. Finally, we are seeing effective marketing of food and drink tourism, and this is increasingly happening through digital vehicles such as online blogs, social media sites like Facebook and Twitter, online review websites, and celebrity endorsement. These aspects are discussed in more detail in the next chapter.

END OF CHAPTER POINTS

- Food and drink tourism marketing should be considered in the context of an extended marketing mix, such as the Services Marketing 4Ps; however, other mixes that include the environment and e-commerce help to cover tangible and intangible aspects.

- It is increasingly rare to find promotional and marketing materials for a destination without reference to its food and drink on offer, as it has a powerful motivational impact and emotional pull.

- Destinations need to stand out, and increasingly their Unique Selling Points (USPs) are drawing on food and drink cultures, traditions and attractions. The intrinsic link between food and regional and national identity make it one of the most powerful vehicles and weapons in the marketing armoury of a destination.

- As there are different types of food tourist, different approaches are needed in marketing to attract different groups. There is opportunity to market food through other tourist segment and markets, and this is increasingly the case with special interest groups (e.g. religious, adventure, culture, ecotourism).

- One of the most popular and effective approaches to creating a strong food and drink brand that attracts tourists is to provide a sense of historic origin and nostalgia.

- Labelling and packaging are key to developing a strong brand, providing a visual mechanism to selling a product, advertising and attracting the consumer

FURTHER READING

Du Rand, G. E. and Heath, E. (2006) 'Towards a framework for food tourism as an element of destination marketing', *Current Issues in Tourism*, 9 (3): 206–34.

Getz, D., Robinson, R.N., Andersson, T.D. and Vujicic, S. (2014) *Foodies and Food Tourism*. Oxford: Goodfellows.

Hall, C.M. (2003) *Wine, Food, and Tourism Marketing*. London: Routledge.

Hall, C.M., Cambourne, B., Sharples, L., Macionis, N. and Mitchell, R. (2003) *Food Tourism Around the World: Development, Management and Markets*. London: Routledge.

Horng, J.S. and Tsai, C.T.S. (2010) 'Government websites for promoting East Asian culinary tourism: a cross-national analysis', *Tourism Management*, 31 (1): 74–85.

McKercher, B., Okumus, F. and Okumus, B. (2008) 'Food tourism as a viable market segment: it's all how you cook the numbers!', *Journal of Travel and Tourism Marketing*, 25 (2): 137–48.

Meler, M. and Cerović, Z. (2003) 'Food marketing in the function of tourist product development', *British Food Journal*, 105 (3): 175–92.

Middleton, V.T. and Clarke, J.R. (2012) *Marketing in Travel and Tourism*. London: Routledge.

Okumus, B., Okumus, F. and McKercher, B. (2007) 'Incorporating local and international cuisines in the marketing of tourism destinations: the cases of Hong Kong and Turkey', *Tourism Management*, 28 (1): 253–61.

Spilková, J. and Fialová, D. (2013) 'Culinary tourism packages and regional brands in Czechia', *Tourism geographies*, 15 (2): 177–97.

Stanley, J. and Stanley, L. (2015) *Food Tourism: A Practical Marketing Guide*. Oxford: CABI.

9

THE ROLE OF MEDIA AND SOCIAL MEDIA IN PROMOTING FOOD AND DRINK TOURISM

CHAPTER OBJECTIVES

- To examine the growth of the media-created 'celebrity chef' and look at how television is bringing food tourism to people's homes and prompting visitation
- To explore the different media channels and vehicles that present and discuss food and drink destinations and thereby inform image development and perceptions (include radio, magazine and the internet)
- To present a discussion on the role of social media and review-based websites in the promotion and marketing of food and drink tourism
- To provide an overview of the impact of international food and drink blogs and examine the role of bloggers
- To provide useful links to resources that can be examined and analysed in terms of marketing and advertising techniques and approaches

CHAPTER SUMMARY

This chapter provides an overview of how place is being promoted, and food and drink tourism is being marketed through the popular media and increasingly through consumer-authored social media channels and web-based vehicles. The chapter starts by examining the evolving promotion and utilisation of the celebrity chef and popular food television programmes and channels, and then moves to look at media forms including radio programmes, magazines and periodicals. It then explores the growth of the internet as a key marketing tool and in particular the massive growth of user-generated content through social media channels. Social media is dominating approaches to online promotion; powered by content generated through review vehicles, blogs, vlogs (video blogs), web-based marketing campaigns and vehicles such as Twitter, Facebook and Instagram. Such channels are undoubtedly now the most influential approach to food and drink marketing food websites. This global, ever-changing and powerful phenomenon is at the forefront of promotional avenues and has become a pervasive and fast-paced method of marketing.

CELEBRITY CHEF AND TELEVISION PROGRAMMES COMBINING FOOD AND TRAVEL

The rise of the celebrity chef has been well documented on television and in the press, with culinary figures enjoying huge cultural and social impact (Henderson, 2011). These culinary personalities have created an industry worth hundreds of millions of pounds. The 1980s saw the birth of a new class of restaurant-goer, the 'foodie' (Getz et al., 2014) and since then a significant market has developed for people wanting to recreate their food experiences at home. People also wanted to ensure they were visiting a restaurant of quality and began to seek out food and drink associated with a well-known personality. Mitchell and Hall (2003) acknowledge there has been significant growth and increasing desire to taste the dishes of the 'celebrity chef'. Several chefs have been credited with being the first celebrity chef, among them historically Bartolomeo Scappi, a sixteenth-century Italian and personal chef to Pope Pius V. He is believed to have written the first modern recipe books (called 'Opera di ricette'); then came the celebrity French chef and food writer Marie-Antoine Carême in the nineteenth century, credited with establishing the 'grande cuisine' and high art of gastronomy in France (Kelly, 2005). With the advent of television several chefs have been described as the 'first celebrity chef', including Julia Child in the USA, who first appeared on American television in 1963, and Fanny Craddock in the UK.

It is perhaps Keith Floyd (1943–2009) who first appeared regularly in television shows 'on location', explicitly linking food, culture and place. Keith Floyd was a British celebrity cook, television personality and restaurateur. His flamboyant presentation made him popular with millions of viewers worldwide. He is widely regarded as the pioneer of taking cooking programmes out of the television studio and into boats on rocky seas, or in hilltop mountain spots in Australia, Spain, Italy, Ireland, France, America and the Mediterranean.

Prominent celebrity chefs who have built up global brands include Gordon Ramsey (Jones, 2009), Jamie Oliver, Ken Hom, Rick Stein, Nigella Lawson and Marco Pierre White. Through the television, these chefs are now often propelled into fame through media appearances, food shows and cookery books. One of the most popular television food programmes in the UK is The Great British Bake Off, which attracts a weekly audience of up to 12 million people and has made the presenters (Paul Hollywood and Mary Berry) household names as in Figure 9.1, which was taken during an autograph signing session by both (the queue was very long!).

FIGURE 9.1   *A book signing by Mary Berry, celebrity baker. Photo by author*

Henderson (2011) argues that celebrity chefs have risen to prominence in countries such as the UK and USA, where they are a powerful commercial force. However, she also argues there is now clear and growing influence in the more economically advanced parts of East Asia, including Singapore. Gordon Ramsay, for example, is certainly reported to have a huge fan base in Singapore, especially after his involvement in the Hawker Heroes challenge in 2013. Celebrity chefs who have opened up restaurants and have attracted consumers from across the globe include the Frenchman Joel Rubuchon, Japanese chef Tetsuya Wakuda, Austrian Wolfgang Puck, Australian Luke Mangan, and American Cat Cora. In South Africa, you find vineyard tours linked to a trip to restaurants run by chef Reuben Riffel, who remains a high-profile and very well-respected member of the South African culinary community.

Television is an extremely powerful vehicle and communication medium linking place and food, enticing and inviting people to visit places with a food story, famous personality or culinary heritage. One popular programme aired in the UK in 2015 was A Cook Abroad, where chefs travelled to destinations and cooked iconic products.

A Cook Abroad, BBC2, UK

One of the most recent television series in the UK to showcase and link place with food is BBC2's *A Cook Abroad* (details at: www.bbc.co.uk/programmes/b052hdnr (21/3/15)). Each week it features a well-known celebrity chef travelling to a country to enjoy its sights, but particularly to investigate its food and drink offer and the dishes it is associated with. Examples have included Dave Myers in Egypt, Rachel Khoo in Malaysia, Tony Singh in India and Rick Stein in Australia. A popular programme, it powerfully promotes the place through its food and the people associated with its production. This close link between place and food is now explicit in these kinds of prime-time television programmes, presenting the delights of different dishes and encouraging the audience to buy the food if at home, but also to visit the place. Holiday and travel shows were once about the quality of the beach, swimming pool or nightlife; now, they are most definitely about the food and drink.

Interested consumers and foodies can see and (almost) taste the world from their armchair, fuelling an ever-present explosion of television programmes and channels dedicated to food and travel. These specialist food-related television channels have become a medium for chefs to become household names. For example, in the USA, the 24-hour Food Network features shows from celebrity chefs flying around the world cooking the unusual and exotic. Many shows feature on channels in more than one country, which has made chefs truly global products with the power to endorse products extremely effectively. Furthermore, channels such as the Travel Channel are increasingly focused on food and the culinary offer of the destinations promoted. It is clear that endorsements by celebrity chefs have led to increased demand for certain food products, but they now also lead to increased visitation of countries and places. For example, Ken Hom's first television series caused a surge in sales of Peking duck, as well as raising awareness of the Far East and its culinary offerings (Halonen-Knight and Hurmerinta, 2010). Powell and Prasad (2010) claim that the celebrity is as a cultural intermediary; they present them as unique tastemakers in contemporary culture and argue that they have a powerful role in ensuring viewers are exposed to particular lifestyles across popular media forms, such as television, print, and advertising. These media construct the stars who transfer knowledge of place and food.

RADIO FOOD AND DRINK PROMOTION

The medium of radio is powerful and pervasive in the promotion of food and drink tourism. For example, in the UK, BBC Radio 4's 'Food Programme' and their Food and Farming Awards (www.bbc.co.uk/programmes/b00zxv3j) are examples not only of how food is promoted, but of how food attractions and consumer engagement are celebrated through awards including 'best food market', or 'best food initiative'. The awards were launched in 2000, to mark the twentieth birthday of The Food Programme. The website gives the mission statement at the birth of the programme (remaining true to this day) as 'to honour those who have done most to promote the cause of good food'. In Australia, there are regular shows on ABC Radio discussing organic and local food and tourism (www.touristradio.com.au/barry_green/ABC_radio_interviews. htm) and SBS Radio Australia also regularly showcase celebrity chefs, recipes and place (www.sbs.com.au/food). Radio programmes are increasingly part of a complex media package of food and drink promotion, evidenced by numerous popular radio shows such the Chef's Table, and Splendid Table (USA). All these shows generally focus on topical issues related to food; a specific food item, such as a particular fruit or traditional dish; health issues in relation to food; and, increasingly, food of a certain geographical area or of certain ethnic peoples, sparking interest in visiting these destinations.

Other mechanisms include radio shows and programmes specifically aimed at supporting and helping the tourist. For example, in New Zealand, Tourism Radio has a section dedicated to food and drink (www.tourismradio.co.nz), claiming to be like:

> having your own personal tour guide sitting in your vehicle with you. Tourism Radio will greatly enhance your travel experience here in New Zealand. As you're driving along, our Tour Guide commentators keep you right up to date with where you are, where to go and what to see and do in the surrounding area.

PRINT MEDIA THAT BRINGS THE WORLD'S FOOD TO YOUR COFFEE TABLE

In addition to radio and television, food and tourism promotion through printed materials has become a significantly lucrative market. The explosion of food as a central story and theme in magazines is illustrated by the increase of specific food editorials and glossy magazines dedicated to food and travel. The increased range of gourmet cooking magazines includes: *Gourmet, Bon Appétit, Food & Wine, Art of Eating, Cook's Illustrated, Fine Cooking, Saveur, Cooking Pleasures, Intermezzo, Gourmet Traveler, Good Food Magazine* and *Food and Travel Magazine* published in the UK (www.foodandtravel.com), *Food Traveler* (www.foodtravelermag.com) from the USA, *Food and Travel* (www.food-travel.com/) from Singapore, offering periodicals, editorials, reviews and advertorials. Travel magazines (such as *Lonely Planet, Condé Nast* (www. condenast.co.uk), *Wanderlust* (www.wanderlust.co.uk/)) are also now full of food and drink articles and advertisements. Wilson's (2003) analysis of these food magazines provides a useful insight into their different readership, market and focus. However, it is beyond doubt that these are popular and reflect a demand for magazines combining food and travel. Newspapers also contain food and travel supplements, regularly promoting a new destination or secret foodie location.

Print media also includes promotional material in inflight magazines, and it is now commonplace to see numerous food articles focused on an airline's destinations. One example is shown in Figure 9.2 from an inflight magazine promoting Madrid as the culinary capital. Every region and destination is in a search for a unique product to differentiate itself from other destinations, and through the power of magazine articles and advertising, it is possible to showcase local food and cuisines that are unique to an area. These are powerful marketing tools to attract more visitors (Stanley and Stanley, 2015).

FIGURE 9.2 *Madrid as a culinary capital promoted in an inflight magazine, easyJet. Permission given*

ACTIVITY   **FOOD AND TOURISM MAGAZINE ANALYSIS**

Purchase a magazine dedicated to food and travel. Think about who this magazine is aimed at and how you can support your answer. What kinds of messages are being relayed in the articles? What kinds of images are used and why?

THE INTERNET

The internet is most certainly the most effective and efficient advertising medium we have today and it is now the most widely used tool for searching for tourism information: 'The information-based nature of this product means that the Internet, which offers global reach and multimedia capability, is an increasingly important means of promoting and distributing tourism services' (Doolin et al., 2002: 557). It goes without saying that the design of government tourism websites, restaurants, attractions and other culinary destinations must consider the adoption and use of presentation methods and web-based technologies that are eye-catching (Sigala et al., 2012). Certainly, to maximise the advantages of web-based marketing (such as travellers accessing information quickly, making immediate bookings, comparing costs, and so forth), destination marketing organisations (DMOs) and tourism companies have developed, redesigned and reconstructed their websites, devised elaborate technological strategies and created advanced digital interfaces (Buhalis and Law, 2008).

Kim et al. (2009b) investigated the effective use of web marketing in food tourism at sites in West Texas that would affect tourists' destination decisions, finding there was little research on food-based web-marketing. They add that, 'with the dramatic growth in the online travel market, the Web sites of destinations have been considered as an important resource to gain information for consumers and as an effective marketing tool for suppliers' (2009: 55). Information on food and drink through destination marketing organisations' websites is significant for food tourists. Kim et al. (2009b) claimed their study took an initial step to look at web marketing on food tourism and their study found information about food festivals, recipes of local and traditional food from the destinations, and food-related events, but suggested the promotion of food and food tourism on websites was still in its infancy. In the intervening years, there has been explosion of web-based activity and one only has to undertake a search for food and place on the internet to be faced with a dizzying array of options and search engine results.

Today, marketers and institutions no longer have ultimate control over the image of their destination or product (Hays et al., 2013), and this is where the power of social media and user-generated content has come into its own. Schegg and Fux (2010) suggest that the evolution of Web 1.0 to 2.0 marks a shift from users rather than organisations taking charge of the internet.

SOCIAL MEDIA AND CONSUMER-GENERATED REVIEWS

A recent phenomenon dominating promotional avenues and marketing is the rapid growth of social media channels, online promotion vehicles and web-based marketing campaigns. Social media is particularly relevant since tourism is an 'information-intensive industry' (Gretzel et al., 2000: 147). Consumers obtain information to assist in the trip-planning process and to make informed decisions about destinations, accommodation, restaurants, tours and attractions (Xiang and Gretzel, 2010). It is a key broadcasting medium (Buhalis and Law, 2008) and we have seen the explosion of eWOM (online Word of Mouth) (Litvin et al., 2008), where consumer-generated media is increasingly the most powerful vehicle for destination marketing. This has challenged and disrupted traditional approaches to place marketing, giving way to instantaneous and informal approaches, including consumer-authored reviews and suggestions through sites such as Trip Advisor and online booking pages. The line of communication is no longer limited to producer-to-consumer, but is increasingly consumer-to-consumer, and consumer-to-producer, as well as many-to-one, one-to-many, one-to-one, or many-to-many (Buhalis, 2003; Hays et al., 2013)

Websites are now dominated by user-driven content and represent what has become commonly known as Web 2.0 technology, where the website is no longer just a static page, but a dynamic platform allowing users to engage with the autonomous generation of content and an opportunity to relay, reflect on, and rate their own experiences (Miguéns et al., 2008). Such platforms host a vast amount of user-generated content, and are proving extremely influential in directing tourists' choices. A study by Xiang and Gretzel (2010) outlines the role of social media in online travel information, confirming the growing importance of social media in the online tourism domain. It also provides evidence for challenges faced by traditional providers of travel-related information. Online restaurant reviews are also increasingly becoming a key part of the pre-research to a trip. The study by Lu and Jun Yi (2014) in China using dianping.com finds these review sites significantly increase traffic to restaurants. It is also noted that Web 2.0 approaches are increasingly used by managers and destinations to understand and accommodate ever-changing consumer preferences, needs and tastes.

ACTIVITY   WRITE AND SUBMIT YOUR OWN ONLINE REVIEW

Register with an online review website such as tripadvisor.com or a restaurant table booker with reviewer sections and provide your own review of a restaurant or food outlet you have visited (a good or bad experience!). Think about providing a balanced, evidence-based and accurate account of your experience. Continue to monitor how many hits/likes you receive over the next few weeks. Can you see how powerful your entry is and how it can influence others?

Many DMOs turn to social media as a relatively low-cost and global reach marketing tool, although there is limited research, according to Hays et al. (2013), which looks at use of social media. They claim that, despite social media being recognised as central to providing a competitive advantage, there remains relatively little understanding of its impact, especially in how using it in a poor manner can be more harmful than not engaging with it at all. Hays et al. claim that DMOs need to exhibit more interactive behaviour on their social media platform, given that it is publicly available, widely accessible information. DMOs need to ensure they are up to date and understand how other tourism professionals and organisations are implementing social media strategies to learn from their achievements and mistakes.

In terms of web 2.0 technology, one growth area has been the emergence of online diaries or regular posted commentaries, better known as blogs (weblogs) or vlogs (video diaries), where social media is providing relevant, fluid and iconic culinary commentary.

▶

in small numbers'. The company are keen that tourists feel that are not 'part of a herd', but are simply travelling with friends on a fabulous foodie holiday. It promises that 'Each day we'll duck and weave through local markets, cafes, roadside stalls and visit the homes of locals. We take time out to sit and enjoy many of the local daily customs and brews, immersing ourselves in our surroundings and soaking the senses, rather than rushing from one sight to the next' (http://tastetrekkers.com.au). The website shown in Figure 9.3 offers a clear example of how a small food company is using social media links and evolving content to engage and interact with potential customers and interested 'foodies'.

The owner and entrepreneur behind the business, Sally Lynch, was keen to state in correspondence that social media can be a blessing and a curse: 'I do food treks to far flung locales – exploring the world of food producers and home cooks with a little bit of foodie rockstar thrown in for good measure :-)'. In social media she claims 'It is one of those issues you don't think about when full of excitement about taking over the world with your new business – but as the technological world takes over names are becoming harder and harder to get so that all your social media is aligned – with the simple replacement of a letter you have a copycat brand on your hands. Difficult to keep on top of it all too – not sure what the solution is?' (Correspondence 10/8/15).

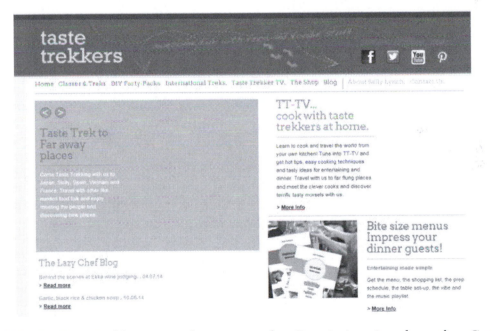

FIGURE 9.3 *Taste Trekkers.au website screen shot. Permission given by author. Credit Sally Lynch*

BLOGGING AND VLOGGING

Blog is an abbreviation for 'web log' and is usually a frequently updated, reverse-chronological single web page using images and links to other social media links and applications. Blogging has become a powerful online marketing approach, with titles such as '10 Iconic Foods of New York City, and Where To Find Them' and 'Sarawak Top 10 Iconic Foods'. This consumer-to-consumer (C2C) medium has become a massive growth area (Pan et al., 2007). Tseng et al. (2015) found that food blogs in China are one of four key themes in destination marketing which prompted tourist visitation. Baker and Green (2008) found that there were 31.6 million blogs on the internet with 40,000 new blogs coming online each day. This form of online publishing has gained more and more popularity, as personal communication or word-of-mouth is viewed as a more credible and honest source of consumer information. There is now a clear need for tourism marketers to understand this new phenomenon and its implications for marketing and promotion of a destination. As Pan et al. (2007) outline, consumers are able to access opinions not only from close friends and family members, but also from strangers from all around the world who may have used the product, visited a certain destination or eaten a certain food.

One example of a website which hosts and promotes food and drink blogs is www.foodies100.co.uk, the UK's largest network for food and drink bloggers, with almost 5,000 members reaching 8 million readers a year. It provides bloggers with opportunities to share and develop their blogs through the website, events and brand partnerships. Or elsewhere in the world, examples from Nigeria include www.dobbyssignature.com, or South Africa www.foodandthefabulous.com; or Spain www.latortugaviajera.com. For example, another site referring to Malaysia (http://kampungboycitygal.com) includes specific information about Malaysia's culinary offerings, supporting research that finds consumer feedback is essential to the success of a tourist offer (Kivela and Crotts, 2006).

To reduce the uncertainty associated with purchase, potential tourists often rely on the opinions and evaluations of a reference group in the decision-making process. The advice of consumers with prior experience of tourism products is particularly valued, and has been identified as the most influential form of word-of-mouth in shaping potential visitors' decision-making (Crotts, 1999). Through a blog or vlog, the consumer can seek more authentic advice from other consumers who have prior experience with the tourist destination. Pan et al. (2007) suggest bloggers are seen as interpersonally available and rank not only as the preferred source of purchase information, but the most influential in travel decision-making for many. One of the methodologies employed to research this phenomenon is netnography (Kozinets, 2010).

Critical Reflections: using netnography as a methodology

Netnography is a methodological approach that analyses the behaviour of individuals on the internet to provide insights into their views and thoughts of places, services and products. Netnography explores cultural and symbolic information on the internet and is increasingly used by tourism researchers (e.g. Mkono (2012a) used this in a study of Zimbabwe). The word 'netnography' comes from 'inter[net]' and 'ethnography' and was a process and term coined and developed by Robert Kozinets. It is an adaptation of traditional ethnography using the internet as a virtual fieldwork site. Data generation takes two forms: data that the researcher directly copies from the computer-mediated communications of online community members, and reflective fieldnotes that capture the ethnographer's observations. Without both parts, it is arguably not ethnographic.

Web-based research is becoming more widely used in tourism research as more tourism consumers become active in online travel communities and social networking forums dedicated to tourism, such as Trip Advisor. Researchers can also find travel-related discussions on general networking sites such as Facebook and Twitter. In particular, post-visit narratives provided on these online platforms offer a way of exploring tourists' subjective travel experiences. Through the blogosphere, they rate tourism suppliers and generate important points of reference for other travellers through their 'word-of-mouse' testimonies.

Think about the advantages and disadvantages of this research method and how you might employ it to gain insights about the food and drink tourism phenomenon.

With magazines, websites, television and Twitter feeds dedicated to food, stories are given new life and traditions transformed to fit new fashions and instantaneous consumer feedback. With advanced web technologies, destinations are establishing real and online spatial and social zones, where food experiences are packaged together into a highly interactive, evolving and enticing offer.

Working with food and drink tourism: social media blogging

There is money to be made and a career to be carved through successful blogging and online food writing. Food and drink writers are in demand, but it is competitive and they often look for experience in blogging and using social media. It is free to

(Continued)

(Continued)

start blogging, and can get you noticed very quickly. Some bloggers are freelance and attract writing contracts and paid advertising on their sites. Others move into jobs like this, recently advertised for an anonymised company in the USA: 'A company is looking for an ambitious, internet- and social-media-savvy editor with a huge passion for cooking to lead its popular food section'. Note the type of work, but particularly the skills and experiences required (listed below). Perhaps this is an area that would suit you?

Responsibilities:

- Write posts about food in a shareable style and tone.
- Come up with smart ideas for food posts to assign to the food team.
- Edit staff posts and generate effective, clever headlines aimed at sharing.
- Drive and oversee the production of cooking tutorial photo and video shoots.
- Grow, diversify, and innovate the food section's presence on Pinterest, Facebook, Twitter, Instagram, and other social media channels.
- Outline and execute a vision for growing and expanding the section to reach new, diverse audiences.
- Line-edit original recipes for clarity and accuracy.
- Establish and maintain relationships with chefs, food writers, and other food-world authorities to bring fresh perspectives and ideas to the section.
- Obsessively track viral trends on Facebook, Pinterest, and Tumblr and create content around those trends.

Requirements:

- Two to four years of website, magazine, or blogging/vlogging experience – or similar experience in the food industry.
- Experience editing and managing writers.
- Proven understanding of the kinds of food and cooking that generate engagement on social media platforms like Pinterest and Instagram, and the ability to articulate those qualities.
- Self-starter and hard worker with tons of smart ideas.
- Obsession with and passion for cooking plus a strong interest in and knowledge of professional cooking techniques.
- Flexibility and enthusiasm about experimenting with unconventional ideas.
- The technical cooking expertise to create new image-based cooking tutorials and write posts full of authoritative tips is a plus.

CHAPTER SUMMARY

This chapter has provided examples and case studies to illustrate the role and impact of the media – whether online, in press or on the television. In its analysis of these communication vehicles, it first looked at the power and influence of the phenomenon that is the celebrity chef and their role in generating interest in places they visit, or dishes they cook on camera. Furthermore, this chapter recognises the plethora of dedicated television channels and programmes across the globe that represent culinary intermediaries, bringing flavour and gastronomic delights from around the world into a viewer's home, simultaneously enticing them to visit the place of its origin and production. The chapter also focused on the increasing space on the radio or in print media dedicated to food tourism, and the explicit promotion and championing of producers and locations. Advertising, periodicals and editorials in printed magazines and publications have become big business. Very few inflight magazines or newspaper magazine supplements do not have food articles or supplements enticing you to visit a city, region or country to savour its culinary offer.

Finally, the chapter focused on the power of the internet and web-based technologies. Widely regarded as the most effective and efficient advertising medium today, it is the most impactful and truly international tool available for searching tourist information and where to eat and visit. Coupled with this online boom, it needs to be recognised that web 2.0 technologies have become the vehicle of consumer choice and communication. There has been an explosion of online word-of-mouth methods, promoting a marketing approach which draws on consumer-to-consumer, and consumer-to-producer influence, adopting social media channels such as review websites, but also Facebook, Twitter, Instagram, etc. and single-authored blog and vlog sites that build on our desire to check out, listen and seek the opinions and evaluations of others to inform our decision-making process.

END OF CHAPTER POINTS

- Celebrity chefs have risen to global prominence and are now a powerful commercial force as a cultural and culinary intermediaries and tastemakers in contemporary culture.
- Television and radio have become extremely powerful vehicles and communication methods to link place and food, promoting a complex media package of food and drink promotion that encourages visitation to places with a food story or heritage.
- The internet is the main research tool for consumers seeking out information and recommendations on place and where to eat and drink.
- Marketers and institutions no longer have control over the image of their destination or product: power lies with the user and consumer.
- Online word-of-mouth mechanisms that promote consumer-generated media are arguably the most powerful vehicles for destination marketing.
- Websites are now dynamic platforms that allow users the autonomous generation of content and the opportunity of relaying, reflecting on, and rating their own experiences.

- Blogs and vlogs provide valuable advice from consumers with prior experience of tourism products to potential consumers and are therefore identified as the most influential form of word-of-mouth in shaping potential visitors' decision-making.

FURTHER READING

Buhalis, D. (2003) *eTourism: Information Technology for Strategic Tourism Management.* London: Prentice Hall.

Halonen-Knight, E. and Hurmerinta, L. (2010) 'Who endorses whom? Meanings transfer in celebrity endorsement', *Journal of Product & Brand Management*, 19 (6): 452–60.

Henderson, J.C. (2011) 'Celebrity chefs: expanding empires', *British Food Journal*, 113 (5): 613–24.

Kim, Y.H., Yuan, J., Goh, B.K. and Antun, J.M. (2009) 'Web marketing in food tourism: a content analysis of web sites in West Texas', *Journal of Culinary Science & Technology*, 7 (1): 52–64.

Lu, P. and Jun Yi, L. (2014) 'The impact of electronic word-of-mouth on the online page view of restaurants', *Tourism Tribune*, 29 (1): 111–18.

Miguéns, J., Baggio, R. and Costa, C. (2008) 'Social media and tourism destinations: TripAdvisor case study', *Advances in Tourism Research*. Presented at Aveiro, Portugal, 26–28 May. Available at: www.iby.it/turismo/papers/baggio-aveiro2.pdf. [Accessed 14/12/15.]

Pan, B., MacLaurin, T. and Crotts, J.C. (2007) 'Travel blogs and the implications for destination marketing', *Journal of Travel Research*, 46 (1): 35–45.

Sigala, M., Christou, E. and Gretzel, U. (eds) (2012) *Social Media in Travel, Tourism and Hospitality: Theory, Practice and Cases*. Farnham: Ashgate Publishing.

Xiang, Z. and Gretzel, U. (2010) 'Role of social media in online travel information search', *Tourism Management*, 31 (2): 179–88.

10

MANAGING FOOD TOURISM: ON-SITE MARKETING AND INTERPRETATION

CHAPTER OBJECTIVES

- To explore approaches to on-site marketing and visitor interpretation at food production sites and attractions
- To provide insightful examples of how food is being marketed and promoted through on-site methods and visitor experiences
- To explore some of the latest technologies and approaches used in food and drink visitor interpretation
- To assess the challenges that on-site interpretation methods bring (including health and safety concerns and risk of contamination)
- To offer a critical assessment of the concept of the 'sanitised' tourist gaze in relation to the use of viewing windows

CHAPTER SUMMARY

This chapter assesses how food and drink sites are now managing and educating tourists (originally, many such sites were food production and processing sites that did not attract visitors). It looks at issues of on-site marketing, product promotion, and interpretation (videos, tastings, viewing windows and guided tours) and assesses the methods used to manage, guide and educate visitors. The chapter also uses examples to highlight the difficulties that some site owners and managers have in assuring the health and safety of visitors, and ensuring food is not contaminated by external sources and visitors. It draws on real-life case study material from more developed sites across Scotland, Ireland and Europe, but will also include examples from less developed countries using food and drink tourism to improve their economies (discussion of the risk management associated with this kind of promotion is also provided). Finally, the chapter looks at the concept of the 'sanitised' tourist gaze, suggesting that although tourism is presented as an embodied and immersive experience, and food and drink are ultimately sensual experiences, the visitor attraction is often sanitised when sites use viewing windows and artificial 'front stages' to entertain and educate, yet simultaneously need to protect the integrity of the products on display.

DIVERSIFICATION OF PRODUCTION SITES: ON-SITE MARKETING AT FOOD PRODUCTION SITES

As food tourism interest increases and destinations employ it as a driver to increase visitor traffic, we have seen the transformation of food production sites into spaces of touristic experience. Food and drink producers are increasingly opening their doors to visitors as the popularity of food and drink tourism increases, negotiating a balance between the operation of their food production business (often small, local, family-run businesses such as bakeries, butchers, farms and dairies), and the drive towards diversification by developing new arenas of consumption. As Everett (2012) argues in her discussion of how production sites are becoming consumption sites, places of food production are now opening their doors to visitors. Unlike many heritage tourism sites that no longer exist for their original purpose, food tourism sites remain active places of work, providing a living for small rural producers whilst simultaneously changing to accommodate visitors who wish to watch food production as part of their tourism experience. Although food tourism sites are promoted as places offering authentic and embodied, multi-sensual experiences of local food, they are increasingly becoming themed spaces undergoing perpetual re-imagining and manipulation.

Live workshops and publicly accessible activities at production sites are now becoming very powerful marketing mechanisms, and these are increasingly supported by investments to recreate food-making and workmanship in museums and heritage attractions. New sites are being created, and many old food sites, which had often been developed with no intention of attracting or accommodating tourists, are being transformed into attractions where people are making a living. Over the past 20 years, commercial sites have become paying attractions, serving a multiplicity of purposes beyond their original design or the owner's intention. It is clear that on-site interaction and *in situ* interpretation is helping to increase visits to farms and factories for the purposes of on-site retail purchases, recreation and education (Blekesaune et al., 2010). These sites promote culinary tourism that embraces practices of exploratory eating and encountering, knowing, and consuming other places and cultures (Long, 2004).

In Everett's (2007) study of food producers and consumers, a number of producers outlined the value of consumer engagement at the sites. One producer suggested that it needs to be a subtle performance: 'People don't like being managed, not in a very obvious way. You can manipulate people, that's what you do with marketing, but they don't like being managed' (2007: 282). Likewise, at a Scottish bakery, the owner claimed:

> They want to see it as a rustic, old fashioned bakers. It's one of the things about the shop, one of the reasons the shop has remained old-fashioned as I quite like the fact that people will come in and see this wooden-type, warm feeling shop. You don't try and make it all spick and span and modern. (2007: 282)

Similarly, at a Scottish distillery, the visitor manager claimed it was all about performance and olfactory engagement:

> It is very tactile. People like to touch and feel and want to be able to touch the barley, they like the smells and on purpose we are producing the whisky in the summer, whereas the traditional way of making whisky is to close down during the summer. (2007: 282)

The provision of some kind of 'experience' on site not only seeks to attract visitors to a place, but attempts to go one step further as it is designed as a marketing tool, to encourage the tourist to buy the product and become a consumer of the product once they return home. For example, on-site attractions inevitably have a shop and established mechanisms to drive traffic to online delivery and repeat orders. It is a well-researched and evidenced area of marketing, that 'try before you buy' approaches are powerful in generating customer trust and loyalty. This added value of showcasing food and production is proving to be a very effective marketing technique. The increase in food sites becoming visitor attractions in their own right is testament to this and certainly investment through grants and funding for such sites is supporting this growth. One such source of funding includes European LEADER funding (see below), which supplied funds for factories and shops to diversify into visitor attractions, and to provide methods of interpretation and visitor engagement.

CASE STUDY

Funding onsite visitor experiences – LEADER Funding

LEADER (*L*iaison *E*ntre *A*ctions *pour le D*eveloppement *de l'E*conomie *R*urale, which means 'liaison among actors in rural economic development') funding supports farmers and food producers to diversify into new types of activity across Europe (see also Chapter 15). The UK website states:

> If you have an idea that will bring some different activities to your farm or small-holding, or add value to the things that

►

you produce, then a LEADER grant may help to almost double your investment. We are not looking to provide new equipment for old, but support genuine new ways of doing things or additional processes that you can do with your core activities to make them sell at a higher value. For example, processing some of the raw ingredients of the food, using some of your space to process green waste or even creating some visitor and tourism interest.

From summer 2015, rural businesses went through a Local Action Group (LAG) for LEADER funding for projects that aimed to create jobs, helped businesses to grow and embrace tourism opportunities, and intended to use their sites to benefit the rural economy.

Source: www.gettingfunding.co.uk/farming_and_forestry.html, and www.gov.uk/rural-development-programme-for-england-leader-funding

Food and drink sites are employing numerous approaches to visitor engagement, and part of the marketing mix has been to develop and offer cookery schools and tastings. These provide opportunities for full immersion and the development of a relationship between product and consumer (attractions are discussed further in Part 3). Once engaged in conversation with a producer, and having tasted the product, a tourist is far more likely to purchase that product. This development of an immediate relationship with the product through a tasting is one of the most powerful marketing methods available to a producer or retailer. This is shown in Figure 10.1, which illustrates how a tea plantation in Sri Lanka invites

FIGURE 10.1 *Tea tasting in Sri Lanka. Permission given and credit for photo: Halpe Tea, UHE Exports (pvt) Ltd*

THE PROMOTION AND BRANDING OF FOOD AND DRINK TOURISM

tourists to see tea production, but also taste the tea; invariably this prompts purchases (see Chapter 17 on tea tourism). This approach is demonstrated particularly well outside the place of production at farmers' markets and events (discussed in Chapter 14).

INTERPRETATION TECHNIQUES AT FOOD PRODUCTION SITES

Interpretation in this context refers to how information is provided to visitors, and how education is used to make connections between them and places, sites, natural areas, wildlife and cultures. Various communication methods, from signs to tours to games. One definition provided by The Association for Heritage Interpretation is as follows: 'Interpretation enriches our lives through engaging emotions, enhancing experiences and deepening understanding of people, places, events and objects from past and present' (www.ahi.org.uk 2015). Interpretation has also been regarded as a set of communication techniques that can get a particular message across to a particular group (Uzzell, 1989). It was perhaps Tilden who first developed the concept of interpretation for educating visitors; he saw it as an art and 'an educational activity which aims to reveal meanings and relationships through the use of original objects, by first-hand experience and by illustrative media, rather than simply to communicate factual information' (Tilden, 1957: 9). At its core is thinking about how artefacts are presented and high-quality accompanying information. At food sites, this supports a process of informal education, or what Light (1995: 117) describes as 'voluntary learning in leisure time', and 'self-motivated, voluntary, exploratory, non-coercive learning and understandings which can take place during a visit to a heritage site'.

INTERPRETATION FOR AN ISLAND: TASTE OF ARRAN

One example of a destination using on-site marketing and interpretation techniques extremely effectively is the Isle of Arran in west Scotland, which has developed a strong food tourism identity (Michaelidou and Hassan, 2010). In a study of the island, Boyne et al. (2002: 97) claim that 'there appears to be a paucity of published research dealing with tourists' related consumption patterns and behaviour', although more studies have since researched this area, including Seo et al. (2014) and Getz et al. (2014). Arran is hailed as a benchmark for subsequent food tourism initiatives, with Boyne et al. (2002) finding that 88% of visitors return to Arran due to the experience and food offer. Visitors to the Isle of Arran can stop off at the attractively named 'Cheese Experience' (Figure 10.2) that is located between other small independent shops as they wind around an island that heavily promotes its food and drink. This is one example of a small shop where chunks of cheese are provided to taste, but also a viewing window and

FIGURE 10.2　*Tourists stop off at the 'Cheese Experience', Isle of Arran, Scotland. Photo by author*

FIGURE 10.3　*Taste of Arran shop, Scotland. Photo by author*

THE PROMOTION AND BRANDING OF FOOD AND DRINK TOURISM

television are installed. The nature of the viewing window is theorised below, and is an example of how food sites are cross-selling and -promoting other food sites. Figure 10.3 shows how the shop has become a visitor attraction, with leaflets, posters, videos and tasters being used to sell cheese and provide a more immersive experience.

Personal guided tours are also a much-employed method of engaging visitors at sites, and the Isle of Arran also provides a number of examples of this, such as the distillery tour, which seeks to encourage visitors to buy whisky in their shop and when they return (see Chapter 17). This is a powerful approach to marketing, which develops loyalty through personal engagement and education. The distillery has installed an interactive visitor centre with videos, croft house recreations, game simulations and even indoor waterfalls to recreate the landscape of Scotland. Figure 10.4 shows a tour guide talking to visitors at the Arran Distillery, which is one of the methods of interpretation used to bring the process to life.

FIGURE 10.4 *Tour guide talking to visitors at the Arran Distillery, Scotland. Photo by author*

LATEST TECHNOLOGIES AND APPROACHES USED IN FOOD AND DRINK VISITOR INTERPRETATION

As competition to attract food and drink tourists intensifies, sites are increasingly looking at more creative and interactive ways to bring visitors through the door, innovating beyond guided tours and tastings. The very latest visitor interpretation technologies are being employed to engage and excite tourists. As outlined above, it is said that visitor interpretation leads to learning (Black, 2005; Hooper-Greenhill, 2013), but it also leads to food and drink purchases. Black (2005) outlines the need for museums in general to provide stimuli, which in turn develops a frame of mind to want to engage, and then the third phase finds visitors wanting to engage more closely with the site or artefacts (i.e. by purchasing the food). There are numerous studies on museum interpretation that should be consulted as they provide excellent reference points to describe how shops and sites are developing stronger brand loyalty than can ever be created online or through newspaper adverts.

Food and drink locations are increasingly using technology to engage. For example, the Alimentarium Food Museum in Switzerland (see the Case Study in Chapter 16) is widely reviewed as engaging with its own courses and iconic structures (www.alimentarium.ch). A review on Trip Advisor highlights the approach they take (Figure 10.5).

"If You Love Food It is a Must Visit"

This was a very interesting museum with a lot of interesting and fun facts about food history and nutrition. It appeals to a wide age group with something for everyone, A good way to spend a casual afternoon. The gardens were just as interesting as the inside.

FIGURE 10.5   *A Trip Advisor review of the Alimentarium highlights the enjoyment they experienced at the museum. Permission given*

THE CHALLENGES AND RISKS OF ON-SITE INTERPRETATION

Despite the effectiveness of welcoming visitors into the food spaces, the introduction of mechanisms that separate the tourist from the food are common, as concern about effective visitor management and safety increases. Shops and production sites use viewing windows to promote their food whilst retaining a healthy distance between producer and voyaging gourmand. Viewing windows are partly a result of intensified business pressure and the need to balance continued production that must meet health and safety requirements with the ongoing management of visiting tourists. However, what is created is a regulated form of embodiment, offering a strange hybrid of the visual and internalised, and a curious space of 'inbetweenness' separating consumer and producer; a postmodern experience that highlights the persistence and sustained influence of Fordist forms of consumption (Everett, 2009; see Critical Reflections). Despite being engaged in an activity that connects consumers more closely with food than would ordinarily be experienced, where tourists are seeking 'up-close and personal' interactions, there is a physical disconnection.

A viewing window helps to market and display the product, but there is also a disconcerting absence of smell or sound that would traditionally be associated with the food item. While it is understandable why sites have installed viewing areas, they have created a sanitised, hygienic bubble (Bauman, 2013 [1993]). As the Isle of Arran's 'Cheese Experience' shows, the concept of an 'experience' is perhaps over-stated, particularly when it involves this barrier of sensory separation in an overly-managed and pure space (Everett, 2009). The window provides a view from the tourist-occupied 'front stage' into the productive 'back stage', and visitors can enjoy food-related activities that they may interpret as real and 'authentic', but it lacks the kind of physical engagement that one might expect from an 'experience'. Although viewing windows are often presented as a way to gaze into the back stage areas of food production, much of the experience is constructed to meet certain marketing objectives and promote regional food and drink needs. For another example from Scotland of this separation see Figure 10.6, which shows tourists observing the fish smoking process through glass – there is little real interaction with the producers. Interpretation is provided through information boards and leaflets, but the concept of bringing the producer closer to the consumer is perhaps compromised here because of safety and hygiene concerns.

FIGURE 10.6 *Visitors at The Hebridean Smokehouse, Scotland. Photo by author*

HEALTH AND SAFETY IMPLICATIONS AND MITIGATING RISK

Findings ways to bring the consumer into a food and drink shop or factory will inevitably create stronger emotional bonds and identification with the produce and the producer. As found with restaurants (Shelton, 1990), food sites have become heterogeneous theatres for thinking and arenas for fashioning identities. However, as outlined above, close physical contact with food also creates significant risk and has led to the growth of viewing windows and more distant forms of engagement – the paradox of food being the ultimate olfactory experience! Producers need to balance continued production (and meeting health and safety requirements) with the ongoing management of tourists. However, what is created is a regulated form of embodiment, offering a hybrid of the visual and internalised, and a curious space of 'in-betweenness' separating consumer and producer and the non-material experience and the material object (Everett, 2009).

Given that one sneeze typically contain as many as 40,000 droplets (some which leave the body at more than 100 mph), it is absolutely business-critical that sites open to tourists are not exposed to this risk. Examples of these kinds of site open to risk are dairies, open-production factories, and open kitchens. Not all countries have strict food regulations, and often visitors are free to enjoy production spaces at their leisure (and peril!). However, generally where food and drink tourism is being formally promoted and supported in developed countries, there are challenges to balance food safety and visitor enjoyment. Approaches and legislation to militate against problems have been adopted across the globe. In Australia, www.foodstandards.gov.au operates to protect the consumer; similarly, the South African Food Safety Initiative (FSI) of the Consumer Goods Council of South Africa (CGCSA) was set up to ensure

> all reasonable steps to collaborate with stakeholders [are taken] to ensure that food produced, distributed and marketed in South Africa meets the highest standards of food safety and nutrition and complies with legal requirements or recognised codes of good practice.

In the UK, the Food Standards Agency outlines food safety regulations for businesses. The key regulations are (EC) No. 852/2004 on the hygiene of foodstuffs. The Food Hygiene (England) Regulations (UK Government 2006) state that:

> Staff should keep hair tied back and wear a suitable head covering, e.g. hat or hairnet, when preparing food; Staff should not wear watches or jewellery when preparing food (except a wedding band); Staff should not touch their face and hair, smoke, spit, sneeze, eat or chew gum when they are handling food.

All of these things are easily managed with staff, but more challenging with members of the public! In England and Wales, 'Safer food, better business' offers an innovative and practical approach to food safety management by the FSA for small businesses (food.gov.uk/sfbb). In Ireland, the Food Safety Authority of Ireland (www.fsai.ie)

performs the same role, providing guidance on starting a food business, including regulations on how to manage visitors and achieve good hygiene standards that comply with the law (see Figure 10.7, which shows visitors in protective clothing visiting a dairy in West Cork, Ireland). The concept of close engagement between food and tourists is good in theory, but the reality at some real production sites is a more difficult balance and investment is needed to support this, for example hair and shoe coverings, educational talks and enhanced washing facilities.

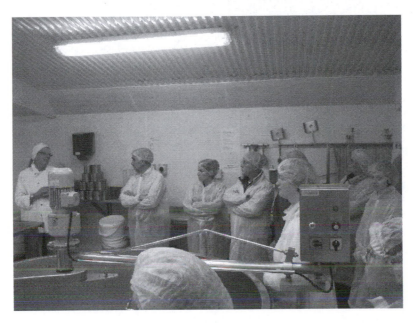

FIGURE 10.7 *Visitors in protective clothing visiting a dairy in West Cork, Ireland. Photo by author*

Critical Reflections: a sanitised visual gaze? Fordist or post-Fordist?

Everett (2009) offers a study that critiques the dominance of Urry's (1990b) concept of the 'tourist gaze', suggesting food tourism affords an opportunity to critically reflect on this statement. This chapter outlines efforts to offer new tourism experiences that bring the producer closer to the consumer as food-related tourism offers a plethora of indulgent multi-sensory experiences. Yet, Urry's 'gaze' privileges the eye, locating other senses in a distinctive visual environment. In claiming that the visual has long been understood as the most discerning and reliable sensual mediator between humans and their environment, Urry suggests practices of tourism can be approached with an emphasis on vision. Although the 'gaze' continues

(Continued)

to provide a seminal concept for contemporary tourism discussions, particularly those that pursue visual-centric approaches that focus on representations, tangible semiotics and the visual consumption of landscape, it has become apparent that visual-centric approaches are limited in their ability to tackle the complex dimension of more embodied postmodern activity (Edensor, 2001).

If you consider the concept of 'new' postmodern forms of tourism activity, the installation of a viewing window perhaps problematises this concept, as there is a paradoxical situation of 'postmodernity', in which a (post) tourist is encouraged to engage sensually with (and physically internalise) a place through its food, yet is simultaneously enjoying the sight through a form of regulated 'tourist gaze' reminiscent of more 'Fordist' and modernist modes of tourism experience.

In shops, staff may be working on food production, yet there is an element of staging and manipulation of space where equipment is carefully located and placed to entertain the public, framed by interpretation panels about the people, product and process. Figure 10.8 shows the situation that a consumer finds themselves in; balancing the power of food standardisation and hygiene legislation, mass production, homogenisation, commercialism and rationalisation, against the inner circle that represents complete multi-sensory and embodied

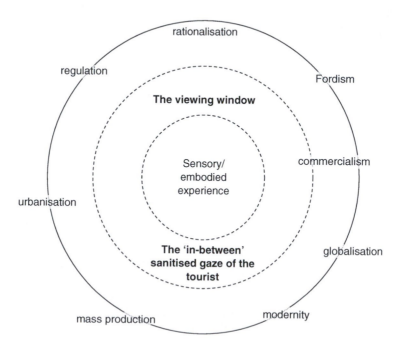

FIGURE 10.8   *The paradox of the viewing window*

THE PROMOTION AND BRANDING OF FOOD AND DRINK TOURISM

immersion in the production site. It illustrates the creation of an interstitial hybrid space of tourism between avoiding excessive immersive sensory experiences whilst also resisting external processes of globalisation, commercialism and mass production.

Working with food and drink tourism: visitor attraction and interpretation

There are a growing number of career opportunities to work within food and drink tourism and heritage interpretation. Although a competitive and niche career path, it is one of creativity and growth. More general positions often include opportunities to present food stories through displays and educational vehicles, research heritage and ways of life, by being a museum curator, in-house marketer or interpretation officer at food tourism sites, or as a tour guide. In general, a museum curator's duties include acquiring items, interpreting their history, exhibiting them to advantage and protecting them from harm. At a minimum, the job requires a related master's degree plus work experience: competition is fierce and food- and drink-specific sites are small in number.

Examples of real jobs and projects recently advertised include:

- Tour Guide: Fredericksburg, Virginia, US. Adverts include 'A Smith Bowman Distillery is seeking a part-time Tour Guide to work weekends, holidays and some weekdays'. As a Smith Bowman Distillery's Tour Guide, one will be responsible for 'mak[ing] every visitor an influential raving fan as they experience the pioneering spirit of our historic family-owned distillery.'
- Education and Interpretation Officer, responsible for recreation of methods of agricultural food production, small folk museum in Adelaide, Australia.
- Museum Officer at The National Civil War Museum (NCWM) in Harrisburg, Pennsylvania – responsible for interpretation of the kitchen including a building with two new masonry bread ovens to attract and educate tourists.

CHAPTER SUMMARY

This chapter has outlined how food and drink tourism is increasingly promoted, marketed and advertised at the place of production. A growing number of food and drink shops are seeking to increase sales through a visitor experience beyond pure display and a more transactional and traditional sales formula. New visitor experiences involve tastings, viewing windows, and multi-media exhibitions plus more formalised experiences such as educational workshops and tours.

At sites such as the Taste of Arran attractions, the latest visitor interpretation technologies are being installed to engage and excite tourists, from extremely interactive multi-media games to visual simulations. With the pressure on attracting visitors, the chapter goes on to discuss one of the most popular interpretation mechanisms being used at shops, factories and production sites: the viewing window. This mechanism is a marketing approach that helps build a close relationship between the tourist and product, but paradoxically the glass leads to an absence of smell or sound, thus creating a sanitised tourist gaze (Everett, 2009). Further, the chapter outlines why business owners and producers are turning to these 'safer' methods as a response to increasingly complex health and safety regulations, put in place to protect the producer and consumer. There is clearly a balance to be struck in creating an engaging and enticing experience without compromising the integrity of the product. Sometimes, the opportunity to dress in lab coats, shoe-covers and hairnets can form part of the overall experience.

END OF CHAPTER POINTS

- Numerous food production sites are transforming their infrastructure and ways of working to accommodate visitors who wish to watch food production as an attraction.

- Interpretation techniques are not only employed in museums and galleries, but are increasingly adopted in food production sites, shops and factories to entertain and educate tourists.

- Tastings, visuals, multi-media tools, tours and exhibitions within shops and sites represent some of the most sophisticated and personalised marketing and promotional techniques, proven to be effective in generating sales and repeat business

- Where food and drink are concerned, there will inevitably be a conflict with food safety, hygiene laws and health and safety.

FURTHER READING

Boniface, P. (2003) *Tasting Tourism: Travelling for Food And Drink*. Aldershot: Ashgate.

Black, G. (2005) *The Engaging Museum: Developing Museums for Visitor Involvement*. Abingdon: Routledge.

Boyne, S., Hall, D. and Williams, F. (2003) 'Policy, support and promotion for food-related tourism initiatives: a marketing approach to regional development', *Journal of Travel & Tourism Marketing*, 14 (3–4): 131–54.

Boyne, S., Williams, F. and Hall, D. (2002) 'On the trail of regional success: tourism, food production and the Isle of Arran Taste Trail' in A. Hjalager and G. Richards (eds), *Tourism and Gastronomy*. London: Routledge, pp. 91–114.

Rand, G.E.D., Heath, E. and Alberts, N. (2003) 'The role of local and regional food in destination marketing: a South African situation analysis', *Journal of Travel & Tourism Marketing*, 14 (3–4): 97–112.

Seo, S., Yun, N. and Kim, O.Y. (2014) 'Destination food image and intention to eat destination foods: a view from Korea', *Current Issues in Tourism* (in press), 1–22.

11

FOOD ASSURANCE SCHEMES, ORGANISATIONS AND INITIATIVES

CHAPTER OBJECTIVES

- To provide an overview of national and multi-national organisations that promote the growth and development of food and drink tourism
- To explore policy development and the role of government organisations in the promotion and regulation of the food and drink tourism offering
- To provide illustrative case studies and examples of organisations and schemes that support producers and provide marketing and networking support
- To explore organisations that promote ethical and responsible food and drink consumption
- To critically assess the impact and role of quality marks and reassurance organisations

CHAPTER SUMMARY

This chapter explores the important and growing role of local, regional and (inter) national agencies. It links the discussion back to the marketing strategies and promotional agendas outlined in this section. Food and drink tourism has developed in tandem with local and regional food groups (producer and tourism promoters), therefore this chapter discusses and outlines the various organisations and stakeholders that have contributed to the growth and development of food tourism and looks at how they have raised consumer interest. It will include a discussion of relevant food actors and non-governmental organisations with consideration for food-related planning policy and localised food policy/food supplier networks. Overviews of the influence and role of such groups are offered with indicative case study illustrations, which include the more established and recognised Slow Food movement (part of the wider phenomenon of Slow Tourism), the Fair Trade movement, the World Food Travel Association, the growth of regional food tourism agencies, 'food sheds' (Feagan, 2007), quality marks and reassurance organisations (such as the Red Tractor scheme), community projects and artisanal groups promoting local food to tourists and local stakeholders through events, publicity and promotion (examples include the Arctic Menu in northern Norway).

The chapter also looks at initiatives and voluntary organisations/charities around the world providing opportunities for individuals to support and celebrate local and distinctive foods, and critically examines the concept of organisational theories in relation to how these bodies and associations might be theorised and understood.

WORKING TOGETHER: THE GROWTH OF (ALTERNATIVE) FOOD NETWORKS

The creation, operation, and evolution of 'new' or 'alternative' food supply chains is one of the key dimensions of evolving rural development patterns, and there has been growth in a variety of new food-production and trade circuits falling outside the conventional model of agriculture (Renting et al., 2003). Many of these bodies have been developed partly in response to an apparent stream and increase of food 'scandals', ranging from salmonella to bovine spongiform encephalopathy (BSE) since the 1980s (addressed in Chapter 5).

Following food scares and concerns over safety and increased regulation, new organisations and food agencies were established, and existing ones reorganised (as outlined in the previous chapter, which looked at the health and safety of on-site food engagement). This chapter focuses on the nature and establishment of non-governmental networks, agencies and assurance schemes, all of which are key stakeholders and players in the delivery and management of food and drink tourism.

Numerous food agencies were established in response to various food crises. Examples include the Food Standards Agency (FSA) in the UK, the European Food Safety Authority (EFSA) in the EU, and the Mattilsynet in Norway, which oversees food safety across the nation. In response to growing concerns in the 1980s, consumers and other stakeholders began to demand transparency about how food is grown and handled throughout the supply chain. This resulted in the concept of 'traceability' becoming central to how food quality and safety were addressed and managed. In the EU, the growth of these networks has been linked with the rise of a new rural development paradigm, discussed by Goodman et al. (2012), which looks at the battle between alternative rural approaches and spatial freedoms, seeking to explain the adoption of alternative social and technical constructions as part of new rural development practices. Watts et al. (2005) found that while alternative systems of food have expanded, the nature of the alternative(s) is often unclear. In a study of Washington by Qazi and Selfa (2005: 45), this development was also found to be fragmented and uneven. The work found the emergence of alternative agro-food, but a question arose as to whether these can be viable alternatives to globalised food systems. Consequently, they wonder if it is 'possible for small farmers to initiate these alternative reconnections with consumers if eaters (as producers or consumers) are resistant to the political implications of their social and/or ecological relations?'

Alternative networks are extremely varied and have a number of different approaches and objectives. Through such networks there are alternative production processes that focus on product quality, local/historical territorial origins, and products with an environmental consciousness (for example, less-intensive processes, organic/bio certification, and biodiversity conservation). From the consumers' perspective, some support consumers as producers (e.g. community gardens) and others support initiatives that bring the consumer closer to the producer through direct sales, such as farmers' markets. Other food networks have a more overt policy agenda and look at public procurement to ensure they link farmers and markets with other industry sectors such as tourism. In general, alternative Agriculture Food Networks (AFNs) focus on promoting improved relationships between people and their food, social justice, environmental awareness and alternative production methods; partnership among producers and consumers; producers' economic independence from a mass industrial system; a political-ethical commitment to production; regional development; and local and community-based food production.

FOOD CERTIFICATION AND ASSURANCE SCHEMES

Food assurance schemes (both mandatory and voluntary) could be said to place an additional regulatory burden on farmers and lead to impacts unfavourable to farming costs, where all additional costs are borne by producers. However, they do provide a powerful marketing scheme and reassurance to the consumer, and are used in promoting food and drink to tourists. In the 1990s, farm assurance schemes seemed to develop in every commodity sector. These schemes set and monitored the compliance of production standards by farmers and food producers nationwide; they operated independently of each other and only the pigs (and eggs) sectors had a consumer-facing logo. The Red Tractor scheme in the UK represents a harmonisation effort for British produce (see the Case Study, Red Tractor, 2015). A similar scheme (Nyt Norge, or 'Enjoy Norway') operates in Norway; Spain ('Baena' for olive oil and 'Dehesa de Extremadura' for ham); and France (the 'Label Rouge' scheme for chicken). A number of EU schemes have been reported and researched.[1] Many

---

[1]See http://agrilife.jrc.ec.europa.eu/s_study10.html or http://ec.europa.eu/agriculture/quality/certification/index2_en.htm

highlight a widespread lack of awareness of how food assurance schemes work at a local level. Other global efforts in harmonisation include the Global Food Safety Initiative (GFSI), a supermarket-owned umbrella body that oversees a number of private standards, including those of the British Retail Consortium (BRC), Safe Quality Food (SQF), the Dutch HACCP (Hazard Analysis and Critical Control Points), and International Food Standard (IFS).

Food assurance schemes have been developed all over the world with the aim of guaranteeing to consumers and businesses that food and drink has been produced to particular standards. These schemes are mainly voluntary arrangements although many food businesses make certification in an assurance scheme a specification requirement for their suppliers. Examples of farm assurance schemes include: organic certification; Non-GMO Project (US organization); the Red Tractor assurance scheme (as outlined below in the Case Study); Freedom Food (animal welfare assurance from the RSPCA); Grainsafe (Indiana-based programme in the USA); the IKB (Integrated chain control system) in the Netherlands; the Australian dairy industry's range of HACCP-based programmes; Quality Meat Scotland; and Farm Assured Welsh Livestock (FAWL) which assures farm standards in Wales.

CASE STUDY

Red Tractor Assurance Scheme, UK

Red Tractor is an umbrella organisation of around 59,075 members (Red Tractor, 2015), covering ten different systems for meat, grain and milk (www.redtractor.org.uk). Set up in June 2000, it is a food-assurance scheme that covers production standards developed by experts on aspects including safety, hygiene, animal welfare and the environment. Red Tractor Assurance is a small organisation, and its administrative costs are met by assurance fees and licence payments from farmers and food companies. Owned by the entire food industry, they operate independently on a not-for-profit basis. The Red Tractor logo is the sign that the food is fully traceable back to independently-inspected farms in the UK (Figure 11.1).

FIGURE 11.1 *Red Tractor logo provided with permission from Red Tractor*

Red Tractor is becoming a key asset of the UK agricultural industry, with over 78,000 farms committed to farming that meets responsible standards under the Scheme. It is the largest farm- and food-assurance scheme in the UK and the only scheme that integrates a range of issues, food safety, animal health and welfare and controls on environmental pollution into a single set of standards and a single inspection. Their annual review for 2015 claims 'We estimate that today the Red Tractor logo is applied to food products with annual sales of £12 billion and the latest YouGov survey has reported a further increase in consumer awareness to 65%' (Red Tractor 2015 :2).

Further details: www.redtractor.org.uk/home

In addition to official food-assurance schemes, there has been growth in demand from discerning tourists for schemes that reassure consumers at a more informal and local level. This interest in being able to identify food from a certain area, producer or location has led to the establishment of a number of small food organisations and alternative networks, including small groups that have come together to promote local community projects, and artisanal groups promoting local food to tourists and local stakeholders, through events, publicity and promotion. In Scotland, one example is the Hebridean Kitchen; in West Cork (Ireland) there is a group supporting local artisan producers; and in Norway, there is the Arctic Menu.

FOODSHEDS

A foodshed is a geographical region that produces food for a particular population, and is a concept embraced by alternative food networks to define what constitutes 'local'. The term is used to describe a region of food flows, from the area where it is produced to the place where it is consumed, including: the land it grows on, the route it travels, the markets it passes through, and the tables it ends up on. A foodshed is described as a 'socio-geographic space: human activity embedded in the natural integument of a particular place' (Feagan, 2007: 26).

Hendrickson and Heffernan (2002: 349) state that there is a need to support the local food system around the world and find ways to support such initiatives:

> Space has been disconnected from place in the dominant food system ... As people foster relationships with those who are no longer in their locale, distant others can structure the shape and use of the locale, a problem that is being explicitly rejected by those involved in the local food system movements across the globe.

Feagan (2007) argues that the movements, practices, and writing about local food systems offer increasingly visible structures of resistance and counter-pressure to conventional globalising food systems. It is suggested that the foodshed concept reconstructs the geography of food systems by compelling social and political decisions on food to be orientated within specific spaces.

The concept and movements of 'field to fork', 'plough to plate' and 'farm to table' are focused on producing food locally within a foodshed, and delivering it to local consumers. Examples with links to tourism that employ the local food shed concept include farmers' markets, which are the centre of alternative food distribution systems (see Chapter 13), roadside stands, pick-your-own (PYO), and tourism-focused farming (diversification through tourism activities such as events, farm stays and animal petting).

THE WORLD FOOD TRAVEL ASSOCIATION (WFTA)

Based in the USA, the World Food Travel Association (WFTA) is a non-profit and non-governmental organization (NGO). Their vision is 'To be the world's leading authority on food and drink tourism issues, ideas and trends. We drive economic development based on the certainty that every traveller must eat and drink' (WFTA, 2015). The organisation was founded as the International Culinary Tourism Association (ICTA) in 2003 by Erik Wolf. In 2012, it changed its name to the World Food Travel Association to clarify its position in the industry and in response to research that found that the term 'culinary' was considered elitist. This is similar to debates in the literature about terms that are a subset of food tourism, such as 'gourmet' and 'gastronomic'.

The WFTA claims to be the world's oldest and largest organisation dedicated to the special needs of food, drink, travel and hospitality professionals: 'The Association is at the forefront of food and drink tourism development with cutting-edge resources for today's food, drink, travel, hospitality and media professionals' (http://worldfoodtravel.org). They define food tourism as simply 'the pursuit and enjoyment of unique and memorable food and drink experiences, both far and near'. The association offers educational tours, an annual conference, a regular blog, business support and advice, and is central in the global promotion and marketing of global food and drink with a cultural and social identity and place association. Increasingly, food and drink tourism has become synonymous with a more ethical approach to consumption, and movements such as Slow Food and Fair Trade have been fuelled by this growth in interest and activity.

THE SLOW FOOD MOVEMENT

The Slow Food movement (www.slowfood.com) should be theorised and considered within the wider concept of Slow Tourism and its philosophy and principles. The Slow Food website claims, 'Slow Food envisions a world in which all people can access and enjoy food that is good for them, good for those who grow it and good for the planet. Our approach is based on a concept of food that is defined by three interconnected principles: good, clean and fair.' The Slow Food movement was founded in 1986 in Italy by Carlo Petrini, a journalist. He was so disgusted by the opening of a McDonald's near the Spanish Steps in Rome that he felt something needed to be done to counteract an apparent destruction of food culture and identity in a country famed for its wonderful food, small producers and quality produce. In 1989, the founding manifesto of the international Slow Food movement was signed in Paris by delegates from 15 countries and it has grown to become a global movement of over 100,000 members in 150 countries. It aims to preserve traditional and regional cuisines and educate people about food whilst promoting local artisans, local farmers, and local flavours at a regional level. Offices have been opened in Switzerland (1995), Germany (1998), New York City (2000), France (2003), Japan (2005), the UK and Chile, and its global headquarters are located in Bra, near Turin, Italy. Its logo is a snail, which summarises its approach to food and drink (see Andrews, 2008; Petrini, 2007), and this image has become iconic. It is now displayed outside restaurants around the world, as shown in Figure 11.2 (the wall of a restaurant in Santorini, by the Aegean Sea).

There are 10,000 small producers involved in 400 'presidia' projects in 50 countries, all designed to protect food biodiversity and save products at risk of extinction in rural areas. In 2010, Slow Food International began its independent Slow Wine project with the release of a wine guide.

FIGURE 11.2 *Slow Food logo on public display on a wall by a restaurant in Santorini in the Aegean Sea.*

Slow Food 'Good, Clean and Fair': the Slow Food Manifesto for Quality

The Slow Food Manifesto is clear: the effort must be common and must be made in the same aware, shared and interdisciplinary spirit as the science of gastronomy. All members are expected to practise and disseminate a broader concept of food quality, based on three basic, interconnected prerequisites (quoted from their website):

1. Good. A food's flavour and aroma, recognizable to educated, well-trained senses, is the fruit of the competence of the producer and of choice of raw materials and production methods, which should in no way alter its naturalness.
2. Clean. The environment has to be respected and sustainable practices of farming, animal husbandry, processing, marketing and consumption should be taken into serious consideration. Every stage in the agro-industrial production chain, consumption included, should protect ecosystems and biodiversity, safeguarding the health of the consumer and the producer.
3. Fair. Social justice should be pursued through the creation of conditions of labour respectful of man and his [sic] rights and capable of generating adequate rewards; through the pursuit of balanced global economies; through the practice of sympathy and solidarity; through respect for cultural diversities and traditions.

'Good, Clean and Fair' is the Slow Food pledge for a better future, and is presented as a tool to improve the food system. More information about its campaign can be found at www.slowfood.com.

Promoted as an alternative to fast food where the origins of the raw product are often unknown, Slow Food is characterised by its ethical, moral and even political stance.

Slow Food has informed the thinking around Slow Tourism, and promotes an alternative mobility and travel mindset that values quality of the investment of time in products. Slow Tourism encapsulates many ways and approaches to slowing down the tourist experience and reducing the impact and intensity of travel. It is a holistic and wide-ranging concept that covers everything from a literal slowing down of activity (spending more time in each location), to the promotion of non-aviation transport methods, to spatial escape, to the pursuit of well-being, and an enhanced quality of life for the tourist and destination communities. Slow tourism is synonymous with using more environmentally benign forms of transport such as walking, cycling, sailing, trains and other public transport. Lumsdon and McGrath (2011) suggest that the literature on slow travel and tourism can be categorised into four main themes or attributes: slowness and the value of time; locality and activities at the destination; mode of transport and travel experience; and environmental consciousness. All of these aspects are central to the notion of Slow Food, where there is a reduction of food miles, an investment of time and artisanal skills, and where the environment is reflected in the product. Catherine Gazzoli, the chief executive of Slow Food UK, says Slow Food's greatest legacy has to be the development of 'the idea that there is an alternative to fast food, and progress doesn't mean bigger, faster and global when it comes to food production and eating'.

Slow Food also manages 'The Ark of Taste' which focuses on endangered heritage foods. The Ark is designed to preserve at-risk foods that are sustainably produced, unique in taste, and part of a distinct ecoregion. There is an 'Ark of Taste' list, which catalogues 1,000 unique 'forgotten foods' threatened by industrial standardisation and which it hopes to save. One method for doing so is through visitor promotion and engagement. Often foods that are becoming lost can be revived through tourism and destination marketing strategies (Everett and Aitchison, 2008). The Slow Food movement also supports and runs campaigns that seek to sustain small-scale fishing (Slow Fish), defend communities' land (Stop Land Grabbing), and resist the development and use of genetically modified organisms in agriculture. It also has a separate network called Terra Madre, which aims to preserve, encourage and support sustainable food production methods around the world.

Despite its honourable vision, the Slow Food (SF) movement is not without its critics. It has been described as elitist and unable to speak for all food workers. Some suggest it needs to think about the population who cannot afford to accept their invitation to the movement and its ethos. These workers include the farmworkers, meatpackers, and restaurant workers whose long hours, low wages, and deplorable working conditions help make the lives of Slow Food members possible. Sassatelli and Davolio (2010: 207) ask, 'to what extent does SF represent a viable critique of contemporary trends in market globalization or a form of elitist association... [to] Put it more bluntly, is SF subversive or elitist?' Social justice must be at the core of the movement, to avoid the danger of narcissism. This is perhaps where the Fair Trade movement sought to make a difference.

THE FAIR TRADE MOVEMENT

The Fair Trade movement goes well beyond the food and drink tourism agenda, but is included in this chapter as one of the organisations and initiatives that has had a profound impact on how food tourism is presented and managed. Increasingly, it has become an attractive component of a holiday for ethically minded tourists. The main aim of the Fair Trade movement is to fight against poverty in the Third World by seeking to re-connect producers and consumers economically, politically, and psychologically through the creation of a transnational moral economy (Goodman, 2004). The movement is represented by numerous international organisations and most commonly uses a definition developed by an informal association of four international Fair Trade networks: Fairtrade La† Organizations International, World Fair Trade Organization (WFTO) † European Worldshops and European Fair Trade Association (EFT. 'fair trade is a trading partnership, based on dialogue, transparency, that seeks greater equity in international trade. Fair Trade organizations, backed by consumers, are engaged actively in supporting producers, awareness raising, and in campaigning for changes in the rules and practice of conventional international trade' (Fair Trade Advocacy Office, 2015).

Fair Trade labelling was created in the Netherlands in the late 1980s and the Max Havelaar Foundation launched the first consumer guarantee label in 1988 on coffee sourced from Mexico. An example of this label used on bananas is shown in Figure 11.3. The Fair Trade Mark Organisation operates in countries including the Netherlands, Switzerland, France and the UK. The charity Oxfam (2015) claim that 'Fair Trade aims to ensure a fairer deal for Third World Producers in international trade.' In their work on Fair Trade in tourism, Cleverdon and Kalisch (2000) outline the increasing awareness of the consumer seeking an experience and sourcing products that are produced and traded fairly and ethically. The Fair Trade movement has sought to redress unequal trading by promoting Fair Trade in commodities with small producers, enabling them to take control over the production and marketing process and challenging the power of transnational corporations. It is suggested that Fair Trade tourism is a 'commitment to finding positive and practical solutions for the tourism industry as well as consumers, local communities and destination governments, so as to benefit local communities through trade, in preference to aid' (Kalisch, 2002: 17).

One of the key components of the wider movement is the focus on ensuring producers get a fair price for the food they grow and supply, with focus specifically on tea, coffee, fruit and vegetables. It puts the consumer in touch with the producer (especially small-scale producers) and often has an educational function for tourists who know little about the people behind the production

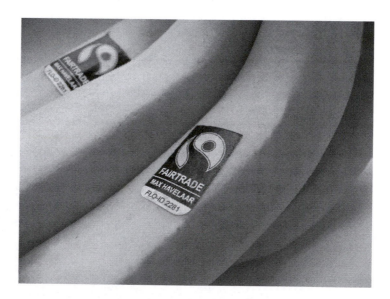

FIGURE 11.3   *Fair Trade bananas. The Max Havelaar label is internationally recognised*

process. Cleverdon and Kalisch (2000) find that NGO projects such as the Global Supermarkets Campaign by Christian Aid, with the competitive advantage a Fair Trade reputation has, are becoming increasingly powerful as they tap into the social consciousness of companies. Fair Trade is now one of the driving forces leading change in relationships with producers.

Some of the world's most exotic destinations are featured on the labels of fairly traded products: Costa Rica for coffee, Sri Lanka for tea and South Africa for wine. Fair Trade has therefore become a global marketing vehicle for ethically aware tourists, with tourism organisations increasingly promoting their Fair Trade ethos and using badges to attract and reassure consumers. For example, in South Africa there is Fair Trade in Tourism South Africa (FTTSA), a national scheme that has awarded its trademark to 30 travel companies in South Africa. FTTSA is a non-profit organisation promoting responsible tourism in southern Africa and beyond. Their aim is to make tourism more sustainable by ensuring that the people who contribute their land, resources, labour and knowledge to tourism reap the benefits (www.fairtrade.travel), with one offering being the Fair Trade Travel Pass, which 'gives you the freedom of choice to visit the most beautiful and culturally diverse parts of South Africa knowing that the community where you spend your money is going to see the benefit'. These kinds of movements are certainly providing a mechanism to influence food and drink choices, although 'direct trade' is perhaps even more powerful as a concept. Direct trade refers to transactions in which the tourist buys directly from the producer *in situ*; perhaps the only way in which you can ensure the income goes straight to the producer.

There are a number of Fair Trade holidays now on offer that capitalise on growing interest in this movement. For example, in Cuba, tourists have a chance to engage with a two-week Traidcraft tour of the island, including hiking in the Topes de Collantes Mountains and stopping off in Ciego de Avila to stay at one of the cooperatives that supply Traidcraft's fairly traded juice. They run similar Fair Trade holidays in India, Thailand and Peru, and provide trips to Vietnam, Ghana, Costa Rica and Nicaragua (traidcraft-tours.co.uk). Another example is Kahawa Shamba, Tanzania, where a coffee cooperative in the foothills of Kilimanjaro was set up with help from the UK Department for International Development, development charity Twin, Cafédirect and Tribes Travel.

FOOD TOURISM MARKETING AGENCIES AND ORGANISATIONS

In the last 20 years, there has been a growth of food tourism agencies and organisations that promote the food and drink of a particular region or location. These bodies can be private, government-funded or cooperatives, organised and with members focused on marketing strategies and plans that promote regions, cuisines and cultures. One example is the Arctic Menu in Norway, which has brought together food providers to develop a recognisable badge of local and quality food establishments around the Arctic Circle (see the Case Study).

Arctic Menu, Norway

Norwegian restaurants are members of the Arctic Menu scheme (arktiskmeny.no), which guarantees top-quality cooking and the use of local ingredients. The 45 members share the same logo: an orange circular icon with two flashes beneath. Arctic Menu boasts that it is an organisation that works to ensure restaurants get high-quality local ingredients, and promotes Arctic food culture to visitors (see Figure 11.4). Arctic Menu is presented as a regional actor that, through skills and training initiatives for restaurants and manufacturers, helps to make northern Norway a food destination. Since its creation, the network has arranged a series of cooking classes for their own members and other restaurants in the region; annual competitions for the Arctic Cook, which picks north Norway's best chef and the best 'Arctic value creation' (northern Norway's most innovative food product); and offers joint marketing. The members of the Arctic Menu serve northern Norwegian dishes and ingredients, make use of fresh produce in season, and are dedicated to the promotion of northern Norwegian food culture. Arctic Menu is owned by the Confederation of Norwegian Enterprise Tourism North Norway, and has an Office in Tromsø, Norway

Source: http://arktiskmeny.no

FIGURE 11.4   *Norwegian produce proudly offered to tourists and the hospitality sector as part of an Arctic Menu. Photo by author*

Many of these organisations are membership-based (including producers, distrib-utors, food service, retailers and marketing specialists), and provide a framework and body, which producers join and use for advice, marketing and consultancy services and networking. Other examples include Taste of the West in the UK, a membership organisation of over 1,000 members promoting food in the south-west of England and which supports marketing and annual awards that celebrate local food and producers (www.tasteofthewest.co.uk). Others include the Taste Council of Ireland (see the Case Study below), and a regional body deliciously-orkshire, a not-for-profit organisation providing vital support to a diverse range of food and beverage producers, retailers and distinguished hospitality operators in the Yorkshire and Humber Region (http://deliciouslyorkshire.co.uk).

Other examples assurance schemes include Euro-Toques, which is recognised by the European Union as an organisation that defends quality food. Euro-Toques forms part of the privileged network of contacts of the European Commission (euro-toques.org), and promotes high-quality food and good practice. In Brazil, there is ABRASEL, The Brazilian Association for Bars and Restaurants, which assists food businesses to maximise opportunities from international sports events hosted in the country, for example the 2016 Olympic Games (abrasel.com.br). Finally, in Spain the Tasting Spain Association is promoted by the Spanish Association of Destinations for the Development of Culinary Tourism, consisting of 23 members that seek to capitalise on the popularity of Spanish cuisine and gastronomy (tastingspain.es); and the Food Association of Denmark (http://the foodproject.dk), a small not-for-profit organisation dedicated to furthering the experience of Nordic food and nature.

CASE STUDY

Taste Council of Ireland, Republic of Ireland

The Taste Council of Ireland is an exam-ple of the many voluntary representative groups that represent the smaller food busi-ness sector, made up of local, artisan and speciality food-producers. It was formally established in October 2003 with a mission 'To empower and enable the Irish speciality food sector at a strategic level to maxim-ise its current and potential contribution to Ireland's food and agri-economy, society,

culture and environment'. Current projects provide a good overview of the kinds of activities these organisations are involved in and support:

- Analysis of PDO/PGI and its application to Irish food;
- Farmers' Markets Strategy paper: strategy for sustainability for Irish farmers markets;
- Middle Farm, a project on the develop-ment of 'middle'-sized farms and their potential for adding value to their primary produce;

- Sustainable fishing, exploring the potential to promote small fishing vessels and improving the route to market for their catch;
- Food Heroes, an umbrella brand for Irish speciality food-producers within the retail market;

- TASTE Council Summer School, working towards the second food summer school.

Further details at www.tastecouncilofireland.com.

Critical Reflections: organisational theories

This chapter has presented a lot of different food- and drink-related organisations, networks, bodies and associations. You may be interested in organisations as a concept and theoretical construct. Organisations are social units of people that are structured and managed to meet a need, or to pursue collective action or interest, and to understand how they work it is useful to explore the various theories developed about them (Clegg et al., 2006; Grant, 2004). Organisational theory describes a number of different approaches. Dwight Waldo (1978: 591) once said, 'Organization theory is characterized by vogues, heterogeneity, claims and counterclaims', although in recent years, even greater differentiation in theory and practice has emerged. It is not a unified body of knowledge in which each development builds on and carefully extends the one before it; rather, theories of organisations evolve, merge and are constantly redefined. Theories include (i) 'bureaucracy', (ii) 'rationalization' (the scientific management approach), (iii) 'administrative', and (iv) 'neoclassical'.

Bureaucracy: Max Weber was a German sociologist and seen as the father of this theory. The bureaucratic approach considers the organisation as part of broader society. The organisation is based on the principles of structure, specialisation, predictability and stability, rationality, and democracy. Weber's theory of bureaucratic management has two essential elements. First, it entails structuring an organisation into a hierarchy. Second, the organisation and its members are governed by clearly defined rules. This form of organisation, comprising non-elected officials who implement rules, is not only common in the public sector but in the business world as well. One obvious example of a bureaucratic organisation is a public university.

Scientific management theory: developed in the early twentieth century by Frederick W. Taylor, the scientific management approach is loosely based on the concept of planning to achieve efficiency, standardisation, specialisation and simplification. Increased productivity is achieved through mutual trust between management and workers. Scientific management theory seeks to improve an

THE PROMOTION AND BRANDING OF FOOD AND DRINK TOURISM

organisation's efficiency by systematically improving the efficiency of task completion, utilising scientific, engineering, and mathematical analysis.

Administrative theory: propounded by Henry Fayol and based on several principles of management, this theory considers management as a set of planning, organising, training, commanding and coordinating functions. Other key thinkers include James Mooney and Luther Gulick. Administrative theory supports a rational way to organisational design, based on a formalised administrative structure, a clear division of labour, and the delegation of authority to administrators in different areas of knowledge and responsibility.

Neoclassical theory: this theory emphasises individual or group behaviour and human relations in determining productivity. The main features of the neoclassical approach are individuals, work groups and participatory management. Neoclassical theorists recognised the importance of individual and group behaviour and emphasised human relations in an informal organisation structure.

ACTIVITY ORGANISATIONAL THEORIES AND FOOD AND DRINK TOURISM

Research the four theories outlined in the Critical Reflections box and think about how different food organisations demonstrate these traits and characteristics. Try to find an example of a food-related or tourism organisation for each theory, and also find an additional two theories not referenced above.

CHAPTER SUMMARY

Food and drink organisations and associations are central to the development, support and growth of the international food and drink tourism offer, whilst also providing effective mechanisms for advertising, marketing and quality assurance. The chapter has highlighted the impact of global food scares and crises (such as foot and mouth disease and BSE) in prompting the establishment of numerous alternative food networks and associations. Many were established to help reassure consumers and support producers in getting their product to market. Organisations such as farmers' networks and the Slow Food movement have sought to bring the consumer closer to the producer and are discussed throughout this chapter and the wider book. Further, food assurance schemes such as Red Tractor highlight the importance of reassurance and badges of quality for marketing purposes, offering traceability and provenance to an increasing population of discerning and ethically minded consumers and tourists. Consequently, food assurance schemes have increased in number, with the aim of providing guarantees that food and drink has been produced to particular standards of quality and skill. Although many of the relevant organisations operate beyond the boundaries of tourism, they have been included here to provide examples of how such organisations support the food and drink tourism offer, and work directly with producers to appeal to tourists and consumers, thereby resisting more globalised, homogenised and mass-produced food.

END OF CHAPTER POINTS

- The emergence of 'new' and 'alternative' food supply chains is a product of new rural development patterns that have emerged in response to growing concerns about the origins and production of food, in light of food crises and scares.

- Tourists and other consumer stakeholders now demand transparency in how food is grown and handled throughout the supply chain, resulting in 'traceability' becoming central to how food quality and safety are addressed and managed.

- Food organisations have been developed to promote improved relationships between people and their food, whilst also pursuing social justice, environmental awareness and promotion of alternative production methods.

- Food certification schemes provide an effective marketing scheme and reassurance to consumer, and are used in promoting food and drink to tourists.

- The Slow Food movement and the Fair Trade movement are examples of international organisations that promote food which is good for people, good for those who grow it and good for the planet. These organisations demonstrate the increasing awareness of the consumer seeking an experience and products that are produced fairly and ethically.

FURTHER READING

Clegg, S.R., Hardy, C., Lawrence, T. and Nord, W.R. (eds) (2006) *The SAGE Handbook of Organization Studies*. London: Sage.

Cleverdon, R., and Kalisch, A. (2000) 'Fair trade in tourism', *International Journal of Tourism Research*, 2 (3): 171–87.

Feagan, R. (2007) 'The place of food: mapping out the "local" in local food systems', *Progress in Human Geography*, 31 (1): 23–42.

Goodman, D., DuPuis, E.M. and Goodman, M.K. (2012) *Alternative Food Networks: Knowledge, Practice, and Politics*. London: Routledge.

Grant, D. (ed.) (2004) *The SAGE Handbook of Organizational Discourse*. London: Sage.

Maye, D., Holloway, L. and Kneafsey, M. (2007) 'Introducing alternative food geographies, in D. Maye, L. Holloway and M. Kneafsey (eds), *Alternative Food Geographies: Representation and Practice*. Oxford: Elsevier, pp. 1–20.

Qazi, J.A. and Selfa, T.L. (2005) The politics of building alternative agro-food networks in the belly of agro-industry, *Food, Culture and Society: An International Journal of Multidisciplinary Research*, 8 (1): 45–72.

Rand, G.E.D., Heath, E. and Alberts, N. (2003) 'The role of local and regional food in destination marketing: a South African situation analysis', *Journal of Travel & Tourism Marketing*, 14 (3–4): 97–112.

Renting, H., Marsden, T.K. and Banks, J. (2003) 'Understanding alternative food networks: exploring the role of short food supply chains in rural development', *Environment and Planning A*, 35 (3): 393–412.

PART THREE
FOOD AND DRINK
ATTRACTIONS
AND EVENTS

12

THE TRANSFORMATION OF PLACE THROUGH FOOD AND DRINK

CHAPTER OBJECTIVES

- To examine how places of production and work are becoming spaces for consumption and visitor experience
- To explore how food and drink tourism has created and transformed places
- To examine how a town, city or region can be branded/re-branded for culinary and gastronomic tourism
- To discuss how destinations are becoming food tourism destinations through investment and strategic projects
- To explore the concept of hospitality servicescapes and how food and drink outlets are changing to provide an experience, ambience and unique offering to consumers

CHAPTER SUMMARY

This chapter introduces Part III of this book, which focuses on specific types of food and drink activity and tourism. It commences by reflecting on how food and drink tourism has transformed destinations and fuelled a growing interest in buying and tasting fresh food local to where is grown and produced. This chapter makes a strong connection to the general marketing concepts 'place marketing' and 'destination branding' discussed in Part II, and also looks at the relationship between production/consumption in changing places and place identity. As discussed in Chapter 10, more and more production sites are opening themselves up to visitors, and shops, factories and processing sites are increasingly considering the impact of consumption taking place in traditional production arenas. It is this transformation of place through the phenomenon of food and drink tourism that is explored in this chapter.

In looking at the changing nature of places, this chapter builds on the issues and concepts raised in Part II and explores place branding and transformation. It suggests that places are now undergoing dramatic reconfigurations and change in the light of new consumer (tourist) demands, interests and practices, with many proclaiming themselves centres or 'capitals' of food. For example, Castle Douglas in Scotland has branded itself a 'Food Town'. Although it offers little more than many similarly sized towns, it has used food to create an attractive and alluring identity for itself, stating on its website that:

> with approximately fifty local businesses involved in either producing or selling food and drink, it is easy to see why Castle Douglas has been designated a Food Town. The vibrancy and appeal of the town lies largely in the draw of the shops and cafés, restaurants and hotels.

Further, UNESCO has also now given some cities (including those in China, Sweden, Colombia and Korea) the prestigious recognition of 'City of Gastronomy'. These are the kinds of identifying labels and 'rebranding' examples that will be discussed and overviewed in this chapter. Others include examples from the USA such as Watsonville as the (not uncontested!) 'Strawberry Capital of the World', Gilroy as the 'garlic capital', Castroville for artichokes (including a festival of artichokes established in the 1940s), and Alma as the 'Spinach capital of the world' with its statue of Popeye.

The chapter will also look at the Sites Remarquables du Goût (Exceptional Food Heritage Sites) across France, which all have an emblematic food or beverage product linked to a landscape or architecture with exceptional aesthetic qualities and specific know-how. They all represent food tourism destinations and demonstrate how a town or region can be branded/re-branded for gastronomic tourism.

The chapter also looks at the phenomenon of the 'gastro-pub' and how destinations without any agriculture or food production heritage are becoming food tourism locations through a cleverly constructed gastronomic offer, comprising menus, gastro guides and celebrity endorsements. Issues of gentrification, the changing nature of the local pub (to serving food as well as drinks) and rural places are outlined, alongside consideration of links to the emerging urban agriculture agenda (for example, the Brooklyn Grange in New York). The chapter also looks at the concept of the hospitality servicescapes in relation to place and food spaces.

Castle Douglas, Scotland, UK

The town of Castle Douglas is a good example of how place has been transformed through adopting food tourism as a theme, and through destination branding (Macleod, 2009). It claims to have about 50 local businesses which produce or sell food and drink, and uses its designation as a 'Food Town' to promote tourism. From a relatively unremarkable town in Scotland, it has developed a new identity and branding using food. This transformation has happened over a number of years as businesses seek to take advantage of this branding. Claiming that 'the vibrancy and appeal of the town lies largely in the draw of the shops and cafés, restaurants and hotels', Douglas hosts an annual 'Food Town Day' to celebrate local produce and producers. Their promotion claims that 'In an age when consumers are often given conflicting advice about what food is good for them and which constituents they should avoid, it is refreshing that Castle Douglas offers high quality local produce which everyone can enjoy'. In a study of the town along with other themed Scottish towns, Macleod (2009) found that that the new themed branding initiatives led to economic growth in the town, and Castle Douglas reported a growth in visitor numbers related to its festival and its increased marketing as a food town. Through the initiative there has been a heightened sense of community through the pursuit of a common goal, and an enhanced sense of unity through the consolidation of an identity. Macleod also found that the theming led to a growth in social capital in terms of formal and informal networks.

Further information from: www.cd-foodtown.org

PLACES OF PRODUCTION AS PLACES OF CONSUMPTION

Everett (2012) suggests that we need to question how work and leisure are perceived in terms of food and drink tourism. It is suggested that work settings and places are increasingly enjoyable and seductive, and the boundaries between work and leisure have become blurred, so much so that leisure happens in the workplace and vice versa. Lewis (2003) has suggested that leisure is increasingly constructed as the antithesis of work, that is, non-obligated time, filled with activities perceived as freely chosen and intrinsically motivated. What has been less researched is the situation where someone at work and someone at leisure occupy the same space at the same time. As outlined in Chapter 10, this can cause issues to emerge in a food setting, such as health and safety considerations, and risk. Sheller and Urry's (2004) work has been particularly informative in examining how places evolve to become sites of tourist consumption; the examples they use include shopping, photography, and eating sites.

In exploring the transformation of work or production places into leisure spaces it may be helpful to acknowledge the contribution of heritage tourism literature, which explores the development of previous places of work and non-tourism purposes, such as hospitals, churches and mines into tourism sites, and identifies the challenges that are faced; it is about the conversion of places of work into places of tourism and leisure (Everett, 2012).

Research into the transformation of places of industry into places of leisure is not new. For example, Edwards and Llurdés (1996) have written extensively about the evolution of industrial installations such as mines into attractions. However, heritage tourism is usually characterised by the consumption of a place once it no longer performs its original purpose. The focus in this chapter is the transformation of place as a result of food and drink, and the creation of places that have multiple identities and functions. It is useful to consider how places that have historically produced foodstuffs are now producing experiences, memories and a touristic offering. For many years, production sites like farms and factories have been popular tourist attractions, but in the last few decades we have seen significant investment into sites of food production which were originally built and used with no plans to attract or accommodate tourists, evolving to embrace the four 'imagescapes' of aesthetics, escapism, education and entertainment (Pine and Gilmore, 1999). Over the past 20 years, commercial sites have become paying attractions, serving a multiplicity of purposes beyond their original design or the owner's intention (see Chapter 10).

CASE STUDY

Tensions within hybrid spaces – A dairy in Scotland

Everett (2012) found a number of examples where turning places of production into tourist experiences caused a lot of tension amongst stakeholders. This tension between operating production facilities and offering something for visitors featured prominently in her interviews with a dairy owner in Scotland who highlighted the impact on his business and outlined how tourism had changed the identity of his place of production:

We are a production factory and when this place was rebuilt in 1993, it seems like yesterday, we got some grant aid at that time to refurbish the place and one of the conditions or strings attached was we had to provide something for tourists, so that was when this area, much to my concern as I could have used a lot more office space, but this space was created.

All it is, well, we are a factory which enables visitors to see what is going on, we are not a visitors' facility that makes something that most of the other places are. There are expectations of tourists on the coach tours etc., well, I try to discourage coach tours as the last thing I need is 50 or 60 people plonked into this room and the driver telling them they are here for one hour. (2010: 545)

Everett (2012) found that food tourism led to the development of hybrid spaces where consumer needs often clashed with production needs when they were co-located. She also found many production places had undergone a physical transformation to become consumption spaces where consumers exert an active agency in influencing the future production and development of food and the transformation of places.

Adapted from: Everett (2012)

As outlined in Chapter 10, producers are aware of the need to provide for increasing tourist interests and have put in windows, viewing areas and interpretation to facilitate this. Consequently, there are new and transformed places to be created. Production and historic trading sites are changing to facilitate tourist engagement, and a number of producers are physically changing the look and feel of their premises to accommodate tourists. One such example is shown in Figure 12.1, where a former Dutch East India Company (VOC) building has been transformed

FIGURE 12.1 *A transformed building – the De Kaaskelder, Amsterdam, Netherlands. Photo by author*

into De Kaaskelder, a renowned cheese shop and museum. Its giant cheeses have given a new identity to the market outside and staff wear traditional dress to try in an attempt to recreate something nostalgic: an inauthentic historic place.

Another such place in the research of Everett (2012) is the bakery on the Isle of Arran (Scotland), where the producer has changed the shop and created a new site specifically for viewing their production:

> I will probably put one [viewing window] in the new place and the oatcakes will be manufactured. It is a tidy operation, it isn't flour and water flying around the place, so it doesn't look awful. Whereas making bread rolls can get a bit messy, so making oatcakes, so I would let them watch that … I would certainly put one in to watch the manufacture of the oat cakes, the baking and even the wrapping of them. (Lindsay, interviewee quoted in Everett 2007: 286)

One example of how the urban landscape is being altered and transformed through food and agriculture is the innovative urban agriculture agenda run by the Brooklyn Grange in New York (http://brooklyngrangefarm.com). Brooklyn Grange has become the leading rooftop farming and intensive green roofing business in the USA, located on two roofs in New York City and growing over 50,000 lbs of organically cultivated produce per year, in addition to growing and distributing fresh local vegetables and herbs. The flagship farm has about 1.2 million lbs of soil on a total rooftop farming area around 2.5 acres (108,000 square feet). It is one example of how food projects are transforming spaces, even those in very built-up urban areas. Agricultural processes and farming are infiltrating urban spaces in the name of tourism.

FOOD CAPITALS AND CULINARY DESIGNATIONS

As outlined in the Case Study above of Castle Douglas, this chapter explores how places are now proclaiming themselves centres or 'capitals' of food and changing to meet consumer demands and interests. There are numerous other examples of how food and drink has been used to make cities more attractive destinations to visitors, creative locations for companies and hotspots for investors. In their research, Lucarelli and Berg (2011) show that elements of food, beverages and gastronomy are used frequently as factors in city branding, and that this is consistent with observations in studies of city branding processes taking place in large metropolitan cities across the globe

In 2008, UNESCO developed the idea of a 'City of Gastronomy' network, recognising places that had a well-developed gastronomy, characteristic of the urban centre and/or region, and 'a vibrant gastronomy community with numerous traditional restaurants and/or chefs' (UNESCO, 2015). The city of Popayán, Colombia was the first UNESCO City of Gastronomy and was awarded this title on 11 August 2005. In February 2010, Chengdu in China joined the Creative Cities Network, followed by Östersund in Sweden in July 2010, and the city of Jeonju, Republic of Korea in May 2012. The criteria to become such a city are listed below as an

Activity, but it is clear that places have invested and changed greatly to be in a position to attract such recognition. For example, Jeonju is claimed to have 'excellence in culinary infrastructure with many unique gastronomic assets and resources promoted through the various food festivals and vibrant local traditional markets' (UNESCO, 2015).

In a multi-site study through the Stockholm Program of Place Branding (STOPP) at Stockholm University, Berg and Sevón (2014) suggest that there are numerous rankings of 'food cities' and gastronomy places in guides such as the Michelin Guide and as a consequence places are developing to enter such rankings and in turn are offering something new to visitors. Berg and Sevón (2014) claim that food is used in many different types of city branding strategies, from event-based strategies (festivals and exhibitions), to excellence competence strategies (for example, City of Gastronomy and City of Origin), to architectural and spatial strategies (for example, iconic food halls and waterfront restoration areas). In the 15 cities they explored, they argue there are three main reasons as to why places are adopting food in their brand. These are: (i) to support food industry; (ii) to protect and amplify identities of places; and, importantly for this chapter, (iii) to change the place.

ACTIVITY   THE NEXT UNESCO GASTRONOMY CITY

There are criteria to guide cities interested in joining the network as a City of Gastronomy. Significant changes to infrastructure and process have sometimes been required to meet such criteria. Using your own knowledge and online searches, try and find a town or city that you think could qualify for this special status and put together an evidence-based proposal to support a nomination to UNESO. The criteria it must meet are:

- well-developed gastronomy that is characteristic of the urban centre and/or region;
- vibrant gastronomy community with numerous traditional restaurants and/or chefs;
- endogenous ingredients used in traditional cooking;
- local know-how, traditional culinary practices and methods of cooking that have survived industrial/technological advancement;
- traditional food markets and traditional food industry;
- tradition of hosting gastronomic festivals, awards, contests and other broadly targeted means of recognition;
- respect for the environment and promotion of sustainable local products;
- nurturing of public appreciation, promotion of nutrition in educational institutions and inclusion of biodiversity conservation programmes in cooking schools' curricula.

Source: www.unesco.org/new/en/culture/themes/creativity/creative-cities-network/gastronomy

One interesting example of the way food has been used to change a place is presented in Shultz et al. (2005), who argue that food can be used for post-war recovery, peace and prosperity. Their work indicates that food can have a transformational impact on places that were previously war zones. Their examples are perhaps the starkest illustration of the transformative power of food – replacing conflict with consumption. Lucarelli and Berg (2011) find other destinations have also used food to change inner-city areas into dense culinary spaces: examples include Darling Harbour in Sydney, Australia, or the World Cup 'fan walk' in South Africa, which was developed into a parade lined with restaurants, cafés and street food trucks to overcome issues of traffic and public nuisance. In Sweden, Berg and Östberg (2008) present the Malmö Festival as a further example of how the city square was redesigned into a food market, and this initiative seems to have contributed to positively changing the identity of this multi-cultural city in the 1990s.

Numerous examples of the way places have branded using food can be found across the globe. There are quirky places such as Watsonville in the USA, which presents itself as the 'Strawberry Capital of the World'. However, such titles are not without controversy and debate, as Plant City branded itself the 'Winter Strawberry Capital of the World'; the region of Ponchatoula in Louisiana also claimed to be the strawberry capital and strengthened their destination theming with an annual strawberry festival. Such titles are important to make a place stand out to visitors and over time places gradually evolve to strengthen their entitlement to make these 'food-place' claims. For example, strawberries are proudly painted on the Ponchatoula fire trucks. Yet, if you go to Poteet in Texas, visitors can see the World's Tallest Strawberry, which is a 130-ft tall water tower. In Europe, similar initiatives are employed to promote place and the strawberry remains a popular choice for the decoration of place (as shown in Figure 12.2, which is one of the many strawberry stalls that line Berlin's main shopping area in Germany).

FIGURE 12.2   *Strawberries transforming the Berlin urban environment, Germany. Photo by author*

Similar developments have been undertaken to create other 'food capitals'. Examples include Stellenbosch in South Africa for wine, and Beardstown and Hope in the USA, both self-declared 'Watermelon Capitals'. One particularly note-worthy example is Alma, the 'Spinach capital of the world'. In 1987, residents George Bowles and Wolf Grulkey thought about how they could put their small community on the map and decided spinach would offer this, as the Alma-based Allen Canning Company canned around 65% of all the spinach canned in the USA. Once agreed, the town built an 8-ft statue of Popeye to welcome its visitors (http://arkansasroadstories.com/alma.html).

ACTIVITY   **THEMING YOUR HOME TOWN WITH FOOD AND DRINK**

How might you consider changing your home town or village to become a culi-nary destination? Would you consider investment in events, restaurants, shops or attractions? Write a plan and how the identity of it might change.

Second, despite the growth and success of ranking, branding and place trans-formation to attract visitors, it is worth considering that food destination branding might become 'fatigued'. Describe how this might happen and why.

FOOD HERITAGE SITES

As outlined above, the identification of place and labelling of destination through food is a global phenomenon, with numerous cities and places drawing on an his-toric connection with food to help build and develop their tourism offer and the place around it. Bessière (1998) discussed the importance of rural destinations becoming food sites, and explicitly the transformation and redefinition of local identity through food. One of the ways that this has been done is through heri-tage protection. As discussed above, UNESCO (2015) has had a clear role in the transformation and sustainability of place through its designations and intangible heritage list, which recognises 'practices, representations, and expressions, and knowledge and skills which are transmitted from generation to generation and which provide communities and groups with a sense of identity and continuity'. One example is Turkish coffee, which was inscribed on the Representative List of the Intangible Cultural Heritage of Humanity in 2013, or shrimp-fishing on horseback in Oostduinkerke (Belgium), which plays a central role in social and cultural events like the two-day Shrimp Festival. The shrimp parade, and a con-test involving hundreds of children being initiated into shrimp-catching, attract over 10,000 visitors every year.

The 100 Sites Remarquables du Goût ('Exceptional Food Heritage Sites') in France is an example of a well-established approach to listing and nam-ing food heritage sites (www.sitesremarquablesdugout.com). Four French ministries (Culture, Tourism, Environment and Agriculture) developed this initiative, which involved selecting the Sites Remarquables du Goût in 1995. These sites are associated with an emblematic food or beverage product linked to a landscape or architecture with exceptional aesthetic qualities and specific know-how. Examples include Le Potager du Roi (the vegetable garden developed for Louis XIV at Versailles); the salt ponds in the Guèrande (sea salt and fleur de sel); the Palais de la Bénédictine in Normandy (Benedictine liqueur); and in the Gard region, the meadows and marshes of the Tour Carbonnière, which produced Camargue bull meat. All sites identified by logo are described in *Les Chemins du Goût* (Site Remarkables du Gout, 2015) and provide examples of how places have used food to strengthen the identity and attractiveness of destinations. Many such places would ordinarily be unremarkable or unseen, if it was not for the recognition of their culinary and gastronomic offerings. Now many have developed the infrastructure and facilities for tourism.

THE EMERGENCE OF GASTRO-TOWNS AND CELEBRITY CHEF-INDUCED DEVELOPMENT

A more recent catalyst to the transformation of place has been the growth and phenomenon of the 'gastro-pub' (many claim this is a result of gentrification, a concept discussed in the Critical Reflections box). Increasingly, destinations that do not even grow or produce food or drink are becoming food tourism locations through a cleverly constructed gastronomic offer, often fuelled by celebrity ownership or association. In 1984, the Spinnakers Brew Pub opened in Victoria, British Columbia, and became the first ever custom-built brewpub in Canada. It marked the start of a new wave of craft breweries in that province following significant deregulation of beer (see also Chapter 17 on beer tourism). Spinnakers also included innovative and new cuisine styles, and claims to be the world's oldest gastro-pub.

In the 1990s, the gastro-pub phenomenon took off in the USA, with leaders such as Dhillons in Las Vegas. In the UK, the term 'gastro-pub' was coined in 1991 with the development of the Eagle pub in Clerkenwell, London. Recently, the British-based *Telegraph* newspaper wrote about 'the great British gastropub – the food-led phenomenon that saved the humble boozer from outright millennial slump' (29 Jan 2015), giving examples of how old pubs facing closure are using food to reinvent themselves, and become new and vibrant spaces of consumption and activity; this phenomenon has altered the identity of place.

Gastro-pub is now a term that has become synonymous with high-end beer and food served in a bar or pub (Farley, 2009), a combination of the words 'gastronomy' and 'pub'. Certainly, until the late twentieth century, English pubs were drinking establishments and little emphasis was placed on serving food or in the offer of anything resembling gastronomy (Bujdosó and Szűcs, 2012; Farley, 2009). However, by August 2012 the term 'gastro-pub' had entered the Merriam Webster's Collegiate Dictionary, thereby not only changing the physical landscape, but also the linguistic one. Gastro-pubs have now been responsible for the transformation of a number of towns and villages (Sims, 2010), with many becoming high-end dining establishments offering wine-tasting, cookery experiences, steak nights and celebrity chef dishes (illustrated in Figure 12.3).

FIGURE 12.3 *Wine tasting on offer outside a restaurant and bar in Cambridge, UK. Photo by author*

Examples of how places have changed as a result of the appearance of a gastro-pub include the impact of the Fat Duck in Bray, Berkshire (www.thefatduck.co.uk). The pub opened in 1995 and acquired a reputation for precision and invention under the flamboyant chef Heston Blumenthal, who has been at the forefront of many modern culinary developments. The town of Bray is now synonymous with food (it contains two of the four three-Michelin-starred restaurants in the UK) and house prices, tourism accommodation and visitor offerings have changed to reflect this and the type of people it attracts. Other examples of the transformation of place include Padstow in Cornwall, as a result of the growing business portfolio of Rick Stein: it has gone from sleepy fishing harbour to gastronomic centre of the north coast. This is in line with academic work, such as Debbage and Ioannides (2004), who claim more attention is needed to how consumer tastes and consumption can significantly reconfigure the geography of place and production, and how such new food offerings are slowly shaping what has been called a 'new culture of consumption' and change (Goodman and Du Puis, 2002; Rojek and Urry, 1997).

HOSPITALITY SERVICESCAPES: PLACES OF HEIGHTENED CONSUMPTION

Gastro-pubs are one example of how hospitality has changed over the past few years, and how food-themed décor and associations have become attractive. It is not just towns, cities and regions that have been transformed by food; this transformation is also happening at a more local level in food outlets as we have seen with (gastro-)pubs and brew houses. The concept of a 'servicescape' can be used to describe the transformation of place into one of heightened consumption and experience. Scholars have published empirical evidence of the influence of servicescape elements on customers' loyalty intentions (Foxall and Yani-de-Soriano, 2005). According to Bitner (1992: 60), the servicescape comprises three distinct environmental dimensions: (i) ambient conditions, (ii) space/function and (iii) signs, symbols, and artefacts. Wakefield and Blodgett (1996) later added the cleanliness of the facility as an important element of the servicescape. This term describes the physical environment such as overall layout, design, ambience, artefacts and décor of a hospitality space, and draws together the physical and intangible, such as the atmosphere which may be influenced and enhanced by music, colours and lighting. These aesthetic components have become increasingly important when creating a service experience, and are apparent in hospitality arenas (Lia et al., 2009; Lin and Mattila, 2010). Hospitality servicescapes are becoming about the incorporation of physical complexity and social interaction (Spielmann et al., 2012).

In hospitality settings, environmental, social and ambient clues can influence customer perceptions. Spielmann et al. (2012) claim these features interact not just with consumers, but also with each other to elicit responses, and they drive the propensity to eat or drink in a certain location. In the case of hospitality services, 'positive (negative) internal responses to the servicescape enhance (detract from) the nature and quality of social interactions between and among customers and employees' (Bitner, 1992: 61). For example, Ha and Jang (2010) claim that the combination of atmospherics, service quality, and food quality are important in influencing consumer satisfaction and quality perceptions. As the environment is increasingly important, modifications to the internal and external physical features in hospitality environments are changed, as they are known to affect consumer perceptions. Increased awareness of food origins and a desire to experience something more unique are driving a push towards altered servicescapes, where food is no longer enough, but must be accompanied by an experience. Thus, we see restaurants, places and venues transforming themselves to appeal to a more ethically-minded consumer.

Critical Reflections: gentrification of place – coffee shop capitalism?

It has been argued that gastro-pubs and new coffee shops are the clearest example of the gentrification of place, and that food tourism has accelerated this process. 'Gentrification' describes the arrival of wealthier people in an existing urban district, which leads to a related increase in rents and property values, and changes in the district's character and culture. It is a highly contested term and a number of books have tried to cover its various facets (Lees et al., 2013; Smith and Williams, 2013).

Ruth Glass has explored the links between housing and class struggle in London using the work of Marx and Engels and raised concerns about the changing housing patterns of ownership, tenurial transformation from renting to owning, property price increases, and the displacement of working-class by middle-class incomers. This led her to coin the term 'gentrification' in 1964. There are numerous theories about the causes of it, but three are:

- *Theory 1*: Individuals cause gentrification by moving into a neighbourhood: the theory of consumer choice finds individual newcomers with more income create gentrification by choosing to move into an urban working-class neighbourhood.
- *Theory 2*: The invisible hand of the capital market causes investment and gentrification so the flows of the capital market create gentrification. As the gap grows between the current profits from land in a depressed neighbourhood compared to the potential profits from development, capital begins to flow in to these areas in the form of new, higher-priced housing.
- *Theory 3*: A group with something to gain purposely causes gentrification and displacement. These power-brokers develop policies of investment designed to produce displacement. It is about who, rather than what, causes it.

Shaw (2008: 2) summarises the apparent link between gentrification and place transformation through food well:

Gentrification extends to retail and commercial precincts, and can be seen in rural and coastal townships as well as cities. Designer shops, art galleries, bars and restaurants form the background to a landscape of people in semi-public space (tables on the footpath they must pay to occupy) watching the passing parade and sipping chardonnay from a boutique winery, beer from a microbrewery, coffee from organic beans grown in the developing country du jour.

Further information: Lees et al. (2013), Shaw (2008), Smith and Williams (2013)

CHAPTER SUMMARY

This chapter marks the beginning of Part III on food and drink experiences, places and types of engagement. It looked specifically at some of the ways in which food and drink are transforming places (rural and urban) and providing the catalyst for some quite dramatic reconfigurations, including rooftop urban farms in New York, food-themed towns, cities of gastronomy, and changes in the buying habits of the consumer and tourist. It illustrated how places have evolved in response to food and drink and begun to brand themselves around this identity, using examples such as Castle Douglas and food 'capitals'. The chapter introduced the concept of blurring production sites and consumption spaces, which is the fundamental principle behind much food tourism development. In examining literature exploring how producers and production sites are now transforming into places of experience, consumption and consumer engagement, it has been possible to problematise the concept of production/consumption (Everett, 2012).

Drawing on the concepts raised in Chapter 10, it has been suggested that production sites and places are changing to facilitate tourist engagement, with producers physically changing the look and feel of their premises to accommodate tourists. Further, global initiatives are supporting this process, with bodies such as UNESCO prompting urban centres and regions to visibly celebrate their gastronomic history and culinary offering. It has been argued that food can be used for recovery, sustainable peace and prosperity, with the power to transform places of war into places of tourism and prosperity. Further, the chapter looked at the concept of food heritage sites, and how places are now capitalising on their history to develop and grow a tourism offer which prompts a change in infrastructure to support it.

Finally, the chapter looked at the transformation of pubs and buildings through gastro-pub development, with some towns being completely changed by the influence of a celebrity chef or new food identity. This spills over into the hospitality servicescapes, which are focused not only on the food offer, but all the elements that contribute to a multi-sensual experience. The chapter concludes with a reflection on the term 'gentrification', which has become synonymous with the evolution and change of urban places and development of high-end (often food-related) consumer outlets and experiences.

END OF CHAPTER POINTS

- Workplaces are increasingly becoming places of play, where the boundaries between work and leisure have become blurred and places evolve to become sites of tourist consumption.
- Sites of food production that were originally built with no plans or future intention to accommodate tourist visit sites are now investing in tourism infrastructure and this has brought change to their physical environment.

- Food, beverages and gastronomy are being used more frequently as elements of place branding. The identification of place and labelling of destination through food is a global phenomenon, with numerous cities and places drawing on an historic connection with food to build and develop their tourism offer and the place around it.
- Sites Remarquables du Goût and similar heritage sites are being developed to capitalise on an association with an emblematic food or beverage product linked to a landscape or architecture with exceptional aesthetic qualities and skills.
- The gastro-pub has become synonymous with high-end beer and food served in a bar or pub; it has also been increasingly linked to the theory of gentrification.
- Hospitality servicescapes draw together the physical as well as the intangible; aesthetic components have become increasingly important when creating a service experience, and are increasingly apparent in hospitality arenas.

FURTHER READING

Berg, P. O. and Sevón, G. (2014) Food-branding places: a sensory perspective, *Place Branding and Public Diplomacy*, 10 (4): 289–304.

Bessière, J. (1998) 'Local development and heritage: traditional food and cuisine as tourist attractions in rural areas', *Sociologia Ruralis*, 38 (1): 21–34.

Bitner, M.J. (1992) 'Servicescapes: the impact of physical surroundings on customers and employees', *Journal of Marketing* 56 (2): 57–71.

Everett, S. (2012) 'Production places or consumption spaces? The place-making agency of food tourism in Ireland and Scotland', *Tourism Geographies*, 14 (4): 535–54.

Lees, L., Slater, T. and Wyly, E. (2013) *Gentrification*. London: Routledge.

Lin, I.Y. and Mattila, A.S. (2010) 'Restaurant servicescape, service encounter, and perceived congruency on customers' emotions and satisfaction', *Journal of Hospitality Marketing & Management*, 19 (8): 819–41.

Lucarelli, A. and Berg, P.O. (2011) 'City branding: a state-of-the-art review of the research domain', *Journal of Place Management and Development*, 4 (1): 9–27.

Macleod, D. (2009) 'Scottish theme towns: have new identities enhanced development?', *Journal of Tourism and Cultural Change*, 7 (2): 133–45.

Shaw, K. (2008) 'Gentrification: what it is, why it is, and what can be done about it', *Geography Compass*, 2 (5): 1–32.

Sims, R. (2010) 'Putting place on the menu: The negotiation of locality in UK food tourism, from production to consumption', *Journal of Rural Studies*, 26 (2): 105–15.

Smith, N. and Williams, P. (2013) *Gentrification of the City*. London: Routledge.

13

FOOD AND DRINK FESTIVALS, EVENTS AND MARKETS

CHAPTER OBJECTIVES

- To outline the development and growth of food and drink festivals, farmers' markets and events
- To provide an overview of the benefits and value of food and drink events, festivals and markets
- To provide case studies that illustrate the importance and contribution of food festivals and events to destinations
- To offer a critical overview of the evolution of events and the apparent benefits to all
- To explore the importance of farmers' markets and examine how they have become tourist attractions

CHAPTER SUMMARY

This chapter explores the role of food and drink festivals and events in the development of tourism destinations, and looks at their role in fostering identity, providing experiences and generating income. It links back to earlier discussions in Part II on destination development strategies, and examines their economic, cultural and social contribution to people and place. Smith and Xiao (2008) suggested that there are three categories for culinary tourism resources: local festivals, restaurants and farmers' markets, but it is suggested here that the key aspects that characterise festivals and markets are similar and they are therefore covered together in this chapter (although the differences will be made clear). Silkes (2012: 327) suggests that 'Farmers' markets can be considered a small-scale food festival in terms of culinary tourism'. The food festival is perhaps the most successful food tourism initiative of the last 20 years, with events being held around the world to celebrate a range of local food or one specific product, such as cheese, wine, garlic, strawberries, asparagus, fish and oysters. Some of the more famous and established festivals are discussed as exemplars of these culinary initiatives, as well as the smaller and more embryonic events which attract tourists, support producers and create unique place identities. Examples of these events include the town of Trujillo in Spain which hosts the Spanish Cheese Festival, the Ludlow Marches Food and Drink Festival in England, or Galway's oyster festival in Ireland. This chapter should be read in conjunction with Chapter 14, which looks at slightly more unusual food events around the world.

This chapter looks at the birth, growth and development of the food and drink festival. In particular it looks at the value of such events, with particular attention on the economic impacts and how they are used for effective destination marketing and place branding. After all, Joanna Blythman writing in the *Observer Food Monthly* (2008) said of Abergavenny of (arguably the most famous food festival in Wales) that: 'Abergavenny is to Food as Cannes is to Film – an annual festival for spotting rising stars in Britain's artisan food firmament'. Festivals and events have a significant impact on the towns, cities and the surrounding areas, often transforming regions into a culinary and gastronomic destinations. However, this chapter also looks at the potential negative impact of these events on people and place and suggests that they might not benefit all.

This chapter then turns its attention to the growth of farmers' markets, as well as fish and local growers' markets. It looks at how these small markets have evolved to become tourist attractions in their own right and the links with the local community and visitors, and how they have developed from small market stalls to large festivals. It explores how many have become branded, professionalised and regulated, such as in Victoria in Australia with the 'Victorian Farmers' Market Accreditation', organised by the Australian Farmers' Markets Association. Another farmers' market Case Study will be 'Pasar Tani' in Kuala Lumpur, Malaysia, alongside other examples including tourist-attracting fish markets in Cornwall (UK), Bergen (Norway) and even the Mogadishu (Somalia) fish markets (which could arguably be presented as the new tourism emblem of Mogadishu). Certainly, it is clear that tourists are seeking more ways to reconnect to local food and pursue opportunities for experiences, and this is being found in food festivals and markets.

THE GROWTH AND DEVELOPMENT OF FOOD AND DRINK FESTIVALS

There is a growing body of literature on the importance and contribution of events in tourism (Dwyer and Wickens, 2014; Getz, 1997; 2014), but more recently we have seen a growing focus and research projects on the contribution of food related festivals and events. Hall and Sharples (2008) suggest that food events lie between at the intersection of key elements of tourism, events and food, finding that events are about external promotion, but also internal drivers relating to the maintenance of communities, local identity, pride and a sense of place. In an article for *The Independent* newspaper (UK) in April 2012 (Gillmore, 2012), Europe's top food festivals were discussed, confirming that 'Across Europe, there's a festival almost every week. Take Sicily, where sagra (local fairs) celebrate everything from cannoli in May (in Piano degli Albanesi) to couscous in September (at San Vito Lo Capo). In Germany they have been celebrating onions with an onion queen, in Weimar since 1653.' The value of celebration and festivity certainly extends to those taking part, as well as those who are selling and showcasing their products at the events.

Events have long been associated with religious, spiritual and cultural festivals, and despite early event literature not specifically focusing on food and drink, it is apparent that food lies at the centre and foundation of the very earliest forms of celebration and festivity. The number of food and drink events is growing quickly around the world (Griffin and Frongillo, 2003; Payne, 2002); however, such festivals are not new, and you only have to look at wine festivals relating to Roman gods such as Bacchus, saints' and pagan days, harvest festivals, or celebrations such as Thanksgiving to see that humankind has celebrated food (and with food) for hundreds of years. Festivals are said to 'resonate with culture and reflect environment' (Rotherham et al., 2008: 48), with a focus on celebrating local foods, drinks and customs. In medieval times, foods were highly significant and symbolic, forming a regular part of the annual cycle and representing a link to the past and an agricultural way of life. Festivals are about the images, emblems and markers, and the experience reaches beyond the physical and material into the intangible and imagination. After all, 'food is art of a physiological, psycho-sensorial, social and symbolic environment' (Bessière, 1998: 23).

At festivals and events, producers demonstrate how they have encoded their produce with meaning which is in turn decoded by the consumer, an idea expressed by Oakes (1999) who felt that food was a crystallisation of the environment, where places are feasts. Such as idea links well to the concept of *terroir*, used in France to denote the special characteristics of geography that bestowed individuality upon the food product. It can be very loosely translated as 'a sense of place' embodied in certain qualities, and the sum of the effects that the local environment has had on the manufacture of the product. Some claim 'a "terroir" is a group of vineyards (or even vines) from the same region, belonging to a specific appellation, and sharing the same type of soil, weather conditions, grapes and wine making savoir-faire, which contribute to give its specific personality to the wine' (Echols, 2008: 14). Some writers include history, tradition, vineyard ownership and other cultural factors. These are the aspects that characterise food tourism, and which underpin a successful food event.

In more modern times, food and drink festivals have become vehicles of income and visitor generation, forming part of a destination's tourism, marketing and visitor strategy, if not part of a wider economic development strategy (Cavicchi and Santini, 2014). Certainly, food events have attracted additional

FOOD AND DRINK ATTRACTIONS AND EVENTS

investment and provided mechanisms to support local people, businesses and products. Although historically great feasts represented a key time of the year such as harvest, it is clear that festivals are increasingly being held at key times of the tourist calendar as a means to extend the tourist season. For example, in the UK, many events take place outside of the busy summer in the quieter months (in the so-called 'shoulder' seasons) of May/June or September/October (Everett and Aitchison, 2008). An example of this is the Abergavenny Food Festival in Wales, held annually in September (see the following Case Study).

CASE STUDY

The Abergavenny Food Festival, Wales (UK)

The Abergavenny Food Festival is one of the most well-known food events in Europe. As outlined in earlier chapters, a number of food initiatives emerged out of the food scares of the 1980/90s, and this festival was one such example, founded in 1999 by two local farmers (Chris Wardle and Martin Orbach) in the aftermath of the BSE crisis. By 2014 it was attracting over 31,000 people over the weekend of events, 'providing an environment for the meeting of minds, out of which new ideas are born' (Heather Myers, Abergavenny Food Festival Chief Executive).

FIGURE 13.1   *The Abergavenny Food Festival, Wales. Photo by author*

FIGURE 13.2 *The Abergavenny Food Festival, Wales. Photo by author*

The festival is now a national sensation, winning the National Tourism Awards 'Best Event in Wales 2013/14' and Finalist of the 'Best Event in Wales (Large) 2015' and is now one of the leading food events in the UK. The event includes around 220 stalls in the centre of Abergavenny, with numerous ticketed events such as tastings, cookery classes and workshops, attracting celebrity speakers and supporting a programme of demonstrations by international chefs. Figures 13.1 and 13.2 provide a flavour of the atmosphere.

Source: www.abergavennyfoodfestival.com/

THE RANGE AND VARIETY OF FESTIVALS

Hall and Mitchell (2008) claim that as a result of greater cultural and economic connectivity between places, food festivals have increasingly become commoditised and are being used more and more extensively to promote products, places and attract visitors – all underpinned by an economic motive. As outlined in previous chapters, some of these events have led to the complete transformation of place and community. Examples vary from small local producer markets to internationally famous annual festivals, such as Oktoberfest in Munich, Germany (see Chapter 4), or the annual garlic festival in Gilroy, USA, which attracts over 100,000 people to its garlic-themed events and stalls (http://gilroygarlicfestival. com), or Europe's largest turnip event in Switzerland on the second Saturday after Halloween. Known as *Rabechilbi Richterswil*, the festival involves 26 tonnes of carved turnips, in all shapes and sizes, being paraded around the village!

There are different approaches to categorising food festivals, but a useful general overview is given in Hall and Sharples (2008: 14), who place the events in a table against size of event and type of product, or in Getz et al. (2014) who present festivals from the perspective of the visitors who attend. Festivals range greatly in size, frequency and focus. Perhaps the simplest way is therefore to categorise events by whether they are local, regional, national or international in focus, and then by the type of products that are on offer from the generic offer of all types of food and drink (like the Abergavenny event outlined above) to the locally produced, multiple (wine, cheese, fruit), to single and specific products (oysters, garlic, and specific foodstuffs like maple syrup).

CELEBRATING THE SEA: FISH AND SEAFOOD FESTIVALS

The lure and importance of the sea and ocean has directly influenced the growth of festivals that celebrate fishing, coastal communities and the powerful relationship people have with the sea. Events such as oyster festivals, fish festivals, and seafood events are increasingly commonplace and bring sleepy harbour towns to life during the celebrations. Perhaps more so than many other festivals, these are steeped in history, celebrating the ocean, and the industries and communities around ports, harbours and the coast. Oyster festivals are among the most popular festivals around the world, with most celebrating the start of the native oyster season and therefore restricted to the seasons (Rusher, 2003). Examples include the Nordic Championships in Oyster Opening in April in Tanumstrand, Sweden, or the Pick n Pay Knysna Oyster Festival, which has become one of South Africa's most popular festivals (www.oysterfestival.co.za). Canada plays host to the Tyne Valley Oyster Festival, an annual festival on Prince Edward Island, featuring the Canadian Oyster Shucking Championship; finally there is the Whitstable Oyster Festival (http://whitstableoysterfestival.co.uk), a week-long celebration representing a modern revival of an ancient holy festival dating way back to Norman times. All such festivals seek to engage tourists with the sea, and reconnect people with the cultural heritage and ways of life associated with coastal industries and fishing.

Fish festivals are increasingly becoming central tourism attractions, with examples such as the Dublin Bay Prawn Festival (dublinbayprawnfestival.com), which puts on food and wine tastings, a prawn-shelling competition and a firework display; or the Newlyn Fish Festival in Cornwall, UK (see Figure 13.3), which began in 1990. Tourists in Iceland enjoy numerous events during Dalvik's Fish Festival (dalvik.is), or 'The Great Fish Day' which is an annual festival in

FIGURE 13.3   *Newlyn Festival, Cornwall. Photo by author*

Dalvíkurbyggð on the first or second Saturday in August. The Great Fish Day has run for eight years and attracted 200,000 visitors. All of these examples can be regarded as ways to educate people on the benefits of fish, sustaining these industries and resisting globalisation and government policy (as outlined in Chapter 6).

Other examples include fish markets in Hamburg (Germany), Bergen (Norway) and Mogadishu (Somalia). One of the more unlikely fish markets showing signs of becoming something of an event, Mogadishu's fish market has received worldwide attention and now is being called the new emblem of Mogadishu (BBC 2012, www.bbc.co.uk/news/in-pictures-17404466). With a coastline of 3,300 km, Somalia's fishermen have access to over 400 different species of fish in both the Indian Ocean in the east, and Gulf of Aden in the north.

ACTIVITY   THE FISH MARKET IN MOGADISHU, SOMALIA

Undertake some desk-based research on Mogadishu and the fish market in Somalia and outline what might be the political, social and economic challenges if the country wished to make their fish market into a tourist event. What might a tourism strategy need to consider before promoting its fish industry and its people? How could this be done?

THE ECONOMIC IMPACT OF FESTIVALS

Food festivals are big business and are effective economic drivers (Cela et al., 2007; Crispin and Reiser, 2008; Hall and Sharples, 2008). In their study of food and drink festivals in Japan, Hashimoto and Telfer (2006) noted that the development of food festivals supported local communities' economic growth and provided valuable income for local people. Likewise, in Wales, an economic report on its 30 festivals suggested that food events are boosting the sales of Welsh producers by more than £16m per year and help support nearly 300 jobs. The Welsh Government found the impact of the direct spend of festivals across Wales was worth £7.3m to the economy per year (reported in the DailyPost 2014). It found that Gwledd Conwy Feast, the second biggest festival in Wales, saw the highest average spend at £28 per head at the festival, plus an extra £15 in the local area. In 2014, it attracted in excess of 25,000 people and generated £1.4m for the local economy and is clearly continuing to be an effective strategy for local economic development and creating a 'sense of place' (Haven-Tang and Jones, 2006). An evaluation of food festivals by the Welsh Government found the net additional spend hit £16.5m on the food and drink sector and £27m in the wider economy (Daily Post 2014). Research has also highlighted a long-term impact, with exhibitors reporting increases in sales due to regular and increased attendance at the showcase events. Another example of economic impact is in the Economic Impact Assessments of festivals conducted at the Shrewsbury Food Festival 2013 in Shropshire, UK (its first year) which found an additional spend of £180,510; 80% of visitors specifically came to the region for event.

Attracting visitors and visitor spend from out of the region is key to the success of festivals. Rong-Da Liang et al. (2013) claim that most visitor expenditure research has focused on wine festivals and tourists; they examined the characteristics of food festival visitors and the determinants of their festival expenditures. They rightly suggest that the key aspect of economic impact is what visitors spend and needs to be understood, as few studies have been conducted on visitors' motivations for attending food festivals and events. Likewise, Uysal et al.'s (1993) study on food festival participants' motivations at the Corn Festival in South Carolina, USA looked at why visitors attended and how likely they were to spend. Çela et al.'s (2007) study of north-west Iowa's festivals (22,806 visitors) found the economic impact of visitors was $2.6 million sales, $1.4 million personal income and generated 52 jobs. These various studies have generally found that spend is positively correlated to the motivations for attending. Çela et al.'s (2007) work indicated that visitors were motivated to simply attend the festival, followed by the motivation factors to support, taste, learn about and purchase local food.

SOCIAL AND CULTURAL BENEFITS OF EVENTS

In addition to economic impacts, festivals have a key role in reconnecting the consumer to food with a local provenance, which in turn has a role in conserving the landscape, protecting traditions and sustaining ways of life (Everett and Aitchison, 2008; Sims, 2010). With the introduction of assurance schemes and speciality food groups (see Chapter 11), consumers are encouraged to patronise local businesses and resist multi-national global distributers. Recent research by Organ et al. (2015) indicates that food festivals are agents for behaviour change and education and found that engagement and positive emotions at a food festival are good predictors of food buying behaviour six months later. However, there was a need to promote consumer awareness and reconnection with local food to rectify a perceived loss of identity with the countryside. In seeking to eat only foods that have been produced through passion, time and quality ingredients, they were taking an active stance against fast foods, mass production and wider elements of rationalisation (as discussed in Chapter 5). For example, a producer in Ireland suggested that through internalised experiences offered at festivals, food tourists decode personal investments through personal engagement: 'that's the input maybe, it's not just the locality but it's the identity, you know like a piano player. Someone knows we are doing it and they emotionally engage in it like we do.' Food reflects the producer's personality and values. Rather than being driven by profit, tourists and producers work to sustain ways of life.

A multi-layered touristic 'foodscape' is developed at such events, where place is experienced through all the senses. Food festivals could be described in the terms that Löfgren uses (1999: 106, cited in Sheller and Urry, 2004) who suggests that:

> The grammar of landscape experiences includes all the different tourist forms of taking in a landscape, to traverse it, pass through it or past it, to dwell in it, sense it, be part of it … landscapes are produced by movement, both of the sense and of the body. (Löfgren 1999: 106)

Furthermore, food and drink initiatives can be central to marketing and branding, and the strategy must consider the market, but also the people and community it presents and projects (Hall and Sharples, 2008). Lee and Arcodia's (2011) study of the role of food festivals in destination branding supports research that has seen such events as important for regional tourism development, adding value to pre-existing products (Quan and Wang, 2004). Lee and Arcodia (2011: 357) state they are a 'great tool for regional regeneration rather than simply as a generator of economic wealth and particularly a major area of interest for regions'.

ARE FOOD FESTIVALS GOOD FOR ALL?

It might seem that food and drink festivals are a wonderful panacea to economic development and social cohesion, but this topic must also be considered critically and with balance. An example is where the income to support festivals has been reduced where other aspects of health, education and public sector funding might be perceived as more important. Despite positive reports from Wales (above) concluding that the festivals were excellent value for money, the level of funding from the Welsh Government has fallen.

There is no guaranteed success with any event. It is worth noting that festivals are not for everyone and the cost of setting up and clearing up often lies with the community. Further, as Slocum and Everett (2014) argue, an event will not revitalise a town alone, and there needs to be a clear communication strategy. Often there is differing commitment of vendors to entrepreneurship and a fragmented approach to effective marketing and destination promotion. Research has found that many producers want to keep things simple and small and actually resist the growth of events which seem to counteract the uniqueness of their product, with producers not prepared to buy into the incubation function and follow up after event (Hilchey et al., 1995; Stephenson et al., 2006). Part of this reluctance lies in the initial outlay and investment required to engage with an event, as well as a perception that producers are not always interested in growing and becoming commercial in their approach.

THE BIRTH OF FARMERS' MARKETS AND PRODUCER MARKETS

Producers selling at market is an ancient human activity and the oldest form of economic exchange, and today hundreds of markets are held across the world every day. Markets form the centre of most trading towns and villages, and yet by the 1970s many developed nations had seen a decline in direct-to-consumer venues with the development and growth of supermarkets and increasingly advanced processing and food preserving technologies. However, over time we have seen the emergence of the concept of farmers' markets, which focus on local food produce in a more organised and structured setting, often accompanied by advertising. Direct marketing of agricultural products at farmers' markets has become an important sales outlet for smaller farm operations nationwide (Wolf et al., 2005).

In essence, farmers' markets are recurrent and regular markets at fixed locations where farm products are sold by farmers themselves. Increasingly such markets bring the rural to urban centres in addition to taking place in rural contexts. They provide a forum where the farmer/producer links directly with the consumer. In response to food scares and risk, we have seen a growth of these forms of market. According to the US Department of Agriculture (2008), farmers' market operations increased by as much as 6.7% annually, with over 1,800 new farmers' markets opening since 2003 (Silkes, 2012). Also, the number of markets in Ontario, Canada doubled between 1980 and 2007. Since 2000, the growth of markets in Australia has also exploded, with over 100 in operation by 2014 (Adams, 2007).

For the purposes of examining their role in tourism, it is useful to focus on how such markets have evolved into tourist attractions. Like festivals, representations of local identity, local food and production methods are culturally attractive and build a sense of identity and recapturing a more authentic life. Jolliffe (2008) looks at the relationship with tourists in Canada, and states that markets appeal as tourists are looking for 'authentic' food experiences. Certainly, established farmers' markets are extending their offer in the light of tourism interest, drawing on historic and cultural links (Holloway and Kneafsey, 2000). We see markets that have existed for years increasingly attracting more tourists, appearing as 'sights to see' on tourism maps and in travel guides. Examples include markets

FIGURE 13.4 *Farmers sell their produce to tourists in Matmata in Tunisia. Photo by author*

in Matmata in Tunisia (Figure 13.4), or Hoi An market in Vietnam, which is now using food as a destination theming mechanism (Figure 13.5).

Hall and Sharples (2008) provide some very insightful chapters on farmers' markets and include a number of indicative examples, such as the Airey's Inlet market in Australia (Hede, 2008) and the Otago farmers' markets in New Zealand (Mitchell and Scott, 2008), which outline the characteristics and approaches to these events around the world. Further, Silkes (2012) looks at why visitors attend farmers' markets, finding that the primary function is to exchange agricultural products and it is crucial in presenting the residents' life and culture. Farmers' markets represent local culture in a social setting and can be viewed as an attraction for culinary tourists (Smith and Xiao, 2008). They are a forum for consumers to try and comment on produce, providing income to farmers and invaluable consumer feedback, as well as contributing to social and cultural goals in sustainability and supporting local networks. This has certainly been in the case with the Pasar Tani markets in Malaysia (see the Case Study).

FIGURE 13.5 *The market in the World Heritage Site of Hoi An in Vietnam attracts thousands of tourists every day. Photo by author*

CASE STUDY

Pasar Tani (Farmers' Markets), Kuala Lumpur, Malaysia

Pasar Tani is the Malaysian name for farmers' markets and they have been set up by the Federal Agricultural Marketing Authority (FAMA). For over 25 years, the Pasar Tani had 17,300 traders with each earning an average monthly income of anywhere between RM700 (approximately US$175) to RM20,000 (US$5,000). The total sales generated from 1985 until 2010 (25 years) from Pasar Tani was recorded at RM11.5 billion. Hamid and Raihan (2011) find that Pasar Tani has been an effective marketing platform for small-scale entrepreneurial farmer to increase sales. Unfortunately, non-farmers started to use the spaces for training and as many farmers are located in rural areas (more than 100 kilometres away from the sites), logistics and time constraints led to lower participation. The dilemma is whether it would be better to relocate the markets closer to the farms to alleviate the logistical problems facing the farmers, but which may remove the touristic attraction. Hamid and Raihan (2011) pose some useful questions to consider in the Malaysian context, outlined in the Activity box.

THE VALUE OF FARMERS' MARKETS

Farmers' markets offer farmers an opportunity to secure an increased profit compared to selling to wholesalers, food processors, or large grocery firms. They are perhaps an easier and more stable and secure income source than an annual 'mega-event' food festival. Markets respond to a move towards more ethical and moral consumption, and increasing demand from consumers to know where food has come from, especially in response to food scares. Holloway and Kneafsey (2000) claim farmers' markets are logical outcomes of these trends, where the consumer is connected with the producer. It is suggested that markets are 'liminal spaces' in that they both reinforce free market idealisms, yet are in a position to challenge multinationals and supermarkets. They are alternative spaces, but also reactionary and nostalgic spaces that are increasingly becoming performance spaces.

The UK National Farmers Retail and Markets Association (FARMA) found that farmers' markets are worth £220 million annually, and 10,000 farmers and producers participate every year (Hall and Sharples, 2008). In Gloucestershire and Wiltshire, there were 112 market days which generated £2.8 million a year in turnover, and Surrey had eight monthly markets (96 market days) which generated £2.6 million (National Farmers' Retail and Markets Association (FARMA), 2006). Markets are appearing all over the country, and are becoming key aspects of a region's tourism armoury. For the farmers, they can secure more of the income and a higher percentage of the higher retail price through markers. The US Department of Agriculture (2015) finds that of the market managers whose markets had been open at least two seasons, 64 percent reported increased customer traffic; about the same percentage reported increases in the number of repeat customers and increases in year-on-year sales. Farmers' markets support business start-ups and growth for producers and retailers. The US Department of Agriculture (2015) adds that farmers' markets 'play a vital role in enabling small to medium sized growers to gain access to consumers. Without this access the existence of many small-sized

TABLE 13.1 *Benefits of farmers' markets for the farmer, tourist consumer and community*

For the farmer	Consumer/tourist	Community
Diversification of income, offering an additional source of income. They give farmers greater control over their economic lives	Access to healthier and more seasonal foods	Attract visitors and tourists to an area, those interested in cultural and authentic experiences who then purchase in other local businesses
Producers and farmers can get higher prices – as the middle businesses such as distribution are cut out	Better variety of foods on offer as they are not tied into contracts like supermarkets. They offer increased choice, and can offer extra fresh, affordable produce in areas with few such options	Provide an outlet for local produce, helping to start new local businesses and expand existing ones. Create local jobs and business networks, maintaining local employment
Connect producer and consumer in closer relationship and therefore provide feedback to both	Place for social networking and meeting others	Promotion of the wider region, town or area and its activities and offerings
Collaborative potential with other aspects of tourism (trails, tours, restaurants)	Cheaper food, e.g. Farmers Markets of America found the prices at a farmers' market are lower than prices at a supermarket 91% of the time	Branding and a colourful set of images and attractions – develops sense of distinction and uniqueness, which can increase pride and encourage visitors to return
Cooperative movements offer group support and partnership to facilitate income generation. Farmers get increased networking and learning opportunities with other farmers	Offers unique insight into local community culture, people and traditions	Lower transportation pollution and reduced congestion as food is not being transported across the world, less 'food miles'
Transport and storage savings: less transport, less handling, less refrigeration and less time in storage	Entertainment and a fun and educational day out	Money stays in the community longer as opposed to the high levels of leakage with supermarkets
Farmers have an opportunity to diversify their skills, which include gaining marketing and business expertise		Improved infrastructure and access to produce and services for local people
Incubator facility – test new products, try new approaches and pilot different methods in a small scale environment. It is a form of entrepreneurship (Hilchey et al. 1995)		

growers would be threatened.' In general, a farmer secures 80% of the final retail price at a market, but if food went to a packer/shipper then a supermarket, the farmer would get only 10–18% of the final retail price. Some of the benefits of farmers' markets are outlined in Table 13.1, which has drawn data from the Friends of the Earth report (2000) and Hall and Sharples (2008). It is also worth asking if such consumerism is just a form of middle-class narcissism and a fashion for ethical consumerism. See the Critical Reflections box below.

ORGANISATIONS THAT SUPPORT AND CHAMPION FARMERS' MARKETS

The growth of farmers' markets has been coupled with the emergence of organisations to support their growth and promotion. For example, the Australian Farmers Market Association (AFMA) brings the country's markets together, although there are also state-run organisations under AFMA. This is operated as a voluntary organisation and supports the development and growth of best practice and sustainable farmers' markets (www.farmersmarkets.org.au). The New Zealand Farmers Market Association (www.farmersmarkets.org.nz) offers a membership organisation of around 25 independently owned and operated

FIGURE 13.6 *Tourists enjoy the farmers' market near Kyrenia, North Cyprus. Photo by author*

FOOD AND DRINK ATTRACTIONS AND EVENTS

farmers' markets; over 1,000 small food businesses attract an estimated 50,000 customers every week. In the UK, FARMA vis a cooperative of around 500 businesses that claim to share one thing: 'a passion to promote food which is grown and sold by the same hands. Each member has a share in the business, this ensures that we all sign up to a clear mission that we all believe in' (FARMA, 2015).

These organisations exemplify the collaborative approach to farmers; this support can be seen growing and becoming more formalised across the world. Another example of a growing and thriving farmers' market culture can be found in North Cyprus (see Figure 13.6, a farmers' market near Kyrenia). A blog focused on food in North Cyprus asks: 'have you tried the fresh vegetables and fruits from a Cypriot farmers' market? It's cheaper. And – in a lot of cases – it's tastier. I, for one, am a convert' (Afrodite's Kitchen, 2015).

Critical Reflections: are markets a middle-class narcissism?

Narcissism is a concept developed by Sigmund Freud with roots in psychoanalytic theory, introduced in his essay *On Narcissism* (1995 [1914]), although the term originated from Greek mythology, where the young Narcissus fell in love with his own image reflected in a pool of water. Narcissism is regarded as the pursuit of gratification from vanity or egotistic admiration of one's own attributes. It is therefore interesting to think about how farmers' markets could be regarded as vehicles that allow narcissistic tendencies to be demonstrated. A newspaper article from the UK questioned the very approach to ethical consumerism that some feel is now characteristic of farmers' markets. What are your thoughts on Jay Rayner's words? Is he right? Rayner writes:

We believe that, in spending ludicrous sums on this wonderful food, we are making a stand against The Man. We are turning our faces against the supermarkets, promoting true British agriculture, supporting a way of life that is in danger of being lost. There is a technical term for all this: bollocks … What we are not doing is harking back to a bygone era. Farmers' markets mythologise Britain, create a version of it that never existed, when horny-handed peasants lived on prime cuts of happy pig and lashings of thick cream the colour of buttercups. Our great grandparents never ate this well. They couldn't afford to. Don't let any of this put you off shopping in farmers' markets: it's a noble way to pass the time. Just don't think you're changing the world by doing so.

Source: Guardian (2011), available at www.theguardian.com/lifeandstyle/2011/jul/17/farmers-markets-jay-rayner

CHAPTER SUMMARY

This chapter has presented food and drink festivals and events as dynamic spaces, spaces of entertainment and education, as well as places that foster interaction and community. The significant growth in the number and types of events is matched by the growth of farmers' markets and their increasing role within a destination's tourism offer. Food events have quickly become the drivers behind the growth of food and drink tourism and form a key role in marketing and destination strategies. Much of the research to date has focused on visitor motivation, economic and social benefit, networking, expenditure, entertainment and enhancing the of sustainability cultural heritage and community identity.

In many ways, a useful summary for this chapter is to recap some of the benefits of food festivals and farmers' markets, which include:

- increased visitation to a place and retaining travellers for longer;
- attracting funds to local economy which then ensures money circulates in the local economy for longer;
- improving and maintaining employment;
- improving image of a destination and enhancing community pride;
- high knock-on spending in other shops on market days;
- extension of visitor season outside of intensive summer months;
- added value to existing food and drink products;
- social, cultural, health benefits;
- building relationships with consumers;
- increased word-of-mouth sales, and business-to-business marketing (B2B), development and networking leading to partnership and new businesses;
- encouraging entrepreneurship and business incubation – stalls are a form of micro entrepreneurship;
- environmental benefits – reduced energy and fuel consumption;
- increased margins through direct sales due to absence of intermediary costs – shorter supply chains;
- increased consumer exposure to products and opportunity to sample;
- building brand awareness and product loyalty between producer and consumer;
- additional sales outlet, especially for small producers who cannot guarantee volume or consistency;
- marketing intelligence on producers – instant feedback and trial new products, growth of innovation and diversification.; and
- raised awareness of food, opportunities for education of consumers.

END OF CHAPTER POINTS

- Food events have enjoyed a long association with religious, spiritual and cultural festivals.
- Food and drink festivals have become key vehicles of income and tourist generation, adopted as central to a destination's tourism, marketing and visitor strategy.
- Festivals are increasingly being held at key times of the tourist calendar as a vehicle to extend the tourist season.
- Food festivals are effective economic drivers which support local communities' economic growth and provide valuable income for local people.

- Festivals also have a key role in reconnecting the consumer to local produce and producers, and in turn can help conserve the landscape, protect traditions and sustain ways of life.
- Farmers' markets are recurrent and regular markets at fixed locations where farm products are sold by farmers themselves. Direct marketing of agricultural products at farmers' markets has become an important sales outlet for producers.
- Events and festivals are not always good news: often there is differing commitment of vendors to entrepreneurship and a fragmented approach to effective marketing and destination promotion.

FURTHER READING

Cavicchi, A. and Santini, C. (2014) *Food and Wine Events in Europe: A Stakeholder Approach*. London: Routledge.

Dwyer, L. and Wickens, E. (eds) (2014) *Event Tourism and Cultural Tourism: Issues and Debates*. London: Routledge.

Getz, D. (2014) *Event Tourism*. New York: Cognizant.

Hall, C. M. and Sharples, L. (2008) *Food and Wine Festivals and Events Around the World: Development, Management and Markets*. Oxford: Butterworth Heinemann.

Holloway, L. and Kneafsey, M. (2000) 'Reading the space of the farmers' market: a preliminary investigation from the UK', *Sociologia Ruralis*, 40 (3): 285–99.

Organ, K., Koenig-Lewis, N., Palmer, A. and Probert, J. (2015) 'Festivals as agents for behaviour change: a study of food festival engagement and subsequent food choices', *Tourism Management*, 48 (1): 84–99.

Wolf, M.M., Spittler, A. and Ahern, J. (2005) 'A profile of farmers' market consumers and the perceived advantages of produce sold at farmers' markets', *Journal of Food Distribution Research*, 36 (1): 192–201.

14

FOOD- AND DRINK-INSPIRED EVENTS: THE WEIRD AND WONDERFUL

CHAPTER OBJECTIVES

- To explore events that use food for fun and frivolity, where food is the focus, but not necessarily for its culinary or gastronomic qualities
- To examine the origins of unusual food events and explore how many have developed from historical events, tradition and myths
- To provide an overview of the many different types of event (including competitions, racing, fighting, sculpture and throwing) and theorise as to why they are so popular and attractive to tourists
- To draw on theories of performativity and engagement to explain how food events can be used to understand motivation and engagement

CHAPTER SUMMARY

In addition to the major food and drink festivals and farmers' markets discussed in Chapter 13, it should be noted that there are numerous global events which attract tourists and involve food and drink, but are not directly promoting a specific cuisine or gastronomy. Rather, the important role and significance of unusual food-inspired events and experiences is demonstrated; using examples, it seeks to explore the fun, weird (often wacky) and wonderful side of events and competitions. It offers global examples of events that might not be considered 'festivals' in the purest sense, but are certainly key dates, drawing crowds of tourists every year. In many cases, the food is not actually eaten, but nevertheless takes centre stage as it is thrown, rolled or shaped and becomes part of a culinary adventure.

The chapter looks at some quirky examples to illustrate key event management issues, cultural issues, the history of such events and development strategies. For example, events that have become part of a region's heritage and identity, such as the cheese rolling event at Cooper's Hill in Gloucestershire (where people are often injured as they chase a cheese down a steep hill). It looks at how events have become embedded in the social fabric of local communities and how they have developed to become tourist attractions in themselves, often harking back to historic events or traditions.

Further afield, it looks at events such as oyster-shucking competitions, and the 'World's Biggest Food Fight' (the Tomatina in Buñol just outside Valencia, Spain). It also looks at why people are drawn to such events in line with much of the work and research on visitor motivation, and links directly to theories about invented tradition and heritage, and the performativity of people and place. It also looks at the concept of ugly and 'scary food' (Gyimóthy and Mykletun, 2009) and outlines how eating the weird and dangerous might become an adventure in itself. Examples include sheep-head-eating, and consumption of potentially poisonous fish.

FOOD AS THE INSPIRATION FOR UNUSUAL EVENTS

Weird and wonderful events that use food to entertain are probably the least discussed and researched type of food and drink events, and very few publications use them as case studies or illustrative examples. There has been a significant amount written about food festivals (for example Getz, 2014; Hall and Sharples, 2008), but it is difficult to find much research about events using food in a way that involves rolling it, fighting with it or throwing it. Such events do not necessarily support producers, and indeed have not been developed with a view to sustaining producers, promoting the purchase of local food or offering alternative distribution avenues. Rather, food is the object used to create fun, to use and to (sometimes) abuse! Despite this, events around the world attract millions of tourists to engage in activities around food – often to celebrate it, but usually to enjoy the impact of its employment and use.

History, and its subsequent interpretation, has a lot to answer for: many of the odd events claim to have emerged from a historic event, rivalry or need, and are now deeply embedded in the cultural fabric of a destination and its people. For example, there is the annual World Black Pudding Throwing Championships in Ramsbottom, UK, where black puddings are thrown at a pile of Yorkshire puddings on a 20-ft-high plinth, and competitors attempt to knock down as many as possible. Although the competition only dates back to the 1980s, it is believed that the ancient grudge between the counties of Yorkshire and Lancashire is played out at this event and the rivalry can be traced back to the Wars of the

Roses (1455–1485), when the two sides used foodstuffs when ammunition ran out! Other examples include the Chinchilla Melon Festival in Chinchilla, the 'Melon Capital' of Australia because it produces a quarter of the country's melons. Every February, the melon is celebrated and tourists enjoy attractions such as melon skiing, melon tossing and melon bungee! This form of heritage and cultural tourism is perhaps not as present in literature as it should be given its clear links to historic events and agricultural history.

CASE STUDY

Fellsmere Frog Leg Festival, Florida, USA

As the Guinness Book of World Records holder for the Largest Frog Leg Festival in the World, the Fellsmere Frog Leg Festival takes place each January in Florida, USA. Originally, like so many such events, it began as a charity fundraiser to support the development of recreational activities for children in the area. The first festival was organised by a small group of local residents, who guessed that frogs' legs might be unusual enough to entice folks to the city, so they made plans to sell frog legs for dinner. In the first year, they caught 400lbs of frogs around Fellsmere, which they thought would be enough for the entire festival. However, they had under-estimated the popularity of the event and sold out of frogs' legs, while the queues for dinners remained. It has grown from a few hundred people to more than 80,000 visitors in 2015. Think about the reasons for this: is it about people looking for something usual? Does it facilitate a temporary escape from 'normal' life?

Source: www.froglegfestival.com.

Another example is the 'Spam Jam' held in early July in Austin, Minnesota. The event provides fireworks, fun and games and, of course, a lot of the tinned meat Spam. A similar event takes place in Waikiki, and despite being the ninth smallest state in terms of population, Hawaii consumes more Spam (7 million cans annually) than any other state in the country. The event has dishes prepared with Spam by local chefs and cans are collected for charity.

VISITOR ENGAGEMENT WITH FESTIVALS AND EVENTS

The concepts and theories behind why people engage in festivals are well published (Crompton and McKay, 1997; Getz, 1993). It has been said that reasons for event visitation vary, although it is often to meet a personal need, whether a push/pull factor, or a desire to escape. It has been said people are 'pushed' into travelling by internal reasons, or 'pulled' by destination attributes (Dann, 1981). Push factors link primarily to internal or emotional factors, such as a desire for escape or relaxation, adventure, or social interaction. Pull factors are linked to external or cognitive aspects in the chosen destination, such as landscape, cultural factors and attractions such as events. Nothing perhaps offers more escape from regulated and structured ways of life than engagement in unusual events that encourage deviant behaviour (Smith and Costello, 2009). Certainly, being allowed to run around the streets throwing tomatoes or wine at each other, or chasing giant rounds of cheese down a hill, or even finding road-kill and putting it on the barbecue offers such escape! These are all activities discussed later in this chapter, but it is important to consider what such events offer to visitors and why they are so well attended. In addition to enhancing local pride, events also provide opportunities for destinations to take advantage of a desire to escape, with novel recreation opportunities using ritual and tradition to generate funds for the local economy and provide employment (Lee et al., 2004). Festivals are part of what Pine and Gilmore (1999) term the 'experience economy', providing a temporary 'creative space' that can attract visitors and generate local income for places with no obvious tourism attraction or infrastructure (Richards and Wilson, 2006).

Back in 1991, Getz (1991) claimed events would be the main type of alternative tourism, one that would contribute to sustainable development and improve the relationship between host and guest. Uysal et al.'s (1993) research on visitors' motivations for attending the Corn Festival in South Carolina found 24 motivation items and five dimensions of motivation emerged: escape, excitement/thrills, event novelty, socialisation and family togetherness. In a later study, Li et al. (2009) find 'escape' the most dominant of the six motivational factors identified from the visitor data collected at a community-based festival in the rural Midwest of the USA. These motivations were escape, novelty, nostalgia and patriotism, event excitement, family togetherness, and socialisation. In terms of food events, these pull factors and a desire for escape can be illustrated in some of the competitions and events that involve food held across the world.

CHALLENGE AND COMPETITION USING FOOD

Food competition events are now big business, with many becoming world record-breaking occasions that attract thousands of visitors. For example, around the world we see numerous oyster-shucking competitions. One of these is the Galway Oyster Festival in Ireland and part of this event includes parading oysters through the street (see Figure 14.1). There are also eating competitions including hot chilli eating, throwing events including the 'Tunarama' (the world

FIGURE 14.1 *Oysters are paraded through the streets of Galway, Ireland.*
Photo by author

championship of tuna tossing in Port Lincoln, Australia), and smaller village events such as Pancake Day races (a 415-yard dash in Olney, UK). It could perhaps be said that such events have more links than might seem obvious with the wider literature on sport tourism.

In theorising sport tourism, you might think about people travelling for the Olympics or other major sporting events, but it can be argued that similar motivation exists for people travelling to engage in food-inspired events. A lot of attention has focused on the economic development potential of sporting events and competitions (Burgan and Mules, 1992). Sport tourism scholars have suggested that positive image and identity, inward investment and tourism promotion through media coverage and televised sport also help to justify hosting sports mega-events. In a study of sport, Higham (1999) claims that little academic attention has been paid to the tourism potential of domestic sport competitions, national championships and local/regional sport. We might take this a step further and suggest that competitive food events are classed as 'food-sport tourism' or a form of 'soft sport tourism' (Gammon and Robinson, 1997), where sport is recreational, whether viewing or participating. Much like Higham (2005) who argues for sport as a way to reduce seasonality, food events have also been developed for a similar reason, with many of the competitions taking place in the 'shoulder' seasons either side of the tourist peak season. One of the most interesting competitive events included in the *Encyclopaedia of Traditional British Rural Sports* (Collins et al., 2005) is the rather bizarre 'sport' of cheese-rolling.

CHEESE-ROLLING: PLAYING WITH FOOD

Events that involve rolling large rounds of cheese have become enshrined in cultural heritage and history in various villages and places around the world. Magliocco (1998) has written about the concept of 'deep play' in her detailed analysis of food cultures in America. In a discussion about 'playing with food', she discusses and outlines the socio-economic importance of the cheese rolling event in Clinton, Indiana, which is part of the Little Italy Festival. Part of her analysis involves an interesting evolutionary history of how the event has developed, which has seen it change from using real cheese out of a desire to be authentic and link to a 'sacred consumption', to the decision to use fake wooden cheese (pseudo-cheese) that helps continue the tradition without wasting food. This illustrates how concepts of authenticity come into such events and where there are 'symbolic inversions of the usual social order' (Magliocco, 1998: 156).

Cheese-rolling is a famous, long-standing food event and an example is discussed by Sharples in Hall et al. (2003) and Jefferies (2002) as a case study. The cheese-rolling festival at Cooper's Hill in Gloucestershire, UK is a unique food-inspired event (www.cheese-rolling.co.uk/the_event.htm). Competitors line up at the at the top of a steep hill and large 8lb wheels of Double Gloucester cheese are rolled down in front of them from the top of the hill; the competitors then race down to catch the cheese (see www.cheese-rolling.co.uk). The cheese has a one-second head start and due to the steepness of the hill can reach speeds of up to 70 mph! This event is famously dangerous, dating back to pagan rituals of the fourth century, and it continued even through food rationing in the Second World War (Daeschner, 2004).

Despite a cancellation under health and safety regulations in 1998 (33 competitors were injured in 1997), villagers continued hosting the cheese-rolling event from 1999 and their defiant attitude has been hailed as a signifier of British identity and pride. In her chapter on constructing a research agenda for culture, Hess (2012) recalls that in 2010 the Cooper's Hill event was cancelled by the 'official' committee as it had become too popular, with 15,000 people attracted to a site in 2009 when it only had a capacity of 5,000 (it now continues unofficially!). In researching the use of common and public spaces, Hess describes this cancellation as an erosion of a 'cultural public good' (2012: 19), illustrating how 'cultural commons' are being eroded. This is yet another example of how food shapes spaces and places (Chapter 12). It is therefore interesting to consider how such events can be researched from a number of different subject areas, including cultural studies and anthropology. This link between food and identity seems ever-present, and continues to act as a lens onto human behaviour and culture (Caplan, 1997). Another example is the cheese-rolling competition in Stilton, UK where rounds of cheese are rolled down a road rather than a hill.

FOOD FIGHT!

Competitions and 'food sport tourism' does not stop at cheese: some of the most spectacular events are the global and public food fights! Ask yourself why visitors want to engage in such activities. It is said that the 'World's Biggest Food Fight' is the very messy event known as Tomatina in Buñol near Valencia, Spain. This event has attracted up to 40,000 people to participate in a huge tomato fight in the streets, significantly increasing the population of the host town Buñol, which normally has a population of 9,000. Again, its origins are historic, with stories suggesting it started as a town fight that has now developed into part of their cultural (and food) tourism offering: heritage has emerged from violence! Food events are becoming emblematic expressions of a place, where people celebrate a region's 'typical' local food products and they are embraced to act as differentiators for destinations otherwise not capable of boasting of flagship attractions.

There are numerous events around the world that seem to encourage people to fight with food and are similar to the Tomatina. Examples include:

- *Potato wrestling*: renowned for its potato production, this annual event takes place within the Potato Day Festival at Barnesville, Minnesota in the USA. Visitors are drawn to the town festival for unusual potato-inspired activities and tastings.
- *Boiled sweet-throwing*: Les Comparses at Festa Major is hosted by Vilanova i la Geltru near Barcelona, Spain and is characterised by the throwing of boiled sweets at one another. The whole town takes part in the sweet wars and parades.
- *Clean Monday Flour War*: this is a massive flour fight which takes place in Galaxidi, Greece. The event is also known as Pure Monday, but it is not pure

or clean! This 'Flour war' precedes the Greek Orthodox Lent and locals and visitors throw handfuls of flour at one another throughout the town.

- *Orange Battle*: a three-day-long symbolic event is held before Ash Wednesday in Ivrea, Italy. People put on helmets before they throw oranges at each other. The battle pays homage to the insurrection against the Holy Roman Empire that took place in 1194. Participants either represent the tyrant guards or join on foot as rebellious commoners. Again, the recreation of what was once a bloody battle with relatively harmless food has kept stories alive, and provided a cultural spectacle!

- *The Batalla del Vino (red wine fight)*: every June in La Rioja, Spain (Haro), the Batalla del Vino takes place. Again rooted in history, this began as a medieval dispute over a mountain range between neighbouring towns and has now become a celebration. People (dressed in white) seek to drench each other by pouring gallons of the Rioja red wine until everyone is stained purple!

FOOD AS ADVENTURE: DANGEROUS AND SCARY FOODS

Food fights are generally safe and fun, though could be regarded as risky if participants were not wearing helmets! On the other side of risk, there is the phenomenon of tourists seeking out 'scary', ugly or dangerous food experiences that challenge and provide personal 'embodied' adventure through food, thereby making an individual event of food and adventure. According to Pliner and Hobden (1992), food neophobia is avoidance of, and reluctance to taste, unfamiliar food, whereas some people go out of their way to try the dangerous, the ugly and scary and it has become a tourism attraction (Gyimóthy and Mykletun, 2009).

For example, in Japan, the delicacy of the pufferfish (blowfish) is both cuisine and personal adventure! It can be lethal if not served properly, as consumption of incorrectly prepared puffer soup (*fugu chiri*) or the puffer meat (*sashimi fugu*) can lead to severe sickness. Eating *fugu* pufferfish is the mealtime equivalent of Russian roulette. The expensive delicacy contains a concentration of poison up to 1,200 times more potent than cyanide, and can cause intoxication, lightheadedness, and numbness of the lips if not cooked correctly. The toxin can induce dizziness and vomiting, followed by numbness and prickling over the body, rapid heart rate, decreased blood pressure, and muscle paralysis. In 2011, a two-star Michelin restaurant in Toyko suspended its head chef after a diner came close to death having eaten the potentially poisonous puffer fish. The customer had apparently asked for the liver of the fish, something that particularly brave diners do, illustrating the adventure and embodied nature of some food experiences. Such food events that can hurt or kill range from this dangerous pastime to eating competitions that lead to hospitalisation (for example, the 2011 hottest chilli-eating competition in Edinburgh, Scotland led to two people being rushed into hospital (*Telegraph* 2011)).

One might wonder what is attractive about such food 'adventures', although it could be said that what is seen as 'disgusting' is socially constructed and depends on the context and country. Fischler (1988) suggested there are two different reactions to unfamiliar food at different ends of a spectrum. This dichotomy encompasses neophilia (a love of tasting novel and untried experiences), and neophobia (abhorrence of the unknown). This could be eating an animal head, or indeed pretending to eat road-kill; see the Case Study below). Gyimóthy and Mykletun's (2009) research captures this approach to 'scary' food, presenting some food 'events' as adventurous and stating that the range of emotional reactions in food tourism resembles that of adventure tourism in general, including novelty-seeking, fear and thrill. The question is how may culinary tourism intersect with adventure tourism, and indeed event tourism? Through a case study of the Voss sheep's-head meal where some of the work included research at the local festivals around Norway that celebrate this, and several private sheep's-head parties, they claim there is an 'innovative potential of combining rural culinary heritage with cosmopolitan consumer trends as a way forward to in order to develop "local food experiences" in tourism' (2009: 263). In 1998, Voss launched a two-day festival, *Smalahovesleppet* ('sheep's-head release'), reminiscent of the Beaujolet Release in France:

> The festival today celebrates local rural food: sheep's head meals as well as other small-scale quality products within the '*Vossamenyen*' culinary heritage project. The festival offers games like 'Lamb Run' for children or contests in wool cutting of live sheep. The climax of the festival is the great public sheep's head meal, which is quite different from Fleischer's elegant societas... There is a sheep's head eating contest, assessing the competitors' aptitude with regard to style as well as speed. (Gyimóthy and Mykletun, 2009: 269)

Similar sheep- and goat-head culinary experiences are sought out by tourists in Tunisia (see Figure 14.2).

Some experiences or food offerings can be both entertaining and enticing. For the Western tourist, the prospect of 'braised clotted duck blood with pig's intestine' (see Figure 14.3) might not sound that appealing, but this offers an experience unlike anything in their home countries. Food has become a way for tourists to engage in 'performative' activities; this concept is discussed in the Critical Reflections box on p. 244.

There is certainly something of the carnival in eating the unusual or the unfamiliar, where the consumption of traditional food becomes a staged celebration of common cultural values (Rusher, 2003) or personal food-related events like eating puffer fish or fiery chillis in a restaurant become part of a dramaturgical performance (Getz, 2007). This is perhaps also true of the RoadKill Grill (below).

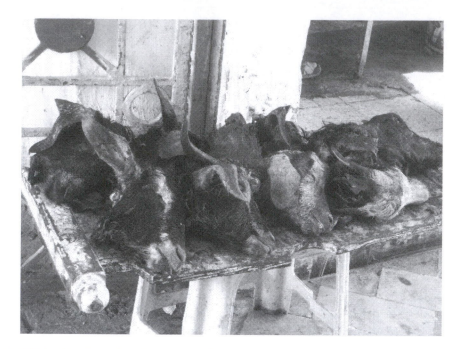

FIGURE 14.2   *Goat-heads ready to be eaten, Tunisia. Photo by author*

FIGURE 14.3   *Braised clotted duck blood with pig's intestine on the menu, Beijing, China. Photo by author*

RoadKill Grill

One particularly gruesome food event is the 'The RoadKill Grill' in Marlinton, West Virginia which happens every September. This event gives visitors the opportunity to eat a wide range of dishes freshly peeled from the nearest road. Its publicity asks, 'Do you ever see a dead raccoon on the side of the road and think, "Man, that looks good!"? If you answered yes to that question, then this festival is for you.' Locals in Pocahontas County poke fun at the stereotypes by adding a Roadkill Cook-Off to their autumn harvest festival. It is worth noting that actual road-kill isn't used in any of the dishes, but the competition requires that the main ingredient must be something commonly found flattened on the side of the road: anything from groundhogs to possum, deer, rabbits, squirrels and snakes.

'INVENTED TRADITION': USING UNUSUAL FOOD EVENTS TO ATTRACT TOURISM

As outlined in Chapter 13, food and drink events and festivals offer a number of economic, social and cultural benefits to a town or region, including economic investment, tourism spend, community pride and identity. Food can provide the foundations of staged celebrations of common cultural values and heritage. This chapter has considered some of the reasons people may be drawn to such events, but it is also useful to consider how such events could be used by countries to generate income and attract tourists, despite often having very little in the way of the historic roots and traditions that some of the events described above enjoy. 'Invented tradition' is a concept extensively discussed by Hobsbawm and Ranger (2012), but also present in tourism literature (Chhabra et al., 2003; Wang, 1999). Not all towns and regions have such a clear heritage to draw on for their events, and increasingly we see 'invented traditions' involving food-inspired events. One example of this more cynical approach to tourism attraction is the Monkey Buffet in Lopburi province, north of Bangkok, Thailand. This 'invented tradition' involves a group of monkeys receiving an extensive lunch at the Pra Prang Sam Yot temple. Tourists enjoy this spectacle (see Figure 14.4), although many have argued that it is probably little more than a scheme to increase tourism spend.

   Many destinations are linking food with art to attract visitors. Even invented events like the monkey buffet have become new cultural sights and can become part of the region's identity. Gastronomy and cuisine are widely acknowledged as an expressive form of art and culture. However, increasingly events are being developed that draw together food and other artistic and cultural forms. In more extreme cases, the food becomes the art to justify events. For example, the Night

CASE STUDY

Monkey Banquet Festival

This quirky event takes place in the town of Lopburi. To pay homage to the hundreds of monkeys that live in this town in central Thailand, a buffet is provided that includes fruit and food for these animals who bring in an enormous amount of money thanks to the tourists that visit to see them. The idea came from a businessman in the 1980s and is now sponsored by a local hotel. Head to the ancient Khmer temple of Phra Prang Sam Yot to see these monkeys that are classed as heroes. To see the festival you need to go there on the last Sunday in November. Legend has it that the monkeys once saved a God and that means they are a symbol of luck and prosperity throughout the country.

FIGURE 14.4 *Advert for the monkey buffet, Thailand in TravelBag magazine*

of the Radishes in Oaxaca, Mexico is a food festival where the main goal is not actually eating. It is celebrated every December and radishes are specially grown and kept in the ground past harvest season, so they develop a strange shape and become large enough that unusual sculptures can be made from them. The festival attracts visitors from outside the area. If we look back at the cheese events discussed above, a more artistic use of cheese (rather than rolling) is perhaps the event at Ellsworth, Wisconsin, the self-proclaimed 'Cheese Curd Capital', which hosts a cheese curd-eating contest and cheese-carving competition every June, in celebration of the century-old Ellsworth Cooperative Creamery and the town's proud dairy tradition.

Critical Reflections: performativity, the drama of food and events as a repertoire of performance

Performativity seeks to explain how tourists enact and inscribe space with their own stories and create their own sense of place. As a dimension of active bodily involvement, performativity has become a powerful discourse, theorised as a way of making sense of self and the world. Edensor (2001) pays particular attention to how tourists play out identities to (re)produce tourist spaces, assigning power to the individual where they are able to redefine their own landscape in a shifting world. Edensor is one of the strongest advocates of the 'performance turn', where we don't just look at the representational world, but move from the semiological realisation of space to what tourists actually do and how bodies are involved (in consuming food, or being covered in it at food fights!). In placing specific emphasis on 'things' (such as food) and their importance in tourism performance in how they enhance the physicality of the body, Bærenholdt et al.'s (2004) and Haldrup and Larsen's (2006) work on tourist performances specifically alludes to the power of the individual to redefine landscape in a shifting world of intersecting spatialisations, socialisations and cultural forms.

Performativity examines place as a series of fluid performances of memory and some of the unusual events outlined above create a distinctive memory of place that is not fixed, but mobile. Pioneered by Goffman (1959), the idea of the dramaturgical everyday is pervasive, fuelling work on tourism places as regulated performance spaces. For instance, Haldrup and Larsen (2006) claim that tourism performances are often subtly choreographed, both by tourists and the tourism industry, and echo Lefebvre (1991: 93) who found space to be an 'image of complex mobilities, [a] nexus of in and out circuits', while Bærenholdt et al. (2004) look at the 'spatial morphology' of tourist performance stages, conceptualising them as hosting complex choreographies of movement. Sites are presented as not just backdrops, but performed and inscribed with meaning. This growing body of work on the embodied creation of space provides a useful basis from which to consider food tourism activities. We need to think about food tourism as a system of performative activities and metaphors, particularly as it has been said that food tourism is a 'complete and performative activity' (Franklin 2003: 245). There is value in drawing on concepts of how food tourism produces regulate 'enclavic' spaces that are constrained and planned as single-purpose spaces, such as restaurants and the events outlined above. As mentioned, such blurred 'heterogeneous' spaces of food events or food-renowned places are often about 'escape' for people and are less openly regulated and constructed against other people's everyday (non-tourist) lives.

CHAPTER SUMMARY

There are hundreds of food- and drink-inspired events around the world, ranging from the dangerous to the bizarre. Although often linked back to a moment in time or specific tradition or heritage, such events have become significant generators of visitors. Such events support tourism theories based on the concept of escape, subversion of the norm and adventure. The 'push' factors link to personal and emotional aims, such as a desire for escape or social interaction, and the 'pull' are the heritage, culture and uniqueness of such occasions. As part of the 'experience economy', it is interesting to think about strange events outside the obvious farmers' markets and festivals, and interrogate the novel, exciting and strange which seem to foster a sense of nostalgia and simplicity.

The concept of 'food-sport tourism' has been introduced in this chapter, building on work in sport and adventure tourism. Food as part of sport is perhaps not obvious, but much of the literature is remarkably similar. Certainly, throwing food at each other and rolling cheese down hills has links to the competitive, but also represents a symbolic inversion of the usual social order. Further, a number of research agendas and subjects can be explored through the lens of weird food events, including the use of common land (cheese), the theory of performativity, the idea of invented traditions to generate a tourism offer, and even resistance by local people who wish to continue cheese-rolling, despite the risks!

END OF CHAPTER POINTS

- Food-inspired events are often deeply embedded in the cultural fabric and community spirit of a destination and its people.
- Few events offer more escape from ordinarily regulated and structured ways of life than allowing people to engage in unusual food events, which encourage deviant behaviour and are thus a symbolic inversion of the usual social order.
- Unusual food events have a role to play in enhancing local pride and community cohesion. They provide opportunities for places to use ritual and tradition to attract visitors and therefore generate income through food-related recreation opportunities.
- Food events are becoming emblematic expressions of a place, where people celebrate the region's 'typical' local food products; embraced as differentiators for destinations otherwise not capable of boasting of flagship attractions.
- Visitor motivations to attend unusual food events include dimensions of motivation such as escape, excitement, novelty, socialisation, nostalgia and patriotism and togetherness.
- Some food events could be regarded as a form of 'food-sport tourism', and 'soft sport tourism', and even some events like chilli- or pufferfish-eating are a form of extreme adventure tourism.
- Food events of the type discussed can be regarded as 'invented tradition' where an element of carnival is prominent and the consumption of traditional food becomes a staged celebration of common cultural values and illustration of performativity.

FURTHER READING

Chhabra, D., Healy, R. and Sills, E. (2003) 'Staged authenticity and heritage tourism', *Annals of Tourism Research*, 30 (3): 702–19.

Crompton, J. L. and McKay, S.L. (1997) 'Motives of visitors attending festival events', *Annals of Tourism Research*, 24 (2): 425–39.

Gyimóthy, S. and Mykletun, R.J. (2009) 'Scary food: commodifying culinary heritage as meal adventures in tourism', *Journal of Vacation Marketing*, 15 (3): 259–73.

Higham, J. (2005) 'Sport tourism as an attraction for managing seasonality', *Sport in Society*, 8 (2): 238–62.

Lee, I. and Arcodia, C. (2011) 'The role of regional food festivals for destination branding', *International Journal of Tourism Research*, 13 (4): 355–67.

Organ, K., Koenig-Lewis, N., Palmer, A. and Probert, J. (2015) 'Festivals as agents for behaviour change: a study of food festival engagement and subsequent food choices', *Tourism Management*, 48 (1): 84–99.

Smith, S. and Costello, C. (2009) 'Segmenting visitors to a culinary event: motivations, travel behavior and expenditures', *Journal of Hospitality Marketing & Management*, 18 (1): 44–67.

15

FOLLOWING FOOD AND DRINK: TOURS, TRAILS AND ROUTES

CHAPTER OBJECTIVES

- To explore and examine the origins and growth of food and drink trails and routes
- To outline the different types and categories of food and drink (usually wine) trails
- To provide international examples and case studies that illustrate the different types of trail and route, and the different management approaches adopted
- To discuss issues of marketing and funding required to support trails and sustain these distributed, itinerary-based initiatives
- To discuss the potential and realised benefits of the development of food and drink/ wine trails, routes and tours, as well as the pitfalls and obstacles in their development and management

CHAPTER SUMMARY

Companies, producer cooperatives, regional agencies, food interest groups, tourist boards and local governments are setting up and promoting an increasing array of organised food and drink tours, routes and trails to help market a destination, attract visitors and showcase different products and producers within specific locales and regions. These trails are usually themed and can take the form of branded signposted routes with self-guided maps, a formal walking tour with a guide, or simply a leaflet or website with named local producers, linked by a logo. Examples of initiatives that bring producers and food sites under one banner include the shellfish journey in Sweden, the wine road in Northern Sonoma County, USA and the Bregenzerwald cheese trail in Austria. Given the rapid increase of this kind of organised food and drink activity, this chapter offers case study examples of this form of tourism attraction to illustrate some of the key management considerations and how they demonstrate high levels of entrepreneurship and business acumen. The chapter discusses the reasons for the establishment of trails, types of initiative, funding mechanisms and the benefits of food trails, and explores the importance of wine trails in terms of their history and character. In looking at wine and culinary routes the chapter discusses how and why they have developed, how local producers can get involved, the importance of stakeholders, and their operation.

The chapter also provides a critical discussion of some of the debates and problems resulting from the kind of networking and collaboration expected (and often imposed) onto regions and destinations. It looks at some rural examples where partners are not equally engaged or where financial and administrative commitment and investment wanes (e.g. the Outer Hebrides Speciality Food Trail in Scotland, which launched with European Union LEADER funding, or regions in Australia that have since lost support). It also draws on recent work on the concept of 'social capital' and looks at the tensions between agricultural stakeholders and tourism organisations who often want different things to achieve differing priorities.

ORIGINS OF THE FOOD AND DRINK TRAIL AND ROUTE

Food and drink/wine trails and routes should be regarded as an itinerary tourism product: often self-directed routes with some form of formal organisation and planning behind them that brings numerous food-themed sites together under one experience or banner. Such trails offer a unifying culinary and gastronomic narrative about people, process, place or product mediated through a series of locations (Timothy and Boyd, 2015). Food and wine trails are characterised by networked spatial separation and provide a way to offer an attractive tourism experience from existing resources that are usually already in place (shops, factories, production sites). They take advantage of increasing consumer interest in culinary tourism and the origins of food (Boyne et al., 2002; Everett and Aitchison, 2008). One of the key drivers behind these initiatives is the desire to strengthen cooperation between agriculture and tourism, and it is this explicit linking of food and tourism that is usefully outlined by Meyer-Cech (2003) in the case study of Austrian food trails. In a study of more than 50 trails (mainly wine), Meyer-Cech traces the wine roads in Austria and outlines their history, noting that the South Styrian Wine Road was built in 1955 with the intention of capitalising on the number of producers to bring strength in numbers and provide an alluring attraction for visitors.

Networked producers under one thematic banner can offer an opportunity for food businesses that lack underlying organisational structures to gain technical support from an organising body or others in the network, and capitalise on a wider customer base who may have only been initially attracted to one of the other partners, but are prompted to visit other affiliated sites. Closer and more strategic agricultural producer-and-consumer relationships are generated through such formal routes, as Getz et al. (2014) claims; they bring producers together to produce meaningful and multi-layered experiences. For example, the strategic food alliances through the Taste of Niagara that Telfer (2001) has written about highlight the financial and social benefits of partnership. However, it is not just about bringing agriculture closer to tourists, as the case studies in this chapter show: trails are working to bring a wider variety of produce to the consumer in an attractive, convenient and branded package.

Trails and tours can attract significant economic investment and become powerful drivers generating enhanced visitor spend in local regions. For example, a report on the Twin Rivers Farm Food and Wine Trail in East Gippsland, Victoria, Australia by Nexus and Urban (2003: 3) found that:

> The Trail makes a significant contribution to the rural community, in terms of additional visitor nights and expenditure. Using known tourist information about the region and Trail member estimates of sales and visitor numbers, it can be estimated that the Trail induces additional visitor expenditure in the region of $3.6 million per annum.

In their study of food trails in Australia, Mason and O'Mahoney (2007: 498) claim that trails offer a 'hedge against economic uncertainty', where such initiatives facilitate the development of shorter supply chains, thereby offering more opportunities for closer collaboration between producers and increased opportunity for access to locally produced food and drink for consumers and the hospitality industry. Food and wine trails are partly a response to concerns relating to distance between the consumer and their food (see Chapter 5), and examples of alternative food networks (AFNs) or short food supply chains (SFSCs) which are approaches and mechanisms that offer an alternative (or supplement) to conventional food supply systems (Marsden et al., 2000). As discussed in earlier chapters, these managed tourism products offer a mode of diversification where there may be uncertainty over the economic future and viability of traditional farming. It is this economic diversification in agriculture through tourism that is now being played out as attractions such as tours, markets, homestays, accommodation and trails. The impact of drawing together (sometimes disparate) producers and processes has meant new and enhanced links between producers and with consumers. It also encourages the hospitality sector to stock and use local food, and undertake promotion of place as part of a wider package presented to tourists.

TYPES OF FOOD AND DRINK TRAIL AND ROUTE

There are numerous types of food trail which range from the organised itinerary-based guided tours and trips involving tour guides and transport, to self-guided tours supported by maps and guidance, to individual production sites unified only by a logo, website or map in a leaflet. Getz (2014: 108) has suggested that trails form a 'cluster' that brings stakeholders together for mutual benefit and cooperation, and this cluster formation is far more effective than disparate and isolated producers seeking to attract tourists and visitor spend on their own. For Rosenfeld (1997: 10) clusters are '[a] geographically bounded concentration of interdependent businesses with active channels for business transactions, dialogue, and communications … that collectively shares common opportunities and threats'. These clusters take on numerous different forms, though they generally group around the key principles of place, process, people and product. Table 15.1 provides an indicative overview of the types of trail and formalised culinary itineraries that exist.

ACTIVITY   **EXAMPLES OF TRAILS, TOURS AND ROUTES**

Take each element of Table 15.1 and provide an example for each one from around the world. Once you have populated the table, think about the aspects which are similar and different in terms of size, scale, focus, membership and objectives.

WINE ROADS: THE OLDEST FORM OF CULINARY TRAIL

Some of the oldest forms of food and drink trails are the wine roads and routes, with most wine-making countries offering a wine road experience (see Chapter 7). In his study of food and wine trails, Mason (2010) finds that the main influences and drivers behind the development of wine trails were those relating to economic pressures including trade liberalisation and globalisation. Although the German Wine Route was established in the 1930s and is believed to have been the first, the recent explosion of such trails in the past 20 years, and their success, has been attributed to the enthusiasm for food and wine tourism and the potential for significant income from visitors looking for something unique, and specific to the region. One example of an established tourism offer is the Case Study below of Sonoma, USA. Likewise, in Greece, the wine route is said to be 'a special form of agritourism aimed at maintaining and promoting this heritage. There are selected routes for travellers to follow, which pass through the most picturesque viticultural areas and wineries' (www.visitgreece.gr/en/touring/wine_routes). There are examples of these initiatives all around the world including the New Zealand Wine Trail, (wellington.nz.com/winetrail) which takes visitors through three North Islands regions, or the Clare Valley Riesling Trail in Australia (http://rieslingtrail.com.au), or the many now appearing in Hungary since they set up the Villány-Siklós (http://villanyiborvidek.hu/en/villany-wine-region), or the popular Mendoza wine trails and tours in Argentina. More countries are embracing the wine trail as an emergent tourism offering and these include Israel

TABLE 15.1 *An overview of the different types of food and drink trail and routes*

Type of trail	Management	Method of guiding	Funding	Access	Form of information	Objective
Themed around specific food product	Private company	Self-guided organised trail through leaflets/website/signs	Membership and fees from producers	Open to all tourists	Road map, e.g. wine roads	Enjoyment
Regional offer (any food/drink produced in area)	Tourism agency	Tour guide (closed group)	External development funding, e.g. LEADER, charity, government	Closed as paid trip / tour	Website or other social media	Educational and instructional
Seasonal	Collaborative membership/network	No guide – just unified by logo	Private company/enterprise	Self-drive	Road signs	Thematic clustering
Wine route	Single member takes leadership and management (committee)		Start up only – basic and embryonic, e.g. road signs only	Walking	Tour guide led	Link parts of the region in identity
Combination (includes other products such as art and crafts from area)				Tour bus		Support producers in marketing and promotion
				Cycling		

(Jaffe and Pasternak, 2004) and Canada (Getz and Brown, 2006). Wine roads and routes are some of the most established and historic of all the tourism initiatives, and exemplify some of the principles and motivations behind the development of other forms of trail. For further examples from around the world see the Best Wine routes (www.bestwineroutes.com).

CASE STUDY

The Wine Road, Northern Sonoma County, USA

This wine road is a success story and illustrates the plethora of tourism activities bundled up into wine routes (Mason and O'Mahony, 2007). Wine has been made in Sonoma County for over 130 years. As a consequence, the route through the wine country in California called 'Wine Road, Northern Sonoma County' is well established and seeks to promote encounters with vineyards and winemakers at California's oldest wineries. From a small group of 9 wineries, it how has 197 wineries and 54 lodging-places. The road encourages visitors to explore uncharted territory and gives them a sense of self (and wine) discovery (and adventure). Founded nearly 40 years ago, it brings together wineries and lodgings in the Alexander, Dry Creek, and Russian River valleys of Northern Sonoma County. It describes itself as 'a treasure map to the many jewels nestled among the hills and valleys of a region where fresh air, fine wine and exquisite cuisine await those who traverse it'. This is a good example of an initiative that has developed not just a route, but a portfolio of programmes, events and services (e.g. three major events: Winter Wineland, Barrel Tasting and A Wine & Food Affair). A dedicated map and accompanying website are offered.

Source: www.wineroad.com

In his study of Australia's food and wine trails, Mason (2010: 26) finds that wine trails exemplify the composition of such trails, formed of multiple small and independent businesses, claiming that they are:

> active on their own behalf as independent producers but also involved in tourism. They exist within highly touristic regions yet also operate in areas where tourists are relatively scarce. Like small businesses everywhere, they appear to be dependent on their own hard work.

It is because of their character that marketing the trail and network is so vital to their 'combined' and collaborative success.

MARKETING AND PROMOTING FOOD AND DRINK TRAILS

Food and drink trails illustrate a bi-directional strategy towards marketing and combined promotion, an approach common in regional tourism which encourages complementary benefits for the tourist and industry sectors. Trails and publicised routes undoubtedly become attractive experiential draw for tourists, and simultaneously enable food and producers to become more visible through the production by a tourism board of maps, guides, signs and leaflets, or through organised tours and specific branding. Certainly, as Boyne et al (2002) points out in his case study of the Arran Taste Trail in Scotland, trails are used to raise awareness of a destination and encourage new visits (projecting an image outside the region), but are also good at encouraging return visits, which Arran has done very successfully. The example of Arran illustrates the importance of a unifying logo supported by a guidebook (produced 1998), distributed by a central tourism body and underpinned by exclusive membership. Arran has used the trail effectively to promote the island as a unique and niche destination, encouraging visitors from mainland Scotland and more directly (good location with Glasgow airports close by and ferry links). The 'Isle of Arran Taste Trail' logo is used extensively on gift packs, leaflets and is proudly displayed at member sites (see Figures 15.1 and 15.2). Interviewed by Everett (2007), the Managing Director of the Isle of Arran Taste Trail explained that their strapline

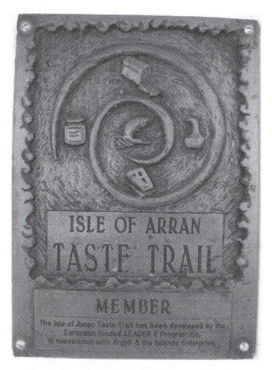

FIGURE 15.1   *The 'Isle of Arran Taste Trail' logo, Scotland. Photo by author*

FIGURE 15.2 *The 'Isle of Arran Taste Trail' logo is proudly displayed at member sites. Scotland. Photo by author*

'Island Time, in No Time' encapsulates the concept of 'escape' whilst still being accessible, which fits well with the motivations of culinary tourists. However, he also was keen to stress the importance of long-term, sustained funding and support for initiatives that involve several partners and an overarching marketing strategy.

Linked with the ideas and strategies outlined in Chapter 8, organised trails can be very effective parts of the marketing and advertising strategy of regional development bodies. For tourism planners, they offer value-added attractions without excessive additional funding and without the development of new infrastructure because there is often opportunity to build on pre-existing cuisines to promote an area as a holiday destination. Bringing producers and food sites under one recognisable identity and initiative helps create a positive image of the region and can in turn increase a sense of local pride. It is this kind of brand cluster that has helped to increase the marketing reach of many trails (Getz, 2014), with some becoming more famous for the trail and its events than the region itself. For example, the Cheese Trail at Bregenzewald (www.kaesestrasse.at) states:

> KäseStrasse Bregenzerwald is a union of farmers and alps, alpine dairymen and cheese-makers, cheese restaurants and inns, museums and railways, tourist organisations and partners from the fields of trade and industry. The thing that unites all 160 partners in the KäseStrasse network is their dedication to the cultivation and the maintenance of culinary delights and regional culture.

Certainly, few people may have heard of Bregenzewald, but the cheese trail is far more well-known; businesses have been able to develop on the back of this new identity, and the region's identity has been exploited to visitors. Meyer-Cech (2005: 139) suggests, 'it is an intricate network of parallel or even intertwined initiatives. In the theme trail network an important role is played by the regional planning congregation, an informal organisation similar to a voluntary regional parliament consisting of the mayors and other political leaders of the region.'

Food trails also offer opportunities to demonstrate entrepreneurship and business acumen, where this distributed form of tourism attraction has become commercially lucrative. It is clear that a number of trails and businesses have been able to profit from an increasing demand for authentic tourist producers and cultural and gastronomic experiences; the packaging together of such businesses into a themed tour is attractive and convenient for tourists. One example is the Shellfish Journey in Sweden, a commercial offering compiled as a tourism package for discerning food tourists (see the Case Study below).

CASE STUDY

The Shellfish Journey, Sweden

The Shellfish Journey in Sweden is a typical example of a company offering an organised commercial food tour. The package suggests that:

> After settling in, you stroll down to the harbour where a local fishing boat picks you up quayside. Once aboard, the experienced captain verses you on the trip and you don a lifejacket. Then it's off to the deep, dark, mineral-rich waters off the coast to prepare and pick up the lobster pots, haul up oysters and catch langoustine, shrimp and blue mussels.

This kind of organised trip is becoming increasingly popular, and offers the entire experience from accommodation to guide to travel.

Source: www.vastsverige.com/en/Food-eng/Articles-Food/The-Shellfish-Journey.

These tours are examples of how different sites can be packaged into an attractive commercial offering, lasting a few hours or days. It is about using the producers and culinary offerings available, and making them into something commercially viable and attractive as a formal tour rather than self-guided trail. Through such offerings, producers attract tourists they previously may not have seen, as tour guides are purposely bringing them to the market, cellar door or production site. Some producers may find association with a commercial 'tour' that draws together businesses in a planned programme more attractive than becoming part of a membership network, as the private tour company funds the trip, and there is little need for producers to fund their own logo or marketing strategy. Rather, this kind of commercial tour relies on the company working with the producers to agree a timetable and generates appropriate rewards (often just in terms of bringing tourists to the door or to their stall who then make purchases) or offers payment per group.

Examples of commercial trails and tours can include bus tours, or walking tours around markets and food establishments (see Figure 15.3).

FIGURE 15.3 *An organised tour around the food sites of the Algarve, Portugal. Photo by author*

More formal packages with itemised itineraries including something like FoodTourMalaysia (www.foodtourmalaysia.com/packages; see Figure 15.4), which offers walking tours and custom tours, boasting that:

> Food Tour Malaysia is operated by a group of passionate food adventurers. Like gourmet Indiana Joneses, we thrash through the concrete jungles of Kuala Lumpur in search of a gastronomic adventure, and want to share the experience with you. We organize (very fun!) excursions to local food fare within the cities of Petaling Jaya and Kuala Lumpur – and would be honoured to have you join us while you are here.

Others include walking tours of specific areas (e.g. in New York: www.foodsofny. com), or week-long tours with a food theme, with Intrepid boasting, 'These are cross-country tours designed to fully immerse you in a destination's food scene.

FIGURE 15.4 *Tourist photographing the food stalls in Jalan Alor, Kuala Lumpur in Malaysia as part of an evening local food tour. Photo by author*

Taste the freshest market produce, meet artisanal producers, find the best street food and learn the subtle changes in regional cuisine' (www.intrepidtravel.com/theme/food). Clearly, these are commercial products taking advantage of the increased interest in food and drink outlined in Chapter 1.

ACTIVITY   **DEVELOPING YOUR OWN FOOD TRAIL**

Collate 4–5 food and drink sites in a region that is well known to you and put together a basic marketing and management strategy for it. These sites could be shops, restaurants, markets, producers, factories or museums. Think of a name for the new trail, and consider how tourists will access the information about the different locations, and how the sites might work together.

PRACTICALITIES AND THE MANAGEMENT OF TRAILS

One fundamental aspect of a food trail is its ongoing management and administration. Although attractive to producers, there are challenges in initiating a new trail, getting producers and stakeholders to work with each other, and offering a product that matches the promotional material and marketing messages given to tourists. The challenges come when disparate small and micro businesses are (sometimes artificially) clustered and expected to work together, as often the 'weakest link' can negatively affect how the whole trail experience is perceived (Mason and O'Mahoney, 2007). For example, if a member site becomes known for rude staff or a poor quality offering, this can taint the entire trail through association (and this can happen quickly through the internet and social media, as outlined in Chapter 9). The difficulties come when trail organisers and members need to manage different stakeholders from the small and large; from privately owned to public. Numerous approaches are required for success including a clear management structure. Successful trails require clear and sustained leadership, and a common purpose, as all too often people's motivations and drivers differ. As previously discussed, research has found that farming and tourism are not always seeking the same rewards, as Getz et al. (2014: 125) observe:

> From a business perspective farming and tourism are complete opposites – farming is supply driven, tourism is market-led; farmers are cost-cutters, tourism businesses are revenue maximisers; farmers produce single standardised products at a given price, tourism businesses diversify into many products and offer a range of prices.

Successful and popular trails rely on effective networking and the cooperation of small and medium-sized businesses, where success depends on working together, sharing logistics, creating offerings that enhance market penetration (Boyne et al, 2002). They need financial support, but also administrative management in place to manage day-to-day requirements. Some trails have failed to realise their aims and have been unable to bring their members into a shared commitment and understanding. An example is the winner of a Highlands and Islands 2005 Food Tourism Award, the Outer Hebrides Speciality Food Trail, which was developed with European funding (LEADER+). It was a tourism-focused initiative consisting of 23 speciality food producers and was widely promoted in tourism literature. The initiative sought to encourage the rejuvenation of artisanal activity and local food promotion on the islands. Significantly, in a study of heritage, food and tourism in Scotland, Burnett (2003) specifically drew on the Isle of South Uist in the Hebrides to illustrate the success of food tourism development where food promotion draws on the idea of the Hebrides as a destination of 'honest representation rooted in local reality' (2003: 33). The trail sought to bring producers across the Hebridean islands together in a joint tourism initiative, but it proved extremely difficult to find some of the sites on some of the published maps (see Figure 15.5), and many were devoid of anything that hinted it might be attractive to tourists.

The 'Outer Hebrides Speciality Food Trail' seems to have disappeared in name and producers listed on the map are promoted through the main Visit Scotland site (www.visitscotland.com/about/food-drink/outer-hebrides). There is little indication that there once was a substantial external investment to establish this trail. The original trail site (www.outerhebridesfoodtrail.com) is now an empty website.

FIGURE 15.5   *The Outer Hebrides Speciality Food Trail map on a member's wall. Photo by author*

Interviews with the original producer who took on its management hinted at the difficulty in securing membership funds from all those who had signed up, and to agreeing on the correct approach for the trail. Another problem was relying on a producer with their own business to also take on the management of the trail – her own business would always take priority, hence the management of the site would often be neglected as a result of her lack of time, limited resources and lack of long-term funding. Significantly, Mason (2010) focuses on the importance of 'social capital' (see Critical Reflections on p. 263) in the success of such trails, and cites Plummer et al. (2006) who identified a range of factors that contributed to the demise of a trail which included differences of trust, commitment, goals, time and decision-making and coordination.

FUNDING TRAILS AND NETWORKS

Most visitor trails and routes require significant financial support and resources to start, and more importantly, to be sustained. One of the most successful funding approaches has been through government and regional development programmes. In the EU, funding for many food trails came from the European Union's LEADER programme, which helped projects with education, advice and grants. LEADER (Liaison Entre Actions de Développement de l'Économie Rurale, meaning Links between the rural economy and development actions) is a local development method that allows local actors to develop an area using its endogenous development potential (https://enrd.ec.europa.eu/en/leader) (see the Case Study in Chapter 10). The programme aimed to revitalise rural areas and create jobs, and LEADER+ was the third phase of this (2000–2006). Initiated through Local Action Groups, the funding had several key objectives that focused on rural development, cooperation between rural territories and use of resources, networking rural areas and information exchange.

LEADER had seven basic principles: area-based; bottom-up; public–private partnership; innovation; integration; networking and cooperation. These all lent themselves to supporting food and drink trails that were innovative, information-sharing and partnership-building. One example was the Styrian Apple Trail in Austria, launched in 1986 (Meyer-Cech, 2003), and the now closed Outer Hebrides Speciality Food Trail discussed above. The 'heritage trails' in the Czech Republic were also sponsored by the EU with the Gastronomia Bohemica Company and Spilková and Fialová (2013) outline its promotion since its birth, as well as how it has evolved to bring in the best regional restaurants and dishes.

Outside the EU, funding has been secured through similarly focused rural development pots, charities and government initiatives, although they have not always succeeded. For example, in Australia, the Albury-Wodonga area launched a 'Legends, Wine and High Country' wine and food trail and promotional campaign, funded through Commonwealth government programmes and receiving significant funding through rural grants (Carlsen and Dowling, 1998). However, by 2006 newspapers were reporting its failure ('The esoteric branding name given to Victoria's North East tourism region two decades ago was yesterday consigned to legend status itself' said a *Border Mail* report on 25 May 2006). It was claimed that it 'soaked up over $13 million of public funds – mainly provided by the ratepayers of Albury-Wodonga. Then there's the one-off payments from the Commonwealth and the like. They were nice little earners as well.' The provision of grants and funding was watched closely, but it did not always lead to the food tourism benefits it was meant to deliver.

Outside government funding, there are more commercial methods of attracting funding to sustain and grow such initiatives. Obviously ensuring producers are selling their product is key and in turn they can generate income to support a membership funding approach or contributions to a formal partnership. Such networks look to generate ongoing management funds and support through collaborative promotion, events, and joint ventures. Membership schemes (for example www.artisanfoodtrail.co.uk) often require fees, which are then used to promote the value of using local and regionally produced goods, and in turn members receive support in the form of legal advice, promotion and networks. Strategic partnerships mean that it is possible to sell more and re-invest in the trail or group.

CREATION OF NEW LANDSCAPES AND 'TASTESCAPES'

Aside from the economic benefits and financial rewards that can motivate producer involvement in trails, trails and tours can alter and shape the landscape, thus creating new 'tastescapes'. The development of food trails provides a new and distinctive narrative to a place and can even provide a new identity, particularly if there was little promotion of the region before the development of a trail (Timothy and Boyd, 2015). In changing how places link to each other, there is a tangible change to place, physical spaces and the environment (Everett, 2012. See also Chapter 12). It could be argued that the branding of an entire region could lead to a loss of the individual character of one specific product, although others would suggest it helps highlight and showcase the offerings of the whole region. A tourist in Arran remarked that his view of the island was enhanced by the trail:

> yes I think there is, that's the strength of it, that's going to give them, hopefully the quality and the flavour in the food will be top notch and the purity and authenticity behind the making of the food, but then there is the making of brand Arran on top of that which you can tell is strong. (quoted in Everett, 2007: 212)

There is also the process whereby we see the creation of new products and offerings from the region, and the creation of new dishes to complement the trail (for example, mixing together local whisky with cheese to produce whisky cheese, or beer and chocolate to create chocolate-flavoured beer). There is a sense that trails that link producers are able to help endow artefacts and places with capital and meaning through association and a unified brand, giving them an enhanced transformative value. The physical surroundings are not only embedded, but a 'sense of place' is constructed from internal feelings and experiences triggered by the environment and the network.

The Isle of Arran Taste Trail director suggested during an interview (Everett, 2007) that 'we sell all of our food and drink on place: people and place. I wanted to bring the profile of people forward on our products as we feel it is the air and people, the ambience and the people that make the product special'; such initiatives are entwined with cultural engagement. There is an emotional bond to place that has been recognised by producers and is not only building a tastescape, but is being utilised in a commercial capacity. Russell and Ward (1982: 654) describe this as the 'psychological or perceived unity of geographical environment'; a partnership of spatial and intangible emotive elements. Through trails, a multi-layered touristic 'foodscape' is being developed that draws together the product, process and place (Ilbery et al., 2005). It is not just about the trail and the fixed locations; trails encourage wider engagement and a different sense of place, where food locations become symbols of the landscape and part of a new and visible tourist narrative; new text and symbols represented by physical signs

FIGURE 15.6 *Signpost to Connemara Smokehouse, Connemara, Republic of Ireland. Photo by author*

(see Figure 15.6), or more semiotic types of sign conceptualised by the Swiss linguist Ferdinand de Saussure (see De Saussure and Baskin, 2011) that are less tangible and more auditory and tactile.

Critical Reflections: Social Capital

The concept of 'Social Capital' is most associated with the work of political scientist Robert Putnam. It is understood to describe the goodwill developed through social interaction that can be harnessed to facilitate action and outcomes. According to Mason (2010), social capital has a two-fold capacity: to bridge, reach out and contact others external to the initial group or individual, and secondly to bond and describe the skills of empathy and understanding within networks. Food trails rely heavily on social capital through partnership, exchange, networking and collaboration.

Social capital has been critically referred to as a 'slippery concept' (Johnston and Percy-Smith, 2003), but has been utilised extensively in sociology and tourism literature (Jóhannesson et al., 2003; Jones, 2005; Zhao et al., 2011). It refers to the

(Continued)

(Continued)

features of social organisation such as networks, norms and social trust that facilitate coordination and cooperation for mutual benefit (Putnam, 1995). Collective action is at the heart of many decisions on the management and development of trails and food networks. There is a recognition that collective action requires networks and flows of information between individuals and groups to help decision-making. These networks are increasingly described as social capital (with similar facets to concepts such as cultural capital and economic capital). Therefore, social capital is based on the premise that social networks have value as interaction and connections develop shared norms, trust, and reciprocity which then deliver common goals and successes. Social capital seeks to explain the degree of connectedness and the quality and quantity of social relations in a population (Harpham et al., 2002) and describes how social relations lead to tangible outcomes.

THE BENEFITS OF TRAILS, ROUTES AND NETWORKED PRODUCERS

There are many benefits to a successful food trail or wine route, and they encompass the financial, social, cultural and structural. These benefits are similar to those outlined in previous chapters relating to wider food tourism initiatives; attracting visitors to a region with an organised trail or route, there is every chance that visitors will extend their stays and increase their spending, directing much of it towards purchasing more local produce as sites become more visible and accessible. One food shop may be interesting, but a networked and themed group of five food sites becomes a full day's experience! It is a mechanism to stimulate backward linkages and minimise the leakages that come from buying products outside the immediate region. Research indicates that trails and organised linked sites also allow for the dispersal of visitors to more remote areas that might not previously have attracted tourists (Meyer-Cech, 2003). They bestow a renewed identity by providing a unifying theme and brand. Trails can also increase visitor satisfaction through experience, as well as raising consumer awareness of the agriculture and gastronomic heritage of a destination. There is certainly an opportunity to enhance cultural understanding, support heritage, and encourage the hospitality sector to look at its own supply chain and use the local products being promoted around them (this is further discussed in Chapters 21 and 22).

Working with food and drink tourism

If you desire to travel, talk about food and meet people, you might consider working as a food tour guide. There are numerous openings around the world as companies seek to meet the growing interest for tours, trails and experiences. An example is the Food Tour Malaysia company (www.foodtourmalaysia.com/about/work-with-us) who seek people 'obsessed over good food and [who] cannot wait to tell someone about your latest find. Have the reputation to talk nonstop (and of course, not boring!). Are you well-travelled, own a car, = [and] love our beautiful country, Malaysia?'

Another advert posted came from the Madrid (Spain) Food Tour company who were looking for a food tour guide in 2015 with the following skills:

> You need to be make a great first impression, be a fantastic storyteller, have an infectious sense of humo[u]r, be adept at thinking quickly on your feet, be responsible and detail-oriented and be empathetic and highly sensitive to people's backgrounds, cultures and differences. We want people who are passionate about Madrid, Spain and this country's cuisine, and who know how to communicate that passion to others and make them as excited as you.

Or, you could look to become a tour leader with a specialism in food tours. An example would be a company like Intrepid known for their global food-themed tours (www.intrepidtravel.com/theme/food). Or you could set up your own company if you are enterprising, like Sally Lynch who set up Tastetrekkers in Australia (see Chapter 9). There are a growing number of opportunities in this area if you have the necessary skills.

CHAPTER SUMMARY

This chapter has introduced food and drink trails and routes that are forming and offering new tastescapes and touristic experiences. It has provided illustrative examples from around the world (wine, cheese, seafood and regional themes) to explain the benefits and attraction of such initiatives and why regions and local communities are developing these trails, and discuss the challenges of setting up and sustaining this kind of spatially distributed attraction. In response to a growing desire to experience more authentic tastes, ways of life and cuisines, we are seeing these types of product being developed across the world. By outlining the different types of trail, the chapter has tried to show how these stakeholder partnership clusters adopt many different forms and approaches, although based loosely on the key principles of bringing place, process, people and product together in one unified and distinctive (often branded) product. Trails and routes offer a powerful marketing strategy if well-funded and supported, providing small and independent food producers and sellers with an opportunity to take advantage of their social capital and work together to share resources, marketing spend, advice and knowledge. Organised tours and trails enable producers to become more visible than might be possible on their own through the production of maps, guides, signs and leaflets and websites.

END OF CHAPTER POINTS

- Food trails are an itinerary-based tourism product with some form of formal organisation and planning to coordinate spatially distributed food sites.

- One of the key drivers behind trails is the objective of strengthening cooperation between agriculture and tourism.

- Trails and tours can attract significant economic investment and become powerful drivers to generate enhanced visitor spend in local regions and can also extend trips.

- There are numerous types of trail but all rely on producers and food/drink sites working together in a themed and collaborative 'cluster'.

- Food and drink trails illustrate a bi-directional strategy towards marketing by networked food and drink establishments.

- The long-term management of trails can be problematic, as successful trails need clear and sustained leadership, and a common purpose, as often farming and tourism are not seeking the same rewards.

FURTHER READING

Barrera, E. and Bringas Alvarado, O. (2008) 'Food trails: tourist architectures built on food identity. Gastronomic sciences', *Food for Thought*, 3 (8): 36–43.

Boyne, S., Hall, D. and Williams, F. (2003) 'Policy, support and promotion for food-related tourism initiatives: a marketing approach to regional development', *Journal of Travel & Tourism Marketing*, 14 (3–4): 131–54.

Jaffe, E. and Pasternak, H. (2004) 'Developing wine trails as a tourist attraction in Israel', *International Journal of Tourism Research*, 6 (4): 237–49.

Mason, R. and O'Mahony, B. (2007) 'On the trail of food and wine: The tourist search for meaningful experience', *Annals of Leisure Research*, 10 (3–4): 498–517.

Meyer-Cech, K. (2003) 'Food trails in Austria', in C.M. Hall, L. Sharples, R. Mitchell, N. Macionis and B. Cambourne (eds), *Food Tourism Around the World: Development, Management and Markets*. Oxford: Butterworth-Heinemann, pp. 149–57.

Spilková, J. and Fialová, D. (2013) 'Culinary tourism packages and regional brands in Czechia', *Tourism Geographies*, 15 (2): 177–97.

Telfer, D.J. (2001) 'Strategic alliances along the Niagara wine route', *Tourism Management*, 22 (1): 21–30.

Timothy, D.J. and Boyd, S.W. (2015) *Tourism and Trails: Cultural, Ecological and Management Issues*. Bristol, UK: Channel View Publications.

For some studies on tourism that utilise the concept of social capital, see:

Jóhannesson, G., Skaptadóttir, U.D. and Benediktsson, K. (2003) 'Coping with social capital? The cultural economy of tourism in the North', *Sociologia Ruralis*, 43 (1): 3–16.

Jones, S. (2005) 'Community-based ecotourism: the significance of social capital', *Annals of Tourism Research*, 32 (2): 303–24.

Zhao, W., Ritchie, J.B. and Echtner, C.M. (2011) 'Social capital and tourism entrepreneurship', *Annals of Tourism Research*, 38 (4): 1570–93.

16

FOOD AND DRINK VISITOR ATTRACTIONS

CHAPTER OBJECTIVES

- To provide an overview of how visitor attractions have been categorised and look at how food and drink attractions might be categorised along the lines of ownership, theme and funding source
- To explore the range of 'spatially fixed' food and beverage attractions using illustrative case studies and examples from around the world
- To provide a critical overview of the academic literature on food and drink visitor attractions and museums
- To introduce issues of financial management and the funding of attractions (income and expenditure)
- To examine how food has been used in temporary art exhibitions and displays
- To offer 'intimacy theory' as a useful critical tool to describe how people are emotionally affected by food and drink encounters

CHAPTER SUMMARY

This chapter commences with a brief analysis of approaches to the study of visitor attractions before it discusses the development and growth of spatially fixed food and drink visitor attractions. These fixed attractions include everything from factories to smokehouses, vineyards, museums, small production sites, breweries, dairies, and theme parks. This chapter should be read in conjunction with Chapter 10, which looked at on-site marketing and interpretation. This chapter extends earlier discussion by focusing on museums and the wider sector of fixed-location food sites beyond concepts relating to on-site interpretation, marketing and sales. It looks at different types of attraction, and links approaches to the wider visitor attraction and management literature. This chapter looks at the sites that the food trails and tours (Chapter 15) link together, i.e. the places people stop at along the trail.

The chapter also introduces food attraction initiatives such as the *Sites Remarquables* in France and provides examples of the more unusual and popular food attractions around the world, including the SPAM museum in Austin, Texas, the fries museum in Belgium (Frietmuseum), Currywurst museum in Berlin, the Burnt Food museum in Arlington, Massachusetts, and Japan's ramen museum. The chapter will discuss the visitor management of these attractions, financial considerations, and the benefits of such places (heritage, celebration, identity, out-of-season tourism, and links to local businesses). In addition to permanent attractions and museums, the role and significance of temporary (art) exhibitions of food will also be briefly discussed.

VISITOR ATTRACTIONS AND THE LITERATURE

Pine and Gilmore (1998) stated in their seminal work that we live in an 'experience economy', where places tailor for the consumer 'imagescapes' comprising the four realms of experience: entertainment, education, aesthetics and escapism. Middleton and Clarke (2001) refer to attractions as permanent resources managed for visitor enjoyment, entertainment and education, although Leask (2010) questions how some of the darker tourism sites (places of death and disaster) might fall into this rather positive categorisation. Visitor attractions have been defined in numerous ways, one of which is as 'a permanent resource, either natural or human-made, which is developed and managed for the primary purpose of attracting visitors' (Hu and Wall, 2005: 619). Lew (1987) simply describes them as 'non-home' places which draw travellers away from their homes, and Pearce (1991: 46) stated that an attraction is a 'named site with a specific human or natural feature which is the focus of visitor and management attention'.

Swarbrooke has also written extensively on the subject of visitor attractions, and states that 'attractions are generally single units, easily delimited geographical areas based on a single key feature. Destinations are larger areas that include a number of individual attractions together with the support services required by tourists' (2002: 9). In terms of food themed sites, Benckendorff and Pearce (2003) were keen not to include festivals in their definition of attractions and specifically highlighted that wineries and retail establishments are temporary and sporadic. However, it could be argued that wineries are semi-permanent, albeit seasonal, given the growth of fixed and all-year, all-weather visitor centres and tours even outside the wine-growing and harvesting season. Alternatively, the definition could go as wide as 'Anything that has sufficient appeal to "attract" a visit' (Cooper, 2012: 148).

There are numerous approaches to the categorisation of visitor attractions in the literature. One useful approach is offered by Swarbrooke (2012) who presents four types of attraction:

- features within the natural environment;
- human-made structures, buildings and sites not designed for visitors e.g. food factories and dairies;
- human-made structures, buildings and sites designed for visitors such as theme parks and new museums; and
- event and temporary attractions such as food festivals.

Swarbrooke (2012) also categorised attractions based on ownership into three types:

- public (government, local authorities) which would include museums, galleries, parks, monuments where the main priority usually conservation;
- private (commercial) such as theme parks, zoos, entertainment, leisure complexes where main motivation is profit; and
- voluntary (trusts and charities) which would cover historic buildings, museums, and steam attractions where the main priority is conservation using visitor income.

It is also possible to categorise attractions on their 'pulling power' (Boniface et al., 2012). This approach uses the concept of the 'First Order' sites, which are the 'must see' and internationally significant sites such as the Eiffel Tower; those of a 'Second Order' (for example, famous vineyards, or global brand factories), and 'Third Order' (for example, local heritage centres showcasing regional produce).

ACTIVITY   CLASSIFICATION OF FOOD AND DRINK VISITOR ATTRACTIONS

Use the grid in Table 16.1 based on Swarbrooke's classification of types of visitor attraction. Think of food and drink attractions that fall into the four main

(Continued)

(Continued)

thematic categories against the three types of ownership. Complete the grid with examples and discuss the reasons for your allocation to the different categories. Are there any food attractions that could fall into several categories? For example, Cadbury's World in Birmingham, UK was a factory and was not made for tourist-related reasons (to make chocolate), but most of the attraction is now a large commercial theme park, built specifically for tourism, and is private and commercial.

TABLE 16.1 *Classification of food and drink visitor attractions. Based on Swarbrooke's (2012) classification of types visitor attractions*

Food and drink attractions type/ownership	Natural environment	Human-made structures not originally designed for visitors	Human-made structures designed for visitors and tourists	Temporary events
Public				
Private			e.g. Cadbury's World, UK cadburyworld.co.uk	
Voluntary				

In a review of research on visitor attractions, Leask (2010) finds effective management of attractions is crucial for their survival in an increasingly competitive marketplace, but this aspect is rarely researched. Mason (2005: 181) further states that the 'conventional approach to visitor management is largely about minimising negative impacts with little research undertaken regarding the visitor experience', and it is clear that often sites are unprepared for ordering spheres of management, which might be financial, or educational (although this is improving; see Chapter 10). Food and drink attractions also have a number of additional management challenges in terms of risk, health and safety and visitor-producer engagement (see Chapter 10). There is certainly an increase in bricks-and-mortar museums being built and dedicated to specific food items or the wider production and celebration of food. In terms of types of food and drink museum, there are private corporate-sponsored sites that promote global brands such as the Dr. Pepper Museum in the USA, or the Jameson Whisky Museum in

Ireland; others are family-run, quirky and small (such as the Burnt Food Museum in Massachusetts, USA), and some have become world-class institutions attracting millions of visitors such as the Shin-Yokohama Ramen Museum or Museum Alimentarium in Switzerland (see the Case Study below). All are now offering interactive activities and exhibitions with immersive tasting, smelling, touching and creating experiences and activities.

STUDIES ON FOOD AND DRINK VISITOR ATTRACTIONS

It is interesting to note that much of the food and drink literature available, including many of the published collections and textbooks (Boniface, 2003; Getz, 2014; Hall et al., 2003; Hjalajer and Richards, 2002; Long, 2004) neglects spatially fixed food and drink museums and attractions. There are many chapters on the types of food tourist, spatially distributed attractions such as routes and trails, festivals and events, cookery schools and the marketing and promotion of food and drink tourism, but very little about fixed mono-location food and beverage-themed sites. Furthermore, a search of articles on this topic fails to unearth many academic articles specifically on food attractions. Interestingly, Pearce (1998: 1) observed that the study of general tourist attractions has 'not received the same prominence as other suppliers and this deserves multidisciplinary research effort', and this remains true of food and beverage attractions. You will find a few useful brief case studies in existing academic texts on places such as dairies, distilleries and wineries, but it is worth spending some time looking at the specific issues relating to these culinary attractions. In their work on the consumer experience of tourism, Mitchell and Mitchell (2001) focused on the growth of food visitor centres, which they claim has helped expand and strengthen links between consumers and a food/drink brand, and such places are certainly key in providing venues that raise awareness and promote learning. As outlined in Chapter 10, such sites have employed highly innovative interpretation techniques and methods to engage, entertain and enthral their visitors, but it is useful to look at the range of attractions, the management of such places, the specific challenges, and the different experiences offered.

Food tourism relies on the spatial fixity of the product, where tourists must physically travel to the locations of production in order to consumer local fare (Hall, et al. 2003), and this is never more true than in the discussion of food and beverage museums and attractions. A number of types of site fall under this category, including breweries, dairies, restaurants with some form of visitor interpretation, factories, distilleries, museums for a specific type of food, agricultural and heritage sites, farm attractions, and even exhibition and art spaces. Williams (2013) states that a food museum is also about celebrating agriculture and does not need to display things like plastic food and vintage tins, because a food museum 'is not a warehouse of a kitschy collection of cute paraphernalia. Given the broadest interpretation, food museums can be found in many forms and food has its place in many types of museums.' For example, she cites the Agropolis Museum in Montpellier in France (www. museum.agropolis.fr) established in 1986 to present the world's food history in a modern day context; we might also cite the Canada Agriculture and Food Museum (http://cafmuseum.techno-science.ca) which supports events and educational activities, and offers a fascinating insight into an agricultural past. Another site is the Yorkshire Museum of Farming, offering photos, artefacts, livestock on site and re-enactments. Attractions that present food history and our agricultural past are increasingly popular around the world, offering an insight into the social, cultural and economic contexts of our ancestors. These sites are good examples of the ongoing debate and theorisation of what (food) heritage and authenticity are. Interestingly, they do not all necessarily have to be physical sites and brick buildings now, as the Case Study below shows.

CASE STUDY

'Foodmuseum.com' – an online food attraction

Tom Hughes and Meredith Sayles Hughes set up a website celebrating food sites, heritages and places (www.foodmuseum. com), clearly 'dedicated to discovering, exploring and promoting the world's foods, their histories, and relevance today', with a wealth of resources, ideas and blogs. Their website states that the founders seek to research, collect, preserve, exhibit and explain the history and social significance of the world's most important foods and package this into a virtual museum. Tom also founded the Potato Museum in Brussels, Belgium in the 1970s, and since then they have managed three major exhibitions about food: the Smithsonian's National Museum of Natural History exhibition 'Seeds of Change'; 'The Amazing Potato' for the National Museum of Science and Technology in Ottawa, Ontario; and the 2010 exhibition, 'Spuds Unearthed!' at the US Botanic Garden in Washington, DC. For those interested in food, this quirky but informative site offers a wealth of information.

FOOD MUSEUMS AND REMARKABLE SITES OF TASTE

Hundreds of food- and drink-themed visitor attractions can be enjoyed around the world. Examples include the Mustard Museum in Wisconsin, the bread museum (in Ulm, Germany), the Dutch Cheese Museum (Alkmaar, Netherlands), and the Kimchi Museum (Seoul, Korea). One relative newcomer to this genre of museum is New York's Museum of Food and Drink (www.mofad.org) (MOFAD). Its purpose is to change how people think about food and inspire curiosity about what we eat. Some of the most famous food sites are those in France, and in particular, the *Sites Remarquables*. In his study of food heritage, Bessière (1998) explains that the French Culture and Agriculture Ministries commissioned a complete inventory of the culinary heritage of the French provinces and granted quality classification marks, including a hundred sites outstanding for their food throughout France in 1995. These were then categorised together under one banner and site (www.sitesremarquablesdugout.com). Meeting in Paris, representatives of the sites created the federation to promote exchanges among members, to support programmes to promote and strengthen the image of quality associated the concept of 'Remarkable Sites of Taste'.

Although more than fixed attractions, the *Sites Remarquables* recognise places with a reputation for celebrating and presenting a food product emblematic of the territory: sites that enjoy a reputation and a history, an exceptional heritage in terms of development and environment, and underpin a public interest in links between food, cultural heritage, landscape and people. The map of these remarkable sites offers a useful visual and interactive list of the permanent attractions, as well as events/festivals (see www.sitesremarquablesdugout.com).

As Chapter 14 indicated, there are many unusual food and drink attractions. Examples include the SPAM Museum in Austin, USA which has also been called the 'Guggenham', 'Porkopolis' and 'MOMA (Museum of Meat-Themed Awesomeness)'. Visitors enjoy the imposing wall of SPAM (4,000 cans of SPAM), the vast advertising exhibits, video displays, and can talk to the 'Spambassadors' who guide visitors around the building. In Belgium, Eddy van Belle opened the Frietmuseum (Fries Museum) in 2008, in a fourteenth-century building in the town of Bruges. There's a collection of vintage chip fryers, pre-Colombian potato artefacts, and fries to buy (www.frietmuseum. be/en), or you might be intrigued by the Burnt Food Museum in Arlington, USA. Containing 'some of the best carbonized culinary artwork in the world', the Burnt Food Museum was founded when curator Deborah Henson-Conant put some apple cider on the stove to heat up, got distracted by a long phone call, and came back to find the cider burnt down to a black crust. Now, people submit their own food 'art' from across the world and it is open to the public on request or online.

Museum Alimentarium in Vevey, Switzerland

Matijaško's (2008) conference paper on the visualisation of food builds on the literature and writings of the Director of the Museum of Food, Schärer (1987, 1996) who has written extensively about the exhibitions at the Museum Alimentarium in Vevey, Switzerland, by Lake Geneva, identified by the iconic fork statues in the lake (Figure 16.1). The Alimentarium is the first museum in the world to be entirely devoted to food and nutrition. The museum is based at Nestlé's first administrative building and its first permanent exhibition was opened in 1985; after refurbishment in 2000–2002, the first floor was reserved for temporary exhibitions, although yet another refurbishment in 2015 may see it embrace ever more innovative approaches. It celebrated its thirtieth birthday in June 2015. The Museum has had over 1.5 million visitors since it first opened. The focus in the museum is the relationship between people and food. It offers culinary workshops, equipment demonstrations, children's activities and historical displays. It is a vast space offering experiences of markets, food safety, information about the digestion of food, agriculture, supermarkets and anything associated with the production, processing, consumption and disposal of food. Matijaško states that it is not about what theme of food is exhibited, but (2008: 35) 'the quality of meaning (aesthetic, informative, symbolic, emotional, allusional, etc.) we have managed to create for the visitors'.

Further information: www.alimentarium.ch/en, and Matijaško (2008).

FIGURE 16.1   *The iconic fork of The Alimentarium in Lake Geneva, Switzerland. Photo by Ji-Elle*

CELEBRATION OF A REGION'S ICONIC CUISINE AND FOOD HERITAGE

Some food museums demonstrate the extreme level of pride people have in their local dishes and cuisines. For example, a nostalgic homage to noodles can be found at Japan's Shin-Yokohama Ramen Museum. Opened in 1994, it offers a permanent theme park dedicated to ramen noodles. It houses a series of educational exhibits about ramen in general, and a food culture retrospective on Momofuku Ando (the inventor of Cup o' Noodles) and proudly offers visitors a recreation of Tokyo in 1958 with ramen restaurants (www.ramen.co.jp). A further example which celebrates a national dish is the Currywurst Museum in Berlin (see Figures 16.2 and 16.3) (http://currywurstmuseum.com). Opened in 2009, on the sixtieth anniversary of the dish's creation, the Museum is dedicated to Berlin's favourite snack: sliced sausage with curry sauce. Costing 5 million euros, the Currywurst Museum was established by Martin Loewer who set out to offer an interactive experience, including a simulated interactive currywurst kitchen (you 'chop' sausages on a screen), detailed maps of currywurst outlets in Berlin, models of currywurst street stalls and kiosks, sniffing stations

FIGURE 16.2 *The Currywurst Museum, Berlin, Germany. Photo by author*

FIGURE 16.3   *The Currywurst Museum, Berlin, Germany. Photo by author*

and 'drawer elements' for visitors to smell and guess the elements of the curry powders, and an eat-in kitchen where guests can sample currywurst. This experience is fully immersive and allows the visitor to engage with a 'tastescape' – ensuring that all the senses are stimulated to entice visitors (Everett, 2009). Of course, when the visitor experience is complete, they are invited to buy and eat the currywurst in the café. It is an excellent example of how food sites are now using tourism to celebrate, sell and market products in one physical site.

The increase of heritage shopping villages and heritage centres that seek to bring food culture back to life demonstrates the growing consumer demand for sites that ignite memories, reflect the past and foster nostalgic resurrection. Bessière (1998: 22) talks of the explicit links between a thirst for heritage and food sites: 'Consequently, studying rural tourism and its heritage component – more specifically gastronomy – leads us to consider rural space as a place to find compensation for lost identity, and as a representation of "the good old days"', and, adds Bessière, (1998: 28) that:

> Heritage must be legitimized in order to be genuine: this means giving the consumer a maximum guarantee of the historical content, origins and roots, which are the most important conditions for a successful

heritage market. Some heritage or traditions may be misunderstood, misrepresented or may even be considered as genuinely inherited, when they are in fact recent artificial constructions void of any historical substance.

Bessière's views link well to the ideas presented in Chapter 3 on food and identity, which suggested that places are in a continuous state of 'becoming' through heritage processes, where identity symbols are produced and exchanged. This kind of folklore therapy and temporal escape is found in folk and agricultural museums. For example, outdoor folk museums seek to demonstrate authentic and traditional ways of providing and preparing food. Examples of these heritage sites include The Black Country Living Museum (UK), Sovereign Hill (Australia), and Norway's Folk Museum – the largest museum of cultural history in Oslo (http:// norskfolkemuseum.no/en) (see Figure 16.4. The experience is perhaps compromised by the less than authentic plastic cups!).

FIGURE 16.4   *Visitors enjoying an 'authentic' drink with a 'local woman' in a traditional home in the Oslo Folk Museum, Norway. Photo by author*

Working with food and drink tourism: museum curator

If you are interested in museums and heritage visitor attractions, you might consider becoming a museum curator. You would manage collections of objects of

(Continued)

(Continued)

artistic, scientific, historical and general interest, and would use these to inform, educate and inspire visitors. Such a role would give you the opportunity to work with food- and drink-themed attractions, although a wider scope may be necessary at the start of your career because food museums remain a very small part of this sector. To gain entry, you will need a degree and may also require a postgraduate qualification in a relevant subject like museum or heritage studies. Paid or unpaid work experience is also now essential.

A curator acquires, cares for, develops, displays and interprets a collection of artefacts or works of art. Other activities include public relations, marketing, fundraising and education programmes. Curators are also expected to prepare budgets, manage staff and build relationships with other museums, partners and stakeholders. The specific responsibilities of a curator can vary from museum to museum, as you might find yourself acting as a manager at a small independent museum or gallery, or in a large museum you may be responsible for one specific area of the collection. Further guidance can be found at the museums association: www.museumsassociation.org/careers

The roles and responsibilities include:

- acquiring and cataloguing objects or collections of interest to the museum/gallery;
- responsibility for a collection of artefacts or works of art;
- undertaking research and writing catalogues;
- displaying objects or collections in way that makes them accessible and engaging;
- writing materials and articles for the website – internal and external publications;
- planning, organising, interpreting and presenting exhibitions and lectures;
- collection documentation, management and interpretation;
- handling enquiries from researchers and the public;
- budget planning, forecasting and reporting, and
- staff management, recruitment, and disciplinary matters.

FOOD AND DRINK AS TEMPORARY ART ATTRACTIONS

This chapter has primarily looked at food and drink attractions where food is spatially fixed; however, there are also exhibitions that reflect food's transient and movable characteristics. Temporary attractions of food and drink in art exhibitions portray food as a multi-faceted cultural artefact that offers an ephemeral focus and inspiration. Such a focus within attractions and exhibitions can often attract visitors interested in art, culture and design rather than only food tourists. Food is central to the exhibition, but is presented in a way that shifts the focus from the qualities of the product or brand to the more artistic and philosophical (Tefler, 1996).

Recent exhibitions in 2015 include the World Expo in Milan, Italy which examined the relationship between art and rituals around food (see Figure 16.5) or the numerous exhibitions for Berlin's 'Food Art Week' which focused on the different connections art can make with food through design, photography, collages, performances, food experiences and books (www.foodartweek.com). You might also consider Ferran Adrià's major retrospective exhibition held in Somerset House, London on gastronomy, where 'The Art of Food' became the world's first exhibition dedicated to a chef and his restaurant showing the art of cuisine and cuisine as art based on his restaurant in Catalan, Spain (www.somersethouse.org.uk/visual-arts/elbulli-ferran-adria-and-the-art-of-food). These sites are testament to the ability of food to be celebrated and to form art (Martin, 2005). Furthermore, food and drink can be used in art to present food-based politics and economic plights. For example, a study by Cook (2006) undertook research at an exhibition aimed at highlighting the plight of banana farmers. The exhibition comprised framed dried banana skins from the real harvests of each of the banana farmers, and visitors at each piece were able to listen to the real recorded voices of the growers of the bananas in the frame. This kind of exhibition which brought art, food and politics together worked powerfully to present political messages of slavery, British imperialism and the importance of Fair Trade.

FUNDING FOOD AND DRINK VISITOR ATTRACTIONS

Swarbrooke (2002: 268) states that, 'In the broadest sense, financial management is concerned with ensuring money is available to allow the attraction to function on a day-to-day basis and making sure that these funds are used in such a way that it allows the organisation to achieve its financial objectives.' There are certainly examples of such sites that illustrate many of the concepts of good and bad visitor attraction financial management. The main sources of income are outlined below, based on Swarbrooke's (2002) categorisation (Table 16.2).

Sometimes the enthusiasm to establish a museum that celebrates food can succumb to poor financial management and planning, despite evidence of a potentially strong visitor market. The noble ambition of one such place dedicated to the discovery, understanding, and celebration of wine, food and the arts was Copia: The American Center for Wine, Food and the Arts. This cultural museum and education centre located in the Napa Valley, California opened with much excitement in 2001, but closed in November 2008 after it accumulated significant debt. From the very beginning, it failed to gain local support, with reporters commenting on the tensions created between locals who viewed the Copia as an invasion by rich out-of-town 'foodies' into their working-class local

TABLE 16.2 *The main sources of income for visitor attractions*

The main agents of (food) visitor attraction development include:

PUBLIC SECTOR	Central/Federal/State government (museums, galleries, historic buildings)
	Non-government bodies given task of allocating funds (ancient monuments, historic buildings)
	Local government (museums, parks, events, leisure)
PRIVATE SECTOR	Transnational commercial organisations (e.g. Coca-Cola, McDonald's)
	Major leisure companies (theme and amusement parks)
	Developers who use leisure as part of mixed use development (waterfront developments)
	SMEs (zoos, garden centres, heritage centres)
	Entrepreneurs (museums, leisure parks, e.g. Ramen museum in Japan)
VOLUNTARY	National voluntary bodies such as the National Trust in the UK (stately homes, historic buildings)
	Local trusts related to specific site or location (industrial heritage, steam, events)

Types of funding and support

DIRECT	Start-up grants, capital investment or voluntary donation
INDIRECT PRIVATE	Private sector, including hire purchase, sale and leaseback, concessions and franchises, and sponsorship
INDIRECT PUBLIC SECTOR	Often through provision of land and buildings, tax allowances, provide transport and infrastructure, duty on imports, and job schemes to provide labour
INDIRECT VOLUNTARY	Often includes gifts or volunteer labour, especially common at local heritage sites or small museums

Based on typologies presented in Swarbrooke (2012)

community and those who felt it offered significant commercial and tourism opportunities (Friedland, 2002). Its original mission was to explore, celebrate, and share the pleasures and benefits of wine, its relationship to food, and its significance to culture. Offering wine- and food-tasting programmes, exhibitions, films, concerts, fine and casual dining, and shopping, its business plan had been based on around 300,000 visitors, but these admissions numbers were never reached and it fell into debt and ultimately bankruptcy. Copia is perhaps an example of a site that had the potential to become like the Alimentarium in Switzerland (see the Case Study above), but its business model was flawed and it failed to manage resources that provided the product in an efficient yet profitable and effective way.

ACTIVITY   SETTING UP AND FINANCING A NEW FOOD AND DRINK ATTRACTION

1. Outline the income and costs for a potentially new food or drink site. Use one of the imaginative projects below. Write up a feasibility study for one of them and note all the problems encountered in preparing the report and identify where and when the financial 'break even' might happen. Expenditure generally falls into two types: capital (usually one-off fixed costs to set up, acquire and install) and revenue costs (ongoing maintenance). Draw up a list of the likely income against the capital and revenue expenditure and use Table 16.3 as an indicative list.

   - large multi-partner, multi-million state of the art food museum
   - inner-city food processing factory
   - local mono-product museum
   - new innovation and technology centre with interactive exhibits on food and drink
   - small rural farm site looking to diversify its product (shop, café, animals)
   - local cultural museum with exhibits of village life and personal stories

TABLE 16.3   *Capital and revenue expenditure considerations*

INCOME

• Entrance charges	Rents and tenancies
• On site attractions and rides	Franchises and concessions
• Food and beverage	Grants
• Souvenirs and shop sales	Sponsorship
• Guided tours	Consultancy services
• Hire of rooms/facilities	Special events

EXPENDITURE

• Salaries and on costs	Training
• Travel	Recruitment
• Purchase of goods	Equipment
• Clothing and uniforms	Services, e.g. cleaning
• Transport	Marketing
• Maintenance	Fuel, heat and light, water
• Rents	Telephone
• Taxes, insurance, fees	Loans and debts (from capital costs)

2. Discuss: what are the three most important factors in determining success or failure of (food and drink) visitor attractions?

Critical Reflections: intimacy theory in food tourism experiences

Trauer and Ryan (2005) have examined the tourist experience in terms of 'intimacy theory'. They suggest many special interest tourism sector (including food) encounters are saturated with emotional attachment. Their focus is on personal relationships and emotional connections, but this theory could be used to explain the emotional connection people have with food and drink. They argue that:

> First, intimacies within a place are created by interaction with those local to that place, and second, that intimacy and meanings associated with a place emerge from the nature of the interaction between those who visit the place; particularly when those people possess meaningful relationships between them. In the latter case, the meaning of place recaptures memories of shared behaviours that reinforce personal intimacies. (2005: 482)

It is possible to see how shared experience and meaning are fostered through food attractions and memories are reignited through exposure to nostalgia-inducing foodstuffs. Tourists' behaviour is often based on commercial and tangible transactions

FIGURE 16.5 *Physical intimacy with a foodstuff – a tourist hugging a jar of Nutella at the food-themed World Expo in Milan, Italy. Photo provided with kind permission from Amanda Brunton*

and not on the intensity of emotional involvement. However, to fully experience another culture or foodstuff, it may be necessary to initiate and encourage intimacy, often created by the willingness to share on the part of the host (or museum provider) (see Figure 16.5). It is about how place becomes a centre for emotional and physical exchange, a felt experience of sensual intensity and complexity.

In looking at intimacy, Trauer and Ryan cite the concept of 'sense-scapes': a heightening in the intensity of an experience, so that a taste can recall a memory or experience. They argue:

Not only does this concept incorporate the other senses of hearing, taste, smell and touch in addition to sight – all which are important in developing a sense of the intimate, but sense-scape can be yet again re-interpreted as sens/e-scape ... tourism providing for escape both from and to a place and/or person. (2005: 487)

CHAPTER SUMMARY

This chapter elaborated many of the concepts and ideas about visitor interpretation and management presented in Chapter 10. Visitor attractions have been given many definitions, without anyone really agreeing on one. This indecision reflects the complex nature and wide range of types of attractions that are on offer around the world. In this chapter, the focus is on spatially fixed, mono-location attractions that require people to travel to visit the specific physical location. They are the points that make up food trails and routes, and without these fixed sites it is unlikely many routes would exist. It is suggested that food and beverage visitor attractions have attracted relatively little academic interest, and few studies have specifically examined their management and development. Sites such as The Alimentarium have been included to illustrate the popularity of food and drink attractions, although it is important to recognise they can also succumb to the same challenges (financial, political, economic) as all other attractions, and some fail (such as Copia in California). Unlike many other visitor attractions, food museums and sites are able to create unique 'sensescapes' which use interpretation techniques to generate intimacy between people and food, and celebrate unique products that represent the very heart of a region or country's identity. This chapter has encouraged you to undertake activities that give you practical insights about the running of an attraction, and to help you reflect on what makes for a truly successful one.

END OF CHAPTER POINTS

- Tourism is part of the 'experience economy' (Pine and Gilmore, 1998) and visitor attractions should contain at least one element of the four realms of experience: entertainment, education, aesthetics and escapism.

- Swarbrooke (2012) outlines four types of visitor attraction: (i) Features within the natural environment; (ii) Human-made structures not designed for visitors; (iii) Human-made structures designed for visitors; and (iv) Event and temporary attractions.

- Food and drink literature covers very little about spatially fixed food and drink museums and attractions. Most concentrate on routes and trails, events and festivals, or on the tourist themselves (motivations, activities and type).

- Food and drink visitor attractions include everything from factories to smokehouses, vineyards, museums, small production sites, breweries, dairies and distilleries. With additional funding they increasingly employ highly innovative interpretation techniques and methods to engage, entertain and enthral their visitors.

- Folk and living history sites provide opportunities to create places that compensate for a sense of lost identity, and representations of the past, usually through recreating food culture and methods of farming and processing.

- Food and drink can form the underpinning element for art exhibitions, and can be used in art to advance political messages and highlight economic injustice.

- Intimacy theory can help theorise how shared experience and meaning are fostered through food attractions and explain how memories are reignited through exposure to nostalgia-inducing foodstuffs at attractions.

FURTHER READING

Bessière, J. (1998) 'Local development and heritage: traditional food and cuisine as tourist attractions in rural areas', *Sociologia Ruralis*, 38 (1): 21–34.

Boniface, B., Cooper, C. and Cooper, R. (2012) *Worldwide Destinations: The Geography of Travel and Tourism*, 6th edn. London: Routledge.

Cook, I. (2006) Geographies of food: following. *Progress in Human Geography*, 30 (5): 655–66.

Friedland, W.H. (2002) 'Agriculture and rurality: beginning the "final separation"?' *Rural Sociology*, 67 (3): 350–71.

Fyall, A., Garrod, B. and Leask, A. (2003) *Managing Visitor Attraction: New Directions*. Oxford: Butterworth Heinemann.

Leask, A. (2010) 'Progress in visitor attraction research: towards more effective management', *Tourism Management*, 31 (2): 155–66.

Martin, E. (2005) 'Food, literature, art, and the demise of dualistic thought', *Consumption Markets & Culture*, 8 (1): 27–48.

Matijaško, N. (2008) Muzej Alimentarium u Veveyu u Švicarskoj (Museum Alimentarium in the Town of Vevey, Switzerland), *Etnološka istraživanja* 12 (13): 341–5.

Mitchell, M.A. and Mitchell, S.J. (2001) 'Consumer experience tourism: a powerful tool for food and beverage producers', *Journal of Food Products Marketing*, 6 (3): 1–16.

Schärer, M.R. (1996) 'Museology: the exhibited man/thing relationship: a new museological experiment', *Museum Management and Curatorship*, 15 (1): 9–20.

Schärer, M.R. (1987) A museum exhibition on food. A new alimentarium in Vevey, Switzerland, *Museum* (155): 145–51.

Swarbrooke, J. (2012) *The Development and Management of Visitor Attractions*, 2nd edn. Oxford: Butterworth-Heinemann.

Tefler, E. (1996) *Food for thought: Philosophy and food*. London: Routledge.

Trauer, B. and Ryan, C. (2005) 'Destination image, romance and place experience: an application of intimacy theory in tourism', *Tourism Management*, 26 (4): 481–91.

Williams, E. (2013) 'Food museums', in K. Albala (ed.), *Routledge International Handbook of Food Studies*. Abingdon: Routledge.

17

BEVERAGE TOURISM: DRINKING TO EXPERIENCE PEOPLE AND PLACE

CHAPTER OBJECTIVES

- To discuss the range and types of beverage tourism (excluding wine tourism; see Chapter 7)
- To outline some of the key literature and research on beverage tourism
- To explore some of the types of beverage tourism and examine the key sectors in detail (including tea tourism, coffee tourism, beer tourism and whisky tourism)
- To use illustrations and case studies to explain how beverage tourism can provide useful insights into approaches to the study of tourist engagement and experience
- To examine how some commodities like coffee and tea are providing effective community development vehicles and local economic benefits

CHAPTER SUMMARY

This chapter looks at the niche tourism sector of beverage tourism. Beverage tourism is similar to culinary tourism in that, just as a tourist might travel for food, visitors travel for a drink experience or product (Plummer et al., 2005). The chapter builds on the discussion of wine tourism in Chapter 7, but focuses on more niche areas of gastronomic tourism including tea tourism, coffee tourism, whisky tourism, and beer and emergent drink tourism sectors such as cider and sake tourism. In discussing these types, the chapter looks at the growing interest in specific activities and offerings such as tea holidays, tea estate stays, tea and coffee tours, coffee festivals, ale trails, cider museums and distillery visitor centres. The chapter also looks at the impact on the growers, the economic and cultural implications, and how it can support community (Fair Trade) development projects and diversification strategies.

The chapter draws on research papers and edited publications from Jolliffe on tea and coffee tourism: *Tea and Tourism: Tourists, Traditions and Transformations* (Jolliffe, 2007) and *Coffee Culture, Destinations and Tourism* (Jolliffe, 2010). Other studies underpinning this chapter include Plummer et al. (2005), Spracklen (2011), Spracklen et al. (2013), and McBoyle and McBoyle (2008). A Case Study is also provided on craft beer in Loudoun County, Virginia by Sue Slocum. Through more in-depth discussion of beverage tourism, issues addressed in this chapter include commodification, authenticity, destination marketing, cultural engagement and identity development.

A GROWING 'THIRST' FOR DRINK-INSPIRED TOURISM?

So far, this textbook has employed a small number of case studies that could be described as 'drink tourism' or 'beverage tourism'. These examples have included coffee and whisky tourism. This limited focus and attention reflects the small (but growing) body of literature on this subject; many of the products you might consider relevant to drink tourism have been under-researched, with most studies focusing on wine, and more recently beer and whisky. However, an increasing number of studies look at beer, whisky, tea, coffee, cider and other spirits such as sake in Japan, or vodka tourism in Russia. According to Plummer et al. (2005), wine tourism has been the prominent form of beverage tourism in the literature, and although there are activities, experiences and offerings similar to wine, there is a need to address this deficiency in the literature. Academic research has begun to look at a wider variety of drinks within what might be considered beverage tourism, and focus on how drink is intimately linked with place and people and can provide insights into the tourism experience (Boniface, 2003; Jolliffe, 2010). Beverage studies now offer a fresh approach to a wide range of issues including class and social interaction (Spracklen et al., 2013), authenticity (Mkono, 2012a), local economic development (Hall et al., 2003; Jolliffe, 2010) and marketing strategies (Boyne and Hall, 2004). The first beverages to be discussed are the most consumed in the world after water: tea and coffee.

WHAT'S BREWING? AN OVERVIEW OF TEA TOURISM

Tea enjoys a long and rich association with exploration, as well as with politics and social upheaval (think of the Boston Tea Party, which fuelled the American

Revolution). Tea has been at the centre of human activity for hundreds of years and has been the focus of exploration and travel because of its value as a commodity. Tea tourism has been defined as 'tourism that is motivated by an interest in the history, traditions and consumption of the beverage, tea' (Jolliffe, 2003: 131), and arguably Jolliffe has generated significant academic interest in this topic. Jolliffe (2007) has provided a comprehensive volume on tea tourism which looks at its relationship to tourism around the world (chapters cover India, Sri Lanka, England, China, Canada and Kenya). Tea now underpins growing tourist demand by offering experiences of tea houses, plantation tours, tea museums, tea souvenirs and tea events.

Tea tourism can also be presented as a niche form of heritage tourism and is closely linked to national identity and cultural heritage (Goeldner and Ritchie, 2006; Jolliffe and Aslam, 2009). Examples of this include China and Japan with their elaborate tea ceremonies, or the quintessential British teashop offering afternoon tea in china cups with homemade cakes (Jolliffe, 2003), or events such as the Tea Festival in Shimen, Taiwan, or the Green Tea Festival in South Korea. Tea drinking is central to many cultures and societies, and around the world, we see enthusiasts searching out tea-based experiences (Boniface, 2003). Jolliffe (2007: 4) goes further and suggests that tea is presented as 'an instrument of hospitality, an influencer in terms of tourism and social change, a component of tourism experiences, and a dedicated focus for tourism attractions'.

Interest in and demand for tea tourism is demonstrated by the growing number of tea experiences on offer, including: assamteatourism.com, teatourindia. com, and the Darjeeling tea garden tours; there are approximately 80 operational tea gardens around Darjeeling (e.g. http://soureneetourism.com). The culture surrounding a huge tea plantation is unique to each one, offering a strong thematic approach to regional tourism development and destination marketing (Heath and Wall, 1992). One clear example of the adoption of tea as a vehicle of economic diversification is the tea tourism industry in Sri Lanka.

Cochrane (2007) suggested that no other destination has been exposed to such a range of long-lasting and serious crises as Sri Lanka. This is a country with the potential to maximise its income from tea tourism, yet it had to delay development as a result of prolonged political unrest and civil war (Jolliffe and Aslam, 2009). During a more recent settled period, the opportunity to develop an offer based on a rich history and heritage of tea has been seized and tourists can enjoy visits to tea suppliers, plantations, factories, museums, gardens, exhibits and tea-themed events. Jolliffe and Aslam (2009: 342) claim that:

> tea heritage tourism could add significant value for the tea and tourism industries in Sri Lanka. It has the potential to contribute to restoring, preserving and conserving the historical buildings, monuments, plantations, culture and traditions related to tea.

Further, Gunasekara and Momsen (2007) identified opportunities for tea-related tourism experiences in Sri Lanka based on its landscapes, tea-related architecture and the heritage traditions of tea picking (plucking), processing, selling and consumption, and it has now embraced tea tourism. Examples include tourist

FIGURE 17.1 *Tea tourism resort in Sri Lanka. Credit for photo: Halpe Tea, UHE Exports (pvt) Ltd and 98 Acres Resort*

FIGURE 17.2 *Tea tourists visit a factory in Colombo, Sri Lanka. Credit for visit and photo: Regency Teas. Photo by author*

accommodation nested in the lush green environment at the 98 Acres Resort in Sri Lanka (www.resort98acres.com; see Figure 17.1), visits to tea factories to watch production (visitors at Regency Teas in Colombo, Sri Lanka in Figure 17.2) and the Ceylon Tea Museum (see the Case Study below)

CASE STUDY

Ceylon Tea Museum

The Ceylon Tea Museum's website proudly quotes Sir Arthur Conan Doyle: 'Not often is it that men have the heart when their one great industry is ruined, to rear up in a few years another as rich to take its place; and the tea fields of Ceylon are as true a monument to courage as is the lion of Waterloo.' This reflects the recovery of their tea industry following major upheaval, as well as the development of this tourist attraction which now claims to preserve 'the heritage of tea'.

Built in 1925, the spacious four-storey Hantane Tea Factory was abandoned for many years, before it became a museum project for the Sri Lanka Tea Board and the Planters' Association of Ceylon. It now offers visitors a 'full tea experience' with tours, exhibitions, visitor centre and restaurant. It exhibits machinery, memorabilia, documents, books, pictures, and tea industry artefacts, and claims to 'exploit the tourism potential of the tea industry, strengthening Sri Lanka's image as the leading Tea Producer'.

Source: http://ceylonteamuseum.com

Another country intimately associated with tea and tea cultures is China, described by Pratt (2002) as the 'homeland of tea'. He presents tea tourism in terms of a 'Pilgrimage to the Holy Land of Tea'. These semi-religious references to tea are perhaps indicative of the relationship between tea and the people of China. Cheng et al. (2012) suggest that tea-based cultural and arts performances are embedded with ethnic and regional characteristics, embracing aspects of the society – history, religion, ethics, music and dance, painting and calligraphy as well as food. For example, tea ceremonies are particularly associated with China and Japan and have been called 'an aesthetic cult' (Shalleck, 1972). Tourists join these symbolic forms of expression, although they are usually performed specifically for those tourists in search of tradition in what has been described as 'performativity authenticity' (Zhu, 2012: 1510). In their study of tea tourism in China, Cheng et al. (2012) claim academic research on tea tourism lags behind other forms of drink tourism and remains an under-researched area from the demand perspective. Their research in the tea-producing province of Xinyang found the more people know about tea, the more positive they were towards drinking it and identifying themselves as 'tea tourists'.

FOOD AND DRINK ATTRACTIONS AND EVENTS

Tea tourism is not just popular in tea-producing countries; demand is also found in consuming countries. For example, the UK is one of the world's greatest tea consumers, with an average per capita tea supply of 1.9 kg per year (Food and Agriculture Organization of the United Nations, 2015). Tea became the drink of the upper classes in the eighteenth century (Fromer, 2008) and in the nineteenth century it was British interests controlling tea production in the sub-continent. Britain boasts hundreds of little teashops that encourage 'nostalgic resurrection' and temporal escape, with many afternoon tea venues becoming tourist attractions in themselves, such as Sally Lunn's in Bath (www.sallylunns. co.uk), or Betty's in Harrogate and York (www.bettys.co.uk). Teashops are often full of signs of the past, such as antique cups and saucers, and present staff in Victorian costume to evoke a sense of a temporal and spatial escape, fuel-ling tourist desires to temporarily leave modern day living. This echoes Crouch et al., who suggest that a sense of temporal escape is only truly realised once the body is physically immersed in 'poetic encounters' (2001: 261).

Hall and Boyne's (2007) study of the teapot trails around England asserts that tea rooms, teashops, and afternoon tea have become powerful national symbols. A quick look at the website of Visit England (2015) supports this: 'There are few things that evoke a sense of Englishness quite like the tradition of afternoon tea. You can take it in a tearoom in a grand seaside resort, the café of a local park or the elegant dining room of a sumptuous hotel.' However, Hall and Boyne (2007) claim that despite there being over 30 regional pub-lications focused on tea tourism sites in the region, they are insufficiently promoted, with collaboration collapsing, like so many collaborative food tourism networks in the UK (Slocum and Everett, 2014). However, despite the international demand for tea experiences, it is increasingly clear we are becoming a planet of coffee drinkers and this is now fuelling the demand for coffee tourism experiences.

COFFEE TOURISM: 'BEAN' THERE, DONE THAT?

Coffee originated in Ethiopia and the cultivation of the first Arabica coffee plant was as early as the sixth century (Jolliffe, 2010), with the first coffee house appearing in 1534 in Constantinople (Tannahill, 1988). Coffee culture has become increasingly popular and central to cultures, identities and ways of life around the world. With 60 countries around the world producing coffee, and most consuming it, the opportunities for tourism development are grow-ing. The world produced around 141.2 million 60-kg bags of coffee in 2014/15, and consumed 149.2 million 60-kg bags of coffee in 2014 (The International Coffee Organisation (ICO), 2015). A growing body of work highlights the incredible diversity of coffee-related experiences, which range from seeing production sites and learning about the harvesting of beans through tours, trails, tastings, events, festivals and routes. In particular, Jolliffe (2010) has provided a comprehensive overview of coffee tourism and offers case studies from around the world. Coffee tourism is certainly an established cultural experience within the tourism offer (Boniface, 2003), and is being enjoyed in bars, shops, cafés, restaurants and coffee houses. There are even coffee museums such as the World of Coffee Museum in Switzerland (see Chapter 16). Jolliffe explains (2010: 8) that, 'coffee and tourism collide where coffee consumption becomes a hospitality product and where tourism activities relate to experiencing aspects of the history and production of coffee'.

Coffee, like cheese, wine or foodstuffs discussed in earlier chapters, is closely linked to place and identity. As Thorn and Segal (2006) outline, with so many different traditions and approaches associated with coffee, the coffee experience is as unique as the place – a kind of 'terroir', where one bean can symbolise a distinctive place, people and process. Jolliffe (2010) simplifies the coffee destinations into three categories: (i) coffee-producing destination (e.g. Vietnam, Colombia); (ii) coffee culture destination such as Seattle (the home of Starbucks); and (iii) coffee history destination such as Vienna or Paris. In looking at a coffee-producing nation, Jolliffe et al. (2010) discuss Vietnam, an emerging coffee-producer (and coffee tourism destination), the second-largest producer in the world of robusta coffee (Vietnam National Coffee Corporation). Vietnam has a strong café culture and unique coffee offerings. For example, coffee has been ritualised here, similar to tea ceremonies (Jolliffe et al., 2010), offered in a small metal one-cup filter (*ca phe phin*) on top of the glass or cup, producing rich coffee after a period of anticipation (see Figure 17.3). One of the most unusual coffee tourism experiences being successfully marketed (and increasingly exploited because of its high market value) is civet coffee (*kopi luwak*). This is made from coffee cherries eaten by weasel-like animals that have been digested, excreted, collected and processed before being cleaned to produce an expensive coffee ($20–$80 per cup). The impact of creating such a high demand experience led to cruel farming of civets and also widespread production of fake beans and commodification (see *The Economist*, 2012; www.economist.com/blogs/prospero/2012/01/coffee-vietnam). Demand has led to the production of fake and inauthentic offerings, diluting the very uniqueness so attractive to tourists.

More and more coffee tourism locations are being developed to capitalise on a global appetite for coffee experiences. For example, in Jamaica the Mavis Bank Coffee Factory Limited offers facility tours before tasting the Blue Mountain Coffee, a 'coffee experience beyond compare' (www.bluemountaincoffee.com). Another is the Kona in Hawai'i (Johnston, 2010) where once again increased demand for a unique offering led to the proliferation of diluted, cheap and/or commercialized alternatives.

As outlined in Chapter 13, there is increasing research on food and drink events and festivals (Hall and Sharples, 2008), and the range of coffee-themed events is growing year on year. For example, the Buon Ma Thuot Coffee Festival in Vietnam takes place during the coffee harvesting period (Jolliffe et al., 2010); there are also 'coffee weeks' in the Dak Lak Province in Vietnam that seek to increase engagement, with coffee tours, farms and local interactions, and the cultural coffee festival for Kona coffee, held in Hawai'i since 1970 (Johnston, 2010).

FOOD AND DRINK ATTRACTIONS AND EVENTS

FIGURE 17.3 *A coffee ritual being enjoyed in Ho Chi Minh, Vietnam. Photo by author*

BEER TOURISM

Beer tourism includes ales, lager, stouts and other yeast-fermented malt drinks flavoured with hops and has become an increasingly popular form of artisan production and alternative tourism offer, attracting interest from many different tourist types and market groups (Brown, 2011). Beer tourism describes the experience when the visitor's primary motivation to travel is to visit a brewery, beer festival, or beer show to experience the beer-making process and/ or tasting of beer (Plummer et al., 2005, 2006). As with tea and coffee, there has been limited research on beer tourism compared to other food and drink tourism types.

In seeking to establish a simple typology of beer tourism, Bujdosó and Szûcs (2012) have presented a two-tier approach to beer tourism, where either 'beer' or 'place' is the primary motivation. If beer is the primary motivation then a tour will include experiences such as routes, beer weekends, lunches, and tastings. Where place is the primary focus, a tourist might expect to enjoy beer festivals, museums, breweries, brew houses and brasseries. In the last 20 years, many breweries around the world have started to open their doors to visitors and support a number of different marketing initiatives. Caffyn (2010) suggests that strengthening links between beer and tourism in this way helps both industries become more sustainable in the long term. Plummer et al. (2005, 2006) examined the visitor profile of beer tourists along the Waterloo-Wellington Ale Trail in Canada and found that the majority of were young and male, significantly different from the typical wine tourist outlined in Chapter 7 and in work such as Hall et al. (2002). Plummer et al. found almost every visitor to the breweries had a positive experience and suggested that breweries working and promoting beer tourism together led to substantial benefits including an enlarged network and a wider marketing reach.

Like tea or coffee, beer demonstrates how a traditional product can be used in a number of different diversification strategies to sustain communities, ways of life and promote tourism. Some public houses have been able to become brands in themselves and destinations in their own right, such as The Signal Box Inn at Cleethorpes, UK, which promotes itself as the smallest pub in the world, or the Pub Na Spilce in Plzen, Czech Republic, the largest pub in the world. These unique selling points allow the owners and managers to create 'beer tourist pilgrimage destinations' (Bujdosó and Szûcs, 2012: 107) and, once again, the language of religion and the sacred is adopted to explain beverage experiences. Not only

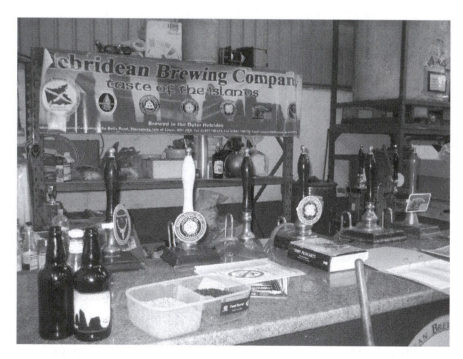

FIGURE 17.4 *The simple visitor centre at The Hebridean Brewery, The Outer Hebrides, Scotland. Photo by author*

FOOD AND DRINK ATTRACTIONS AND EVENTS

FIGURE 17.5 *A sample of 'Moo Cow Brew' awaits the visitor in The Outer Hebrides, Scotland. Photo by author*

do 'pilgrimage' destinations offer unique experiences, but many breweries have invested in visitor centres and tours. Examples include multi-million-pound interpretative installations such as the Guinness Brewery in Ireland, and much smaller micro-breweries in the infancy of building their tourism offering. One smaller example is the Hebridean Brewery (part of the Speciality Food Trail discussed in Chapter 15; see Figures 17.4 and 17.5).

Beer tourism offers many tourism experiences, from beer-themed lunches where different types of beers are offered to accompany dishes to beer weekends that can offer the acquisition of beer brewing skills, or even a spa day at the 'Beerarium' that offers beer therapy treatments (Bujdosó and Szűcs, 2012). Like tea and coffee, beer museums are also appearing around the world, with famous examples such as the Plzen Brewery Museum (www.prazdrojvisit. cz/en), or the Saky Brewhouse and Brewery Museum in Tallin (www.alecoq. ee/en). Museums are just restricted to brewing (see Chapter 16) and examples include the Beer Can Museum in East Taunton, Massachusetts showing over 4,500 different beer cans (Caffyn, 2010). In Belgium, monasteries involved in beer-making are even opening up their abbeys to tourists, and monks now serve the visitors (Bujdosó and Szűcs, 2012). One example of this is the Belgian Abbey town of Leffe which has an international reputation for its beer (Figure 17.6).

Beer festivals are probably the most popular beverage events and generate overnight and day visitors (Wilson, 2006). For example, the Munich Oktoberfest

FIGURE 17.6 *Signs in the abbey 'beer' town of Leffe, Belgium. Photo by author*

(see Chapter 4) is enjoyed by more than 6 million people every year; the Czech Beer Festival in Prague attracts over a million people every year; and the Craft-Beer Festival in Budapest showcases Hungarian craft-beer (Bujdosó and Szûcs, 2012). More tangential events on the spectrum of beer tourism include a beer bike competition in Houston, USA (a bicycle race and drinking competition dating back to 1957) and beermat tourism (collecting beermats is also known as tegestology).

THE RISE OF CRAFT BEER TOURISM

A craft brewery is defined as a small, independent brewery that produces fewer than 6 million barrels of beer annually (Brewers Association, 2011). The craft beer industry consists of four markets: brewpubs, microbreweries, regional craft breweries and contract brewing companies. These sites are appearing around the world and attracting a growing following of 'beer hunters' who travel to collect these craft beers as souvenirs. In his study of beer tourism in the USA, Alonso (2011) suggests legislation changes in Alabama allowed the establishment of a craft and micro-brewing sector across the USA (see the following Case Study). His study gives the perspective of six 'nascent' entrepreneurs and how drink tourism is encouraging an entrepreneurial spirit, illustrating how food and drink facilitate enterprise and 'creative tourism' (Richards, 2011a).

Craft Beer Case Study: Loudoun County, Virginia

The craft beer industry is currently undergoing extraordinary growth across the USA. In 2012, there were almost 2,400 craft breweries throughout the country and the retail sale of craft beer generates $14.3 billion in sales annually (Goddard, 2015). However, the Commonwealth of Virginia, located firmly in the 'Bible Belt' has traditionally regulated alcohol production and distribution, limiting the opportunities for craft beer sales. This changed in 2012 when the General Assembly allowed breweries to sell their product for on-site consumption (Commonwealth of Virginia, 2012). Today, nearly 100 breweries are open around the state resulting in $623 million economic impact for Virginia (Virginia Craft Brewers Guild, 2015).

Loudoun County neighbours the Washington, DC metropolitan area and consists of a densely populated suburban area in the east and a rural farming region in the west. The area is known for its superb wine production and boasts over 40 wineries. Since changes in agricultural regulation, Loudoun County now also houses fourteen craft breweries. The dilemma facing Loudoun County is whether to combine a new craft beer trail with the existing wine trail as a means to promote more tourism to the area. In 2014, Loudoun County conducted a survey to better understand the craft beer visitors and to determine whether this emerging market is similar to the typical wine tourists they already attract. Their results showed that craft beer tourists are generally nine years younger than wine tourists (averaging 39.5 years of age), mostly male (66%) and married (68%). Furthermore, while craft beer tourists to the area reported above-average incomes, they were substantially lower than other studies of wine tourists (Alebaki and Iakovidou, 2011; Pratt, 2011). Nearly 75% of the survey respondents reported visiting three breweries during their visit to Loudoun County; 58% reported staying overnight; and reported spending, on average, $290 per visit. These tourists also participated in local culinary dining (68%) and outdoor recreational activities (50%).

This study is one of the first to provide an understanding of the distinct traits of craft beer tourists, a profitable emerging market niche that is growing in Virginia. Loudoun County has promoted itself as DC's Wine Country for many years, and the addition of craft beer to the tourism offer appears to be a natural partnership. In 2015, a local winery hosted a 'Beer, Bacon and Pig' event as a partnership between the wineries and breweries. However, their research shows that craft beer tourists are different from wine tourists, requiring Loudoun County to promote each drink trail separately to appeal to the different market segments.

For more information, see Visit Loudoun's website at www.visitloudoun.org (Loudoun County, 2014)

Case study kindly contributed by Susan L. Slocum, George Mason University, USA.

WHISKY TOURISM

Whisky tourism illustrates the multi-layered nature of special interest tourism (see Chapter 4). It is closely associated with Scotland, although distilleries are appearing around the globe. However, in Scotland the whisky tourism industry is a success story like no other, growing exponentially since the 1960s. Like the wine tourism industry in Australia, New Zealand, South Africa and Italy, the Scottish whisky tourism industry is now extremely experienced in promoting its brand through experiential and highly engaging methods. Whisky is very effectively promoted to visitors at on-site facilities which fosters long-term relationships with brands and builds powerful connections to places (McBoyle and McBoyle, 2008).

CASE STUDY

Whisky tourism in Scotland

The Scotch Whisky and Tourism report commissioned by the Scotch Whisky Association (2011) identified a 'distillery effect' that describes the formation of tourism and cultural clusters in production areas. In 2015, 115 distilleries were licensed to produce Scotch whisky and over half had established visitor facilities. The report found around 1.3 million visitors visited 52 Scotch Whisky visitor centres and distilleries in 2010; 86.1% of them came from outside of Scotland and 62.3% from outside of the UK. The report found that visitor centres and distilleries provided 640 jobs, and £30.4 million in value to the economy (GVA). Nearly £14 million is generated in income for employees across Scotland with overall turnover of £47.7 million. The May 2015 report (www.scotch-whisky.org.uk/news-publications/news/scotch-whisky-distilleries-attract-around-15-million-visitors/) found more than 1.5 million people were coming to visit, spending a total of almost £50 million in 2014 on tours and in their shops and cafés, up from £27 million in 2010. The average spend per visitor in 2014 was around £32.50.

In terms of indirect benefits, the report found that clusters of tourism and culture-related activities developed around whisky distilleries, which supported an additional 60 jobs in the local community and an additional 70 jobs in accommodation around each distillery. Scotch whisky also accounts for around a quarter of UK food and drink exports, with every £100 million of Scotch Whisky exports associated with £20.6m of direct tourism spending, so with exports of more than £3bn, the industry could be said to generate £640m of direct tourism. After accounting for multiplier effects, the overall impact exceeds £1 billion each year (Scotch Whisky Association, 2011). For example, Laphroaig Distillery Visitor Centre received visitors from at least 61 different nationalities from June 2010 to May 2011; the Arran distillery has a visitor centre and offers a wonderful tasting experience after the tour (see Figure 17.7).

FIGURE 17.7 *A 'wee dram of whisky' at the end of a tour at the Arran Distillery, Scotland. Photo by author*

In addition to the distilleries themselves, the whisky trails in Scotland are some of the most well-known whisky tourism experiences. They have been used as conceptual vehicles to explore a number of key tourism concepts, from heritage to olfactory engagement, from entrepreneurship to industry collaboration, and from marketing strategies to 'serious leisure' (Spracklen, 2011). These trails have become heritage attractions in their own right (see Chapter 15). These 'themed routes' (Richards, 2007) offer cultural heritage experiences that help spread tourism demand and utilise the whisky resources around the country; packaging distilleries to create a new collaborative offering (Martin and McBoyle, 2006; McBoyle and McBoyle, 2008). Whisky routes also illustrate the concept of the 'tastescape' (see Chapter 10). The promotional material for the Scottish trails claims that,

> whisky tasting is done principally with the nose – a far more acute organ than the tongue, although the two interrelate as the sample is swallowed. While there are only four primary tastes, there are 32 primary smells. These are aromatic volatiles, which are detected by a small fleshy bulb called the Olfactory Epithelium, located at the back of our noses and having a direct link to the brain. (www.maltwhiskytrail.com, 2015)

Critical Reflections: Habermasian rationalities in whisky tourism and ale tourism

Spracklen uses Habermasian rationalities in his studies of both whisky tourism and ale consumption. Habermas, the German sociologist known for his work on theories on communicative rationality and the public sphere, is referenced in this work to add new perspectives to these forms of touristic activity and engagement. Habermas is associated with the Frankfurt School, and focuses on the foundations of social theory and epistemology. Spracklen (2011) suggests that in critical studies of leisure, there have been three key theoretical projects applying a Habermasian lens: Scambler (2005) to understand the development of modern sport and its relationship to commodification; Morgan (2006) who used normative ethics of communicative agency to propose a new morality in sport; and Spracklen (2009) who used Habermas's rationalities to explore leisure at the end of modernity. The fundamental Habermasian concern is to protect the project of modernity and provide a new critical approach to understanding society.

Habermas is adopted to help understand the tensions between agency and commodification in whisky tourism around Scotland (Spracklen, 2011). Spracklen claims that whisky tourism is part of Scotland's wider tourism because of the globalisation of blended whisky products, but also because of the quest for the supposedly authentic cultural experience of single malt. He explores the (re)inventions of space, history and place associated with the Highlands and west coast of Scotland and the unofficial whisky trail of distillery visitor centres. He adopts the theoretical framework of Habermasian rationalities to look at tensions between agency and commodification in the authenticity-in-tourism literature. Using the lens of whisky tourism, he argues that the globalisation and commodification of tourism, and the communicative backlash against these trends typified by the search for authenticity, is representative of a Habermasian struggle between two irreconcilable rationalities (Habermas, 1984 [1981]; 1987 [1981]). Following research at several distilleries including Arran (see Figure 17.7), Spracklen suggests that whisky tourism is experienced through an apparatus of Habermasian instrumentality, where authenticity is marketised and 'whisky tourists are still caught in a dialectic of control' (2011: 114).

A similar approach is used in his study of ale tourism (Spracklen et al., 2013), assessing the social and cultural value of real ale to tourism in the north of England. Through ethnographic work and research on real ale tourism, despite its origins in the logic of capitalism, Spracklen claims that they become spaces where people can perform Habermasian, communicative leisure. Spracklen finds that real ale fans demonstrate agency in their performativity. Habermasian theories are used to examine the relationship between leisure choices, the search for authentic food and drink, and tourism. Looking at cultures of consumption and the shaping of identities and social order in tourism, he suggests that leisure choices express individual agency around the maintenance of taste, boundaries, identity and community: what Spracklen identifies as a Habermasian struggle over the lifeworld between communicative rationalities and instrumental rationalities. Drinking alcohol is both a marker of belonging associated with the construction of gendered identities and a strategic use of leisure space that excludes others

Spracklen states that leisure in late modernity is increasingly the product of a Habermasian instrumentality, the logic and practice of global capitalism, neo-liberalism and Western hegemony. Real ale and whisky tourism are examples of leisure practices and spatial performances that, to use Habermas's (1987 [1981]) framework, are both communicative and instrumental. Those who become beverage tourists do so because they feel that real ale or whisky is an expression of authenticity, real food, small capitalism and locality.

CASE STUDY

Luang Prabang Whisky Village in Laos

Whisky tourism is not just about Scotland; it is growing in countries that may not have the same history with whisky, but nevertheless have a thriving industry following strategies to harness the benefits of this niche tourism offer. For example, Laos is home to the 'whisky village' and it has become a 'must-see' stop for many visitors to Laos. In Luang Prabang, whisky is produced from fermented sticky rice called *lao lao* (see Figure 17.8). This is a key part of the Laos tourist trail, where bottles of *lao lao* are sold, some containing snakes, scorpions and insects. Such items are sold to tourists, offering doubtful medical properties.

FIGURE 17.8   *Tasting in Luang Prabang Whisky village Laos. Credit: Julie Pottinger*

TABLE 17.1 *Categories and examples of beverage tourism*

Attraction type	Tea	Coffee	Whisky	Beer
Factories	Tea estate factories	Coffee factory tours and tasting rooms e.g. www.stonecreekcoffee.com/tours, www.tannacoffee.com,	Distilleries	Factory tours, e.g. Guinness, micro-breweries
Tours	Tea tours (e.g. www.worldteatours.com)	Plantation	Guided tours around distilleries	Tour guides, Bavarian 'Bier-Tour durch Munchen', or in Belgium 'bellmen' (Ghent)
Trails and routes	Tea trails, e.g. www.teatrails.com	Coffee routes – even local ones from coffee shop to coffee shop	Whisky trails, e.g. Scottish Malt whisky tour	Beer trails, e.g. Waterloo–Wellington Ale Trail, Canada, Scottish Stockport Ale Trail
Retail	Souvenirs of teas	Coffee pots, jugs, percolators	Bottles of whisky	Beer factory shops – beer accessories (glasses, bottles, mats)
Fixed attractions (museums)	Museums, interpretative centres, tea estates, e.g. Ceylon Tea Museums	Coffee museums, centres and exhibitions	Whisky museums	Museums (e.g. Plzen Brewery Museum, Saku) and largest/smallest/highest pubs in the world – Pub Na Spilce in Plzen – the largest pub in the world
Hospitality/service	Afternoon tea, tea ceremonies	Coffee shops, bars, and houses	Pubs	Public houses, alehouses
Accommodation	Tea bungalows, tea gardens	Coffee plantations	Whisky inns, e.g. www.whiskyinn.com/	Public houses with rooms, brewhouses,
Recreational activities	Tea trekking	Coffee plantations walks	Whisky tasting	Beer weekends, tastings, races, e.g. Beerarium-Offers spa and beer therapy treatments. Also beer marathon in Lithuania beer bike competition (Houston, USA)

NICHE BEVERAGE TOURISM: CIDER AND SAKE

Beverage tourism is an extremely varied form of niche tourism. It seems that
regions with any kind of drink production have attempted to develop a tourism
product, and the options do not stop at tea, coffee, whisky and beer. Examples
include tourism based around sake (fermented rice wine) in Japan, or cider
(alcoholic juice from fermented apples), popular in England, France and Spain.
These niche drink experiences are helping countries and regions further differentiate themselves, and provide marketing approaches that meet growing consumer
groups and interests, and foster discourses of heritage, tradition and identity.
For example, Sharples (A.E., 2003: 57) finds that individual cider producers in
Somerset, UK 'have utilized tourism as a means of establishing a closer relationship with their customers and maintaining, or even growing their sales base'.

The findings and importance of marketing such experiences are echoed in
attractions such as the Cider Workshop (www.ciderworkshop.com), and around the
Herefordshire Cider Route (www.ciderroute.co.uk), which includes the Weston's
Cider experience, demonstrating the entrepreneurial and innovative strategies
employed to grow interest and market share (Augustyn, 2000). In Spain, tourists
can enjoy the Basque Cider Museum (www.sagardoetxea.com), which states:

> The perfect accompaniment to Basque cuisine is the locally produced
> cider. It is one of the region's oldest traditional drinks, a tradition that
> can be savoured in every sip, whether it's from a bottle sipped in a
> glass clinked together in a friendly toast or whether it's straight from
> the 'txotx' or barrel.

This seems to capture the idea that 'tradition can be savoured in every sip'; a sentiment at the heart of food and drink tourism (Everett and Aitchison, 2008; Sims,
2009). Whether local hops, rice or apples, these products are steeped in history and

tradition and represent marketing opportunities. As Sharples (2003: 58) states, 'the realization of a food or drink product that has an unmistakable link to a geographical area can be a powerful tool for both individual businesses and the region as a whole', an idea supported by Muñoz de Escalona (2011) who uses the term 'cider culture' to describe how Asturias has formed a rich folk tradition around cider, including apple cultivation, cider processing, and cider consumption in its public celebrations. Like other drinks, these offerings can enhance brand image, sell more produce and build longer purchasing relationships with the consumer. In return, tourists gain a sense of experiencing something 'authentic' and engage in something different, unique and set apart from others (Kim and Jamal, 2007; Zhu, 2012).

Similar concepts about heritage, identity and tradition can be found in sake. There are about 1,300 sake breweries in Japan (www.japansake.or.jp/sake/english). Although very few are currently set up for tourism, this is rapidly changing as producers see the benefits experienced by whisky distilleries. For example, Fushimi's traditional sake-brewing district has been designated as one of 'Kyoto's top 100 scenic areas' (www.gekkeikan.co.jp/english/products/museum), and the Nada district offers the Hakutsuru Sake Brewery Museum where tourists learn the process of sake brewing. Sake tourism is another demonstration of how a beverage becomes symbolic of a nation's people and history, offering a unique 'tastescape' for discerning tourists.

PROVIDING BENEFITS TO LOCAL COMMUNITIES AND SUSTAINING LIVELIHOODS

It has been noted by Wolf (2006) that food and drink are some of the most overlooked components of the travel experience, yet offer the greatest potential for further research on their contribution to global industries, offering significant potential as instruments of social and economic change to low-income families and communities. Many of the beverages discussed in this chapter are supplied by developing nations, especially tea and coffee. There is a clear pattern that producing countries are often the poorest nations, and the consuming countries those in the developed (Western) world. Farming does not always provide enough income for living, and therefore tourism experiences such as opening farms or plantations for visits or guided tours by local villagers can provide valuable income and routes into formal education. In the earlier chapters, Fair Trade tourism and pro-poor tourism were outlined, but buying through direct trade is perhaps the shortest supply chain you can support as a tourist. Valuable income and living wages are increasingly difficult to gain in some of the least developed countries through export earnings, so food and drink tourism encourages the visitor to travel to the original source (Baffes, 2006). In turn, this supports sustainable development in less developed countries and provides steady and proportionate income (Tourism Concern, 2005).

Jolliffe (2007) suggests that where tea-growing communities are experiencing life below the poverty line, they seek to penetrate pro-poor tourism through the implementation of community-based tourism projects. Given its turbulent history, Sri Lanka was slow to embrace this (Jolliffe and Aslam, 2009), but has since sought to support low-income rural families through cooperatives to practise sustainable land use, through the Sri Lanka Ecotourism Foundation (SLEF). This has included diversification into tourism offerings, presenting itself as 'the pioneer national ecotourism organization, dedicated to promote ecotourism in Sri Lanka and to build a strong and professional Ecotourism Network in the Asia-Pacific Region' through the 'noble ideals and principles of Ecotourism' (SLEF, 2015).

Coffee is said to be one of the most valuable commodities in the world, second only to oil. Like tea, it can boost development, stabilise income, provide diversification avenues, and work as a counter to structural and political forces (Karlsson and Karlsson, 2009). Coffee provides a livelihood for 25 million farming families, with coffee accounting for around 75% of their export earnings (International Coffee Organisation (ICO), 2015). With a few exceptions, coffee is produced in developing countries, including a significant number of the most underdeveloped countries. Consequently, tourism is offering much-needed diversification opportunities. The ICO has outlined that the coffee crisis from 2000 to 2004 saw prices fall to their lowest levels in nominal terms since the late 1960s and led to dramatically reduced rural income, the abandonment of plantations, replacement by other crops (including illegal drugs), and migration from rural areas (ICO, 2010). Tourism provides an opportunity to mitigate the effect of such falls. Research indicates that coffee tourism is providing local incomes, with farmers taking good care of the environment and plantations, as these are the attractions and vehicles of income generation (Jolliffe, 2010) (see Figure 17.9).

FIGURE 17.9   *Coffee producer in the coffee village in Bali. Credit Julie Pottinger*

Linked to work by Chesworth (2010) on cooperative coffee tour ventures and corporate social responsibility, Hall (2010b) has also explored the sale of coffee in the context of Fair Trade and tourism, where organisations such as Tourism Concern are ensuring a fair and equitable price is paid for products. A good example of a more explicit link to tourism is given in Goodwin and Boekhold (2010) who look at Tanzania and the Kilimanjaro Native Cooperative Union (KNCU) which supports farmers in developing tourism activities (www.kahawashamba. co.tz). For example, one business developed a coffee tour in which tourists meet the coffee farmer. It is an encounter where tourists can pick berries, separate, roast and grind them and promotes the experience of tourist as 'producer' (see Chapter 19), and where the farmer becomes guide and manager, rather than an invisible producer (see Figure 17.10).

FIGURE 17.10   *Tourist grinding coffee beans during a local tour in Bali. Credit Julie Pottinger*

ACTIVITY   **RESEARCHING OTHER BEVERAGE TOURISM PRODUCTS**

Find and research a beverage tourism product not mentioned in this chapter. What is it? Where is it offered? Outline the customer market. What products are on offer as part of the experience? What opportunities are there for growth of this niche tourism product?

CHAPTER SUMMARY

Beverage tourism studies have looked at a wide range of experiences including whisky tourism, ale tourism, tea tourism, beer tourism and even sake and cider tourism (Jolliffe and Aslam, 2009; McBoyle and McBoyle, 2008; Plummer et al., 2005; Spracklen, 2011, 2013). Beverage tourism offers a multi-faceted vehicle for fostering economic and social investment, and supporting community development. It is a form of heritage and cultural tourism that offers unique diversification opportunities for agricultural and rural communities to earn direct income from tourism and visitors. It is clear that local drink promotion to tourists helps increase consumer exposure, brand awareness and loyalty; develops relationships with customers and increased margins; offers an additional sales outlet; generates valuable marketing intelligence on products, and supports enhanced educational opportunities for host and guest. Through examples from the industry and academic research, this chapter has shown that something as everyday as tea or coffee can become embedded in the history or identity of a place, and from this be transformed in a unique tourism experience through ritual, performance, heritage messaging, marketing and advertising, and visitor interpretation techniques.

END OF CHAPTER POINTS

- Beverage tourism is a growing sector of the niche culinary tourism market and is driven by a tourist desire to seek out unique and authentic cultural experiences.

- There is a plethora of drink-based experiences which range from fixed visitor sites such as museums, to trails, tours, lunches, tastings and accommodation options, such as tea gardens, pubs and coffee plantations.

- Beverage tourism offers many opportunities to showcase connections between products, cultures, peoples, histories and a product brand.

- Tea, coffee, beer, whisky, cider, sake, vodka, and other drinks are increasingly being recognised and adopted as instruments of social change; becoming lucrative and attractive components of new 'tastescapes', innovative tourism experiences and a fresh focus for tourism attractions.

- Beverage tourism is offering much-needed diversification opportunities and income for some of the least-developed nations and the poorest agricultural communities.

FURTHER READING

Jolliffe, L. (ed.) (2007) *Tea and Tourism: Tourists, Traditions and Transformations.* Bristol: Channel View Publications.

Jolliffe, L. (ed.) (2010) *Coffee Culture, Destinations and Tourism* (Vol. 24). Bristol: Channel View Publications.

McBoyle, G. and McBoyle, E. (2008) 'Distillery marketing and the visitor experience: a case study of Scottish malt whisky distilleries', *International Journal of Tourism Research*, 10 (1): 71–80.

Plummer, R., Telfer, D., Hashimoto, A. and Summers, R. (2005) 'Beer tourism in Canada along the Waterloo-Wellington ale trail', *Tourism Management*, 26 (3): 447–58.

FURTHER READING BASED ON CASE STUDY ON CRAFT BEER

Alebaki, M. and Iakovidou, O. (2011) 'Market segmentation in wine tourism: a comparison of approaches', *Tourismos*, 6 (1): 123–40.

Commonwealth of Virginia (2012) *SB 604 Alcoholic Beverage Control Privileges of Brewery Licensees*. Available at: http://lis.virginia.gov/cgi-bin/legp604.exe?121+sum+SB0604. [Accessed: 07/02/2015.]

Goddard, T. (2015) 'The economics of craft beer', *SmartAssets*, 23 Jan 2015. Retrieved 31 January 2015 from https://smartasset.com/insights/the-economics-of-craft-beer.

Loudoun County (2014) *2014 Virginia Craft Beer Visitor Profile Report.* Available at: www.visitloudoun.org. [Accessed 04/05/15.]

Pratt, M. (2011) *Profiling Wine Tourists, More Than Just Demographics*. 6th AWBR International Conference, Bordeaux Management School, 9–10 June 2011.

Virginia Craft Brewers Guild (2015) Virginia Craft Brewers Guild. Available at: http://virginiacraftbrewers.org/default.aspx. [accessed 7/2/2015.]

FURTHER READING ON HABERMASIAN RATIONALITIES

Habermas, J. (1984 [1981]) *The Theory of Communicative Action, Volume One: Reason and the Rationalization of Society*. Cambridge: Polity.

Habermas, J. (1987 [1981]) *The Theory of Communicative Action, Volume Two: The Critique of Functionalist Reason*. Cambridge: Polity.

Spracklen, K. (2014) 'Bottling Scotland, drinking Scotland: Scotland's future, the whisky industry and leisure, tourism and public-health policy', *Journal of Policy Research in Tourism, Leisure and Events*, 6 (2): 135–52.

Spracklen, K. (2011) 'Dreaming of drams: authenticity in Scottish whisky tourism as an expression of unresolved Habermasian rationalities', *Leisure Studies*, 30 (1): 99–116.

Spracklen, K., Laurencic, J. and Kenyon, A. (2013) '"Mine's a Pint of Bitter": performativity, gender, class and representations of authenticity in real-ale tourism', *Tourist Studies*, 13 (3): 304–21.

18

THE ROLE OF FOOD AND DRINK TOURISM IN SUSTAINABLE DEVELOPMENT

CHAPTER OBJECTIVES

- To present 'sustainability' as a contested term and provide definitions of sustainability in the context of food and drink tourism
- To examine how food and drink tourism contributes to the 'triple bottom line' of environmental, economic, and socio-cultural sustainability
- To critique the concept of 'local' in the context of food and drink tourism consumption
- To provide an overview of the concepts of 'weak' (soft) and 'strong' (hard) sustainability discourses against food and drink themes and issues

CHAPTER SUMMARY

This chapter examines how food and drink tourism can create economic, social, cultural and environmental sustainability. It first looks at what sustainability means before drawing on examples to illustrate how food tourism serves to retain and develop traditional heritage, skills and ways of life, thus contributing to sustaining regional identities by enhancing what has become known as the 'triple bottom line' of environmental, economic, and socio-cultural sustainability. The chapter outlines research that finds food tourism offers a means of enhancing and extending tourist spending without destroying the environmental, social or cultural fabric of a region, and gives examples of food tourism strengthening a region's identity; sustaining cultural heritage; contesting globalisation; and facilitating the regeneration of an area's socio-cultural fabric (namely through education, skills development and community engagement).

The chapter also discusses aspects of environmental sustainability from the perspective of food miles, reduced carbon emissions, promotion of seasonal and local foods, and reducing mechanised production. Whilst there is evidence that food and drink promotion benefits the triple bottom line, there is also evidence that it leads to environmental damage where local communities are unable to develop or change because tourists want to see 'fossilised' and 'authentic' living. Furthermore, it offers a critical and more challenging perspective to the concept of local food and associated approaches to its promotion and development. It is an opportunity to question the discourses over what is 'local' and explore concepts of food mileage, where 'local' is not necessarily better for the environment if grown out of season or with pesticides (the contested concept of 'local' is also raised in Chapters 20 and 21).

WHAT IS SUSTAINABILITY IN A TOURISM CONTEXT?

The original concept of sustainable development was defined in the 1987 Brundtland report which came out of the World Commission on Environment and Development (WCED) as 'development seeking to meet the need of the present generation without compromising the ability of future generations to meet their own needs' (WCED, 1987: 8), and was recognised by the United Nations Environmental Programme (UNEP) and United Nations World Tourism Organization (UNWTO). The Commission further emphasised that sustainable development is not a fixed state, but rather dynamic processes of change that 'are all in harmony and enhance both current and future potential to meet human needs and aspirations' (WCED, 1987: 46). It is the concept that we all need to protect and secure the future of 'people, planet and profit'.

Since the late 1980s, 'sustainability' has become a buzzword in development studies and tourism research (Liu, 2003). Maxey argues that sustainability is socially constructed and that is one of its greatest strengths as an analytical concept, because 'sustainability encourages us all to consider what we want to sustain and to assess the ways we wish to go about this' (Maxey, 2007: 59). In tourism research, five major principles have been presented on sustainability: environmental preservation, economic wellness, social justice, institutional reform and inclusive policy development (Richards and Hall, 2003). The World Tourism Organisation (UNWTO, 2001) defined sustainable tourism development as follows:

> Sustainable tourism development meets the needs of present tourists and host regions while protecting and enhancing opportunities for the future. It is envisaged as leading to management of all resources in such a way that economic, social and aesthetic needs can be fulfilled while maintaining cultural integrity, essential ecological processes, biological diversity and life support systems. (2001: 1)

In the 'Critical Reflections' box at the end of the chapter, the concepts of 'strong' and 'weak' sustainability are described to illustrate how sustainability is highly multi-dimensional and multi-layered. In brief, there are a number of interpretations of this strong/weak categorisation. Neumayer (2003) suggests that 'strong' sustainability implies that human capital and natural capital are complementary, but not interchangeable and not substitutable, so this strong 'non-substitutability paradigm' indicates we must conserve our natural resources. Neumayer (2003) refers to 'weak' sustainability as the 'substitutability paradigm', in which human capital is regarded as being able to substitute for natural resources to sustain life (see Critical Reflections box for details). From a slightly different stance, Opio-Odongo (2003) suggests that 'strong' sustainability implies that the economy must be constrained by basic ideology and institutional changes as regards economic growth, the environment, culture and society. Yet 'weak' sustainability focuses on observable impacts on the environment and suggests the environment can be controlled through human intervention, such as strategies like 'carrying capacity' and implementing thresholds.

From a food tourism perspective, Bramwell (1994) argues that gastronomic sustainability in tourism studies should be considered just as important as environmental sustainability, economic sustainability, cultural sustainability and political sustainability. Further, Scarpato (2002: 140) claims that 'gastronomy studies adds a missing perspective to the quest for sustainable tourism'. Food is central and, in looking towards sustainability and key sectors, it is worth remembering that food is never far away in any study of society. After all, 'Food touches everything. Food is the foundation of every economy. It is the central pawn in political strategies of states and households' (Counihan and van Esterik, 1997: 1).

Like the umbrella concept of sustainability, there is no consensus regarding the definition of 'sustainability' in food and drink tourism, but it is helpful to adopt the concept of a triple bottom line of environmental, economic, and social sustainability (Everett and Aitchison, 2008). Sims (2009) also claims that there are three key aspects (or pillars) for sustainability in culinary tourism. These are the *environmental* (reducing the carbon footprint), the *economic* (buying local food to increase tourist expenditure), and the *socio-cultural* (developing a local identity). Yurtseven (2011) describes this holistic approach as 'sustainable gastronomy', where every aspect of the food experience needs to be considered and be sensitive to the environment when offering an experience. Yurtseven and Karakas (2013) put forward the concept of 'sustainable gastronomic tourism' which focuses attention on agricultural and culinary factors to promote food tourism. Although discussed in this chapter as environmental, economic and socio-cultural, they are interlinked and Gössling et al. (2011) and Hjalager and Johansen (2013) suggest that food production easily bridges the gap between the three sustainability dimensions, and therefore blurs any differences that might lead us to consider them as separate spheres.

Sidali et al. (2013: 1) offers seven dimensions that elevate food products to an appealing culinary niche which could enhance rural tourism without altering historically, socially, and environmentally layered culinary traditions: coherence, anti-capitalistic attitude, struggle against extinction, personal signature, mutual disclosure, rituals of spatial and physical proximity, and sustainability-related practices. However, Slocum and Everett (2014) suggest that there is a lack of consensus on the practicality of sustainability principles in terms of application by organisations and industry sectors. Given that there is no concrete definition of sustainable development, the goals within any food tourism policy framework may be unrealisable. Although local food is regarded as central for the sustainable development of the regional food tourism offer, the very concept of 'local' is often adopted uncritically. Rather, all aspects from cultivation, through to production, distribution and consumption should address and acknowledge the economic, environmental, cultural and social demands of sustainable development (Wang, 2015). Too often, food tourism may only be regarded as 'consumption', which is the final part of a complex story.

ENVIRONMENTAL SUSTAINABILITY: 'PLANET'

In turning to the pillars of sustainability, the first to be considered is the environmental. There is an obvious paradox here in food tourism because at the very heart of tourism is the concept of people travelling (usually using high carbon-emission transport modes such as cars and 'planes) to get to a location before they then eat the food. Food tourism may be environmentally sustainable on the local level (seasonal, no food miles, bought from producer), but it may not be sustainable from a global point of view if people are travelling around the world to enjoy it. We know that human travel is a significant element in carbon-footprint calculations (Whittlesea and Owen, 2012), and yet this is often overlooked in food tourism studies. However, if we accept that people will travel, there is still a significant amount to be gained if tourists buy produce from the region they are travelling to. Pretty et al. (2005) found that agricultural and food produce accounts for 28% of goods transported on UK roads, currently imposing estimated external costs of £2.35 billion/year on the consumer. Although this transport secures jobs, the environmental implications of transporting foods via processing to retail outlets and then to the point of consumption is significant if compared to the cost of people travelling to the 'local' producer whilst in that region.

Gössling et al. (2011) indicate that food service providers and tourism services need to be closely linked to environmental issues and global climate change, and the industry needs to find ways to reduce carbon and waste for food service providers. Sustainability in promoting food and drink tourism involves thinking about the environmental impact of each and every stage of its production, and not just transportation or the people who travel to enjoy it. The elements that need to be considered in the wider concept of environmental sustainability include growth (the use of pesticides or fertilisers that can destroy and disrupt the natural ecosystem), preparation (the energy used in cooking and processing it), seasonality (ensuring products do not use energy unnecessarily if out of season or not native to the country, i.e. avoiding greenhouse heating costs or excessive water resources where they might be scarce), transporting the elements for the food (reduce food miles), using suitable packaging (recycled and reused) and ensuring waste is dealt with appropriately (recycle, reuse and reduce it). So fruit and vegetables may be local, but are often cultivated in large glasshouses requiring lots of water and fuel so that food can be harvested out of season (see Figure 18.1).

FIGURE 18.1 *Peppers being grown in heated greenhouses, British Colombia. Photo by author*

Everett and Aitchison (2008) found that purchasing local food at farm shops, festivals and other food outlets was acknowledged as an important channel in reconnecting the tourist with the landscape and reducing the negative environmental impact caused by excessive food mileage, carbon emissions and transportation. One example of this thinking was the UK 'Eat the View' strategy (Countryside Agency, 2002, see Chapter 20), which built on a concept of 'reconnection': linking consumers with the countryside by encouraging them to purchase locally, stating 'we are looking at the potential to market products that will help to sustain the special qualities of England's protected areas' (2002 10). This was substantiated by Enteleca Research (2001: 21) that found that 65% of holiday-makers believed purchase of local produce helped the local environment and 59% were interested in buying local food. In Danish national parks, Hjalager and Johansen (2013) also found opportunities to combine environmental protection and an agricultural revitalisation strategy through food tourism.

ECONOMIC SUSTAINABILITY: 'PROFIT'

Turning to the second pillar of economic sustainability, food tourism has been regarded as a vehicle that promotes direct sales, helps tourist-generated income circulate in the local economy for longer, develops and sustains local employment, encourages entrepreneurship, and provides valuable income. Food and drink tourism can directly contribute to the survival of distinctive and uniquely local traditions, whilst also ensuring an adequate income for suppliers and producers (Hall et al., 2003). Direct income from tourists is enjoyed by many producers around the world who would not have the social or economic capital to get involved in global distribution or large commercial supplier contracts. An example is shown in Figure 18.2; these small-scale farmers now supply the many cookery schools, tourism tours and hotels in Hoi An, an offering that did not exist 20 years ago. Many of the benefits have been included in previous chapters (see Chapters 5, 8 and 13).

In terms of employment, food tourism is encouraging people to sustain food traditions and skills by learning about the processes through tours, and buying straight from the producer. It encourages the development of new skills, facilitating the continuation of local crafts and fostering the reinvention of

FIGURE 18.2 *A local fruit and vegetable market seller, Hoi An, Vietnam.* *Photo by author*

traditional foodstuffs. In stimulating sustainable gastronomy, food and drink tourism has also assisted the retention of a local food identity and struggling farms and rural businesses have been saved through tourism engagement (Sims, 2009). Everett and Aitchison (2008) find food tourism has a role to play in re-educating and training the younger generation, and reviving skills as risk of being lost. For example, fishing in the south-west of the UK has been affected by draconian fishing quotas and regulation, but tourism has provided a vehicle to supply local hotels, restaurants and markets. Skills are being passed on to youngsters and there are funds from tourism to support re-education, skills and people in agriculture. Clearly, better use of tourist income and improved formal education is key to developing a better-educated local workforce that will sustain the next generation in traditional industries.

Cuba and Hummon (1993) claimed that the culture and identity of communities are often bound up in the very industries being lost, but food tourism is going some way in ensuring the survival of small farms and sustaining ways of life (Garrod et al., 2006; Gössling et al., 2011). Food and drink tourism has a more profound influence than simple geographic and economic figures can suggest. With family farms being seen as the glue holding rural communities together, and where diversification often offers a clear route to survival, tourism is a way that small producers, family businesses, and farmers can extend activities beyond growing crops and rearing animals to include tourism activities, such as stays, trips and shops. One example of a project that has proved extremely successful in terms of local economic development and community job creation is the Eko Mosaik social enterprise operating in Bosnia Herzegovina.

CASE STUDY

Eko Mosaik social enterprise in Bosnia Herzegovina

Eko Mosaik is situated in the hills of Bosnia Herzegovina and adopts a similar approach to ecotourism initiatives in the Philippines (Okazaki, 2008) and Botswana (Mbaiwa and Stronza, 2010). All these projects focus on good governance to reach sustainability goals, through a 'bottom-up' tourism agenda that links social capital creation to stakeholder participation.

With rural development grants from the government and overseas agencies such as USAid, Eko Mosaik offers local people employment (mainly women who have lost husbands and fathers in the civil war 1992–95), and a chance to earn their own income and develop skills. It welcomes tourists and seeks to create thriving rural communities by enhancing the local environment, economy and culture in ways that can be enjoyed by hosts and guests (Clark and Chabrel, 2007).

The Director's enthusiasm is infectious, and she is keen to explain that their main focus is on local job creation. They have created jobs in one of the poorest and

FIGURE 18.3 *The Eko Mosaik sign welcomes visitors, Bosnia Herzegovina. Photo by author*

FIGURE 18.4 *Tourist visitors are given a tour where the bee hives are made, Bosnia Herzegovina. Photo by author*

most rural communities in Bosnia. It is run by the Mosaik Foundation and uses food and income from visitors to provide sustainable jobs and finance community projects for the young and disabled. With a greenhouse area of just over 5,000 square metres for the cultivation of seedlings, it is one of the largest greenhouses of its type in the country and uses the latest environmental approaches to watering and heating. Around 70 women from nearby villages are employed (Eko Mosaik has employed more than 160 seasonal workers during its existence). They are the largest individual owner of bee colonies in the country and employ seven professional beekeepers, who all use organic approaches to honey production (see Figure 18.4). Tourists are welcome and income is reinvested in further development. In recognition of its ethics and responsible approaches, it received an award from the Schwab Foundation and the World Economic Forum (Davos).

Further details: www.ekomozaik.ba (will need translating)

SOCIAL SUSTAINABILITY: 'PEOPLE'

The Eko Mosaik project is not only a good example of a sound economic project, but in meetings its goals it supports people, communities and social justice. Sustainability is a transition and learning process that incorporates elements of adaptive management, such as collective learning, stakeholder engagement, environmental adaptation and social justice. Everett and Slocum (2013: 790) suggest that:

> food tourism studies must foster a multi-agency approach and acknowledge the importance of nurturing social capital within a connected supply chain and integrated regional policy arena to ensure food tourism can truly help underpin a sustainable economy.

The model they develop is helpful to see how food tourism development fits within a social and environmental sustainability framework. Based on de Boer and Heuting's (2004) key sustainability principles (a strong and just society, good governance, sustainable economy, working within environmental limits and using sound science responsibly), the model links these to five themes of social capital: embracing knowledge exchange and networking; supply chain constraints (including consistency in food supply and economies of scale); fear of change; regionalisation of governing bodies; and marketing, all within a food tourism context (see Figure 18.5). In seeking sustainability for food and drink tourism in line with the principles outlined above, the model makes three recommendations to help improve the effectiveness of food tourism initiatives: developing distribution networks; undertaking joint marketing campaigns; and promoting engagement with new reforms (Everett and Slocum, 2013: 804) .

FOOD AND DRINK ATTRACTIONS AND EVENTS

The principle behind the model is that increased social capital between sectors will realise key sustainability principles through food tourism and address the major challenges identified, including a lack of knowledge, competing promotion and ineffective supply chain networks. It is argued that a high level of social capital can facilitate the diffusion of information and lower transaction costs, which are central in the delivery of food and drink tourism. The concept of social justice must be central to discussions about sustainability, offering equal opportunity for all those involved in tourism initiatives and the equitable distribution of benefits.

Mooney (2004) claims social justice and nurturing social capital can in turn help to reduce conflict over resource use, further enhancing the sustainability of environmental and economic advancements (see Chapter 15). Alternative food

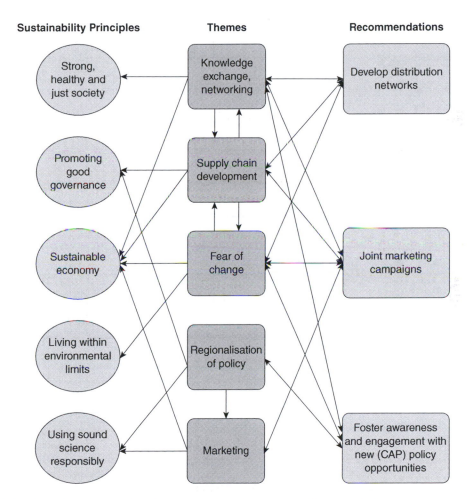

FIGURE 18.5 *Reproduced model of food tourism challenges and recommendations against sustainability principles in Everett and Slocum (2013). Permission given as author's own work. Credit:* Journal of Sustainable Tourism

networks have been extensively examined and theorised in agri-food research (Holloway et al., 2007; Lockie and Kitto, 2000; Sage, 2003). The relevance here is how networks act as vehicles of social resistance, particularly at an informal level, because social networking is vital in helping producers find avenues of influence to retain local food identities. In focusing on taste, quality and culture, artisans are actively seeking to displace the iron law of price. Placing themselves in spaces that fall between sites of resistance and exploitation, individual/community pride is fostered whilst ensuring businesses remain viable.

CULTURAL SUSTAINABILITY AND IDENTITY

Although not directly mentioned as a pillar of sustainability, the 'cultural' often falls under the social. We have seen in Chapter 13 that food tourism events can offer instruments of education and culinary transmission. Tourism is often regarded as a way of contributing to the survival of distinctive and uniquely local traditions including arts, craft and food; tourists are in a position to help preserve and sustain local craft traditions (Cave et al., 2013). This is also the case with food tourism and its ability to contribute to the emergence and extension of new products and skills. It is increasingly apparent that producers are taking advantage of the growing public interest in food, and old recipes and ways of working are being reinvented (Everett and Aitchison, 2008). Bessière (1998) claimed that local food provides a resurrected effect of memory, an object capable of re-establishing an apparently severed connection to nature and times past. Boniface (2003) echoed this, claiming that people who fear they are losing a connection with the past are travelling to the margins to resist processes of delocalisation through food consumption.

These findings are illustrated by a growth in rural partnerships and acts of sustainability against perceived homogenisation, all noted in food tourism research (Hall et al., 2003; Richards, 2002). For example, Haukeland and Jacobsen's (2001) study on food tourism in Norway is indicative of a rising awareness of the role of food as a heritage ingredient in peripheral tourism. They claim that 'peripheral areas may offer opportunities in terms of imagery based on what is perceived as traditional and authentic food' (2001: 10). Food tourism stimulates and regenerates rural, disadvantaged and peripheral areas and therefore has a role in 'preserving and rejuvenating cultural methods and practices' (Boniface, 2003: 37). After all, 'it is the memory and recreation of such unremarkable things as a herring with onions that puts together a history of people and a place' (Jochnowitz (2004: 112).

Rusher (2003: 193) suggests that food tourism has provided communities with a means of affirming their cultural and regional values and identities, and states that tourism interest in local food festivals is an effective instrument of regional development and sustaining cultural identity. Scarpato (2002) also finds in her analysis of food festivals that 'gastronomic tourism products enhance the local tourism on offer not only by promoting the local gastronomic culture but also by building on diversity, multi ethnicity…' (2002: 132). She adds that these 'promote sustainable gastronomy and can encourage the survival of local food production and the transmission of culinary knowledge'. In a study of the Peak District, Sharples (2003b) found that food attractions encourage the development of new skills, facilitate the continuation of local crafts and foster the reinvention of traditional foodstuffs. Her study of the Chatsworth Farm shop found that new products are being made in the small kitchens; old derelict buildings are converted into workshop spaces for local people, and renewed demand for locally sourced products is keeping farms alive. For example, Caudwell's Mill in Rowsley was left to decay in 1978, but is now a popular tourist attraction (www.caud wellsmill.co.uk). The mill provides an educational resource where visitors learn traditional milling methods as well as offering an example of how food tourism facilitates the conservation of a unique heritage site.

Timothy and Ron (2013a, 2013b) also see heritage cuisine as a tool for socio-economic development and pride, offering cultural integrity and community cohesion in Israel. Another example demonstrating the intersection of food, culture and sustainable agriculture is the small island of Maui in Hawai'i, which offers food tours. Visitors interested in culinary and agricultural tourism take tours of the lavender farm, goat dairy, and an organic farm. Tourists can visit the Kapahu Living Farm on a cultural tour led by native Hawaiian guides, and observe traditional crops, including taro, in the Kipahulu section of Haleakala National Park (http://localtastesofmaui.com). This is one of many global examples of small communities seeking to gain their share of incoming tourist spend to support the region's growing sustainable agriculture movement by offering tourists local cuisine, history and culture.

Although it can strengthen culture and support cultural preservation, research has also suggested that food tourism has the potential to unnaturally fossilise, restrict or commodify ways of life and traditions in the name of cultural sustainability (Greenwood and Smith, 1989). This echoes findings in Everett (2007): 'Food producers found themselves the focus of tourism and increasing expectations on how they should look and behave, even though producers had previously not intended (or wanted) to entertain or educate visitors.' One interviewee was particularly vexed that the dominant images of Ireland as a place of difference and escape meant that tourists expected to see them in 'straw hats living in huts'. This was echoed by another interviewee, a dairy owner, who felt the tourist desire to see an historic culture was perhaps unhelpful (Everett 2007):

> I have a funny feeling that they [tourists] expect to see poverty. In fact I think they expect to see noble poverty. I think Ireland has had the most extraordinary branding in America, we have become very branded, old songs and Celtic mysticism, veracious revolutionaries, the princely arrogance of the noble force: that's what the American Irish come back for and there we all are: overweight, driving around in a Mercedes Benz, ruining our landscapes with totally inappropriate planning.

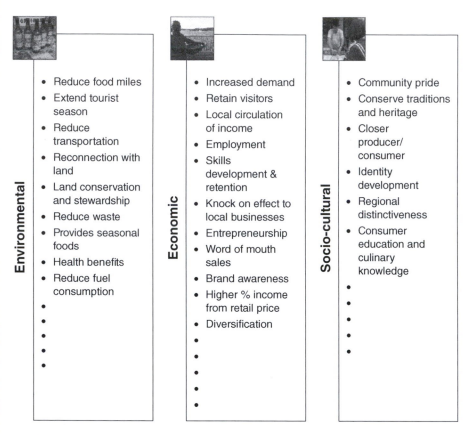

IS LOCAL FOOD REALLY LOCAL?

A lot of the discussion stresses the importance of 'localness', and indeed food tourism marketing relies on the concept of 'local'. However, we should be wary of putting forward a local/global dichotomy (Hinrichs, 2003), as 'local' is a problematic hegemonic discourse and socially contested as a concept and process. The concept of 'local' is as contested as the term 'sustainability' and builds on some of the discussion from Chapter 5 about localisation and globalisation. The concept of local food underpins many food tourism studies (Dougherty et al., 2013; Everett and Aitchison, 2008; Hillel et al., 2013; Kim and Eves, 2012; Moskwa et al., 2015; Sims, 2009) and serves as a local brand identity to show the origin of its primarily produced or processed food (Kim et al., 2009a). Futhermore, Eriksen (2013) talks of 'geographical proximity' and focuses on food miles. For Hall and Wilson (2008) it is about minimising food transportation mileage to ensure 'low carbon' emissions.

Theorising of localisation has become a powerful liberating project for agro-food research, which dilutes the common concept that globalisation is somehow ineluctable. Hines (2000: 4) describes it as 'the ever increasing integration of national economies into the global economy through trade and investment rules and privatisation, aided by technological advances', where 'localisation is a process which reverses the trend of globalisation by discriminating in favour of the local'. There is ambiguity surrounding what people understand as 'local' food and Boniface (2003: 31) also adds that 'local is defined according to perception'. Morris and Buller (2003) suggest it can be understood either in terms of a bounded region within which products are produced and sold, or in terms of 'speciality' or 'locality' foods which are then sold outside the region or country. For example, Sims (2010: 107) asks whether gingerbread (a popular local speciality in the county of Cumbria, UK) can 'ever really be considered a local product in the UK if the sugar and spices used to make it come from overseas?'

Coley et al. (2009) ask whether the carbon emissions of someone who drives a round-trip distance of more than 6 km in order to purchase organic vegetables are greater than the emissions from the system of cold storage, packing, transport to a regional hub and final transport to customer's doorstep used by large-scale vegetable box suppliers. There are clear links to the concept of food tourism where the consumer travels to eat, and research indicates that travelling to local food may well generate more carbon emissions (of course there are always slow tourism transport options such as walking or cycling too). Saunders et al. (2006) looked at food miles from New Zealand and stated that food transported long distances is sometimes perceived as being more harmful to the environment than food from the same country as the consumers. They claim the distance should be assessed, but the total energy used in the process of production to plate including transport is a better and fairer indicator of the environmental costs. Their results show that New Zealand products compared favourably with lower energy and emissions per tonne of product in terms of the whole process to get it delivered to the UK compared to other more 'local' sources.

ACTIVITY   FOOD MILES CALCULATOR

Calculate the food miles of your food and drink. Make a note of the food you eat in one day and where it comes from. Use the food miles calculator (www.foodmiles.com) to see how far your food has travelled. Do the results surprise you? You may also be interested in your own carbon footprint and there is a quick and easy online tool to work this out: www.organiclinker.com. How might you reduce your food miles and your carbon footprint?

'Local' can describe the place of processing, geographical proximity, spatial-lylimited production, local tradition and histories and stories, low carbon, and/or family- and homemade. Ultimately, it is also about trust, community, and a local distribution network. The most local is arguably direct from the grower when it is in season and does not travel using any fuel-powered vehicle (see Figure 18.7, where oranges are sold and squeezed for tourists outside an orchard near Kyrenia in North Cyprus; see also Figure 18.8 outlining the localness of the fish shed in Aldeburgh, UK who sell directly to passing tourists. See Chapter 20).

Sims (2009: 322) suggests that:

> 'local' food and drink products can improve the economic and environmental sustainability of both tourism and the rural host community by encouraging sustainable agricultural and fishing practices, supporting local businesses and building a 'brand' that can benefit the region by attracting more visitors and investment.

There is an increasing desire to buy local and ethically and attendance at farmers' markets and food/fish sheds by visitors from industrialised and economically

FIGURE 18.7 *Direct local income? Oranges being squeezed sold and for passing tourists in North Cyprus. Photo by author*

FOOD AND DRINK ATTRACTIONS AND EVENTS

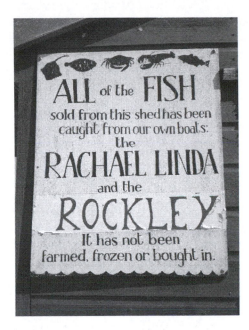

FIGURE 18.8 *Explicit statement that the fish on offer is local in Aldeburgh, UK. Photo by author*

advanced countries is evidencing this growing ethical consumerism (Nabhan, 2009; see also Chapter 13).

In discussing the concept of buying and consuming 'local' food (a concept that underpins the ethical rationale behind food and drink promotion), it is important to look at sustainable food production and not just focus on the consumers and consumption. As Gössling and Hall (2013) suggest, the study of food production (for tourism and more generally) needs to consider land use, biodiversity, ecological systems, the use of fertiliser, greenhouse gas emission and transport. It is not just about the travel and food miles: different foods leave different carbon footprints, are processed differently, and produce different levels of waste (Beer and Lemmer, 2011). It may be possible to cultivate and grow a foodstuff locally in terms of geographical location, but it could involve large-scale production and fuel-heavy processing methods (Eaton, 2008). To achieve local sustainable food tourism, Gössling and Hall (2013) propose that food and tourism should be considered under the framework of 'sustainable food'. However, sustainable food has no formal definition, although similar concepts exist, such as 'green food' in Taiwan, in which health and fairness are central to every stage of production (Wang, 2015). There is a need to look at the whole life-cycle of the process to truly understand what really constitutes 'local' sustainable food tourism. Food tourism may provide the benefit of reviving the local economy (Everett and Aitchison, 2008; Hillel et al., 2013), but can also be dangerous if the food production system does not follow basic sustainability principles (Beer and Lemmer, 2011; Eaton, 2008). It is important to develop a local distribution network and promote 'buying local' (Hall and Wilson, 2008) through networks, social media and marketing activities. At the very least it creates a positive image and market opportunity; 'offering visitors a way to experience some form of authenticity through food can assist the development of sustainable tourism in a number of ways' (Sims, 2009: 333).

To be successful, food and drink tourism initiatives need to support and foster direct channels of distribution that deliver locally targeted benefits, decrease distribution costs, and help producers avoid middlemen (Hall and Wilson, 2008). There is a degree of considering consumer identity and their motivations here. As outlined in earlier chapters, tourists interested in food tourism generally feel they are supporting ethical consumption (Getz et al., 2014). This desire for sustainable consumption is why the branding and marketing that exploits local discourses is so successful, but such messages should not be accepted uncritically. For example, 'all-round sustainable tourism' is difficult to achieve in reality as it involves an impossible balancing act that focuses on achieving social, economic and environmental benefits on the understanding that:

> the best form of tourism would be one which achieves gains on all dimensions and for all groups. It would not, for example, protect the environment by disadvantaging businesses, or benefit businesses at the expense of the host communities. (Clark and Chabrel, 2007: 372)

Critical Reflections: 'weak' and 'strong' sustainability

Weak sustainability has been discussed in environmental economics, putting forward that human capital can substitute natural capital. It is based upon the work of Robert Solow and John Hartwick. The weak sustainability paradigm stems from 1970s neo-classical welfare economics, accounting for non-renewable natural resources as a factor of production. Sustainability can be evaluated based on a 'soft', flexible (weak) standard that allows natural capital (i.e. natural environmental resources and ecological systems) to be replaced by human capital. Turner (1993) finds that weak environmental sustainability is a perception that welfare is not normally dependent on a specific form of capital and can be maintained by substituting manufactured for natural capital with some exceptions. Although weak sustainability measures are better than no measures at all, it is sometimes called the 'substitutability paradigm' (Neumayer, 2003) and is regarded as unhelpful. The concept of weak sustainability attracts a lot of criticism, with some scholars dismissing the entire concept of sustainability altogether. Beckerman (1995) concludes that weak sustainability is redundant and illogical and he effectively launches a demolition attack on its very premise.

'Strong' sustainability assumes that human capital and natural capital are complementary, but not interchangeable and not substitutable. Neumayer (2003) refers to it as the 'non-substitutability paradigm'. It accepts there are certain functions that the environment performs that cannot be duplicated by humans or human-made capital, such as the ozone layer (essential for human existence, and difficult or impossible for humans to duplicate). Strong sustainability puts the emphasis on the ecological over the economic. This implies that nature must be passed from one generation to the next in its original form. Hard/strong sustainability places emphasis on environmental preservation and ecological preservation over industrial growth. Turner (2003) states that strong sustainability derives from a perception that substitutability of manufactured for natural capital is seriously limited by such environmental characteristics as irreversibility, uncertainty and the existence of 'critical' components of natural capital, which make a unique contribution to welfare.

Ekins et al. (2003: 168) claim:

> If sustainability depends on the maintenance of the capital stock, then an important issue is whether it is the total stock of capital that must be maintained, with substitution allowed between various parts of it or whether certain components of capital, particularly natural capital, are non-substitutable, i.e. they contribute to welfare in a unique way that cannot be replicated by another capital component.

Turner (1993) identifies four different kinds of sustainability, ranging from very weak (which assumes complete substitutability) to very strong (which assumes no substitutability at all, so all natural capital must be conserved). Fossati and Panella (2000) also stress the importance of 'irreversibility' with regard to certain critical aspects of natural capital, while 'weak' sustainability allows for the substitution between man-made and natural components. This is an argument unlikely to be resolved. Consider your own views on this controversial debate.

CHAPTER SUMMARY

There is no agreed definition of sustainability, and even less agreement on what constitutes sustainable tourism development, or indeed whether it is even possible with tourists travelling around the globe in such large numbers. However, overall it has been suggested (based on most work on sustainable tourism) that there are three pillars of sustainability to consider: the environmental, economic and the social/cultural. The link with food is clear: food and beverage constitutes around a third of tourism expenditure, and sustainable tourism is only possible when local food production and distribution are linked to food tourism (Dougherty et al., 2013). The additional problem for academics looking at this is what then constitutes 'local', as this is a term almost as controversial and contested as 'sustainability'.

This chapter has sought to outline some of the key relationships and concepts regarding food and sustainability with some examples of social community projects and figures to illustrate 'local' food provision. Overall, food tourism offers a means of supporting declining industries and ways of life, retaining traditional skills, strengthening a region's cultural heritage, encouraging environmental awareness and fostering the outward transmission of regional cuisine, whilst simultaneously countering the inward influence of globalisation (Everett and Aitchison, 2008). The concept of 'localness' and supply chains are discussed in subsequent chapters.

END OF CHAPTER POINTS

- The Brundtland report (1987) defined sustainability as 'development seeking to meet the need of the present generation without compromising the ability of future generations to meet their own needs' (WCED, 1987: 8).
- There is no agreed definition of 'sustainability', but it is helpful to adopt the concept of the triple bottom line of environmental, economic, and social sustainability.
- In thinking about the environmental impact of food tourism, the whole process should be considered in the analysis (not just the transport). These elements include growth, preparing, cooking and processing, transporting, packaging and disposal.
- In terms of economic sustainability, food offers a vehicle to generate direct sales, helps income circulate in the local economy for longer, develops and sustains local employment, encourages (social) entrepreneurship, provides employment and encourages the retention of skills and traditions.
- In seeking sustainability for food and drink tourism, the principles of a strong and just society, good governance, sustainable economy, working within environmental limits and using sound science responsibly should be followed.
- Local food is associated with local culture and rural areas, but there is no agreement on what 'local food' actually means. Local food tourism could have links to a global production system even though its production, processing, transportation and preparation might be more geographically 'local'.

FURTHER READING

Eaton, E. (2008) 'From feeding the locals to selling the locale: adapting local sustainable food projects in Niagara to neocommunitarianism and neoliberalism', *Geoforum*, 39 (2): 994–1006.

Everett, S. and Aitchison, C. (2008) 'The role of food tourism in sustaining regional identity: a case study of Cornwall, South West England', *Journal of Sustainable Tourism*, 16 (2): 150–67.

Everett, S. and Slocum, S.L. (2013) 'Food and tourism: an effective partnership? A UK-based review', *Journal of Sustainable Tourism*, 21 (6): 789–809.

Gössling, S. and Hall, M. (2013) 'Sustainable culinary system: an introduction', in M. Hall and S. Gössling (eds), *Sustainable Culinary Systems*. Abingdon: Routledge, pp. 3–44.

Gössling, S., Garrod, B., Adall, C., Hille, J. and Peeters, P. (2011) 'Food management in tourism: reducing tourism's carbon "foodprint"', *Tourism Management*, 32 (3): 534–43.

Kim, Y.G., Eves, A. and Scarles, A. (2012) 'Empirical verification of a conceptual model of local food consumption at a tourist destination', *International Journal of Hospitality Management*, 33 (1): 484–9.

Sims, R. (2009) 'Food, place and authenticity: local food and the sustainable tourism experience', *Journal of Sustainable Tourism*, 17 (3): 321–36.

Yurtseven, H.R. and Karaks, N. (2013) 'Creating a sustainable gastronomic destination: the case of Cittaslow Gokceada – Turkey', *American International Journal of Contemporary Research*, 3 (3): 91–100.

FURTHER READING ON WEAK AND STRONG SUSTAINABILITY

Beckerman, W. (1995) 'How would you like your "sustainability", sir? Weak or strong? A reply to my critics', *Environmental Values*, 4 (2): 167–79.

Ekins, P., Simon, S., Deutsch, L., Folke, C. and De Groot, R. (2003) 'A framework for the practical application of the concepts of critical natural capital and strong sustainability', *Ecological economics*, 44 (2): 165–85.

Liu, Z. (2003) 'Sustainable tourism development: a critique', *Journal of Sustainable Tourism*, 11 (6): 459–75.

Neumayer, E. (2003) *Weak versus Strong Sustainability: Exploring the Limits of Two Opposing Paradigms*. Cheltenham: Edward Elgar.

19

WHEN CONSUMERS BECOME PRODUCERS

CHAPTER OBJECTIVES

- To problematise the concepts of production and consumption in the context of food and drink tourism
- To explore how the spheres of production and consumption blur to allow the tourist to become a producer
- To examine the concepts of 'co-creation', 'co-production', 'creative tourism' and the growth of 'voluntourism' (volunteer tourism) and 'agri-voluntourism' as examples of productive tourism
- To discuss tourist activities such as 'pick(ing) your own', foraging, and cookery schools to illustrate how consumers (tourists) produce their own tourism experiences

CHAPTER SUMMARY

Food and drink tourism is more than consumption: it can involve tourists as producers as well as consumers. Increasingly, tourists are engaging in work and methods of creation and production of food as part of their leisure and recreational activities. The blurring of production and consumption is theorised in this chapter, where production and consumption are presented as mutually constitutive rather than separate. Many producers who engage with visitors have become food tourism providers, yet tourists are now paying and volunteering to get involved in the 'work' of production, becoming 'co-producers' and 'co-creators'. This relationship is a fascinating example of how food and drink activity is changing leisure patterns and processes; in some spheres, labour has become leisure, production has become consumption.

In discussing the merging and fluidity of the production/consumption spheres, the chapter looks at concepts of co-creation, co-production and the growth of volunteer and working holidays based on agricultural and farm labour (voluntourism). One of the most popular examples of the 'tourist as producer' concept is the growth of cookery and alternative culinary activities which invite tourists to try their hand at skills such as butchery, fish-filleting and cake-decorating. Such activities link closely to the concept of 'creative tourism' and can include making and producing foodstuffs such as wine, cheese, beer and bread. Further, the chapter looks at the rising interest in and use of 'pick your own' fruit and vegetables as a method of farm diversification, as well as a way for the tourist to become closer to the production of food; an interest also illustrated by the popularity of foraging for food such as berries, truffles and seaweeds.

BLURRING PRODUCTION AND CONSUMPTION IN TOURISM

The concepts of production and consumption are often treated as separate entities. Academic writing and literature has tended to reflect this simplistic societal division, where production is associated with work, and consumption with leisure (Jackson and Holbrook, 1995). Ateljevic (2000) suggested that much academic work in tourism had shown a prioritisation of the economic over the cultural, where production and consumption were presented as separate categories of tourism, rather than mutually constitutive. Research into production and consumption in tourism regularly developed economic chains of supply and demand that placed production and consumption as polar opposites. These simplistic linear approaches generally prioritised production over consumption, supporting Bærenholdt et al.'s. (2004: 25) summation that tourism research has long been caught in 'territorial traps and linear metaphors of scale'. Gold and Gold (1995: 22) also advocate that the promotion of tourism must be regarded as more complex than 'a linear chain of cause-and-effect linking production to consumption'. During the 1990s new developments in social and cultural geography opened channels which explored new paradigms and embraced a transformation in how tourism was conceptualised as an encounter. Dualisms such as production and consumption have become openly problematised (Everett, 2012).

In terms of food and drink tourism, it is helpful to critique the theorisation of the production and consumption relationship and look beyond it as a linear and dualistic relationship. It is possible to see that production and consumption are more integrated as the barriers between work and leisure become blurred. Tourists have a co-productive role in developing a food identity and the identity of place. In terms of consumer-as-producer, it is useful to consider that the structures of food delivery and production can be altered in a process of 'productive consumption' (de Certeau, 1988). Fieldwork undertaken by Everett (2007) revealed instances in which consumer and producer agency represented a mutually constructed social resistance (thus further blurring concepts of producer and consumer). A dairy owner explained that both groups work together within an 'interactive tissue' formulated through local food tourism activity, adding that 'it's marvellous what a smart, interesting tourist can do for you' (2007: 248). In thinking of the tourist as a producer, they become an effective agent of change for conservation and creation, not a despoiler of the natural and social environment through consumption alone (Boyle, 2003). If the social interaction between producer and consumer intensifies, food tourism can grow as a sector because confidence levels rise for all those involved in its development and delivery.

CREATIVE TOURISM

Richards (2011a: 1225) has theorised the relationship between tourism and creativity, arguing that there has been a 'creative turn' in tourism studies, where tourists have 'greater involvement with the everyday life of the destination'. Where place-making and co-creation offer a more flexible and authentic experiences for host and tourist, creativity is a means to develop distinction, economic spin-off and authenticity (Zukin, 2010). Although there is no agreed definition, Taylor (1988) groups approaches into '4Ps' of creativity: creativity through the person, process, product and place (the environment). 'Creative tourism' was first mentioned as a potential form of tourism by Pearce and Butler (1993), although they did not fully define the term. Richards and Wilson (2007) suggest the 'creative turn' in the social sciences developed out of the earlier 'cultural turn' in tourism studies.

The United Nations Educational, Scientific and Cultural Organization's (UNESCO) Creative Cities Network (UNESCO, 2006: 3) produced its own definition of creative tourism as:

> travel directed toward an engaged and authentic experience, with participative learning in the arts, heritage, or special character of a place, and it provides a connection with those who reside in this place and create this living culture.

Raymond's (2007: 145) definition of creative tourism from work in New Zealand describes tourist involvement in production very effectively and builds on concepts of sustainability (see Chapter 18), presenting it as:

> a more sustainable form of tourism that provides an authentic feel for a local culture through informal, hands-on workshops and creative experiences. Workshops take place in small groups at tutors' homes and places of work; they allow visitors to explore their creativity while getting closer to local people.

Crewe and Beverstock (1998) claim places are increasingly trying to distinguish themselves through their 'consumptional identities' via the manipulation of culture and creative resources (Richards, 2011a, 2011b). MacCannell (1976) argued that tourism offers opportunities to explore different identities and take on 'new' roles, and it could be suggested that becoming a baker, chef, or farmer allows for this momentary transformation of self, facilitating escape from the everyday. Furthermore, Edensor (2001: 61) notes that:

> the fragmentation of tourist specialisms into niche markets entails a proliferation of stages, activities and identities. The growing social and economic importance of leisure and a blurring between work and leisure in post-Fordist economies further obscures the distinction between tourism and the everyday.

It has been suggested by Richards and Wilson (2006) that creative developments in tourism fall into three basic categories: creative spectacles, spaces and tourism. In terms of creative spectacles for food tourism, these could be food events and festivals (see Chapters 13 and 14) that provide opportunities for the tourist to engage in, and contribute to, creative experiences. Second, creative spaces can be seen in terms of clusters of activity or spaces of creativity that might include food and wine routes and trails, museums and attractions. Finally, creative tourism describes the process of producers meeting consumers, the engagement of visitors in the food and drink process and their role in creating, transforming and influencing offers.

The concept of creative holidays is based on creative tourism discourses, offering hands-on experiences where tourists are encouraged to learn and engage in arts and handicrafts, instead of passively 'consuming' the work or produce of others. Activities that might have previously been just a tour around a tea plantation or brewery are now two-way interactive encounters which provide productive opportunities for tourists to make their own wine, smoke their own meat, mature their own cheese, or brew their own beer or tea. Examples include the Gotthard Cheese Factory at the foot of the Gotthard Pass in Switzerland, which invites tourists to 'Prepare some delicious cheese with your own hands. Starting from fresh milk you are followed in the procedure by a professional cheese maker',[1] or brew your own beer in Prague: 'brewing lasts 9 hours and includes the whole process from crushing through mashing to hopping followed by subsequent cooling of the wort and fermentation. It is possible to brew 50 litres of beer' (www.private-prague-guide. com/prague-beer-experience-brew-your-own-beer).

TOURISTS AS CO-CREATORS AND CO-PRODUCERS

Toffler (1980) talks of 'prosumption' to conceptualise customers' participation in both the production and consumption of the experience, and Meuter et al. (2000)

---

[1] Available from Lugano Tourism (2015) http://luganotourism.ch/en/384/cheese-factory---make-your-own-cheese.aspx

propose the concept of 'co-creation' to reflect the fact that the host and guest are jointly creating value. It has been said that customer satisfaction depends on the degree of customer participation in the production process (Bendapudi and Leone, 2003), yet Prebensen and Foss (2011) argue that few studies have explored how the consumer actually adds value to the final experience of the product, using the concept of 'coping' to explain how tourists act and deal with situations. Furthermore, Prahalad and Ramaswamy (2004: 4) talk about the 'co-creation of unique value' where the consumer has gone from being unaware to informed, and from a passive stance to an active one. A useful way of looking at this transformation in consumer patterns is through the lens of food and drink tourism. With access to more information through the internet, better transport and social media sharing experiences, tourists are now seeking out opportunities that would not have previously had the marketing budget to entice people to visit and stay.

Developing practices of production and consumption are at the forefront of the creative turn, with a symbiotic relationship between a productive drive towards developing new experiences and consumer desires for new sources of 'fun' and distinction (Pantzar and Shove, 2005). Richards (2002) has suggested food tourism has gone beyond just eating and now includes a wide range of courses and experiences aimed at developing cooking and productive skills, which help develop new cuisines, techniques and innovative produce

FIGURE 19.1   *Local homes allow tourists to engage in creative and productive tourism activities such as soya bean grinding, outside Yangshuo, China. Photo by author*

(Cohen and Avieli, 2004; Everett and Aitchison). For example, a brewery owner in Arran, Scotland reported (Everett, 2007: 248):

> It was one of the tourists who then said, 'I think you should think about doing it this way', and that is the way we have done it ever since. Exchange of ideas. I definitely hear things and learn things from customers. Definitely a two-way thing going on there.

There is now co-creation of experiences across activities such as art, music and gastronomy (Williams et al., 2014), and an evolution of cultural tourism towards more engaged and authentic experiences (Fernandez, 2010). Such experiences can lead to the transformation of spaces, which can include a person's home changing into a site of tourist creativity and productivity (see Figure 19.1). The normally private space of the home has been transformed into one of creative production and tourist experience. In a study of Lijang, in north-western Yunnan, China, Wang (2007) refers to the 'customized authenticity' of commercialised versions of such spaces, describing how local hosts renovate their houses to re-create versions of ancient or traditional Chinese living culture and despite being simulations, tourist demand has brought about significant changes in the space and its use.

CASE STUDY

Cook it yourself! Steak houses in Australia

Many restaurants around the world encourage visitors to pick their raw produce and then cook it themselves. This offer includes shared barbecues, boiling water in a steam boat (popular in South East Asia), or a hot plate in the centre of a table. Australia has a long tradition of public houses where people can cook the meat and meal themselves. Examples of this are the 'Kingo' (The Kingston Hotel) in Griffith, Canberra, Australia (http://kingstonhotel.com.au) where 'The Steakhouse invites customers to "Cook your Own" steak', and The Oaks Hotel in Neutral Bay in Sydney (www.oakshotel.com.au), which has been open since 1885 to offer a space where 'guests are invited to prepare it themselves at The Oak's signature cook-your-own steak station'. These venues have become iconic pub settings that facilitate the opportunity for tourists to get directly involved in the production and creation of their food; a clear disruption of the traditional producer–consumption dichotomy.

COOKERY SCHOOLS AND CULINARY CLASSES

Cookery schools as a form of niche tourism were introduced in Chapter 4. Many locations around the world offer culinary classes that teach tourists how to prepare local food, with home cooking classes and homestays providing alternative tourist products that encourage visitors to participate in domestic activities usually unavailable to outsiders (Bell, 2015). Examples of the dizzying array of schools can be found on sites such as www.tastingplaces.com, or a simple internet search for 'cookery schools' will retrieve thousands of examples. Sharples (2003a) has looked at the motivations of people attending cookery schools, acknowledging that working in a kitchen may not appeal to all, but they have increasingly become a popular and attractive tourist activity. A number of cookery schools have been established in South-East Asia (including Thailand, Vietnam, Bali, Indonesia and Malaysia), and Figure 19.2 shows a tourist in Thailand preparing the ingredients before cooking a dish.

FIGURE 19.2 *A cookery school tourist enjoys the produce at a Thai cookery school, Thailand. Photo given with permission. Credit Julie Pottinger*

Landscape, environment and the 'creative space' that Richards (2011a) theorises are important in the examination of cookery schools, given that they are often in rural locations and link the tourist to the produce and origins of the ingredients (farms, markets, the sea). Experiences are then deeply embedded into the culture, traditions and geography of the area in which they are situated (Sharples, 2003b), although increasingly we see cafés, restaurants and shops offering culinary experiences to diversify income, improve their overall brand recognition, drive up sales and boost their reputation. As Figure 19.3 shows, a bakery in Suffolk (UK) advertises its bread-making class to raise its profile, attract additional income and offer visitors a unique experience. There is also undoubtedly a link between rising demand and the increasing numbers of cookery programmes on the television (see Chapter 9).

FIGURE 19.3 *A bakery in Suffolk, UK offering baking classes to visitors. Photo by author*

There is an educational element to the experience, where techniques are learnt and knowledge is gained about produce, recipes and approaches, although it is primarily about fun for the tourist. However, some schools will be intensive and require a high level of skill before even putting on the apron (for example, Le Manoir: see the brief case study in Sharples, 2003a). Brotherton and Himmetoğlu (1997) claim that tourists are increasingly looking for more challenging experiences, and the special interest tourist is now looking at enrolling onto courses to increase their 'cultural capital' (Bourdieu, 1984, Chapter 4), and sense of exclusivity. Cookery holidays are expensive experiences, whether this be undertaking a course like seafood classes in Padstow, Cornwall (£30 for a skills workshop; up to £1,690 for a four-day course), or a market cookery school in Vietnam (approximately £50/day), or a week-long culinary stay in Kerala, India for around £800–£1000. With increased leisure time, disposable income, an interest in knowing where food has come from, and desire for exclusive leisure activities, the growth of cookery schools is set to stay.

Bell's (2015) research is based on her own fieldwork attending *warung* cookery schools in Bali (in people's homes rather than professional separate kitchens), and provides insight into the experience and how tourists are co-creating and producing though a process of 'participant consumption' (Everett, 2012: 2). Tourists are able to occupy spaces that are intimately encountered through immersive physical engagement and activities that demonstrate the value of the sensual economy (Bissell, 2009; Everett, 2009). Bell (2015: 90) outlines the offer: 'The entrepreneurial women running the warung cooking school enterprises used their everyday skills (cookery, hospitality) and facilities (kitchens, dining tables) for "economic empowerment".'

Increasingly, cookery schools are established as vehicles of diversification. Bell (2015) highlights this in her Balinese study, outlining the motivations of the women who run them, described as female entrepreneurs taking advantage of a growing tourist market interested in engaging with something authentic and creative. Bell recalls the importance of the tourist income (2015: 92):

> One warung owner had no signage at all to indicate that she ran classes. She explained that if she advertised in the street, then she would have to pay tax. Her cooking classes came purely from verbal inquiry at her warung or mentioned perhaps as she served food and chatted to guests.

She goes on (2015: 93) to say that:

> Cookery is literally a hands-on activity which takes time … Together, we chopped and stirred, ground and grated, sharing the same small space on the table. Senses were activated as we smelled and tasted; this was certainly beyond the visual gaze.

What Bell outlines in this meal preparation is the tourist as both consumer and producer. Another example is the growing number of cookery classes in Turkey (see the Case Study below).

CASE STUDY

Cookery schools in Turkey, Ozlem's Turkish Table

There is a huge variety of culinary offerings around the world in the form of cookery schools taking advantage of tourists wanting to gain a more immersive experience of different cultures, peoples and places. One such example is Ozlem's Turkish Table, which offers cookery classes in Istanbul, Turkey, plus other locations around the world. She has been teaching Turkish cookery in the

USA, Jordan, Istanbul and England for the past eight years and has a popular Turkish recipe blog. In email correspondence with Ozlem (see Figure 19.4) she stated, 'I am a Turkish culinary expert and teach my passion, Turkish cuisine, through private lessons as well as through cookery schools all around the world'. She explains:

> I love Turkish food and would love to my share my homeland's healthy, delicious, easy Turkish recipes with the home cooks and foodies at my blog. Having lived in Turkey over 30 years, I am also very passionate about the amazing history, landscape and heritage that my country offers. I look forward to sharing photos and stories of my culinary and cultural trips to Turkey and some wonderful Turkish recipes that you can easily create in your home.

During the class, she explains that visitors will see how easy it is to recreate Turkish dishes, 'From courgette fritters with feta and dill to stuffed vine leaves, from aubergines, lentils and peppers cooked in olive oil to Pide'. Like many cookery experiences, more than just cooking it also offers food-inspired boat trips,

FIGURE 19.4 *Ozlem Warren is proud to share Turkish cuisine with culinary tourists. Photo provided with permission by Ozlem Warren*

conversations with producers, heritage walking experiences and food markets.

Source: http://ozlemsturkishtable.com, and via private correspondence.

PICK YOUR OWN (PYO) AND FORAGING FOR FOOD

One component of many cookery school programmes is the opportunity to go out into the fields or rivers to find, catch and pick local produce before even using a knife or saucepan. This concept of 'pick your own' (PYO) has become an increasing popular tourist and recreational activity. If you travel through the countryside or agricultural rural areas in fruit or vegetable growing seasons, you may well see signs promoting 'PYO fruit and/or vegetables'. This illustrates how the tourist can become a producer, in harvesting the fruit, vegetables, fish, etc. themselves, rather than buying pre-picked and packaged food from the farm gate, market or supermarket. For producers, PYO offers important alterative income mechanisms and offerings. In Roth's (1999) study of farming in the USA, he finds the need for alternative marketing channels for farm goods, along with a challenging economic and social climate in the 1960s and 1970s of increased fuel and food prices that made shopping at a farmers' market, farm stands or pick-your-own farms more economical and attractive for consumers.

Consumers increasingly alienated and dissatisfied with produce picked too early for transport to supermarkets turned to local farms for in-season fresh quality, and by the 1970s, direct farm marketing at farm stands, pick-your-own farms, and farmers' markets was well established. PYO has become one of the most popular recreational activities in agri-tourism (farm tourism), as indicated in a study of Virginia by McGehee and Kim (2004). In a study of farmers and owners of rural tourism businesses in Hiroshima, western Japan, Ohe (2002; 2010) found there were increasing numbers of requests from visitors for accommodation and pick-your-own produce. Through interaction with people outside the rural community, the business grew and was able to diversify its income base. From the host's perspective, this new farm activity became a product innovation that reduced the need for employers to pay staff to pick tomatoes and cucumbers, yet it also simultaneously promoted social interaction and achieved what he refers to as 'multifunctionality'.

In terms of the visitor or tourist, PYO meets a number of interests and motivational issues discussed in earlier chapters, such as seeing where the food has originated from (particularly following food scares) and reducing the supply chain. It also offers opportunities for learning, social interaction and closer physical engagement with the land and environment (Boniface, 2003). Tourists are often seeking escape from their urban lives, using PYO as a way to ease the stress by engaging with the countryside and rural lifestyles (Ohe, 2002; 2010). Clarke (2005: 90) talks about activities in rural tourism in terms of a portfolio of attractions, offering 'seeing', 'buying', and 'being' from the leisure consumers' perspective. He claims the 'being/doing' aspect is often neglected and although PYO is put into the 'buying' category, you could argue that getting in amongst the crops with PYO is appealing to tourists who are 'doing' and want to spend their leisure time pursuing self-development and even transformation (being); they therefore get involved with activities that fit with their sense of bodily engagement and 'doing'.

PYO is a good example of 'doing tourism' (Crouch, 1999), where tourists are not just presented as passive consumers, but are active in 'sense-making' where they become co-producers and co-performers in a process of 'productive consumption' (de Certeau, 1988). One could argue that PYO allows tourists to connect to a place in terms of 'feeling, empowerment, attachment and value', illustrating what Harré calls a 'feeling of doing' (1993: 68). Space is intimately encountered through immersive physical engagement and the encounters represent moments of bodily expression that are required to activate and understand places. As outlined in Chapter 10 in the discussion of the 'tourist gaze', food may be mediated materially, but the multi-dimensional experience and sense of place, in its totality, can only be apprehended imaginatively and multi-sensually.

A similar activity that is increasing in popularity and fostering closer engagement with food is foraging. It is perhaps an under-researched aspect of food tourism, but 'foraging-tourism' has become very popular, with numerous organisations offering tours and 'edible walks'. Historically, people have always foraged or fished for food to survive, but now tourists from developed economic nations are turning to it for leisure and fun. Many people may just go out into the countryside independently looking for berries from bushes, fruit from trees or fish in rivers/oceans, but others are joining organised trips such as Fungi Forays that focus on collecting mushrooms for cooking:

> We drive from here to a local fungal hotspot and wander for three hours through the trees identifying and talking about fungi. This is followed by a mushroom-based meal, preserving and tasting sessions in Daniel's converted 17th century milking parlour. (www.fungiforays. co.uk)

David Scott (2013) predicted that foraging would take off in Australia and parts of Europe. Foraging certainly links back to the concept of self-sufficiency. Scott states: 'It's going past the idea of engaging with the grower to being able to fend for yourself', providing a clear statement that describes a shift from tourist as consumer to producer. Wild Edible Identification Trips in Vancouver, Canada are another example of a growing visitor interest in foraging (Scalza, 2012):

> From Toronto to Vancouver, foraging – the art of harvesting and preparing Mother Nature's wild delicacies – has emerged as a new pastime with ancient roots. Dedicated locavores across the country pick and prepare everything from wild blueberries to greens like watercress and cicely and even fiddleheads, the curled tips of fern fronds.

In their research on coastal foraging, Mossot and Duvat (2013) look at the management issues involved in foraging as a recreational pastime rather than what used to be a method of survival (although it remains such in some of the least developed countries). In outlining a typology of type and role in the sustainability of coastal areas, they outline particular challenges of the 'amateur' and opportunistic forager (the tourist) and how tourism authorities need to manage this growing (and potentially ecologically damaging) demand on natural resources fuelled by tourist interest (see also Carruthers et al., 2015).

VOLUNTEERISM AND VOLUNTOURISM

Originally referred to as volunteer tourism, the term 'voluntourism' is now increasingly used. This sphere of tourism has been defined by Wearing (2002: 240). as:

> those tourists who, for various reasons, volunteer in an organized way to undertake holidays that may involve the aiding or alleviating the material poverty of some groups in society, the restoration of certain environments, or research into aspects of society or environment.

The concept of 'voluntourism' covers the activity of working for no wages (usually board, lodging and basic expenses are provided), usually on a charitable, social or environmental project in a less developed country. Often the visitor actually pays for the experience to work. Originally targeted at young adults from the developed world as part of a gap year, it started to be promoted as an alternative to a classic backpacker trip from the 1990s (Brown and Morrison, 2003; McGehee and Santos, 2005; Mustonen, 2006; Stoddart and Rogerson, 2004; Wearing, 2004). The market today goes beyond this to include many experiences, variations and lifestyles where many people of all ages volunteer for longer periods of time – often without a clear altruistic agenda, although they usually hope to contribute to poverty alleviation or an increase in environmental awareness (Daldeniz and Hampton, 2011).

In looking at the tourist as a producer in a food tourism context, volunteering on farms, or 'agri-tourism' has become very popular. In terms of agricultural work, this might be called 'agri-voluntourism'. Many examples can be found via a simple internet search and most have very similar missions. An example is the Himalayan Voluntourism organisation, who provide an overview of the kind of activities they support (www.himalayanvoluntourism.org, 2015):

> Nepal is an agricultural-based country. More than 80 percent of the total population is involved in agriculture. New methods and techniques in agriculture can play an important role in supporting and increasing local livelihoods. HV encourages volunteers with some interest and skills in farming to get involved in Nepali farming. HV also promotes agriculture by identifying the potential market and linking them to rural communities.

Regarded as a way to directly help and contribute to poor rural communities, experience local culture and life, and get fit, tourists are becoming food producers on farms. Other examples include: www.projects-abroad.org/voluntourism, http://govoluntourism.com, and http://planetvolunteer.org/voluntourism.

CASE STUDY

Working on a farm – Sustainable Rural Tourism Project in Haryana, India

The Community Development Farm Tourism Project is specifically aimed at developing the village as a sustainable tourism destination to provide economic and social opportunities for poor local villagers. It is a clear example of a project seeking to facilitate productive consumption, where tourists contribute to its growth and help local people. Currently it has ten families directly attached to the project

▶

and gaining direct income from it. By offering voluntary work to tourists, it hopes to provide them with authentic rural life experience where they cook, grow crops and stay in the village. The small farm has a fishing lake, and grows sugar cane, rice, wheat and vegetables. It welcomes 'people to come and enjoy with us to develop the concept and project rather just help us with daily work'. Their online advert for volunteers clearly indicates they want people who can support the business:

We are also looking for long term volunteers. Nature of work offered – very much depends on volunteer[s] personal/professional skills and liking. We welcome volunteer[s] who ha[ve a] high level of creativity and passion to work for people, learn and is driven to achieve targets and see results/implementation of their work/idea before they fly back. We

prefer Volunteers with special-Personal/ Professional skills like – marketing, communication, project management, conservation of nature, sustainability or any other skill[s] which can fit in a tourism project.

This is an example of one of the many projects in the area of Haryana seeking to develop tourism that benefits the community and is focused on agricultural work, encouraging people to work on the farm so they can produce, contribute and make a difference.

Source: www.workaway.info/353461211272-fr.html

http://tourism.gov.in/writereaddata/Uploaded/Misc/101120111149330.pdf

www.responsibletravel.com/accommodation/13400/haryana-farmstay-in-rural-india

One of the most well-known ways to engage in voluntourism is via the WWOOF Organisation (World Wide Opportunities on Organic Farms) as outlined in the box below.

Working with food and drink tourism: become a WWOOFer!

You might like to consider volunteering on an organic farm through a WWOOF Organisation (World Wide Opportunities on Organic Farms). It is a popular way to see the world and gain valuable work experience and skills (McIntosh and Bonnemann, 2006). Originally called 'Working Weekends on Organic Farms', WWOOF came into being in England in 1971 when Sue Coppard saw a need for people who could not easily access the countryside but who wanted to support the organic movement. The idea started with a trial working weekend for four people at a bio-dynamic farm at Emerson College, Sussex. Given its success, many more

(Continued)

(Continued)

organic farmers and smallholders were willing to host people keen to work on their farms in return for food and accommodation.

A volunteer will usually live with a host and is expected to cooperate with the day-to-day activities, based on 4–6 hours help in exchange for a full day's food and accommodation. Tasks might include sowing seed, making compost, gardening, planting, cutting wood, weeding, harvesting, packing, milking, feeding, fencing, making mud-bricks, wine, cheese and bread.

Source of information: www.wwoof.net.

In looking at what might motivate a tourist to volunteer, it is useful to categorise 'push' and 'pull' factors (Coghlan, 2007). 'Push' factors include the desire to travel with a purpose, helping to improve the environment, and working with communities in less developed countries. Non-altruistic motives to volunteer abroad are self-enhancement, enhancement of one's CV or to develop skills (Callahan and Thomas, 2005; Terry 2014). The development of personal skills and the increase of knowledge, self-confidence and independence were found to be important to many voluntourists volunteering in building, teaching, growing, caring, and farming (Wearing, 2004; Webb, 2002).

According to Lupoli et al. (2014) and Moscardo et al. (2013), one of the most important parts of voluntourism is that it should have a positive effect on the site, and generate cultural exchange and increased understanding between locals and volunteers, with the aim of reaching a final position where volunteers are no longer needed in that location (Stebbins and Graham, 2004). Benefits to host and guest vary considerably, and it has been argued that in some cases, voluntourism can be damaging and counterproductive. It may seem that voluntourism is intrinsically good, but it is important to look at the activity critically as well. Issues may arise when tourists do not have the skills required for a project, when there is poor management, when tourists take up job opportunities that could have gone to local people instead, or when it seems to foster moral imperialism with people from richer nations feeling they know better (Guttentag, 2009). Some of the most controversial projects that opponents of volunteerism use to illustrate the unethical nature of Western tourists coming into developing nations relate to volunteering with vulnerable children in orphanages.

Even in less sensitive projects, Mark Watson, the Executive Director of Tourism Concern (Worldtravelguide, 2005), voiced concerns after speaking with a volunteer:

> She told me the volunteers always gossiped about how lazy the locals were because they slept for most of the morning. It was only at the end of the placement that they discovered that every day, after they finished building a wall, the locals had to come and rebuild it again.

A useful overview of research on voluntourism is provided by McGehee (2014) who reviews the 30-year evolution of volunteer tourism as a phenomenon, industry, and research area.

Working with food and drink tourism: becoming a volunteer

As briefly outlined in Chapter 4, volunteering is an excellent way to develop skills and build up your CV. However if you are interested in voluntourism, you should consider the advice provided by Tourism Concern on how to choose the right volunteer project, to make informed decisions about which organisation to work with:

1. Who is organising the project? Are they a bona fide, registered UK charity, or a business that contributes a small proportion of profits towards a charity?
2. What is their motivation? Are they primarily a business, or were they established to achieve a specific, worthwhile goal?
3. Does the organisation have a written policy on ethics and responsibilities?
4. What level of evidence is provided to demonstrate how the organisation implements its stated good intentions? Look for hard facts: don't be fobbed off by PR flannel such as 'thousands of volunteer pounds has aided the local economy'.
5. Is a wildlife project designed with specific conservation goals or is it a glorified safari and/or an opportunity to pet captured wildlife?
6. What has the organisation actually achieved so far, beyond painting the same school again and again or counting the same sea turtles?
7. Is a reputable NGO or government agency involved?
8. If 'no knowledge or experience is required' why don't they use local people? Is it because they just want your money?
9. Source of information and advice: Tourism Concern, 2015. Website: http://tourism concern.org.uk/volunteer

---

You may wish to think about the benefits for the tourist and host in the Activity below.

ACTIVITY   THE BENEFITS OF VOLUNTOURISM

Draw up a table with two columns as shown in Table 19.1. From your reading, write down some of the benefits that 'agri' voluntourism provides for both host and guest.

(Continued)

(Continued)

TABLE 19.1   *List the benefits of agri-voluntourism*

For host (local people and community)	For guest (tourist)

Complete the table: The benefits of voluntourism for host and guest.

Critical Reflections: De Certeau and the tactics of resistance as productive consumption

The concept of a tourist becoming a producer can be theorised as people engaging in small acts of social resistance to create a sense of identity; this is particularly the case when tourists may choose to buy from a local farmer to resist multinational supermarkets, volunteer to resist normative economic structures, or buy produce that is seasonal to resist an overly globalised and mechanised food offer (Everett, 2007). Ewick and Silbey (2002: 3) suggest that 'resistance represents a sort of practical theory of social processes, of social transactions and their accumulated consequences' and it is through the small acts of living that individuals maintain dignity, self-respect and identity (Goffman, 1961).

De Certeau (1988: 36) put forward an approach to resistance:

I call a strategy the calculation (or manipulation) of power relationships that becomes possible as soon as a subject with will and power … can be isolated. It postulates a place that can be delimited as its own and serve as a base from which relations with an exteriority composed of targets or threats … can be managed.

De Certeau's formulation suggests that tactics can be adopted to resist the strategies of the powerful, so that 'the space of the tactic is the space of the other' (1988: 37).

Tactics can be employed to work within the system to create and produce personal meanings and constructs, thereby manipulating and diverting spaces and processes. De Certeau's interest was in how space can be appropriated through everyday practices such as walking through a city or food purchasing, clearly recognising the expressive nature and power of (tourism) bodies.

CHAPTER SUMMARY

This chapter has introduced the concept of the tourist as a producer that challenges the view of consumption and production as separate and dichotomous entities. By employing examples such as cookery schools, voluntourism, PYO, foraging and creative tourism, it is suggested that tourists engage in co-creation, co-production and productive activities in food and drink tourism for fun, development and altruistic purposes. Tourists can have a co-productive role in developing a food and drink identity that contributes to the development and evolution of place and peoples. Developing and researching production and consumption practices is at the forefront of the creative turn, illustrating a symbiotic relationship between a productive drive towards developing new experiences and consumer desires for new sources of entertainment and unique experiences.

END OF CHAPTER POINTS

- The production and consumption relationship should be critiqued and conceptualised as mutually constitutive rather than linear or dualistic (i.e. as 'productive consumption' (De Certeau, 1988).

- Some food tourists are not passive consumers, but are active in sense-making and become co-producers and co-performers through co-creation, co-production and creative tourism.

- There has been a 'creative turn' in tourism studies, where place making and co-creation provides a more flexible and authentic experiences for host and tourist.

- Cookery schools are an increasingly popular and attractive tourist activity, fuelled by a desire for more challenging experiences that enhance 'cultural capital' and provide a sense of exclusivity. For the host, they offer a vehicle of economic diversification.

- 'Pick your own' (PYO) and foraging has become increasingly popular with tourists and is a recreational activity that shows how food tourism can provide an avenue for bodily engagement with the landscape and active 'doing'.

- 'Voluntourism' has become a popular form of holiday that grew out of the 'gap year' for young adults. Tourists of all ages are now volunteering by becoming food producers on farms (agri-voluntourism). Although voluntourism is usually associated with positive benefits for host and guest, it should be examined critically as there can be negative consequences.

FURTHER READING

Carruthers, C., Burns, A. and Elliott, G. (2015) Development, sustainability and applications – a case study of County Cork, Republic of Ireland, in P. Sloan, W. Le Grand, and C. Hindley (eds), *The Routledge Handbook of Sustainable Food and Gastronomy*. Abingdon: Routledge, pp. 360–9.

McIntosh, A.J. and Bonnemann, S.M. (2006) 'Willing workers on organic farms (WWOOF): The alternative farm stay experience?', *Journal of Sustainable Tourism*, 14 (1): 82–99.

Richards, G. (2011) 'Creativity and tourism: the state of the art', *Annals of Tourism Research*, 38 (4): 1225–53.

Sharples, L. (2003) 'The world of cookery-school holidays', in C.M. Hall, L. Sharples, R. Mitchell, N. Macionis and B. Cambourne (eds), *Food Tourism Around the World: Development, Management and Markets*. Oxford: Butterworth-Heinemann, pp. 102–20.

Terry, W. (2014) 'Solving labor problems and building capacity in sustainable agriculture through volunteer tourism', *Annals of Tourism Research*, 49 (1): 94–107.

Williams, H.A., Williams Jr, R.L. and Omar, M. (2014) 'Experiencing-the-experience: an examination of the significance of infrastructure, co-creation and co-branding within the transnational gastronomic tourism industry', *Transnational Marketing Journal*, 2 (1): 21–37.

20

THE FOOD AND DRINK TOURISM SUPPLY CHAIN

CHAPTER OBJECTIVES

- To discuss the concept of the supply chain with specific focus on food and drink tourism supply chains
- To outline different food and drink tourism supply chains and their various stages, using illustrative case studies, activities and examples
- To analyse how leakage from the tourism supply chain can be reduced and how efficiencies might be achieved
- To explore the evolution and reshaping of supply chains when elements such as health and safety legislation or information technology join the chain
- To introduce a discussion of the supply chain in the hospitality and restaurant sector

CHAPTER SUMMARY

This chapter looks at the nature of the food and drink industry from a supply chain perspective, and illustrates how the links within these chains dominate and drive the tourism and hospitality industry. Following an overview of the concept of supply chains and their management, it traces the full supply chain from the initial production of food and drink to its final disposal, and beyond into customer feedback. The chapter will illustrate how actions taken in one part of the food supply chain can affect another part (such as health and safety legislation and regulations, and information technology). Examples and visual representations of supply chains will be provided to conceptualise how products come through the supply chain. The chapter also looks at the concept of (external) leakage from the supply chain and suggests how efficiencies might be achieved through reduced transport, better waste management, cooperation between producers, joint marketing, and consumer education.

As restaurants and hotels seek to create competitive advantage, finding ways to offer local specialities has become increasingly important to provide differentiation, and demonstrate commitment to the local economy, people and culture. This chapter looks at some of the issues and challenges of sourcing local food and how the hospitality sector might reduce supply chains to provide greater benefit to those involved (including a better price to the consumer). This is also an introduction to the issues addressed in Chapter 22, which looks at the role of restaurants and the hospitality sector in promoting more sustainable supply chains.

WHAT IS A SUPPLY CHAIN?

A supply chain describes the linkages of producers and distributors involved in the creation of a commodity and its consumption. It includes all the systems and links of organisations, people, activities, information and resources involved in getting a product or service from production to consumption (and also to waste and disposal). It is about the transformation of natural or raw resources and components into a finished product that is delivered to, and consumed by, the final consumer. Supply chain descriptions sometimes use the term 'upstream' to indicate processes that occur before manufacturing or production (i.e. processes involved in getting raw materials from suppliers), and 'downstream' to indicate processes involved in getting goods/services to customers and consumers after the production stages. Supply chain theory refers to the body of concepts, models and relationships describing chains, and to ensure these chains operate effectively, there is a need for appropriate supply chain management (SCM), defined by Ho et al. (2002: 4422) as:

> A philosophy of management that involves the management and integration of a set of selected key business processes from end user through original suppliers that provides products, services, and information that add value for customers and other stakeholders through the collaborative efforts of supply chain members.

It is also described by Simchi-Levi et al. (2004a, 2004b: 14):

> Supply chain management is a set of approaches utilized to efficiently integrate suppliers, manufacturers, warehouses and stores, so that merchandise is produced and distributed at the right quantities, to the right locations, and at the right time, in order to minimize system wide costs while satisfying service level requirements.

The concept of the SCM appeared around the 1980s and replaced the concept of logistics management to more accurately include business operations and integration of business processes including research development, marketing and advertising, finance, and consumer input which may have been overlooked in the more simplistic 'dirt to dirt' approach of logistics management (Cooper et al., 1997). SCM is not only about the tangible elements that logistics tends to concentrate on, but considers the people involved, the activities and the functions of the chain, focusing on the network of organisations that are linked to produce value in terms of products and services (see the international journal *Supply Chain Management* or the *SAGE Handbook of Strategic Supply Management* (Harland et al., 2013), which provides a useful general overview of supply chains from a non-tourism perspective).

The supply chains in the tourism industry are arguably some of the most complex and confusing, given the large numbers of actors, organisations and components involved in providing an experience that is both tangible and intangible. Although the body of work on tourism supply chains is increasing, it is claimed that there has been limited research (Zhang et al., 2009). In terms of supply chains, research has traditionally focused on what could be measured, i.e. the tangible, but tourism relies on the intangible and invisible to provide experiences. Tourism supply chains need to consider key aspects including accommodation, food and drink, activities, transport, and so forth. The complexity lies in the fact that many relationships are international, unrecorded or completely invisible (for example, female labour in less-developed countries (Pritchard 2007)). Smith and Xiao (2008: 293) state that:

> Tourism services are not only invisible, but involve chains that are far from the relatively simple linear relationships typical of manufacturing. Rather, tourism involves intricate networks of many different types of relationships.

In other research on tourism supply chains, Font et al. (2008) elaborate the concept of the sustainable supply chain management (SSCM). Similar to the standard supply chain, they argue that SSCM has been primarily used to explain work processes in manufacturing rather than service sectors like tourism. SSCM in tourism needs to be about more than the purely economic and should focus on socio-cultural issues as well as environmental aspects, such as sustainable transport development; sustainable use of resources; and reducing, minimising and preventing pollution and waste. Font et al. (2008) suggest that chains must have sustainability at their heart, and achieving sustainability in tourism requires the development of better linkages between supply and demand. In terms of influencing this, tour operators must use their position to influence destination management on the supply side, and consumers need to exert their power on the demand side.

SSCM also links into discourses of Fair Trade tourism (see Chapter 11), where long-term partnership, fair pricing and a consistent volume of operations must be a priority at all stages. However, some of the challenges to implementing SSCM for tourism, and specifically for food, include 'supplier availability and capacities, time, expertise and financial resource availability' (Font et al., 2008: 270) and these need to be addressed. In terms of priority areas for implementation in the food and drink sector, the focus must be on environmental performance, infrastructure at the destination (especially for management of solid and liquid waste), sustainable production methods including production and training, quality, reliability and distribution, and better access to markets. As Cobb et al. (1999: 209) recognise, 'the food chain as a whole is the ultimate framework for a scrutiny of sustainability'.

THE FOOD AND DRINK TOURISM SUPPLY CHAIN: STAGES OF THE CYCLE

In their study of the culinary tourism supply chain, Smith and Xiao (2008) claim that there is a gap in the research on food and drink tourism supply chains. They state (2008: 291):

> Culinary tourism, as with other forms of economic production, depends on a series of upstream suppliers for the commodities required for the creation of the experiences desired by visitors. Culinary tourism products are then delivered to consumers through various distribution channels, such as markets, festivals, or restaurants.

Hall and Page (2005: 248) identify five types of culinary supply chains:

- direct sales where consumer buys direct from the producer;
- the industrial food supply chain where consumer buys from a retailer, who buys from a wholesaler, who buys from a producer;
- a cooperative where a group of producers cooperate and work together to sell to the consumer (a market for example and joint marketing activities);
- a restaurant supply chain – consumer buys meals from the restaurant that obtains supplies from producers; and
- a network of producers who supply markets and restaurants who cooperate in promotions, join marketing and branding.

This is a starting point, but the details of these different chain models should be interrogated to understand how they work and can be improved. In terms of a supply chain relevant to food and drink tourism, the core relationships are illustrated in Figure 20.1. This figure provides an overview of a simple chain in terms of food production, demand, supply, consumption and waste. A short local tourism chain (without the details of 'who' or 'what') can be organised into key areas: primary food production, food manufacture/processing, food tourism marketing and distribution, food tourism transportation/communication, food service provision/consumption/ food tourism service, and lastly food waste/recycling. However, as Figure 20.1 indicates, it is helpful to add an additional element to the chain to better reflect the consumer's role in providing feedback on the entire experience. With widely accessible online social and print media, customer feedback can now last longer than the chain itself; long after the food has been disposed of. As outlined in Chapter 9, it is important to think about the flow of information in the supply chains and they may be more accurately considered as circular chains, circuits or loops; beginning and ending with the customer and their feedback in a standard supply and demand model. The idea of a chain is now regarded by many as too linear and mechanistic, with production and consumption appearing as abstracted entities occupying either end of the chain (Everett, 2012; Jackson, 2002).

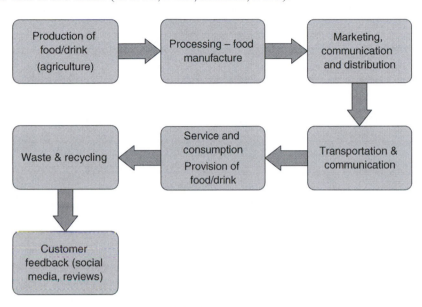

FIGURE 20.1 *A simple food and drink tourism supply chain (with the additional element of consumer feedback)*

As outlined in Chapter 18, there are a number of different stages in the life-cycle and supply chain of food, but each stage is complex and multi-faceted. Beer and Lemmer (2011) suggest that basic headings in food chains often hide significant complexity: (i) different foods involve very different supply chains (i.e. fish, meat, vegetables require different initial inputs); (ii) production methods vary (for example tomatoes can be grown outside naturally, in greenhouses, in/out of season, with/without pesticides, with/without use of technology); (iii) there are many ways to transport food (road, rail, ship, air); (iv) the waste and disposal of food varies depending on the process (landfill, reuse, recycling); and (v) the costs to businesses and individuals vary. Ultimately it is about the stages between the 'plough to plate', or 'field to fork' that make the difference. Effective supply chain management is the integration of these aspects and their relationships with each other to achieve a sustainable competitive advantage (economically, but also environmentally, politically, socially, and technologically).

A supply chain at its most simplistic in food and drink is presented by Atkin and Affonso (2004) in their study of American wineries. Their model consists of three simple components: (i) suppliers (those who provide grapes, barrels, corks, and bottles); (ii) processes (supply procurement, vinification, and the delivery); and (iii) customers (including distributors, retailers, and consumers), as translated into Figure 20.2.

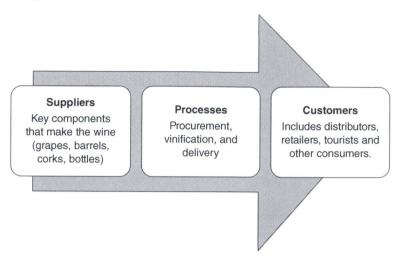

FIGURE 20.2 *Illustration of Atkin and Affonso's (2004) three-stage wine supply chain*

As outlined in Chapter 5, consumer reaction to global food crises and scares in the food supply chain triggered significant interest in all stages of the food and drink cycle, coupled with consumer demand that all steps could be identified. This concern with the supply chain prompted a move to more integrated control and cooperation (Van der Vorst and Beulens, 2002). As evidenced by the growth of farmers' markets, food attractions and local food purchasing, there have been shifts away from price, packaging and appearance and towards food products that can be traced to particular people and places (Ilbery and Kneafsey, 1998; Ilbery and Maye, 2005). For example, the 'Eat the View' project from the UK's Countryside Agency (2002: 12) introduced in Chapter 18 aimed to

> build awareness and trust among consumers, enhance marketability and economic benefits to producers and demonstrate significant environmental benefits … bringing producers closer to consumers within a more localised supply chain can lead to a higher proportion of the value of the produce being retained within the local community.

Part of its remit was to improve local economic linkages between tourism and food production and included 'the development of new supply chain partnerships between retailers/producers, which will increase the proportion of locally sourced/sustainable products'. Hall (2005) argues that altering the supply chain is key to developing sustainable rural tourism, where new relationships are needed between producers and consumers at different scales, and most explicitly by strengthening direct relations between food producers and consumers to

FOOD AND DRINK ATTRACTIONS AND EVENTS

bypass wholesalers and retailers. Better local distribution networks can reduce leakage from the chain and provide more local food through cooperatives, community projects, food sheds, farmers' markets, restaurants and speciality food shops. To work with shorter and more sustainable supply chains, there is a need to build stronger relationships, trust and community (Hall and Wilson, 2008). These things illustrate what has been called an 'ecological paradigm' for rural development, and in terms of tourism actions can disrupt long impersonal chains to create a multifunctional rural space (Ilbery and Maye, 2005).

As more research is being undertaken on food tourism supply chains, it is clear that there is a need to move from the old linear mode of food production (wholesale–retailing–food services–food tourists) to look at different and more diverse ways of direct trading or interactions among food services providers, tourists and food production. Gössling and Hall (2013) suggest that food tourism needs to be explored in terms of sustainability, culinary culture and tourist experience (i.e. the intangible elements); they also advocate a move from just focusing on the economic aspects of the chain to the social, cultural and environmental (Everett and Aitchison, 2008).

An illuminating exercise by Beer and Lemmer (2011: 240) was undertaken on the life-cycle of a meal within an event-catering context in the UK. It looked at four different supply chains to obtain the final meal: the 'commercial chain', a specifically local chain, an organic chain and a biodynamic chain. They found tracing all stages very difficult as information was hard to find, and there was significant complexity in all parts of the chain. Overall they found that commercial supply chains are cheaper than local ones, which are cheaper than organic, which are cheaper than biodynamic. In terms of producing chips (potato fries), they found the organic alternative 35% more expensive than the commercial, and the biodynamic 70% more expensive than the commercial. Overall, non-commercial supply chains tend to be more expensive and this is reflected in much of the local/food tourism research, but the authors suggest that mechanisms can be put in place to reduce this gap, including planning seasonal menus and collaboration between growers. In terms of using food tourism to improve supply chain relationships and maximise opportunities for local providers, a Case Study is provided below.

CASE STUDY

The shrimp-tourism supply chain, South Carolina

Deale et al. (2008) assessed the viability of positioning the local, wild-caught shrimp industry as a feature of tourism in South Carolina using the 2004 *South Carolina Coastal Tourism Survey*. The most popular seafood in the USA is shrimp, but researchers found that fewer shrimp were being landed because of high levels of foreign imports, higher operating costs, reduced progressing and packing plants, and lower economic returns. Researchers wanted to look at different supply chain components to better exploit the 25 million visitors each year to South Carolina, which generated $7.8 billion in 2004. They found that different areas marketed and used the local produce differently, but locally and regionally owned restaurants were much more likely (than national chain restaurants) to purchase local shrimp. Price was a major concern to restaurateurs, but restaurateurs purchasing local shrimp generally did so because they believed the taste and quality were superior.

Supporting local fisherman was found to be the most important motivation for tourists, so researchers concluded it was important to improve relationships between local fishermen and tourists to better promote the local product. The Beaufort Shrimp Festival, for example, worked closely with the local chamber of commerce and the local shrimp industry to promote shrimp. Deale et al. (2008: 18) suggested that:

Attempts need to be made to provide multiple opportunities for people to buy fresh shrimp at coastal venues. Higher visibility of local shrimp in coastal areas through farmers' markets or in this case seafood markets might provide more opportunities for shrimp fishermen to sell their products and for tourists to buy them. … Vertical coordination in the shrimp supply chain, which lies between complete vertical integration and open markets, may also improve the prospects of selling local shrimp. Vertical cooperation requires successful partnerships between producers, marketers, sellers, and perhaps other newly created positions, for example liaisons between the shrimp fishermen and the sales venues.

In offering a new hypothetical shrimp supply chain that favoured the local shrimp fishermen, they demonstrated how tweaks to the supply chain could help sustain an industry. Overall, it was about diversifying the market and making it more visible through new markets, events and festivals, and communication channels such as online marketing.

Source: Deale et al. (2008).

LONG AND SHORT SUPPLY CHAINS

Supply chains vary considerably in length, detail and global reach. Long or conventional supply chains are characterised by multiple actors, nodes and complexity, and this has often been the case with tourism. Food and drink tourism promotes and supports the reduction in these chains into simpler, more direct chains that reduce leakage (i.e. to outside the local economy) and is positioned to maximise the economic benefits to those along the chain. Telfer and Wall (2000) illustrate the vast network of linkages involved in supplying food to a Sheraton hotel in Lombok, Indonesia (Figure 20.3). Their study illustrates a number of different supply chains in terms of hotel size and market.

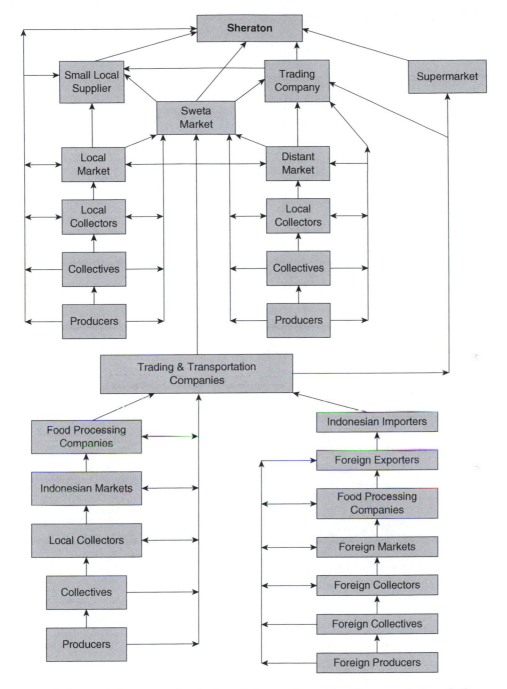

FIGURE 20.3 *A long supply chain – linkages from the Sheraton in Lombok, Indonesia (Telfer and Wall, 2000: 436).*

In their discussion of Short Food Supply Chains (SFSC) Ilbery and Maye (2005) argue that terms including 'local', 'alternative' and 'traditional/speciality' agro-food systems have been used interchangeably, but ultimately priority should be given to reducing the number of nodes between the primary producer and the final consumer so the length is minimised. They have suggested that there needs to be a 're-spatialisation' of food supply chains that provide opportunities for food and drink small businesses to retain added value, improve employment benefits, strengthen regional imagery and help local industries such as tourism (Ilbery and Maye, 2005: 334). Marsden et al. (2000) and Renting et al. (2003) suggest that there are different approaches in SFSCs, including 'face-to-face', where consumers buy a product direct from the producer; 'spatially proximate', where local outlets sell local produce in the area; and 'spatially extended', where products are sold to consumers located outside the immediate area who may know little about where it came from (these might include products such as Champagne, Parma ham, Rioja wine or Parmigiano Reggiano cheese). This can be simply illustrated as a pyramid, where the distance becomes greater at each point, although it remains sold as a Short Food Supply Chain (Figure 20.4).

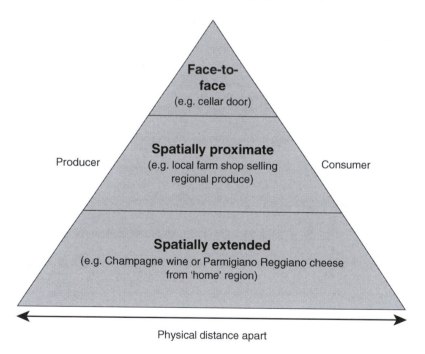

FIGURE 20.4   *Three types of Short Food Supply Chain*

There may be additional 'upstream' components. For example, with online shopping growing so quickly, a consumer could buy directly from a small producer, but the product may need to travel and will generate food miles and transport costs.

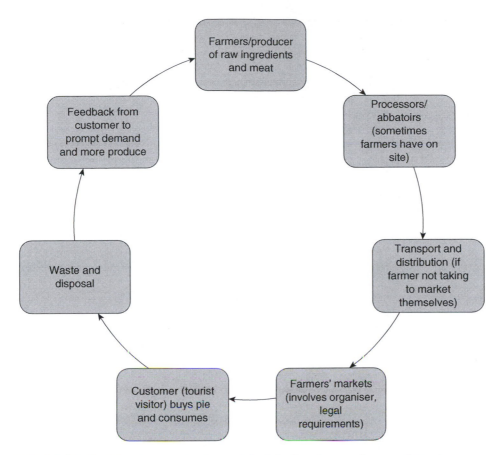

FIGURE 20.5 *Simple supply chain (circle) of a pie at a farmers' market*

It is worth noting that many vendors at farmers' markets are not all producers, but may include those who buy their products from producers or wholesalers. For example, sometimes you will see items such as exotic fruits and vegetables that are not grown in the location of the market. Smith and Xiao (2008) suggest that the supply chain for farmers' markets consists of four main categories of suppliers: food producers, other food retailers, prepared food retailers (e.g. snack bars), and business services. Each of these elements has an extensive supply chain behind it. These additional 'actors' include regulators, seed distributors, fuel providers, abattoirs, veterinarians, waste management, marketing bodies, and lobbying and advocacy organisations. Furthermore, factors such as entertainment and parking are important aspects of the process in their interviewee responses.

Another example of a supply chain is shown in Figure 20.7. It provides an indicative outline of the chain leading up to a tourist buying a flavoured 'local' ice-cream on holiday.

FIGURE 20.6 *The consumer at the end of the farmers' market supply chain, Wales. Photo by author*

WORKING TOWARDS SHORT SUPPLY CHAINS IN THE RESTAURANT SECTOR

Wolf who leads the World Food Travel Association (WFTA) (2015) claims that tourism marketers always want to work out the spending multiplier in a local economy, but we also need to look at how much money stays in the local economy if the impact of food tourism is going to be properly measured. According to the American Independent Business Alliance, chain restaurants only re-circulate 34.5% of their revenue, while locally owned restaurants re-circulate 65.4%. In other words, money spent in independently owned restaurants is nearly twice as valuable to the community as cash spent in chains, because more of the money stays in the community. Is the key premise trying to keep money in the region or community? In a report on tourism in Rwanda, Ashley (2007) states what is needed:

> Work on the food supply chain to hotels, lodges and restaurants to boost product quality and volume, and increasing help so poor farmers can access this market; practical initiatives to help businesses

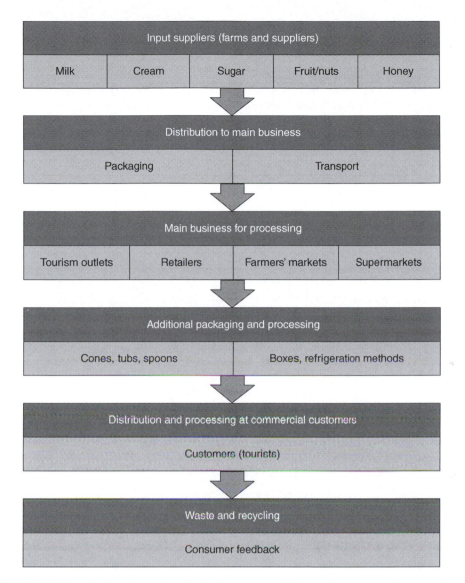

FIGURE 20.7 *Indicative supply chain to provide local ice cream for tourists (based on Ilbery and Maye, 2005: 338)*

enhance their own 'inclusive business' models; and partnerships with tour operators, lodges and hotels, conference organisers, artisans and farmers to make a range of cultural experiences is an integral part of a Rwandan visit.

Research suggests that smaller hotels and restaurants are better at retaining income in the local economy and have a higher multiplier effect (Telfer and

Wall, 2000). In their study of the supply chain of USA beverages in tourism, Jackson and Singh (2015: 27) claim it is essential that 'hospitality firms adhering to the principles of green or environmental management pay close attention to the green practices of their food and beverage suppliers'. In seeking to achieve green supply chain management as an integral component corporate strategy, it was found that companies can gain financial reward alongside developing healthier chains for the local environment.

Torres's (2003: 547) study of tourism linkages in the Yucatan Peninsula, Mexico, looked at what was constraining the development of local chains, and despite the general belief that tourism can strengthen agriculture, she reminds us that:

> Tourism development is also often associated with increased demand for imported food, resulting in foreign exchange leakages and competition with local production. Tourism typically fails to stimulate local agriculture, and in some cases it is associated with a relative decline in production.

She found the popular holiday destination of Cancún, Mexico has reduced leakage in the restaurant/hotel chain unlike other popular tourism locations, yet the majority of fruit and vegetables, dairy products and commodity goods are still imported from other regions of Mexico. Some of the factors disrupting and weakening linkages include poor local growing conditions (soil, climate and landscape), tourist demand for familiar foods, failure to develop 'strategic alliances' (Telfer, 2000), limited access and funding for marketing, and expensive transport caused by all the toll-motorways around Mexico. These kinds of problems along the supply chain push hotels, who rely on consistent and regular produce, to turn to those outside the local area. However, increasingly customers are wanting to see local produce used and local producers' names explicitly mentioned in menus, and this has become a powerful marketing tool (see Chapter 21).

THE EVOLUTION AND RESHAPING OF FOOD AND DRINK TOURISM SUPPLY CHAINS

Ilbery and Maye (2005: 331) claimed that little research has examined whether 'local' or 'alternative' food supply systems are sustainable in environmental, economic and social terms. They claim that:

> [the] agro-food system has undergone significant modernisation and mechanisation, a process heightened by the rise and increasingly monopolistic power of large-scale food processors and retailers who seek to control most parts of lengthening and globalising food supply chains.

Moreover, they raise concerns that rather than shortening chains, in the food sector there has been an increasing disconnection between farming and food and thus between farmers, the traditional producers of foodstuffs, and final consumers. However, as discussed in Chapter 5, global food scares and crises prompted the creation of 'local' and 'shorter' food supply chains; and fuelled a rise of a more ethically minded, discerning and reflexive consumer who appears in the food tourism typologies. However, the success of these chains relies on many elements working together, or tightening up. There needs to be better and more efficient integration of the various links (or nodes) along these chains.

There are numerous 'nodes' along food and tourism supply chains, and many are added or removed without the consumer really noticing – some links that are less obvious than simply the producer and consumer. For example, the introduction of additional health and safety regulations and legal safety requirements have added complexity and additional components to the food tourism supply chain at all stages, from the production of the raw materials to processing to consumer purchase and consumption. Of course, in an era of growing food terrorism and contamination, a problem can cause severe economic disruption in direct costs due to the culling of livestock and the compensation paid to growers (Manning et al., 2005), but prevention can also cause problems. A balance is needed between food safety and the cost of implementing food safety (Renting et al., 2003). Food security and safety are important, but when legislation is enforced (and often rightly so to protect the consumer), it adds cost and time to the production process. This added time can have a significant impact on the smaller and poorer producer, whereas the larger and richer producers can change systems easily and invest funds into addressing what is required in legislation. Countries or individuals that cannot afford to meet compliance requirements or costs, especially for infrastructure requirements, will find that certain markets are unavailable to them. Compliance may require capital investment, knowledge and finances to change management practices, as well as certification or assurance. It is suggested that if legislation is necessary to protect people and promote standards, then they should be considered in terms of risk management and laws introduced that can be enforced. After all, not all countries have similar laws and this provides an uneven playing field for producers of the same product, and therefore food chains vary with every situation.

Renting et al. (2003) outlines the irony in trying to reduce the supply chain to simply producer to consumer, claiming the delinking of food production, processing, and consumption inherent to the old industrial mode of food supply created a structural necessity to establish some kind of institutionalised food quality guarantee. They state that when food was produced in the direct surroundings or even by the household itself, the need for regulation was less apparent, quoting a Dutch proverb ('What the farmer does not know, he will not eat'), indicating that the perception of food quality in former times was founded on personal observation and local social networks. If the food supply chain breaks now, the impact can be internationally damaging and very public, so laws are put in place. However, adhering to these can be expensive and cumbersome for small producers. For example, a fish smoker in Ireland said in an interview in Everett (2007: 232) that she believes her cultural contribution is being compromised by regulatory procedures that are targeted at controlling the large industrialised food factories. She explained that she had attempted to work around these, but faced obstacles:

> We were renting accommodation, so there was a limit to how much renovation and refurbishment you could do to someone else's shed as you want to produce food, so I worked outside off the record for years. The local health inspectors caught up with me and said it was an offence to sell food.

Other examples include an interview with a dairy owner, who said:

> that kind of regulation slows you down. The regulation is very tight nowadays that we have to form fill, you know, which we didn't used to do. Some of it is for good reasons. A lot of it is over the top and we are powerless to change that.

Other local producers highlighted the restrictive power of external bodies and cost to the small producer: 'the girls who live next door to us collect the cockles for us, the only problem with that is we are always fighting legislation', and a baker was quoted as stating, 'then regulations came in and they had to be packed in plastic and the sales fell by about 50%, and I am sure part of that is the smell of it, that's what sells' (Everett, 2007: 232).

The use and introduction of information technology (IT) to the supply chain has transformed processes and ways of working. IT can be exploited to give competitive advantage, as well as create supply chain efficiencies (Marinagi et al., 2014). Johnson and Whang (2002: 413) describe e-business as 'the marriage between the internet and supply chain integration', claiming 'this marriage is transforming many processes within the supply chain from procurement to customer management and product design'. In terms of a more effective and local tourism supply chain management, it provides a cost effective way to share information and develop links with other producers (Zhang et al., 2009). The internet offers cheaper and easier marketing avenues which facilitate the building of networks between restaurants, hotels and retailers and local producers that they might never have known about otherwise. Social media can attract (ethically minded) consumers to products more easily, although poor practices can be communicated just as easily in a matter of seconds. IT has shortened some aspects of supply chains significantly (i.e. buying from the producer online), but may have lengthened others such as transport and delivery once bought.

LEAKAGE FROM THE SUPPLY CHAIN

Tourism has been accused of having high levels of external leakage, with research finding that large hotels and restaurants often have very little contact with local economies. Therefore, it is easy to question the benefit to local people if there is a high external leakage (Telfer and Wall, 1996, 2000). Leakages exist 'when revenue leaves the destination as profit to non-local businesses or for the purchase of external goods and services' (Sandbrook, 2010: 21). There is a need to look at how efficiencies might be achieved through reduced transport, better waste management, IT, education and people management. In their study of Indonesia, Telfer and Wall (2000) argue that the key to improving the efficiency of supply chains in the relationship between tourism and food and drink is to strengthen ties through better backward linkages. They state (2000: 422):

> If a destination area is to maximize the benefits from tourism and generate additional income and employment, attempts must be made to strengthen backward economic linkages, thereby reducing leakages and increasing the indirect and induced impacts of visitor expenditures.

Everett and Slocum (2013) further suggest that where there are limited local producer partnerships across a wide geographical spread (mostly in rural areas that depend on tourism), it is difficult for producers to join forces and create a steady supply of regional produce for tourism outlets, so businesses look outside the local economy. They found businesses struggled to maintain regular supplies when working with a single or small group of local farmers. An interviewee (a food consultant in Scotland) stated that:

> Often suppliers are so small that they can't guarantee regular delivery quantities. It can be a real problem. Some produce is seasonal, so

restaurants have to adapt their recipes to whatever is available. They just don't have the manpower to be that flexible.

Traditional distribution strategies in agriculture have employed brokers or distribution centres, and reduced the interaction between regional or neighbouring farms (see the Further Reading section for other examples that look at reducing leakage).

There is a positive picture in most studies, as many indicate that high leakage along the supply chain can be reduced, despite some concerns about the ability of producers to provide the quantities of food required for large numbers of tourists. Sometimes just changing a chef, buyer or manager to one with a different approach to local procurement can greatly reduce leakage. Another way to improve the chain is to improve education for tourists: advising them on the impact of requesting exotic foodstuffs, offering seasonal menus based on what is locally available, and supporting producer cooperatives in the vicinity of the hotel.

WASTE AND DISPOSAL OF FOOD AND DRINK – THE FINAL STAGE?

Waste is the disposal of something that has/had value and it is a key part of the life-cycle of food, but it does not need to be the end if there are opportunities for recycling and reuse. However, the food and drink industry does produce a lot of waste. Food waste causes several environmental problems, such as climate change, land exploitation, water exhaustion and biodiversity loss. Beer and Lemmer (2011) suggest that the UK wastes £10 billion-worth of food every year. On a domestic level, 8.3 billion tonnes of food waste is sent to landfill, costing the average UK family with children £690 per year and producing as much carbon dioxide as 25% of the UK's cars.

Making the best use of food materials is the first choice in reducing waste. Some waste materials should be recycled and possible alternatives can be sought for its utilisation, saving resources and money. Examples include using old deep-frying oil as biodiesel, running kitchen-food collections, the creation of organic fertiliser by certified companies, and using recycled materials for future plant cultivation. Nielsen and Green Restaurant Association (2004) found 95% of restaurant waste could typically be recycled or composted. In 2000–2001, a medium-sized restaurant in San Diego saved US$ 2220 per year in garbage disposal costs after implementing a comprehensive recycling programme (Kasim and Ismail, 2012), a picture replicated across the industry. Other effective approaches have been waste separation schemes that use bins for organic and recyclable waste (Tapper and Font, 2004), recycling waste water for irrigation, and using renewable energy technologies that use waste as fuel. How waste in tourism is dealt with is a key area of research, as can be seen in the following Case Study.

Getting rid of waste on the Maldives

The Maldives archipelago consists of 26 islands (atolls) in the Indian Ocean, and has experienced rapid tourism growth. Its total receipts rose from $15 million (1981) to $94 million (1991), to a massive $2,333 million in 2013, representing 82.3% of the country's international tourism receipts (Ministry of Tourism, Arts and Culture Republic of Maldives, 2013; WTTC, 2014). Despite its reputation for pristine beaches and high-end tourism, Scheyvens (2011) has highlighted issues of environmental degradation, human rights abuses, connections between the political and economic elite, and huge economic disparities associated with tourism here. Tourism in the Maldives illustrates the tension between tourism income and damage to fragile ecosystems by tourists. Specific concerns have been raised about how it deals with its waste (the end of its tourism supply chain). Brown et al. (1995) found that solid waste production by resorts was considerably higher than the Maldivian average, with resorts producing up to 16.5 kg of solid waste per visitor per week. Large tourist resorts created 204.40 tonnes of waste per year, with much dumped at sea or incinerated, which was found to be costing operators US$300–500 per month on beach cleaning. In 1991, the government decided to use an island called Thilafushi for the waste, which soon became known as 'Rubbish Island'. However, this was far from sustainable. More than 330 tonnes of rubbish was brought to Thilafushi each day. By December 2011 a ban was put on waste transportation to Thilafushi and better regulations were introduced (included a building code, sanitation codes, electricity codes and carrying capacity limitations for resorts). These kinds of strategic measures are vital in destinations like the Maldives; however, they must be supplemented with education for tourists about their impact and the consequences of their actions and consumption requests.

Source of information: Ministry of Tourism, Arts and Culture Republic of Maldives (2013), World Travel and Tourism Council (WTTC) (2014), Scheyvens (2011), and Brown et al. (1995).

IMPROVING AND SHORTENING SUPPLY CHAINS

Improving supply chains relies on reducing leakage to external 'faceless' (international) providers and creating symbiotic relationships between the local producer and consumer, and key sectors of agriculture/fishing and tourism (Everett and Slocum, 2013). What has been lacking is shared knowledge and networking, both within and between food and tourism sectors, and the limited levels of knowledge exchange and networking in many countries have consequently failed to bring the benefits that tourism could provide to local communities and regions in terms of economic, social, political and environmental gains. A shift towards closer relationships and cooperation in all aspects of the chain has been described as 'social embeddedness', where a complex web of social relations must become stronger and more collaborative (Ilbery and Maye, 2005: 334). It has also been described by Sage (2003) as a concept of 'regard' across all links of the chain. However, despite a desire for local food economies being driven by interpersonal ties, trust and reciprocity, it is inevitable that they will carry undercurrents determined by relations of power, inequality, conflict and personal gain which must be identified and addressed (Ilbery and Maye, 2005). Social capital linkages must be nurtured before many of the food tourism diversification strategies and initiatives outlined in government policies and tourism destination offerings can be realised.

New distribution systems and improved governance are needed to help increase social capital and ensure that a reliable, affordable supply chain exists for local produce. However, in Everett and Slocum's research, this demanded new and unknown ways of working which raised concern and fear amongst providers. Taylor and Fearne (2006: 379) proposed the food supply chain from farm to fork required 'more collaboration aid information sharing and joint planning beyond the manufacturer-retailer interface', which they considered to be 'critical if retail food supply chains are to function efficiently and effectively in retail environments where promotional activity creates significant uncertainty'. Everett and Slocum (2013: 805) emphasise the need for policy support and cooperation to improve food tourism supply chains:

> Policy agendas promote and support local distribution networks in line with many existing and successful food cooperatives. Limited or erratic supply of local produce creates barriers to food tourism. Without a cooperative mentality, each enterprise is fighting alone, against its neighbours, to reach and attract tourists.

FIGURE 20.8 *Direct selling- a vegetable market seller, North Cyprus. Photo by author*

FOOD AND DRINK ATTRACTIONS AND EVENTS

If local producers like the one shown in Figure 20.8 worked with each other in a cooperative, then issues of quantity, consistency and flexibility would be significantly reduced.

Working with food and drink tourism: supply chain management

There are many career paths in supply chain management, both in large multinational companies and small businesses who are looking to improve their overall sustainability and efficiency. Recent jobs advertised include a 'Supply Chain Planning Manager' job offering £35–50k ($US 45–70k) that asks if you are 'up to the challenge of planning the supply chain process for a large multinational organization?' The company are looking for a person with 'Higher level general background education (degree level or equivalent), supply planning experience, experience of working across all levels of organizations; experience of working in different cultures/countries would be an advantage, and highly numerate.'

You might wish to work up to a career as 'Head of Supply Chain' for a large health food company. A recent job advert for this role expected the post holder to:

- Produce a supply chain strategy in conjunction with Head of Buying and Buying Director that supports the business objectives of sales and profit attainment
- Form links between Procurement and Production teams
- Ensure the supply of raw materials and components so that our internal packing units meet commercial and production schedules
- Achieve stock holding and supply chain targets
- Attend commercial, quality and production meetings to understand the business needs, drive supply chain efficiencies through teams at all levels.
- Work with supplier base on in-bound logistics and relationships

Requirements:

- Advanced Excel user
- High level of analytical skill
- Strong presentation skills
- Management skills and negotiation Skills – able to gain buy in from senior managers and directors within the business
- Influence and persuasion – able to present business cases and perspectives
- Ideally degree qualified from business background
- Must have experience from similar role
- High level of learning ability due to wider than normal scope of the role.

(Continued)

These are demanding, but can be rewarding and fascinating roles. What is very clear is the expectation that the post-holder will have excellent people skills, numeracy and analytical skills, experience and a relevant degree.

Useful sources for supply chain jobs: www.supplychainrecruit.com, or www.supplychain-jobs.com.

CHAPTER SUMMARY

Tourism supply chains are complex, dynamic and difficult to conceptualise and manage given their lack of research to date and the invisible nature of many aspects of their service delivery. To achieve sustainability, food and drink tourism supply chains need to reduce external leakage outside local economies and cultures to retain economic, social and environmental gains from tourism. To do this, it has been suggested that that there needs to be a development of better linkages between supply and demand where tourism providers influence destination management on the supply side, and consumers on the demand side (Font et al., 2008). The key to developing sustainable rural tourism is in altering supply chains, where different relationships between and among producers and consumers can strengthen the position of food producers and consumers to effectively bypass (external) wholesalers and retailers. Effective supply chain management and the reduction of leakage relies on the success of relationship management: relationships are core to a supply chain (Zhang et al., 2009). Supply chains that focus on consumers' needs and that seek to deliver simpler and more local modes of production could hold the key to improving relationships between agriculture, fishing and tourism – thereby creating a healthier and more sustainable supply 'circuit' that is symbiotic and mutually beneficial to all.

END OF CHAPTER POINTS

- Supply chains describe the systems and links of organisations, people, activities, information, and resources involved in moving a product or service from production to consumption to disposal.
- There has been very limited work to date on tourism supply chains beyond those that consider the economic aspects, and therefore it is an important area for future tourism research.

- Tourism has been accused of having high levels of external leakage (i.e. not retaining income in local communities) but food and drink tourism offers a way to reduce supply chains and increase benefits for those involved.

- Key phases of a basic food tourism chain are: primary food production, food manufacture/processing, food tourism marketing and distribution, food tourism transportation/communication, food service provision/consumption/ food tourism service, and food waste/recycling. Consumer feedback (and increasingly social media) could be added to complete a 'circuit' back to production based on demand.

- Information technology can facilitate supply chain coordination and improve relationships throughout the chain as it is an effective means of promoting collaboration between supply chain members and enhancing supply chain efficiency.

- Improved levels of information sharing and collaboration will aid the development of more sustainable supply chains and reduce external leakage.

FURTHER READING

Deale, C., Norman, W.C. and Jodice, L.W. (2008) 'Marketing locally harvested shrimp to South Carolina coastal visitors: the development of a culinary tourism supply chain', *Journal of Culinary Science and Technology*, 6 (1): 5–23.

Everett, S. and Slocum, S.L. (2013) 'Food and tourism: an effective partnership? A UK-based review', *Journal of Sustainable Tourism*, 21 (6): 789–809.

Hall, C.M. and Gössling, S. (eds) (2013) *Sustainable Culinary Systems: Local Foods, Innovation, and Tourism & Hospitality*. London: Routledge.

Smith, S.L. and Xiao, H. (2008) 'Culinary tourism supply chains: a preliminary examination', *Journal of Travel Research*, 46 (3): 289–99

Telfer, D.J. and Wall, G. (2000) 'Strengthening backward economic linkages: local food purchasing by three Indonesian hotels', *Tourism Geographies*, 2 (4): 421–47.

Torres, R. (2003) 'Linkages between tourism and agriculture in Mexico', *Annals of Tourism Research*, 30 (3): 546–66.

Zhang, X., Song, H. and Huang, G.Q. (2009) 'Tourism supply chain management: a new research agenda', *Tourism management*, 30 (3): 345–58.

FURTHER RESEARCH ON HOW TO REDUCE LEAKAGE AND STRENGTHEN TOURISM AND AGRICULTURAL PARTNERSHIPS

- *Australia*: Knowd (2006: 39) focuses on diversification in Sydney, where 'tourism is an integrating force ... sets the scene for establishing new relationships between agriculture and other industries'.

- *Barbados*: Momsen (1998) explored the linkages between the food production sector and tourism, looking at ways to reduce the leakages in the Caribbean tourism industry. A project is seeking to help small farmers increase the quality and quantity of fresh, regionally grown fruits and vegetables for tourism.

- *China*: Yuan (2013) explores the 'tourism-agriculture' partnership in China. Coupling seems to stimulate interaction between the rural tourism industry and agriculture, which shapes new products, extends rural tourism and agriculture industrial chains, and fosters closer coordination.

- *Mexico*: as outlined in this chapter, Torres (2003) looks at the Yucatan Peninsula in Mexico and assessed how linkages might be strengthened, and examines the challenges to shorter, more localised chains.

21

LOCAL FOOD AND DRINK IN THE HOSPITALITY SECTOR

CHAPTER OBJECTIVES

- To explore the relationship between local food and the hospitality sector (hotels, resorts, public houses and restaurants)
- To examine how local food and drink can be used as an effective marketing vehicle and how it offers unique selling points for businesses in the hospitality sector
- To assess some of the barriers, challenges and obstacles to sourcing and using local produce in the hospitality sector
- To provide case studies of successful hospitality businesses who have committed to local food purchasing and strategies with sustainability principles at their core

CHAPTER SUMMARY

This chapter builds on the previous discussions of supply chains and local food procurement, by looking more explicitly at food and drink tourism in the context of the hospitality industry. Not only are some restaurants, resorts and hotels becoming tourist attractions in their own right (utilising celebrity chefs, offering unusual dishes or providing unique environments through design and décor), but they are increasingly using local produce, regional menus and community food events to attract the more discerning hotel guest or diner looking to raise their cultural and social 'capital', whilst actively supporting local economies (see Chapter 4). This chapter looks at hospitality businesses that have committed to sourcing local food and working with local producers as part of their strategic growth plan (such as the Sandals Resorts in Jamaica, and the Scandic Hotel chain in the Nordic countries). Undoubtedly, this strategy has given many businesses a 'competitive advantage', but not without challenges.

SOURCING LOCAL FOOD IN THE HOSPITALITY INDUSTRY

As Chapter 20 indicated, supporting local economic development by buying local is not just about consumer choice, but powered by the procurement decisions and buying patterns of owners and managers in the hospitality industry (accommodation and food providers). This large industry sector is key to reducing external leakage and has a central role in promoting locally sourced food products to tourists (Sims, 2010; Torres, 2002). Given the size and scale of the industry, hotels and restaurants are central to the sustainability of local food production, where 'the use of local foods may add to the perceived authenticity of the restaurant experience as well as wider experience of the destination' (Smith and Hall, 2003: 248). The different markets are reflected in the types of establishment and their likely interest in building relationships with local producers and farmers. The hospitality sector needs to exploit local providers to create an experience that can only ever be enjoyed in that location. For example, the 98 Acres Resort, which lies high in the tea plantations of Sri Lanka, provides local produce as well as a 'cooking with chef' culinary experience (see Figure 21.1).

FIGURE 21.1 *Local food is offered at the 98 Acres Resort, Sri Lanka. Photo and permission to reproduce kindly given by the 98 Acres Resort, Sri Lanka*

FOOD AND DRINK ATTRACTIONS AND EVENTS

To date, there is very limited research by geographers, sociologists, tourism scholars and cultural historians on the role of restaurants and cafes in promoting local food (Duram and Cawley, 2012). Studies on 'meaningful sustainability' strategies in the hospitality sector have received relatively limited attention (Moskwa et al., 2015), particularly when compared to more obvious food and drink tourism experiences discussed in previous chapters (events, festivals, trails and attractions).

It is widely argued that local food is an important tourist attraction and central to the tourist experience (Boniface, 2003; Hall et al., 2003), both for travellers looking for food experiences and also for those who have a more casual attitude to food (Seaman et al. 2014). However, not all consumers are driven by a desire to eat local food (as the food tourism typologies in Chapter 1 showed), and this needs to be considered by the hospitality industry as well. Sometimes tourists will actively avoid local foods in host destinations for various reasons, ranging from fear to health concerns (Pizam and Sussmann, 1995; Telfer and Wall, 2000). Tourists often demand foods that are not necessarily sourced locally, are not seasonal and may have to be imported from overseas markets. These different categories of consumer link closely to the typologies of different types of restaurant. Kivela (1997) suggests there are four restaurant types: (i) fine dining/gourmet; (ii) theme/atmosphere; (iii) family/popular; and (iv) convenience/fast-food, with different customer bases in terms of the tourist interest in local food and drink. Arguably all these types have the potential to make different buying choices to help sustain local economies, and even 'fast' food does not need to come from distant markets: it is not a zero-sum game (as argued in Chapter 5). Although there is variation across the sector and not all consumers are interested in pursuing a local food or food and drink tourism experience (or paying more for it), the hospitality sector has a role to play in bringing consumers closer to producers, for the reasons outlined in Chapter 20.

In a study of French restaurants, Bessière and Tibere (2013: 3423) claim restaurant owners are central and their decisions impact the entire agro-food promotion system. They find that product tasting in a restaurant leads directly to new purchasing practices and tourists are encouraged to visit the production location, and continue to purchase regionally identifiable foods after they leave the destination (Montanari and Staniscia, 2009). Similar findings by Amuquandoh and Asafo-Adjei (2013) in Ghana find international tourists patronise a great variety of Ghanaian foods and they identify a substantial market of food-interested visitors that should be nurtured and better supported. For example, they calculate that there could be high economic gain if more popular local foods were provided for visitors. Finding that tourists could identify the local foods they consumed and were able to recall them demonstrates that tourists have a good level of knowledge of local foodstuffs; consequently hotels and restaurants need to exploit this demand more effectively. Government has a role to play in this, and the sector must be supported (Amuquandoh and Asafo-Adjei, 2013: 998):

> the government needs to support the improvements in productivity and production systems of these products. Often, the support required by such small scale farmers includes the improvement of infrastructure in rural areas, the provision of loans, and the provision of extension services.

In terms of accommodation providers (hotels, resorts, and guest houses), Ashley et al. (2007: 18) claim limited analysis has been undertaken of the extent to which hotels use local produce, finding that it is 'is still lacking in many countries', where 'most resorts and hotels do not yet maximise their use of local products and services'. Likewise, in a study of accommodation providers in KwaZulu-Natal in South Africa, Pillay and Rogerson (2013) found that, despite the government encouraging the development of responsible and sustainable tourism approaches, inter-sectoral linkages between tourism and other economic sectors were weak and more could be done to integrate tourism more closely into local economies. The supply of local food to tourism establishments was hailed as a potential business opportunity for poor communities. It was clear that some hotels in South Africa's major cities were pursuing initiatives in expanding local food sourcing and procurement as part of their wider adoption of 'green' or 'responsible' business practices, but it remains limited and reflects the patchy global adoption of sustainable buying practices by the industry. Their research found accommodation establishments were procuring the majority of their food suppliers through a single intermediary supplier on the grounds of efficiency and convenience. Only 12% of the establishments surveyed sourced fresh produce themselves, finding working with one single supplier to be easier and quicker. This is where a well-managed cooperative of producers (see Chapter 20) could provide a solution, where hotels could still deal with one organisation or contact, but the cooperative or umbrella organisation could bring together numerous local providers (see the Case Study below).

CASE STUDY

Scandic Hotels, Nordics

Scandic Hotels are a franchise of around 230 hotels in the Nordics. It was on the verge of collapse in the early 1990s, but a new CEO (Roland Nilsson) turned the company around by introducing two business principles: decentralised management and sustainable development. The new value system embodied the concept of sustainability, and linked customers and employees, who were calling for more environmental responsibility (Goodman, 2000).

By 1993 Scandic Hotels were one of the first hotel chains to put in place far-reaching green practices and were recognised as exceptional in their adoption of products that recognise the importance of ecological food and the local economy. It buys foods that are organic, local, Fair Trade, non-genetically modified, climate-labelled and ecologically harmless. Two of the many commitments they make are to 'Serve organic food and reward sustainable fishing', and 'Place environmental requirements on suppliers'. It claims 'We want to find the balance between the physical, emotional and spiritual needs that all people have. It is a holistic approach and a great way to relate to life, we think.'

In 1999 they gained the Nordic Ecolabel for Scandic Sjølyst in Oslo (the Swan) and work with the EU Ecolabel (a tough environmental label to gain for hotels). Their website has very detailed information on their commitment to sustainability, including promises about their waste (Scandic Hotels, 2015). They claim,

> We throw away as little food as we can. The food waste from our breakfasts has been reduced by over 25% since we started working in a smarter way in terms of how much food we put out on the buffet at a time, and weighing and recording every day … Many of our hotels have food waste disposers, and wherever the municipality offers the opportunity, we recycle food waste and send it to compost or for biogas production.

Their commitment is an extremely powerful and effective marketing tool for the hotel chain. They are not only supporting local people (including homeless shelters), but can use their sustainability principles to attract ethical consumers. This commitment undoubtedly saved the business from bankruptcy. As Bohdanowicz et al. (2005) found, environmental responsibility can become a top corporate priority and lead to significantly decreased environmental impact, excellent economic performance, and a considerably upgraded image.

Source: www.scandichotels.com, Goodman (2000) and Bohdanowicz et al. (2005).

It is clear from the Scandic Hotels example that hotel managers, owners and staff all have a role to play in ensuring the hospitality industry is engaging with sustainable food practices. Work by Duram and Cawley (2012) on restaurants in Galway, Ireland further suggests that the role of the chef is key where, 'chefs are indeed revalorizing "local" in the cuisine that they serve which may involve products that are not per se "alternative" but the provenance of which is more closely sourced than in the past' (2012: 23). However, the adoption of 'local' is perhaps more fluid than consumers might expect and challenges in sourcing produce results in a more pragmatic definition of 'local' (Duram and Cawley, 2012: 23):

> Even when chefs are deeply committed to using food grown and processed locally, artisan products may be imported from outside the immediate area or from overseas for particular dishes and to meet consumer expectations. The reputation of artisan producers serves as a guarantee of quality and trusted intermediary importers are used … differentiation may be sought through methods of cooking and the use of condiments to create more exotic dishes. A restaurant may participate in the stretching of local food to incorporate artisanal food in order to create a differentiated market niche.

This approach is not just about hotels and restaurants, but has an increasingly important role for other players in the hospitality industry such as public houses (pubs). This was highlighted by Jones and Rowley (2012) in Wales, who found people were buying more alcohol from supermarkets, and many pubs were closing down. People are no longer going to pubs just for a drink; the food offer is increasingly important and provides a strong marketing tool. The emergence of successful pubs and public house chains based on buying local has been quite a phenomenon and is illustrated by the reduction of drinking-only pubs and the rise of the 'gastro-pub' (see Chapter 12). The emergence of the gastro-pub has become a powerful way to emphasise the quality of food at public houses and revitalise the industry in those countries with a pub tradition (such as the UK, Ireland and Australia).

LOCAL PURCHASING AS A MARKETING AND PR VEHICLE

The Scandic Hotels example demonstrates the importance and reputational value of ensuring there is explicit promotion of local producers, responsible practices and regional brands. The powerful marketing impact of this was exploited effectively in the New Zealand and Australia wine industry (Mitchell and Hall, 2001), although it has taken longer for food to be explicitly linked to place. Research by Smith and Hall (2003: 250) in Iowa, USA found upscale and high-end restaurants were willing to pay 10–20% more for locally sourced produce, finding customers willing to pay more for high-quality local produce as consumers perceive local products to be fresher, tastier and more trustworthy (Roininen et al., 2006). Other studies show that local food is regarded as more authentic, pure and traditional, with many tourists stating it is a welcome and important 'ingredient' in their overall holiday experience (Seaman et al. 2014).

Restaurants are in a position to change menus to match seasonal produce. They are often privately owned, so are not tied to large contracts, and demand and turnover is much lower than for large supermarkets, which provides greater levels of flexibility. In research on New Zealand restaurants by Smith and Hall (2003), they found that two-thirds of restaurants wanted to increase local food use. A move to more local procurement has significant advantages (Gibson, 1995). From the growers' side, restaurant contracts provide more market certainty as prices can be fixed; there are then greater returns for the restaurants which would pay more if they went through a supplier. Additionally, closer personal contact between restaurants and growers facilitates more immediate and honest two-way feedback about the produce, so issues can be dealt with immediately. Furthermore, there is a greater level of brand recognition if producer names are used in menus.

The consumption of locally produced food and the utilisation of local ingredients on tourist menus reduce imports and leakage of tourism revenue from the local economy (Torres, 2002). Moskwa et al. (2015: 126) use examples from Adelaide, Australia to argue that cafés and restaurants can become 'sites for experimentation in profitable and just sustainable hospitality, and places for sustainability engagement and education'. The key aspect is 'profitable', where sustainable practices can lead to a wide range of benefits to the business. Some of the most effective ways to generate new business are to include on a menu or restaurant window the names of producers, place of origin, how far the food has travelled, or a regional 'badge' or logo. One of these 'badges' may be a locally identifiable mark of quality and authenticity (see Figure 21.2) or a more globally recognised logo, like the snail of the Slow Food movement. As discussed in Chapter 11, Slow Food messages are increasingly used to confirm the use of local ingredients and traditional cooking methods, and can help the hospitality industry make claims to authenticity and cultural capital. Mkono (2012b: 152) states: 'food choice and consumption are not viewed simply as acts in dining, but perhaps as a microcosm of a much more complex "slow tourism" phenomenon'.

Some marketing approaches to build identity and reputation if a business is committed to local food purchasing are outlined in Table 21.1.

FIGURE 21.2 *A Bridgestone Guide Award in a restaurant window in Galway, Ireland acknowledges that authentic and local food is sourced and used. Photo by author*

TABLE 21.1 *Marketing approaches to help build identity and reputation based on local food purchasing practices*

Target communications to appeal to specific groups of customers (requires good understanding of the current and intended customer base)

Effective pricing strategies – structure pricing to reflect portion size and quality

Even if local food more expensive, use the principals of sustainability and place distinctiveness to place premium on retail price

Consider promotional meal deals and loyalty programmes

Offer incentives at the point of purchase on popular services to encourage the guest to try your restaurant another time (bounce backs)

Innovative and regular use of social media via Twitter, Facebook, etc.

Promote food quality and reliability in all key marketing messages

Negotiate with local suppliers and use locally sourced, in season ingredients. Invite them to visit and eat at the hotel/restaurant so they understand what is needed and why

Create visible signs of food quality on menus, display awards, editorials, pub guides, signage, website, etc.

Use unusual and innovative approaches to develop new food and drink combinations

Ensure there is good manager and employee knowledge of food and drink create upselling opportunities (key to success for Scandic Hotel group)

Update menus regularly and display menus on the website and all other relevant information sources

Create a theme and inviting environment – appeal to the customers that you want to attract and keep

Train employees to be welcoming and effective marketers, armed with sustainability and local messages

Build links with your destination and community; promote other activities and business near your pub

Host food and drink events – this is a great way to position a restaurant and raise its profile – encourages free PR through local media channels

Even if sustainable purchasing decisions are not used to raise a business's profile, there are still ethical and sustainability dimensions to the procurement and use of local food. Most hotels and guesthouses generally provide key daily meals (most usually breakfast). Although there is often little choice for the consumer during this meal and is not often advertised as a distinctive experience in itself (although some hotels do this with locally sourced meats), hotels could achieve a great deal for the local economy if breakfast produce was locally sourced, thereby building relationships with farmers, cereal and fruit providers and drink producers. Often this is the invisible 'back kitchen' part of consumer engagement with food in the hospitality industry, yet it can be the most significant. However, sometimes this local message can be exploited and consumers need to be aware as the industry has ways to promote 'local' even when the relationship to a local supplier is very distant or tenuous. A farmer producing breakfast meats in Ireland (Avril, West Cork) described how her business is challenged by dubious practices during an interview in Everett (2007: 231):

> We prefer to make quality all of the way, but that's what you have to do as a small producer, particularly in the breakfast meat market. It's a very competitive market, you have got people that are hugely bigger than us, the volumes, they are probably using imported meat, either bacon or pork and once you put your knife through a piece of meat; let's say if you have a piece of loin bacon you have changed its appearance so from being one piece of meat it has become two pieces of meat and you can put down 'produced in Ireland'!

CASE STUDY

Newburgh Inn, Aberdeenshire, using 'local' as a unique selling point

This hotel and restaurant dedicates much of its promotional material to their commitment to sustainability (http://briggies.co.uk 2015):

> Where possible we source all of our suppliers come from within a 50 mile radius of our premises, in reality a lot of our suppliers are within 20 miles of our doorstep, reducing our food miles. We ensure we visit our suppliers, farms and producers every 6 weeks to ensure produce and livestock are well looked after.

Their explicit commitment to a short and responsible supply chain is clear:

> Ethical procurement is high on our agenda, not only is it the right thing to do it also makes great business sense too. Helping to build long term relationships with our suppliers, this in turn can ensure quality and security of our supplier. We ensure that we develop agreements and code of conduct to ensure a better supply and service.

The five key areas of focus that make up their clear sourcing policy are (from their website):

1. We promote environmentally positive farming which helps to protect the landscape, reduce pollution and combat biodiversity loss, and encompasses the LEAF marque system.
2. Promoting local and seasonal food is essential to our menus and eating sustainably. Making use of what we produce ourselves throughout the year is better for the environment than importing out of season produce from far and wide.
3. Ensuring that we have sustainable fish choices is important since stocks of some fish are seriously at risk.
4. Working with farmers to ensure ethical meat and dairy forming a cornerstone of responsible sourcing within our kitchen. If

▶

you buy free range or Freedom food at the supermarket or farm shop, you'll want to know that your local restaurant meal is of the same or better quality.

5. For all of our overseas produce Fair Trade or fairly traded is important. We buy products from communities in the developing world that haven't disadvantaged the producers. It's about ensuring that market price is paid and that working conditions are of a decent standard.

Newburgh Inn is an excellent example of how the hospitality industry can use 'local' to the advantage of the planet, as well as to its own business.

Source: http://briggies.co.uk

ACTIVITY   **A LOCAL HOSPITALITY BUSINESS USING LOCAL FOOD**

Find an example of a hotel and/or restaurant like the Newburgh Inn near you that openly promotes its commitment to sustainability through local food and drink sourcing.

1. What marketing methods does it use to promote itself and its ethical commitment to its customers?
2. How effective is their marketing strategy in engaging and encouraging you to visit?
3. What more do you think it could do to promote the local economy and community development?

THE CHALLENGES OF SOURCING 'LOCAL' PRODUCE

To facilitate the purchase of local food (in its widest definition), key things need to be addressed and this is where some hotel and restaurants owners and managers raise concerns. Quality and freshness need to be consistent, reassurance on quantities provided to meet demand, and prices need to be competitive (although it has been found that consumers in high-end establishments will pay more for local food). In their study of Durban, South Africa, Pillay and Rogerson (2013) claim the key obstacles were the quality of the food, health and safety issues, reliable service and affordability. They also found difficulties in owners being able to communicate with local farmers, and the high turnover of staff meant consistency and staff understanding of key sustainability principles were difficult to retain.

In a study based in Jamaica, Belisle (1984a: 3) asked 'Why is local food production not increased in order to supply hotels with a greater share of their requirements?' and found Jamaicans only produce a fraction of the food they consume.

He summarises the reasons for not buying more local as 'availability, quality, price, regularity of supply, convenience, and taste'. Some of the reasons are interrelated (i.e., unavailability and irregularity of supply) and generally a combination of reasons (as opposed to a single reason) explains the use of imported food. The explanations included historical evolution of the role of food production (focus on sugar cane and not food crops), physical obstacles (poor soil due to landscape and climatic patterns), behavioural characteristics (attitudes toward agricultural work and change and also lack of awareness by farmers of what hotels actually want), economic constraints (landownership structure is very uneven with most land in ownership of the few), technological limitations (limited access to farm machinery, fertiliser and pesticides), and marketing inadequacies (difficult to predict demand, and attempting crop forecasting so hotels aware of what is available). Over 30 years ago, Belisle (1984b) noted that 'It remains to be seen, however, whether Jamaica will succeed in providing more food to its tourist industry' (1984b: 16). The Case Study below of Sandals in Jamaica may indicate it has been possible.

CASE STUDY

Sandals Resort purchasing local food through The Farmers' Programme, Jamaica

Belisle painted a bleak picture of local food usage in Jamaican hotels in 1984. However, the Farmers' Programme initiated and supported by the Sandals Group (large all-inclusive resort chain with 6,000 employees) in the Caribbean demonstrates how a private sector accommodation provider actively engaged in (a) channelling and creating demand for local products among its staff and customers; (b) supporting the supply side to deliver quality and quantity required; and (c) establishing workable communication structures between supply and demand. In 1996, the Sandals Group developed agricultural supply linkages, beginning with support from the Rural Agricultural Development Authority (RADA) to improve the quality and diversity of produce local farmers could supply to its hotels. The project included an officer who worked with farmers to improve production; collaboration with key organisations and hotel management teams visiting farmers to improve quality and marketing procedures. Farmers visit the hotels to see how their products are being used and the focus is on improving pricing and contractual arrangements. Problems included production issues (e.g. lack of water supply, lack of packing materials) and sale of the produce (e.g. inconsistent supply orders and lack of communication regarding demand).

The project began with ten farmers supplying two hotels and by 2004 it involved 80 farmers across the island. Within three years sales rose from US$60,000 to $3.3 million. Farmers' income increased and hotels gained a wider variety of good-quality local produce and made savings. The programme was

▶

expanded to St Lucia and Antigua, although in 2009, there was concern when Sandals reduced the number of fruit and produce buyers who deal with them directly from 60 to 16 in Jamaica. Reported in 2008, Sandals spent over J$370 million on local produce to supply its resorts across the country (*Jamaica Observer*, 19/04/09), although by 2014 the *Jamaica Observer* (24/01/14) was reporting, 'Sandals Group, which spends over $5.3 billion on local purchases, remains keen on the prospects of new tourism linkages to grow its local agriculture purchases for the regional hotel chain.' Unfortunately, it reports 'Then, as now, hotels were reluctant to source produce locally because of inconsistent volume, quality and price of supply ... Poor packaging and transportation often led to damaged produce.' Significant strides have been made, but some of the same issues of local purchasing by hotels need to be overcome.

Source: Pro Poor Tourism Pilots (Southern Africa) Programme, funded by DFID's Business Linkages Challenge Fund, facilitating adoption of pro-poor practices by tourism companies in Southern Africa. Available www.odi.org/sites/odi.org.uk/files/odi-assets/publications-opinion-files/3790.pdf, and the *Jamaica Observer* websites (2009 and 2014).

Inconsistent quality and quantity are problematic. Restaurant and pub owners still have a hazy definition of 'local' that could include the region or county. Sims (2010) found the definition of 'local' changed on a regular basis to accommodate what was available at any particular time. Her interview findings are very similar to those referenced earlier from Everett (2007) with the Irish producers. Sims (2010: 111) finds:

> Inconsistent product availability [the interviewee] is also having to negotiate the minefield that is his suppliers' understandings of local, where meanings can vary from pork bred and reared two miles down the road, to imported pork that has only spent two weeks in the county before it is slaughtered and labelled as 'local'.

Sims (2010) indicates that sometimes restaurant owners may adopt more flexible definitions of 'local' and the many tensions present in the concept need to be critically explored. There is a conscious reconstruction of what is 'local' by café and restaurant owners, where 'concepts were being constantly formed and reformed in response to material and symbolic interactions with producers, consumers and suppliers operating in other parts of the food network' (2010: 112). Some owners widened definitions of local from 'using locally supplied ingredients' to 'locally made' to try and retain the confidence of customers. This kind of discourse clearly illustrates the tension experienced by some hospitality owners, where the reality of offering local food and drink is often in conflict with initial intention of supporting local producers.

Financial power and budgetary controls are also significant obstacles. For example tenants of public houses are not always in control of their budgets and some that try to source local produce can find themselves at the mercy of large breweries who have ultimate financial control. For instance, Jones and Rowley (2012: 261) reported that in one of their case studies the tenant had built up the food sales, but,

> when the brewery in this case discovered how much money she had made, they changed the lease terms so that she had to hand over most of the profits over to the brewery. Therefore the incentive was lost and she abandoned the additional food promotions.

Competition for customers is a very real challenge in popular tourist areas. Jones and Rowley (2012) claim there are 14 million consumers in the UK for pubs, so competition is high and many engage in price wars or find it difficult to create unique selling propositions.

More generally across the hospitality sector, competition is severe in popular tourist areas. As outlined in Table 21.1, uniqueness can be found and used, and this comes from local menu innovations, food presentation and the atmosphere, but customers need to hear about this, and the business needs to know its market. Hotels, restaurants and pubs all have differing investment structures and the challenges of sourcing quality seasonal local ingredients at competitive prices is fundamental to business success. In busy areas, sometimes food and drink are not the reason for the visit. For example, Mkono's (2012b: 147) study of restaurants at Victoria Falls, Zimbabwe illustrates the competitive challenges in buying and promoting local food to passing tourists, claiming that 'Victoria Falls has become a "slow food versus fast food" battleground': tourists used to enjoy local food at a leisurely pace, but now fast food chains have moved in and taken a lot of business away from the smaller restaurants. There is therefore not only competition between the same types of restaurant (i.e. small and local restaurants) but significant competition across the types of restaurant outlined in the categories referenced above by Kivela (1997).

PROVIDING A 'LOCAL' INTERNATIONAL AND ETHNIC OFFERING

Another challenge is providing locally sourced produce for dishes that may not be originally from the destination. Aside from tourists demanding locally identifiable food, there is also a market for ethnic foodstuffs that might be from their home countries or a more international marketplace i.e. ethnic cuisines. Wood and Muñoz (2007) argue that ethnic-themed restaurants serve as conduits of foreign cultural images and are increasingly offered to locals and tourists. These could include offering Indian food in Australia, Chinese in the UK, or Italian in China. In their study of Indian restaurants in the USA, Chhabra et al. (2003: 146) state that 'Ethnicity is often conveyed in a purpose-driven staged manner in spaces beyond its place of origin'. Molz (2004) claims that ethnic restaurants construct varied forms of cultural settings to create a traditional ambience and provide a venue for an authentic 'eatertainment' experience, regardless of the country a visitor is in. Of the authentic 'servicescapes' Chhabra et al. (2003) outline, in terms of 'provenance' they claim this emphasises that ingredients, locally sourced and unique, stand-alone ingredients, or those that compose a dish, are reflective of a culinary heritage and history of the food. Consequently, the challenge is for hotels and resorts to provide a wide range of (ethnic) cuisines whilst still ensuring the raw ingredients are sourced locally and contributing to the local economy. In their Irish study, Duram and Cawley (2012: 20) found that 'local' was often extended to include artisanal produce from other European countries. This international dimension of 'local' procurement is less well-documented. Grains, lentils, chickpeas and wine were sourced through speciality importers, but were not for traditional Irish dishes. Rather, Duram and Cawley (2012: 23) find 'differentiation may be sought through methods of cooking and the use of condiments to create more exotic dishes. A restaurant may participate in the stretching of local food to incorporate artisanal food in order to create a differentiated market niche.'

This 'stretching' of the definition of 'local' highlights how sourcing local food appropriate for some tourism groups can be challenging. Cultural and religious culinary requirements for tourists are also increasingly important to consider. Although it is beyond the remit of this book to discuss religious tourism, it is worth noting that tourism must consider the growing numbers of people from different religions who are becoming significant tourist populations. For example, one of the most important target markets for certain destinations is Muslim tourists and their (culinary) needs must be considered by the global hospitality sector (Battour et al., 2012). Muslims now make up more than 25% of the populations in Marseilles and Rotterdam, 20% of Malmo (Sweden), 15% in Brussels and more than 10% in London, Paris and Copenhagen (Masci, 2005). Globally, there are between 1.5 to 1.8 billion Muslims who form at least a fifth of the world's population and Islam is today the second-largest religion in the world after Christianity. As a result, there is increasingly research on obtaining halal food for Muslim tourists. Certainly, sourcing appropriate halal or kosher food is problematic in many remote destinations and Christian or secular countries and this adds to the complexity of sourcing food, let alone ensuring it is also local to the region (Wan Hassan and Awang, 2009).

Critical Reflections: 'competitive advantage' through differentiation

Michael Porter is Professor of Business Administration at Harvard Business School and is best known for the business concept of 'competitive advantage'. This term describes the attributes that allow an organisation to outperform its competitors through either cost or differentiation. It involves assessing what aspects make up a

FOOD AND DRINK ATTRACTIONS AND EVENTS

company's value chain and thinking strategically about its positioning and overall value system. Porter suggests that strategic management should be concerned with building and sustaining competitive advantage. In terms of the hospitality sector, it can be argued that local food and drink sourcing can provide businesses with this competitive advantage through differentiation and a value system that gives superior benefits to the customer. Based on Porter (2011 [1985]) and studies of industry structure and competitive positioning, the resources to take into account when assessing the comparative advantages of a tourism business or destination are: human, physical, knowledge, capital, infrastructure and tourism superstructure, technologies and historical and cultural resources.

In using a 'resource-based' view Porter suggests a business can pull together its resources and capabilities to create differentiation. In an article on competitive advantage and corporate social responsibility (CSR), Porter and Kramer (2006) suggested that 'the prevailing approaches to CSR are so disconnected from business as to obscure many of the great opportunities for companies to benefit society'. In embedding hospitality businesses in local supply chains and working with producers, where local resources are used with local knowledge and skills, it is possible to create the differentiation sought by culinary tourists, i.e. the escape, difference and cultural capital identifier (see Chapter 4), thereby providing high levels of competitive advantage in a very competitive sector. As indicated in the case studies, Scandic Hotels in the Nordic countries, Sandals in Jamaica and the Newburgh Inn in Scotland are examples of hospitality businesses that have managed to do this.

Source: Porter (2011 [1985], Porter and Kramer (2006).

Working with food and drink in the hospitality sector

If you enjoy hosting and entertaining people, a hospitality career might be for you. Entry-level positions range from catering assistants, bar team members and room attendants, and all these positions offer opportunities to quickly progress to general managers and more senior positions if you have the right attitude. Some sectors of the industry provide traditional career paths. For example, in a hotel kitchen you can move from being an apprentice chef through various positions that include head or executive chef. Many chefs move on to become owner/operators of their own restaurants, or move into management positions in hotels. Career paths may be less linear and more sideways, enabling progression to a similar level position in a different part of the industry.

In hospitality, the hours can be long. Hotels are essentially 24-hour businesses and restaurants are often open long hours and on weekends. Hospitality jobs typically

(Continued)

(Continued)

require at least a secondary school diploma and extensive on-the-job experience. Larger restaurants and hotels may require their managers to have a bachelor's degree in business management, and some restaurants may prefer their managers to have tertiary training in the culinary field. Degrees in hospitality management are now offered by many universities around the world, and language skills are always useful (the most useful are English, Mandarin, Cantonese, French, Spanish and German).

Salaries in the hospitality industry can be good, but they often start off low and you work your way up. Some indicative salaries are provided here in US dollars and UK sterling (currency conversions based on 2015 rates). Accommodation and food service managers average US$45–55k (£30–35k) annually, although many who own their own hospitality businesses can do very well indeed! Some of the highest-paid hospitality jobs according to Monster.com (2015) include a corporate chef job where you set the menu, purchase food, and train senior leadership and chefs on new menu items (salary around US$175,000 (£110k)), hotel manager at US$112,400 (£75k), regional restaurant manager at US$95,800 (£60k), or a wine sommelier $50,400 (£32k) who shares their knowledge about wine with consumers with the intention of selling it to them.

The Hospitality Guild website provides a unique and interactive career map to help you think about which area of this vast industry might interest you (look for the 'career map' on www.hospitalityguild.co.uk). Hospitality is an engaging, sociable working environment, with career opportunities around the world. In this sector you may get the chance to make purchasing decisions and I hope if you find yourself in this position you will always try to buy local and support the local community and producers around you!

CHAPTER SUMMARY

As outlined in earlier chapters, the World Travel and Tourism Council (WTTC, 2015) estimates that by the end of 2015, the travel and tourism sector will contribute US$7,860 billion, 10% of global GDP (including all direct, indirect and induced impacts). It will account for 284 million jobs, 9.5% of total employment, or one in eleven of all jobs on the planet. Given that the hospitality industry makes up the majority of this large industry, it is clear that it has a key role to play in the sustainability of local economies and regional development. Given its global reach and direct contribution to world GDP, it has the power to reduce external leakage around the world and support local economies.

Some of the challenges to significantly increasing the use of local produce by the hospitality industry and ensuring economic gains stay within local economies include the ability of small producers to meet demand and provide the quantities required for larger hotels and resorts; the lack of convenience working with lots of providers rather than one supplier; greater exposure to higher risks of climate or political impact (as opposed to a global market); decision-makers not necessarily working 'on the ground' as seen in some hotels and public houses; tourist demand for exotic and overseas ethnic produce (education is the key here); and providing consistent quality. It is suggested that none of these issues are insurmountable and the case studies have provided ideas on how this can be achieved. There is a need to foster direct supplier and marketing relationships between producer and hotels and restaurants, thereby shortening the supply chain, and ensuring better returns for producers and communities. Producers need to work together in networks to share resources and information and undertake joint marketing approaches. This more collaborative type of working can open new markets and economic opportunities in the hospitality industry (Everett and Slocum, 2013). Finally, there is significant value and worth in embedding practices of local purchase behaviour in the mind-sets of hospitality leaders, owners and managers. It is through their decision-making that meaningful sustainability can be achieved in the hospitality industry.

END OF CHAPTER POINTS

- Better inter-sectoral linkages between tourism and other economic sectors could be more effectively nurtured, and more done to integrate the hospitality sector with local economies and communities.

- Ethical tourists and customers are willing to pay more for high-quality local produce as there is an association between local and quality and authenticity, but the hospitality sector needs to make more of this through marketing and promotion.

- The concept of 'local' must be assessed critically. The adoption of 'local' as a descriptor is often extremely fluid, as difficulties in sourcing produce lead to businesses resorting to a more pragmatic definition of 'local'.

- Local food purchasing offers the hospitality business significant growth'opportunities if it is built into a marketing strategy that focuses on differentiation in line with the values underpinning the concept of 'competitive advantage' (Porter, 2011).

- Some of the reasons given by the hospitality industry for not purchasing more local food include guarantees of the quantities needed, availability, quality, price, convenience and taste. These obstacles are not insurmountable and examples exist where these challenges have been translated into reputational gains for the business and income for local economies.

FURTHER READING

Amuquandoh, E. F. and Asafo-Adjei, R. (2013) 'Traditional food preferences of tourists in Ghana', *British Food Journal*, 115 (7): 987–1002.

Mkono, M. (2012b) 'Slow food versus fast food: a Zimbabwean case study of hotelier perspectives', *Tourism and Hospitality Research*, 12 (3): 147–54.

Moskwa, E., Higgins-Desbiolles, F. and Gifford, S. (2015) 'Sustainability through food and conversation: the role of an entrepreneurial restaurateur in fostering engagement with sustainable development issues', *Journal of Sustainable Tourism*, 23(1): 126–45.

Pillay, M. and Rogerson, C.M. (2013) 'Agriculture-tourism linkages and pro-poor impacts: The accommodation sector of urban coastal KwaZulu-Natal, South Africa', *Applied Geography*, 1 (36): 49–58.

Porter, M.E. (2011 [1985])*The Competitive Advantage of Nations*. New York: Simon and Schuster.

Porter, M.E. and Kramer, M.R. (2006) 'The link between competitive advantage and corporate social responsibility', *Harvard Business Review*, 84 (12): 78–92.

Sims, R. (2010) 'Putting place on the menu: the negotiation of locality in UK food tourism, from production to consumption', *Journal of Rural Studies*, 26 (2): 105–15.

Telfer, D.J. and Wall, G. (2000) 'Strengthening backward economic linkages: local food purchasing by three Indonesian hotels', *Tourism Geographies*, 2 (4): 421–47.

22

THE FUTURE OF FOOD AND DRINK TOURISM

CHAPTER OBJECTIVES

- To provide a summary of key points about food and drink tourism
- To discuss the potential future growth and key priorities for the development of food and drink tourism
- To suggest how issues and challenges regarding social justice, local economic development and sustainability might be addressed and mediated
- To offer ideas on potential areas for future research and project topics relating to food and drink tourism

CHAPTER SUMMARY

It is hoped that you have found this book a useful and informative overview of food and drink tourism. It has explored the many dimensions of the culinary tourism experience and has sought to discuss more concepts, examples and themes than many other published books or previous articles on the subject. It has addressed and raised many issues and hopefully inspired you to find out more about how this important tourism sector could develop and contribute to the sustainable growth of local economies and communities. I hope it has encouraged you to consider how you might personally contribute to the industry as a consumer, researcher and perhaps even as a producer. By employing case studies from around the world, this book has addressed, highlighted and illustrated a wide range of topics and aspects of food and drink tourism that characterise and represent its international reach, evolving nature and the many people involved in its growth and delivery.

Some of the principal issues and challenges addressed throughout this book are briefly revisited in this chapter, with some reflection on the chapters in which key points were made. It outlines some significant areas where this sector could develop, offers predictions on how this food and drink tourism might expand into new countries, and assesses what the consequences of this growth might be for people and the planet. It looks at some of the key drivers of the future of food tourism, potential demand, the search for exclusivity and social capital, social justice and sustainability, the impact of social media and new marketing channels, and considers where future academic research might be most usefully expanded.

THE DRIVERS OF FUTURE FOOD AND DRINK TOURISM

The appetite for studying and interrogating food and drink tourism continues to grow. This seemingly insatiable interest in the subject is illustrated by a recent publication by Yeoman et al. (2015), an edited collection of chapters on *The Future of Food Tourism*. This insightful book should be consulted if you are interested in finding out more about how and where this tourism phenomenon might develop further, and what the implications might be in terms of the industry and for academic researchers looking at the future of the subject. Their edited collection paints a very positive picture of the direction of this food and drink tourism, and the authors suggest that there is little sign of the interest in this sector of tourism activity waning. It is beyond doubt that food and drink tourism has become the fastest-growing sector of the tourism industry, and this is set to continue. After all, we all need to eat and drink – whether we are at home or on holiday. There are very few tourism activities that are so fundamental and non-negotiable. Yeoman et al. (2015) have summarised their book by presenting a series of key 'drivers of change' that affect discourses, actions and behaviours in food tourism. These drivers provide a useful framework to help us think about the future of the subject; they are listed here with added explanations in parentheses to further expand their meaning (2015: 8):

- Food tourism as political capital (discourses of economic, social and cultural benefit)
- Food tourism as a visionary state (a collective utopia, addressing global problems)
- What it means to be a 'foodie' (cultural and social capital, shaping identity)
- The drive for affluence and exclusivity (redefining luxury, higher-value and -spend tourists, and reshaped social and economic capital)
- Fluid experiences in a postmodernist world (wide range of experiences, flexibility and fluidity in activities and types of engagement).

It is acknowledged that some driving forces of change cannot be reversed or stopped, and these may include climate change, increasing scarcity of oil and other fuels, and global economic and political upheaval. This chapter addresses many of these drivers by focusing on key areas of change and development covered in earlier chapters. Discussing the architecture needed to support the future of food tourism, Danielmeier and Albrecht (2015: 94) outline eight drivers for food and drink tourism:

- cultural capital and differentiation
- social significance of food
- luxury experience
- technology and natural environment
- urbanisation and population density
- globalisation and 'glocalisation'
- climate change (e.g. droughts affecting wine regions, or agricultural challenges)
- competition among attractions and destinations.

This final chapter looks at the likely future demand for food and drink tourism, a search for exclusivity and capital, the power of the consumer and social media, the impact and influence of technology, how social justice and sustainability may be realised through food tourism, and what the future might look like for research in this subject.

THE FUTURE DEMAND AND GROWTH FOR FOOD AND DRINK TOURISM

As an industry, tourism is growing at an exponential rate and the demand for food and drink from these tourists will certainly follow. As outlined in Chapter 1, the latest WTTC reports (2015: 1) indicate that the tourism sector has been growing at a faster rate than any other global industry, including the automotive, financial services and healthcare sectors. It finds that tourism generated 277 million jobs (1 in 11 jobs) for the global economy in 2014. Furthermore, international tourist arrivals reached nearly 1.14 billion in 2014, and in terms of its direct contribution to the world's Gross Domestic Product (GDP), tourism contributed US$2,364.8bn (3.1% of total GDP) in 2014, which rose by 3.7% in 2015. It is set to rise by 3.9% per year from 2015–2025, to US$3,593.2bn (3.3% of total GDP) in 2025. The money spent by foreign visitors to a country (or visitor exports) is a key component of the direct contribution of tourism, although to get a picture of the total spend, domestic visitor spend should also be included. In 2014, the world generated US$1,383.8bn in visitor exports. In 2015, this is expected to grow by 2.8%, and the world is expected to attract 1,172,740,000 international tourist arrivals (WTTC, 2015). If a third of this spend is on food and drink, this would offer significant opportunities for food and drink tourism providers to exploit this growth. As Chapter 1 stated, of all possible areas of expenditures while travelling, tourists are least likely to make cuts in their food budget. The World Travel Association has found that the food tourism industry generates over $150 billion per year. Some of the research is illuminating; for example, in a report on gastronomic tourism, Mintel (2009) found that out of 160 million leisure travellers from the USA alone, 27.3 million (17%) were considered culinary travellers.

There are a number of reasons why food tourism is becoming so popular. The formal media and informal social media channels are playing an important role in shaping how we view food; celebrity chefs are also a major part of this trend; and increasingly holiday brochures and packages are giving attention to the food and drink offerings available at destinations. As people become more aware of the culinary choices available, they become more willing to travel long distances to try different types of cuisine and beverage. People are also increasingly willing to pay more, try more and eat more. It is clear that food tourism will continue to offer destinations an attractive vehicle of new streams of revenue based on pre-existing resources such as agriculture, history and traditions. It is being added to the destination marketing portfolio of numerous regions and countries to provide unique selling points and places of specific interest. For example, in their study of Door County in north-east Wisconsin, Green and Dougherty (2008) note that culinary tourists there spent about $1,000 per trip, which represented a massive injection of funds into the local and regional economies. They claim that there will be significant growth in the culinary traveller market, as the number of travellers interested in culinary travel grows, and as people want unique experiences and build their social and cultural capital. In meeting these demands, destinations have an increasing menu of products and experiences that can be offered, from events and festivals (Chapters 13 and 14), routes, trails and tours (Chapter 15) to more fixed visitor attractions and museums that celebrate and showcase food and drink (Chapter 16). Furthermore, the changing tastes and needs of tourists will need to include greater awareness of ethnic and religious requirements, such as kosher and halal food, as the population of tourists from Muslim and countries with a growing tourism industry increases (Chapter 21).

THE SEARCH FOR EXCLUSIVITY AND DEVELOPMENT OF SOCIAL CAPITAL

Much of the literature suggests that the focus of future destination marketing and tourism strategies will be on attracting high-value, high-spend food tourists through unique and exclusive experiences that will not put excessive pressure on infrastructure and limited resources (Everett and Aitchison, 2008; Sims, 2009). In delivering the unique and exclusive, destinations will need to capitalise on their distinctive character, culture, traditions and landscapes to give them competitive advantage (Chapter 20). The demand for more unusual items, a wider range of foodstuffs, and unique experiences is set to grow and the food and tourism sector is set to become even more differentiated. Yeoman et al. (2015: 9) suggest that, 'increased affluence alters the consumer balance of power as new forms of connection and association allow a literal pursuit of personal identity which is fluid and less restructured by background of geography'. There is a growing thirst for luxury and the unique, where a drive towards postmodern experiences needs to be accommodated by those offering tourism experiences (Chapter 1). This offering reflects the desire for greater social capital (Chapter 15), cultural capital (Chapter 4) and more explicit engagement with the experience economy, including the weird, bizarre and outrageous (Chapter 14).

One of the key drivers behind the demand for distinctive food and drink offerings is the growing level of outbound tourism from emerging economies and destinations with new-found influence and affluence. These nations are what Jim O'Neill, the global economist at Goldman Sachs, has labelled the BRIC economies (Brazil, Russia, India and China) and this thinking has expanded to include the MINT (Mexico, Indonesia, Nigeria and Turkey) nations. These new markets and groups of consumers are increasingly keen to bolster their levels of cultural and social capital, and food tourism is offering a vehicle through which to pursue and achieve this. The WTTC (2015) claims that visitors from emerging economies now represent a 46% share of overall international tourist arrivals (up from 38% in 2000), proving the growth and increased opportunities for travel from those in these new markets. Countries are now leveraging and exploiting their own capital, to a point where Mulcahy (2015: 83) states that, 'spatial fixity has also created one of the "new" forms of independent and sustainable tourism that enables tourists to enhance their cultural capital while providers increase their social and economic capital'. This thinking directly links to what Laing and Frost (2014) refer to as the emergent 'food explorer': someone who seeks out authenticity, and is committed to supporting local producers and keeping heritages and traditions alive (Everett and Aitchison, 2008). It is clear that this desire to 'show off' and promote public demonstrations of exclusivity and experience is being fuelled and facilitated by the rapid growth in web technologies and social media.

SOCIAL MEDIA AND THE GROWTH OF CONSUMER POWER

Food and drink tourism will undoubtedly continue to grow and expand into many more spheres of interest, new locations and destinations, and will impact more people who are offering experiences and/or enjoying them. One of the central ways that this growth will be supported and expanded is through the proliferation of social media technologies and usage (Chapter 9).

The importance of social media in the online tourism domain is beyond any doubt (Xiang and Gretzel, 2010): we now see extensive use of handheld smart devices and mobile technology around the world, and people are able to instantaneously share experiences in words, video and images (including pictures of food and drink) on platforms including Facebook, blogs, Instagram, Twitter, and other social network platforms, as well as sharing images with cloud-based technology or file-sharing systems. This offers instant reviews, feedback and recommendations, thereby generating more interest from others to try different places and different food and drink. As outlined in Chapter 9, consumer-generated media has become the most powerful vehicle for destination marketing and it is imperative that managers and destinations grasp and use the full range of web 2.0 technologies to meet a multitude of tourist demands and tastes. It is clear that interest in food tourism will accelerate as geographical barriers continue to dissolve through social media, and effective use of it will lead to successful results for those destinations that understand and utilise it effectively. Technology in all its forms is one of the most powerful drivers of food and tourism growth and development.

TECHNOLOGY, INNOVATION AND TOMORROW'S FOOD SCIENCE

Technological developments will inevitably change the character of our eating and drinking experiences, at home and abroad. There are a number of areas of development in which technology has a key role to play and this now goes beyond the initial (online) research about where to go, and feedback on the experience via social media. These technological advances might include ordering food on touch screens (popular in some restaurants), or utilising advanced interactive experiences that allow the tourist to become more involved with the preparation of food, in line with some of the interpretation techniques already employed (Chapter 10). Examples of emerging interpretative visitor technologies include multi-player culinary game simulations, virtual kitchens, interactive streaming to smart devices of food being prepared, and live streaming of cooking shows that support the preparation of meals in real time.

Another area of food tourism made possible by technology is the growth of molecular and experimental gastronomy. This approach to food certainly offers consumers something novel and unique: a style of cuisine in which chefs embrace sensory experiences and food science (also called modernist cuisine, culinary physics, and experimental cuisine). Borrowing tools from science and ingredients from the food industry, chefs concoct unusual and futuristic experiences for their customers. Around the world, molecular gastronomy restaurants are appearing, making the chef and location famous and alluring. For example, the Moto in Chicago illustrates this approach to offering 'future food' very clearly.

Molecular and experimental food at Moto, Chicago, US

Moto is located in a nineteenth-century warehouse in the Fulton Market area of Chicago's meatpacking district. It attracts adventurous diners and the media with an imaginative interpretation of postmodern cuisine and molecular gastronomy. Described on Trip Advisor as 'adventurous, modern cuisine-as-art with exotic ingredients and futuristic presentations', this Asian-influenced restaurant is dedicated to the avant-garde cuisine of Chef Homaro Cantu. It proudly states that 'using science, technology and art in nouveau ways, the Moto team continues to astound and astonish with novel, interactive dining experiences, redefining the boundaries of established culinary traditions of taste, texture and technique'. Their blog boasts, 'Moto Restaurant in Chicago is not the place to go if you're looking for the ordinary. The restaurant, which specializes in molecular gastronomy, prepares its food in a lab, not a kitchen, complete with centrifuges and laboratory equipment.'

Techniques used at this and other similar 'molecular' restaurants include using carbon dioxide to add bubbles and make foams, liquid nitrogen for flash freezing and shattering, thermal immersion circulators for low temperature cooking, food dehydration, spherification (giving a caviar-like effect), syringes for injecting fillings, edible paper, using aromatic gases and highly unusual presentation techniques, where things are suspended, hidden, immersed, filled, exploded and theatrically inspired. In line with the increasing demand for experiences that generate social capital through unusual and exclusive gastronomic experiences, many restaurants around the world are now pushing the boundaries of what is possible, and attracting customers in search of something futuristic, different and daring.

Source: http://motorestaurant.com

Technology has also supported a shift in how people question and monitor the food they eat. Yeoman and McMahon-Beattie (2015: 31) state that consumers' interest in food and health has spawned a technological revolution in how people manage their heath. The smartphone has become the personal trainer, the diet monitor and the calorie counter. Technology and new products that help assess lifestyle, measure fitness and calculate food intake levels are increasingly being offered as self-monitoring tools for those actively engaged in what they refer to as the 'smart food revolution', linked to what Crawford (1980) has described as 'healthism' and a drive towards a healthier lifestyle and intake of better foods and supplements in the hope of a longer and healthier life.

There is a clearly a major role for science, innovation and technology in changing the food offer and our relationships with it. Its role is increasingly multi-faceted, on the one hand providing the unique and different, but on the other, ensuring there is enough food for the planet as the global population grows. According to

United Nations (2015) estimates, the human population of the world is expected to reach around 8 billion people in early 2024. Yeoman and McMahon-Beattie (2015: 27) use scenario planning to look at what they call the 'Star Trek Replicator', a term used to describe the advancement of food science into fields that include the development of *in vitro* meat and laboratory-grown food, genetically modified (GM) foods that resist disease and poor climate, the creation of artificial flavours, advanced technology in greenhouses that can produce food all year round, and the ultimate solution to the world's food crises: a replicator that can produce food from (re)arranging atoms. In all discussions about food and drink tourism is the overarching message that the exclusive and luxury is not available to everyone. Access to food and opportunity is not equally spread around the world, and technology may have a role to play in rectifying this inequality.

SOCIAL JUSTICE, EQUALITY OF ACCESS AND SUSTAINABILITY

As argued in Chapter 6, it would be misleading to present food and drink as the panacea to the world's problems. There are certainly some less 'digestible' messages about this form of tourism that need to be considered and addressed. These include a growing concern over the widening gap between rich and poor, the need for mechanised production to feed the world's growing population, and realising food sustainability. However, these aspects need to be achieved at the same time as offering the unique experiences and exclusive gastronomy that food tourists and culinary explorers are demanding. There is a need to balance the search for uniqueness and expensive ingredients that attract and excite affluent the Western tourist market (products include truffles, champagne, caviar and rare meats) and prestigious places such as luxury restaurants that are places of cultural capital accumulation (see Figure 22.1) against a fundamental requirement for basic levels of nutrition and sustenance.

Hansen (2015: 49) has called this situation an 'evolution of fault lines' where a gap has emerged between two poles. It describes the increasing gap between the need for a standard global food offer to feed the world and the search for the unique, distinctive and individual in food tourism. It is clear that there is need for industrialised agriculture and (post-)Fordist (Chapter 4) production with food being mass produced with technology and a small number of core ingredients like water or cellulose, alongside the polar opposite of the food tourism experience where individuals search for the novel and non-uniform. Ells (2015) further suggests there will be complex agri-food global supply chains responding to a shift from local and seasonal to supply chain 'funnelling'. This situation is certainly driven by the tensions of local/global and through processes of globalisation (Chapter 5) where a complex mixture of homogenisation (similarity) and heterogenisation (difference) is negotiated in most developing countries around the world. As outlined in Chapter 6, the main problem is inequality in distribution and in equal and fair access to land to grow food and income to purchase it;

FIGURE 22.1 *The Ritz, London, UK. The luxury hotel and restaurant offers a place to demonstrate cultural and economic capital. Photo by author*

it is not about whether the world is producing enough, because it already is. It is argued in this book that providing enough food for the world's growing population is not about increasing the number of multi-nationals, but supporting local producers and ensuring local opportunities are provided for retaining income and reducing external leakages (Chapter 20). As outlined in Chapter 4, a move towards 'market niching' (Meethan, 2015) will find consumption can act as an active and informed process, fostering a shift to the local and regional within a globalised society, where small scale can be effective and efficient if provided with sector and government support, branding and promotion (Chapter 8).

Hurley (2015) explores what agri-tourism might look like in 2115. In her hundred-year vision, some of the more visionary and utopian 'dreams' for food tourism are presented and conceptualised. For example, it has already been stated that we need a global vision of enough food for everyone, where governments are localised, and where there is less economic disparity: only possible when agriculture is a flourishing sector. Furthermore, invisible components of supply chains and food production have to be acknowledged and supported. For example, the work of women needs to become more visible in the global workforce and the contribution of the poor and under-represented must be reflected in final retail prices and considered within government schemes and policies. It is in this utopian desire for social transformation that there is a role for community-based tourism to provide the kinds of partnerships discussed in Chapters 20 and 21. Social and economic sustainability through partnership should become the operating standard for businesses and there needs to be a clear and committed shift to corporate social responsibility where there is increased pressure to adopt sustainability practices (Moscardo et al., 2015; Tolkach and King, 2015).

PREPARING FOR THE FUTURE: SLOWING TOURISM DOWN

The projected growth in food and drink tourism brings opportunities, but also significant challenges for regions seeking to maintain their local character, traditions and identity. Destinations and businesses will need to ensure they are changing to meet the growth of food tourism and the evolving (and increasingly demanding) nature of consumer tastes and interests. It is important that the hospitality industry accommodates this growing sector of food and drink visitors, but this has to be in line with balancing and addressing the triple bottom line of sustainability (economic, environmental and social). It has been argued that for food tourism to benefit all, collaboration is key (Bianke and Chiesa, 2008; Everett and Slocum, 2013). What is central to this goal is the importance of demonstrating to the business sector and wider global industries the benefits of food and drink tourism and how it can be ethically exploited to develop connections and significant economic benefits for everyone (Chapter 21). To be successful and sustainable, it will require businesses, governments and society to work together to achieve a 'virtuous circle' for all (Mulcahy, 2015: 84). Closer links between production and consumption are necessary, both to maintain distinctness but also provide a robust network of people that can resist faceless food production and an externally controlled food and drink offering (Meethan, 2015; see also Chapter 19).

To achieve balance and sustainability, we need to look at different models of tourism development cognisant with the ethos of sustainable food and drink tourism. A movement with increasing visibility to achieve this is the Slow Food movement (Chapter 11). As outlined, the philosophy reflects a wider desire to develop a slower and more sensitive tourism offering with wider-reaching local benefits. The lessons learned from food and drink tourism are certainly applicable to the wider tourism industry and are increasingly being adopted in slow tourism strategies through the establishment of slow towns and cities (see Lumsden and McGrath (2011), Dickinson et al. (2011) and Fullager et al. (2012)). Overall, the general principles of shorter supply chains, ethical consumption, sustainability, local economic development and support, stronger relationships between producer and consumer, and host and guest underpin this philosophy. The slow movement approach has clear applicability to the tourism sector, and addresses what is becoming a louder call for a change to leisure practices and longer, more meaningful immersive engagement.

The idea and pursuit of slow tourism is certainly not new, despite the term being a relative newcomer to tourism research and it is only in the past 50 years that it has really been necessary to distinguish between 'fast' and 'slow' travel. Slow tourism is about the pursuit of less intensive consumption patterns and approaches which promote concepts of immersion, dwelling, value, healthy living, engagement and sustainability. It encapsulates more than just speed, reflecting also a state of mind, the mode of travel chosen, alternative engagement with spaces, how time is spent at a destination, and issues of environmental consciousness. In providing the consumer with an informed choice between 'fast' and 'slow' tourism, it is possible to offer engaged modes of critical consumption that require some reflection on the type of tourist we want to be, and the places we want to be on offer.

The concept of 'slow tourism' is not without its paradoxes. There is an irony as slow tourism can actually be booked very quickly through the internet (including booking trains, ecotourism stays, and walking holidays). There is also a school of thought that suggests slow tourism may be merely a veneer for sustainability, and provides yet another marketing tool to generate commercial gain for businesses offering new and 'unique' experiences (Weaver, 2007; Wheeller, 1994). Despite some cynicism, there is mounting evidence that it is a significant market and slow tourism, slow cities and Slow Food have growing numbers of people prepared to pay a premium for them. These alternatives to fast-paced, high-impact, aviation-based holidays and leisure experiences will be part of the future tourism sector. One way to assess these changes and the impact on destinations is to use a PESTLE analysis tool.

ASSESSING FOOD AND DRINK TOURISM WITH A PESTLE

In thinking about developing food and drink tourism, it is useful to reflect on the supply chain and examine the factors that might affect food and drink tourism potential and development in a destination. A method commonly adopted to undertake these assessments is the PESTLE framework, a mnemonic in marketing and business used to assess the market for a new product or process. It is an analysis framework formed from the letters: P for Political, E for Economic, S for Social, T for Technological, L for Legal and E for Environmental, sometimes also called 'PEST' (see Tribe, 2010 for an explanation within a tourism context). It is a useful tool when thinking about the wider factors that might affect food and drink tourism development in a specific country. It is important to understand the wider meso-economic (one in which we operate and have limited influence or impact) and macro-economic environments (all factors that influence an organisation, but are out of its direct control). It is vital to assess and evaluate political dimensions and government responses and responsibility (Yeoman et al., 2015: 78) before deciding how to respond to social, economic and cultural changes in society.

Figure 22.2 outlines the key aspects that should be considered within a PESTLE analysis. Use this to inform your own analysis in the Activity that follows.

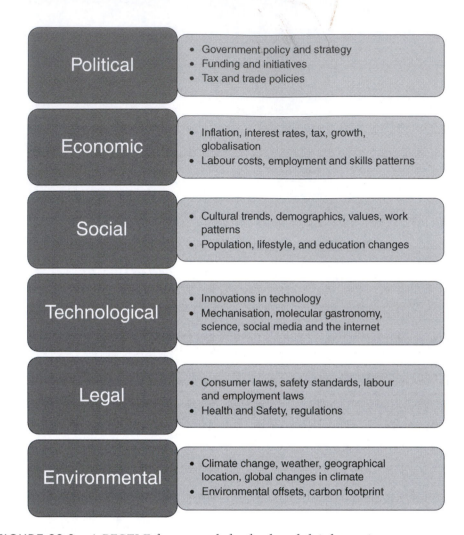

FIGURE 22.2 *A PESTLE framework for food and drink tourism*

ACTIVITY **PESTLE ANALYSIS FOR FOOD AND DRINK
DEVELOPMENT**

Complete a PESTLE analysis for a destination, country or region of your choice that
might consider expanding and developing its food and drink tourism offer. Based
on the chapters in this book, what 'PESTLE' aspects need to be considered and
addressed in a strategy? Use Figure 22.2 to help you think about what specific
aspects you will need to include, e.g. what are the destination's laws and taxes?
What natural resources and technologies does it have?

FUTURE RESEARCH IN FOOD AND DRINK TOURISM

Food and drink tourism is undoubtedly a growing area for research (academic, policy and market research). This book has presented food tourism as an insightful and illuminating area of research, as well as core to the global tourism industry. It has examined food and drink tourism by drawing on a number of theories and concepts, and has sought to provide a comprehensive overview utilising spatial, social and cultural discourses and ideas. It has provided critical reflections from a wide range of subject areas including business, cultural studies, sociology, economics, marketing, anthropology and politics. However, there is much research that is needed and it is hoped that this has 'whetted your appetite' to progress its study through new lenses and from different perspectives.

There is value in conducting more culturally and critically underpinned studies of the subject and some of the following research suggestions should provide useful project or dissertation ideas for you. It is clear that more research is needed on the social and cultural aspects of the experience, and new socio-cultural perspectives are necessary to truly understand the phenomenon and the people involved in its growth. Interrogation and exploration of the inter-relationships between food, tourism and culture will undoubtedly generate new knowledge of its contribution to people and the planet, and move the discourses beyond the focus on profit. For example, it would be valuable to conduct a detailed semiotic analysis of food tourism marketing literature investigating elements of food tourism promotion. In-depth content and discourse analyses of promotional materials would contribute knowledge on how place is performed, promoted and presented. Questioning tourists on their response to such materials would provide insightful studies of the importance of symbols and images in evoking a sense of place. Furthermore, examination of the motivations for food-related travel would help uncover the elements that encourage people to become culinary tourists when they are deciding on a holiday. It would also be useful to examine the consumption patterns of people once they have returned home. This kind of study would ascertain whether the experience had influenced tourists to continue engaging in resistant practices (against multi-nationals and food from homogenised production methods) at home through their food purchasing patterns and choices, or returned to their previous patterns of purchase and consumption.

Another area of research is investigating different forms of 'capital'. Different types of capital have been discussed, but there may be value in examining additional types of capital such as 'eco' (environmental) capital, which can be linked with developing a more experiential perspective on (food) tourist typologies and distinction. Furthermore, it would be useful to examine the social impact of food tourism on locations in regard to employment generation, business development and skills regeneration (the hospitality industry was discussed in Chapter 20). It would be worth investigating other tourism outlets and supply chains that inform specific types of hotels, bed and breakfasts and guesthouses. These accommodation providers are often where tourists eat the majority of their food and although guests may not regard themselves as food tourists, the entire process and delivery of food to tourists is worthy of attention.

Research in other countries not mentioned in this book that have become popular food tourism destinations would build knowledge of the relationships between food and 'sense of place' from a number of different perspectives and contexts. Further, studies in locations that do not traditionally or currently exploit their food and drink history or identity will provide new perspectives and test some of the concepts and theories raised in the published literature. Food tourism has gained global popularity and more case studies from Africa, Asia, and less developed countries would unearth additional perspectives, opportunities and challenges. In addition to the marketing and business advantages that new case studies may provide, the work on sensuous tourism geographies will also be advanced if new places are examined and it will be possible to explore how embodied knowledge may be obtained from different places offering this immersive tourism experience (Everett, 2012).

Another useful research avenue is to examine the 'mobility of food' (the journey of food and its removal from its original place of origin) as perceived by tourists and producers. This research could trace the mobilities of culinary touristic products, as opposed to the movement of people and tourists (Sheller and Urry, 2004). Such research would draw on the geographical food studies by Cook (2006) and Cook and Harrison (2007) who have undertaken multi-site ethnographies exploring the complex relations between commodity producers, consumers, and those 'in-between' by following and 'animating' foods such as pepper sauce and papaya. Following the food and drink, rather than following the people will offer new perspectives to food and drink production and consumption.

CHAPTER SUMMARY

Food and drink has been presented as far more than a necessity in the tourism experience. Rather, this book has presented this key aspect of the tourism experience as a fascinating and multi-dimensional sector and research area in its own right. It is important that food and drink tourism is acknowledge and recognised as a highly complex phenomenon and eclectic experience which must be studied from a multi-disciplinary perspective to fully understand its character, breadth and contribution. As travelling for food and drink becomes ever more popular, it is important that the people who are privileged enough to be able to travel take more time to consider the implications of their consumption choices and patterns, and how it benefits others. It is clear that there is a need to engage in tourist education, promote sustainability discourses, and seek authenticity and shorter supply chains to ensure more benefits are felt by more people, more locally around the world. To conclude this chapter and book, a quote from George Bernard Shaw (Irish playwright and a co-founder of the London School of Economics) neatly summarises the focus of this book (and my driver for writing it): 'there is no sincerer love than the love of food' (2000 [1903]). So, get out there – eating and drinking as your travel, but also researching it and even working with it!

END OF CHAPTER POINTS

- Food and drink tourism is the fastest growing sector of the tourism industry. Growing levels of outbound tourism from emerging economies with new-found wealth and affluence will influence how the sector evolves.

- Drivers for the future of food and drink tourism development include cultural and social capital and differentiation, technology, urbanisation and population density, globalisation and 'glocalisation', climate, competition among attractions and destinations, and ethical consumption demands.

- People are increasingly willing to pay more, try more and eat more. Food tourism offers destinations new streams of revenue and income that can be based on pre-existing resources such as agriculture, history and traditions.

- Destination and marketing and tourism strategies are increasingly focused on attracting high-value, high-spend food tourists through unique and exclusive experiences.

- Food and drink tourism will be expanded through social media technologies and usage. Providers must understand and be conversant with social media technologies if they hope to develop their offer and marketing strategy.

- Technological developments will change the character of our eating and drinking experiences. It will have a role to play in rectifying inequality, as currently access to food is not equally spread around the world.

- A PESTLE framework is useful in analysing the context for food tourism development.

- To ensure the sector grows sustainably, it is important to demonstrate and evidence the benefits of food and drink tourism to the business sector and build partnership and closer connections.

FURTHER READING

Getz, D., Robinson, R.N., Andersson, T.D. and Vujicic, S. (2015) *Foodies and Food Tourism*. Oxford: Goodfellows.

Hjalager, A. and Richards, G. (eds) (2002) *Tourism and Gastronomy*. London: Routledge.

Kim, Y.G., Eves, A. and Scarles, C. (2009a) 'Building a model of local food consumption on trips and holidays: a grounded theory approach', *International Journal of Hospitality Management*, 28 (4): 423–31.

Yeoman, I., McMahon-Beattie, U., Fields, K., Albrecht, J. and Meethan, K. (eds) (2015) *The Future of Food Tourism. Foodies, Experiences, Exclusivity, Visions and Political Capital*. Bristol: Channel View Publications.

REFERENCES

Acott, T. G., Trobe, H. L., & Howard, S. H. (1998) `An evaluation of deep ecotourism and shallow ecotourism', *Journal of Sustainable Tourism*, 6(3): 238–253.

Adams, J. (2007) *A guide to farmers markets: Australia and New Zealand*. Mosman: R.M. Williams Classic Publications.

Afrodite's Kitchen (2015) *Cypriot Inspired Receipes from my Family's Kitchen*. Available at: www.afroditeskitchen.com. [Accessed 11/12/15.]

Aktas, G. (2011) 'Thailand tourism', *Annals of Leisure Research*, 14 (1): 102–3.

Alcock, J. (2005) *Food in the Ancient World*. Westport, CT: Greenwood Press.

Alebaki, M. and Iakovidou, O. (2011) 'Market segmentation in wine tourism: a comparison of approaches', *Tourismos*, 6 (1): 123–40.

Alonso, A.D. (2011) 'Opportunities and challenges in the development of micro-brewing and beer tourism: a preliminary study from Alabama', *Tourism Planning & Development*, 8 (4): 415–31.

Alonso, A.D. and Northcote, J. (2009) 'Wine, history, landscape: origin branding in Western Australia', *British Food Journal*, 111 (11): 1248–59.

Alonso, A.D., Fraser, R.A. and Cohen, D.A. (2008) 'Exploring wine tourism in New Zealand: the visitors' points of views', *Tourism Analysis*, 13 (2): 171–80.

Amuquandoh, E.F. and Asafo-Adjei, R. (2013) 'Traditional food preferences of tourists in Ghana', *British Food Journal*, 115 (7): 987–1002.

Andrews, G. (2008) *The Slow Food Story: Politics and Pleasure*. London: Pluto Press.

Appadurai, A. (1986) *The Social Life of Things: Commodities in Cultural Perspective*. Cambridge: Cambridge University Press.

Armesto López, X.A. and Martin, B.G. (2006) 'Tourism and quality agro-food products: an opportunity for the Spanish countryside', *Tijdschrift voor economische en sociale geografie*, 97 (2): 166–77.

Arsenault, N. (1998) `Typologies and the leisure learner', *Ageing International*, 24(2-3): 64–74.

Arsenault, N. (2001) *Learning travel: Canadian Ed-ventures: Learning vacations in Canada: An overview (Vol. 1)*. Vancouver, BC: Canadian Tourism Commission.

Ashley, C. (2007) *Pro-poor Analysis of the Rwandan Tourism Value Chain: An Emerging Picture and Some Strategic Approaches for Enhancing Poverty Impacts. ODI Report to SNV and ORTPN*. London: Overseas Development Institute. Available at: www.odi.org/sites/odi.org.uk/files/odi-assets/publications-opinion-files/6105.pdf. [Accessed: 23/09/15.]

Ashley, C., De Brine, P., Lehr, A. and Wilde, H. (2007) *The Role of the Tourism Sector in Expanding Economic Opportunity*. Massachusetts: John F. Kennedy School of Government, Harvard University.

Askegaard, S. and Kjeldgaard, D. (2007) 'Here, there, and everywhere: place branding and gastronomical globalization in a macromarketing perspective', *Journal of Macromarketing*, 27 (2): 138–47.

Ateljevic, I. (2000) 'Circuits of tourism: stepping beyond the "production/consumption" dichotomy', *Tourism Geographies*, 2 (4): 369–88.

Atkin, T. and Affonso, J. (2004) 'Wine supply chain management', in L. Thach and T. Matz (eds), *Wine A Global Business*. New York: Miranda Press, Chapter 12, pp. 123–68.

Augustyn, M. (2000) 'From decline to growth: innovative strategies for manufacturing small cultural tourism enterprises – Westons Cider case study', *Tourism Culture & Communication*, 2 (3): 153–64.

Bacardi (2014) *Established in Santiago de Cuba in 1862, BACARDÍ Rum is the World's Favorite and Most Awarded Rum.* Available at: www.bacardilimited.com/our-brands/bacardi-rum. [Accessed 14/05/14.]

Bærenholdt, J.O., Haldrup, M., Larsen, J. and Urry, J. (2004) *Performing Tourist Places*. Aldershot: Ashgate.

Baffes, J. (2006) 'Restructuring Uganda's coffee industry: why going back to basics matters', *Development Policy Review*, 24 (4): 413–36.

Baker, S. and Green, H. (2008) *Social media will change your business.* Available at: <www.bloomberg.com/bw/stories/2008-02-20/social-media-will-change-your-business-businessweek-business-news-stock-market-and-financial-advice. [Accessed: 18/6/15.]

Baipai Thai Cooking School (2015) *Baipai Thai Cooking School.* Available from: www.baipai.com. [Accessed 05/06/14.]

Balmer, J.M., Powell, S.M. and Balmer, J.M. (2011) 'Corporate heritage identities, corporate heritage brands and the multiple heritage identities of the British Monarchy', *European Journal of Marketing*, 45 (9/10): 1380–98.

Baloglu, S. and McCleary, K.W. (1999) 'A model of destination image formation', *Annals of Tourism Research*, 26 (4): 868–97.

Banks, G., Kelly, S., Lewis, N. and Sharpe, S. (2007) 'Place "from one glance": the use of place in the marketing of New Zealand and Australian wines', *Australian Geographer*, 38 (1): 15–35.

Batra, A. (2008) 'An exploratory study on specific preferences and characteristics of wine tourists', *Anatolia*, 19 (2): 271–86.

Battour, M.M., Battor, M.M. and Ismail, M. (2012) 'The mediating role of tourist satisfaction: a study of Muslim tourists in Malaysia', *Journal of Travel & Tourism Marketing*, 29 (3): 279–97.

BBC (2012) *Teaching tourists to cook in a Thai slum.* 24 August 2012. Available at: www.bbc.co.uk/news/world-radio-and-tv-18704670. [Accessed 20/5/14]

Bauman, Z. (2013 [1993]) *Liquid Modernity.* New York: John Wiley & Sons.

Beasley, R. and Danesi, M. (2002) *Persuasive Signs: The Semiotics of Advertising.* Berlin: Walter de Gruyter.

Beckerman, W. (1995) 'How would you like your "sustainability", sir? Weak or strong? A reply to my critics', *Environmental Values*, 4 (2): 167–79.

Beckford, W. (1783) 1760-1844: *Dreams, Waking Thoughts, and Incidents, in a Series of Letters From Various Parts of Europe* (Gutenberg text and illustrated HTML). Available at: http://onlinebooks.library.upenn.edu/webbin/gutbook/lookup?num=7258. [Accessed 20/02/16].

Beer, S. and Lemmer, C. (2011) 'A critical review of "green" procurement: life cycle analysis of food products within the supply chain', *Worldwide Hospitality and Tourism Themes*, 3 (3): 229–44.

Beerli, A. and Martin, J.D. (2004) 'Factors influencing destination image', *Annals of Tourism Research*, 31 (3): 657–81.

Beeton, S. (2010) 'The advance of film tourism', *Tourism and Hospitality Planning & Development*, 7 (1): 1–6.

Belisle, F. J. (1984a) 'Tourism and food imports: the case of Jamaica', *Economic Development and Cultural Change*, 32 (4): 819–42.

Belisle, F. J. (1984b) Food Production and Tourism in Jamaica: Obstacles to Increasing Local Food Supplies to Hotels. *The Journal of Developing Areas*, 19 (1): pp. 1–20.

Bell, C. (2015) 'Tourists infiltrating authentic domestic space at Balinese home cooking schools', *Tourism Studies*, 15 (1): 86–100.

Bell, D. and Valentine, G. (1997) *Consuming Geographies: We Are Where We Eat.* London: Routledge.

Benckendorff, P.J. and Pearce, P.L. (2003) 'Australian tourist attractions: the links between organizational characteristics and planning', *Journal of Travel Research*, 42 (1): 24–35.

Bendapudi, N. and Leone, R.P. (2003) 'Psychological implications of customer participation in co-production', *Journal of Marketing*, 67 (1): 14–28.

Berg, P.O. and Östberg, J. (eds) (2008) *City Branding as an Organizing Concept: Co-creation of Strategic Identities.* Presented at SCANCOR 20th Anniversary Conference Stanford, CA, November.

Berg, P.O. and Sevón, G. (2014) 'Food-branding places: a sensory perspective', *Place Branding and Public Diplomacy*, 10 (4): 289–304.

Bessière, J. (1998) 'Local development and heritage: traditional food and cuisine as tourist attractions in rural areas', *Sociologia Ruralis*, 38 (1): 21–34.

Bessière, J. (2001) 'The role of rural gastronomy in tourism', in S. Boyne, F. Williams and D.R. Hall (eds), *Rural Tourism and Recreation: Principles to Practice.* Wallingford, Oxford: CABI, pp.115–118.

Bessière, J. and Tibère, L. (2013) 'Traditional food and tourism: French tourist experience and food heritage in rural spaces', *Journal of the Science of Food and Agriculture*, 93 (14): 3420–5.

Beynon, J. and Dunkerley, D. (eds) (2000) *Globalization: The Reader.* London: Athlone Press.

Bianke, J. and Chiesa, T. (2008) *The Travel & Tourism Competitiveness Report 2008: Balancing Economic Development and Environmental Sustainability.* Geneva: World Economic Forum 2008. Available at: http://www3.weforum.org/docs/WEF_TravelTourismCompetitiveness_Report_2008.pdf. [Accessed: 25/08/15.]

Bissell, D. (2009) 'Visualising everyday geographies: practices of vision through travel-time', *Transactions of the Institute of British Geographers*, 34 (1): 42–60.

Bitner, M.J. (1992) 'Servicescapes: the impact of physical surroundings on customers and employees', *The Journal of Marketing*, 56 (2): 57–71.

Black, G. (2005) *The Engaging Museum: Developing Museums for Visitor Involvement.* Abingdon: Routledge.

Blekesaune, A., Brandth, B. and Haugen, M.S. (2010) 'Visitors to farm tourism enterprises in Norway', *Scandinavian Journal of Hospitality and Tourism*, 10 (1): 54–73.

Bloomberg Business (2004) *Online Extra: Jeff Bezos on Word-of-Mouth Power.* Available from: http://www.bloomberg.com/bw/stories/2004-08-01/online-extra-jeff-bezos-on-word-of-mouth-power. [Accessed 22/5/14].

Blythman, J. (2008) 'Anyone for pudding?' *Observer Food Monthly*, *Observer* 30 March.

Bohdanowicz, P. (2005) 'European hoteliers' environmental attitudes greening the business', *Cornell Hotel and Restaurant Administration Quarterly*, 46 (2): 188–204.

Bohdanowicz, P., Simanic, B. and Martinac, I. (2005) 'Environmental training and measures at Scandic Hotels, Sweden', *Tourism Review International*, 9 (1): 7–19.

Boniface, B., Cooper, C. and Cooper, R. (2012) *Worldwide Destinations: The Geography of Travel and Tourism,* 6th edn. London: Routledge.

Boniface, P. (2003) *Tasting Tourism: Travelling for Food and Drink.* Aldershot: Ashgate.

Boserup, E. (1965) *The Condition of Agricultural Growth. The Economics of Agrarian Change under Population Pressure*. London: Allan and Unwin.

Bourdieu, P. (1984) *Distinction: A Social Critique of the Judgement of Taste.* Cambridge, MA: Harvard University Press.

Bové, J. and Dufour, F. (2001) *The World is Not For Sale: Farmers Against Junk Food*. London: Verso.

Boyle, D. (2003) *Authenticity, Brands, Fakes, Spin and the Lust for Real Life.* London: Perennial.

Boyne, S. and Hall, D. (2004) 'Place promotion through food and tourism: rural branding and the role of websites', *Place Branding*, 1 (1): 80–92.

Boyne, S., Hall, D. and Williams, F. (2003) 'Policy, support and promotion for food-related tourism initiatives: a marketing approach to regional development', *Journal of Travel & Tourism Marketing*, 14 (3–4): 131–54.

Boyne, S., Williams, F. and Hall, D. (2002) 'On the trail of regional success: tourism, food production and the Isle of Arran Taste Trail', in A.M. Hjalager and G. Richards (eds), *Tourism and Gastronomy*. London: Routledge, pp.91–114.

Bramwell, B. (1994) 'Rural tourism and sustainable rural tourism', *Journal of Sustainable Tourism*, 2 (1–2): 1–6.

Bramwell, B. and Lane, B. (2000) *Tourism Collaboration and Partnerships: Politics, Practice and Sustainability.* Bristol: Channel View Publications.

Brewers Association (2011). *Craft Brewer Defined*. Available at: www.brewersassociation.org/statistics/craft-brewer-defined/. [Accessed 11/12/15.]

Brillat-Savarin, J.A. (1825/2009) *The Physiology of Taste: or Meditations on Transcendental Gastronomy.* New York: Vintage.

Brotherton, B. and Himmetoğlu, B. (1997) 'Beyond destinations – special interest tourism', *Anatolian International Journal of Tourism and Hospitality Research*, 8 (3): 11–30.

Brown, K., Turner, R.K., Hameed, H. and Bateman, I. (1995) *Tourism and Sustainability in Environmentally Fragile Areas: Case Studies from the Maldives and Nepal.* London: Centre for Social and Economic Research on the Global Environment.

Brown, P. (2011) *Man Walks Into A Pub: A Sociable History of Beer (Fully Updated Second Edition).* London: Pan Macmillan.

Brown, S. and Morrison, A.M. (2003) 'Expanding volunteer vacation participation: an exploratory study on the mini-mission concept', *Tourism Recreation Research*, 28 (3): 73–82.

Brunori, G. and Rossi, A. (2000) 'Synergy and coherence through collective action: some insights from wine routes in Tuscany', *Sociologia Ruralis*, 40 (4): 409–23.

Bruwer, J. (2003) 'South African wine routes: some perspectives on the wine tourism industry's structural dimensions and wine tourism product', *Tourism Management*, 24 (4): 423–35.

Buhalis, D. (2000) 'Marketing the competitive destination of the future', *Tourism Management*, 21 (1): 97–116.

Buhalis, D. (2003) *eTourism: Information Technology for Strategic Tourism Management.* Harlow: Pearson Education.

Buhalis, D. and Law, R. (2008) 'Progress in information technology and tourism management: 20 years on and 10 years after the Internet—the state of eTourism research', *Tourism Management*, 29 (4): 609–23.

Bujdosó, Z. and Szűcs, C. (2012) 'Beer tourism–from theory to practice', *Academica Turistica-Tourism and Innovation Journal*, 5 (1): 103–11.

Buller, H. and Morris, C. (2004) 'Growing goods: the market, the state, and sustainable food production', *Environment and Planning A*, 36 (6): 1065–84.

Burgan, B. and Mules, T. (1992) 'Economic impact of sporting events', *Annals of Tourism Research*, 19 (4): 700–10.

Burnett, K.A. (2003) 'Taste of tradition: a critical examination of the relationship between heritage, food and tourism promotion in Scotland', in *Local Food and Tourism*. Larnaka, Cyprus: World Tourist Organisation/CTO, pp.28–38.

Burnett, K.A. and Danson, M. (2004) 'Adding or subtracting value? Constructions of rurality and Scottish quality food promotion', *International Journal of Entrepreneurial Behavior & Research*, 10 (6): 384–403.

Caffyn, A. (2010) 'Beer and tourism: a relationship worth fostering', *Tourism Insights* (February). Available at: www.insights.org.uk/articleitem.aspx?title=Beer%20and%20 Tourism:%20A%20Relationship%20Worth%20Fostering. [Accessed: 13/03/14.]

Callahan, M. and Thomas, S. (2005) 'Volunteer tourism: deconstructing volunteer activities within a dynamic environment', in M. Novelli (ed.), *Niche Tourism: Contemporary Issues, Trends, and Cases*. Oxford: Butterworth-Heinemann, pp.183–200.

Caplan, P. (1997) 'Approaches to the study of food, health and identity', in P. Caplan, *Food, Health and Identity*. London: Routledge, pp.1–31.

Caplan, P. (2013) *Food, Health and Identity*. London: Routledge.

Carlsen, J. and Dowling, R. (1998) 'Wine tourism marketing issues in Australia', *International Journal of Wine Marketing*, 10 (3): 23–32.

Carlsen, J. and Dowling, R. (2001) 'Regional wine tourism: a plan of development for Western Australia', *Tourism Recreation Research*, 26 (2): 45–52.

Carmichael, B. (2005) 'Understanding the wine tourism experience for winery visitors in the Niagara region, Ontario, Canada', *Tourism Geographies*, 7 (2): 185–204.

Carruthers, C., Burns, A. and Elliott, G. (2015) 'Development, sustainability and applications – a case study of County Cork, Republic of Ireland', in P. Sloan, W. Le Grand and C. Hindley (eds), *The Routledge Handbook of Sustainable Food and Gastronomy*. Abingdon: Routledge, pp.360–9.

Carter, J., Dyer, P. and Sharma, B. (2007) 'Dis-placed voices: sense of place and place-identity on the Sunshine Coast', *Social & Cultural Geography*, 8 (5): 755–73.

Cave, J., Jolliffe, L. and Baum, T. (2013) *Tourism and Souvenirs: Glocal Perspectives From the Margins*. Bristol: Channel View Publications.

Cavicchi, A. and Santini, C. (2014) *Food and Wine Events in Europe: A Stakeholder Approach*. London: Routledge.

Çela, A., Knowles-Lankford, J. and Lankford, S. (2007) 'Local food festivals in Northeast Iowa communities: a visitor and economic impact study', *Managing Leisure*, 12 (2–3): 171–86.

Chambers, R. (2014) *Rural Development: Putting the Last First*. London: Routledge.

Charters, S. and Ali-Knight, J. (2002) 'Who is the wine tourist?', *Tourism Management*, 23 (3): 311–19.

Charters, S. and O'Neill, M. (2001) 'Service quality at the cellar door: a comparison between regions', *International Journal of Wine Marketing*, 13 (3): 7–17.

Cheng, S., Hu, J., Fox, D. and Zhang, Y. (2012) 'Tea tourism development in Xinyang, China: Stakeholders' view', *Tourism Management Perspectives*, 2: 28–34.

Chesworth, N. (2010) 'Canada's just us! Coffee Roasters Co-operative coffee tour venture', in J. Jolliffe (ed.), *Coffee Culture, Destinations and Tourism*. Bristol: Channel View Publications, pp.172–80.

Chhabra, D., Healy, R. and Sills, E. (2003) 'Staged authenticity and heritage tourism', *Annals of Tourism Research*, 30 (3): 702–19.

Chhabra, D., Lee, W., Zhao, S. and Scott, K. (2013) 'Marketing of ethnic food experiences: authentication analysis of Indian cuisine abroad', *Journal of Heritage Tourism*, 8 (2-3): 145–157.

Choo, H. and Jamal, T. (2009) 'Tourism on organic farms in South Korea: a new form of ecotourism', *Journal of Sustainable Tourism*, 17 (4): 431–54.

Church, A., Ball, R., Bull, C. and Tyler, D. (2000) 'Public policy engagement with British tourism: the national, local and the European Union', *Tourism Geographies*, 2 (3): 312–36.

Clark, G. and Chabrel, M. (2007) 'Measuring integrated rural tourism', *Tourism Geographies*, 9 (4): 371–86.

Clarke, J. (2005) 'Effective marketing for rural tourism', in D. Hall, I. Kirkpatrick and M. Mitchell (eds), *Rural Tourism and Sustainable Business*. Bristol: Channel View Publications, pp. 87–102.

Clegg, S.R., Hardy, C., Lawrence, T. and Nord, W.R. (eds) (2006) *The SAGE Handbook of Organization Studies*. London: Sage.

Cleverdon, R. and Kalisch, A. (2000) 'Fair trade in tourism', *International Journal of Tourism Research*, 2 (3): 171–87.

Clift, S. and Carter, S. (2000) *Tourism and Sex: Culture, Commerce and Coercion*. London: Pinter.

Cloke, P. and Perkins, H.C. (1998) '"Cracking the canyon with the awesome foursome": representations of adventure tourism in New Zealand', *Environment and Planning D*, 16 (2): 185–218.

Cobb, D., Dolman, P. and O'Riordan, T. (1999) 'Interpretations of sustainable agriculture in the UK', *Progress in Human Geography*, 23 (2): 209–35.

Cochrane, J. (2007) *Asian Tourism: Growth and Change*. London: Routledge.

Coghlan, A. (2007) 'Towards an integrated image-based typology of volunteer tourism organisations', *Journal of Sustainable Tourism*, 15 (3): 267–87.

Cohen, E. (1972) 'Toward a Sociology of International Tourism', *Social Research*, 39(1): 164–182.

Cohen, E. (1979) 'A phenomenology of tourist experiences', *Sociology*, 13 (2): 179–201.

Cohen, E. and Avieli, N. (2004) 'Food in tourism: attraction and impediment', *Annals of Tourism Research*, 31 (4): 755–78.

Coley, D., Howard, M. and Winter, M. (2009) 'Local food, food miles and carbon emissions: a comparison of farm shop and mass distribution approaches', *Food Policy*, 34 (2): 150–5.

Collins, F.L. (2008) 'Of kimchi and coffee: globalisation, transnationalism and familiarity in culinary consumption', *Social & Cultural Geography*, 9 (2): 151–69.

Collins, T., Martin, J. and Vamplew, W. (2005) *Encyclopedia of Traditional British Rural Sports*. Abingdon: Routledge.

Commonwealth of Virginia (2012) *SB 604 Alcoholic Beverage Control: Privileges of Brewery Licensees*. Virginia: Virginia General Assembly.

Cook, I. (2006) 'Geographies of food: following', *Progress in Human Geography*, 30 (5): 655–66.

Cook, I. and Crang, P. (1996) 'The world on a plate: culinary culture, displacement and geographical knowledges', *Journal of Material Culture*, 1 (2): 131–53.

Cook, I. and Harrison, M. (2007) 'Follow the thing "West Indian hot pepper sauce"', *Space and Culture*, 10 (1): 40–63.

Cooper, C. (2012) *Essentials of Tourism*. London: Pearson.

Cooper, M.C., Lambert, D.M. and Pagh, J.D. (1997) 'Supply chain management: more than a new name for logistics', *The International Journal of Logistics Management*, 8 (1): 1–14.

Cosgrove, D. (1989) 'Geography is everywhere: culture and symbolism in human landscapes', in D. Gregory and R. Walford (eds), *Horizons in Human Geography*. New York: Barnes and Noble, pp. 118–35.

Counihan, C. and van Esterik, P. (1997) *Food and Culture: A Reader.* London: Routledge.

Countryside Agency (2002) *Eat the View: Promoting Sustainable Local Products.* West Yorkshire: Countryside Agency Publications.

Craik, J. (1997), 'The culture of tourism sites', in Rojek, C. and Urry, J. (Eds), Touring Cultures: Transformations of Travel and Theory, Routledge, London, pp. 113–136.

Crawford, R. (1980) 'Healthism and the medicalization of everyday life', *International Journal of Health Services,* 10 (3): 365–88.

Cresswell, T. (2004) *Place: A Short Introduction.* Oxford: Blackwell.

Crewe, l. and Beverstock, J. (1998) 'Fashioning the city: cultures of consumption in contemporary urban spaces', *Geoforum,* 29: 287–308.

Crispin, S. and Reiser, D. (2008) 'Food and wine events in Tasmania, Australia', in C.M. Hall and L. Sharples (eds), *Food and Wine Festivals and Events Around the World.* Oxford: Butterworth Heinemann, pp. 113–31.

Crompton, J.L. and McKay, S.L. (1997) 'Motives of visitors attending festival events', *Annals of Tourism Research,* 24 (2): 425–39.

Cronin, M. (2003) 'Next to being there: Ireland of the welcomes and tourism of the word', *Irish Tourism: Image, Culture and Identity,* 1 (1): 179.

Crotts, J. (1999) 'Consumer decision making and prepurchase information search', in A. Pizam and Y. Mansfield (eds), *Consumer Behavior in Travel and Tourism.* New York: Haworth Hospitality Press, pp. 149–68.

Crouch, D. (1999) *Leisure and Tourism Geographies: Practices and Geographical Knowledge.* London: Routledge.

Crouch, D., Aronsson, L. and Wahlström, L. (2001) 'Tourist encounters', *Tourist Studies,* 1 (3): 253–70.

Cuba, L. and Hummon, D.M. (1993) 'A place to call home: identification with dwelling, community, and region', *Sociological Quarterly,* 34 (1): 111–31.

Curtin, P. (1969) *The Atlantic Slave Trade: A Census.* Wisconsin: University of Wisconsin Press.

Daeschner, J. (2004) *True Brits: A Tour of Twenty-first-century Britain in All its Bog-snorkelling, Gurning and Cheese-rolling Glory.* London: Random House.

Daily Post (2004) *Food Festivals in North Wales Boost Economy by £16m.* Available at: www.dailypost.co.uk/business/food-festivals-north-wales-boost-7814206. [Accessed 04/11/15.]

Daldeniz, B. and Hampton, M. (2011) 'VOLUNtourists versus volunTOURISTS: a true dichotomy or merely a differing perception?' in A.M. Benson (ed.), *Journeys of Discovery in Volunteer Tourism.* Wallingford, Oxford: CABI, pp. 30–41.

Dalgic, T. and Leeuw, M. (1994) 'Niche marketing revisited: concept, applications and some European cases', *European Journal of Marketing,* 28 (4): 39–55.

Danielmeier, T. and Albrecht, J.N. (2015) 'Architecture and future food and wine experiences', in I. Yeoman, U. McMahon-Beattie, K. Fields, J. Albrecht and K. Meethan (eds), *The Future of Food Tourism: Foodies, Experiences, Exclusivity, Visions and Political Capital.* Bristol: Channel View Publications, pp.87–100.

Dann, G.M. (1977) 'Anomie, ego-enhancement and tourism', *Annals of Tourism Research* 4 (4): 184–194.

Dann, G.M. (1981) 'Tourist motivation an appraisal', *Annals of Tourism Research,* 8 (2): 187–219.

Dann, G. and Jacobsen, J.K.S. (2003) 'Tourism smellscapes', *Tourism Geographies,* 5 (1): 3–25.

Davidson, J. and Milligan, C. (2004) 'Embodying emotion sensing space: introducing emotional geographies', *Social & Cultural Geography,* 5 (4): 523–32.

de Boer, B., and Hueting, R. (2004) 'Sustainable national income and multiple indicators for sustainable development', in Organisation for Economic Co-operation and Development OECD) (eds), *Measuring Sustainable Development: Integrated Economic, Environmental and Social Frameworks* (pp. 39–52). Proceedings of the May 2003 workshop for accounting frameworks in sustainable development. Available at: www.oecd.org/site/worldforum/33703829.pdf. [Accessed 05/05/13.]

De Certeau, M. (1988) *The Practice of Everyday Life.* Berkeley: University of California.

De Grazia, S. (1962) *Of Time, Work, and Leisure.* The Twentieth Century Fund. New York.

De Saussure, F. and Baskin, W. (2011) *Course in General Linguistics.* Columbia: Columbia University Press.

Deale, C., Norman, W.C. and Jodice, L.W. (2008) 'Marketing locally harvested shrimp to South Carolina coastal visitors: the development of a culinary tourism supply chain', *Journal of Culinary Science & Technology*, 6 (1): 5–23.

Debbage, K.G. and Ioannides, D. (2004) 'The cultural turn? Toward a more critical economic geography of tourism', in A.A. Lew, C.M. Hall and A.M. Williams (eds), *A Companion to Tourism.* Oxford: Blackwell, pp. 99–109.

Demoncracy Now (2011) Every 30 Minutes": Crushed by Debt and Neoliberal Reforms, Indian Farmers Commit Suicide at Staggering Rate. Available at: www.democracynow. org/2011/5/11/every_30_minutes_crushed_by_debt. [Accessed 06/12/13.]

Department for Environment, Food and Rural Affairs (DEFRA) (2002) *The Strategy For Sustainable Farming and Food – Facing the Future.* London: DEFRA.

Department for Environment, Food and Rural Affairs (DEFRA) (2007) Consultation on the Rural Development Programme for England 2007–2013 (27 February 2006 to 22 May 2006). London: DEFRA.

Department for Environment, Food and Rural Affairs (DEFRA) (2010) *Food 20,30.* London: DEFRA.

Dickinson, J.E., Lumsdon, L.M. and Robbins, D. (2011) 'Slow travel: issues for tourism and climate change', *Journal of Sustainable Tourism*, 19 (3): 281–300.

Dodd, T.H. (1995) 'Opportunities and pitfalls of tourism in a developing wine industry', *International Journal of Wine Marketing*, 7 (1): 5–16.

Dodd, T. and Beverland, M. (2001) 'Winery tourism life-cycle development: a proposed model', *Tourism Recreation Research*, 26 (2): 11–21.

Doolin, B., Burgess, L. and Cooper, J. (2002) 'Evaluating the use of the web for tourism marketing: a case study from New Zealand', *Tourism Management*, 23 (5): 557–61.

Dougherty, M.L., Brown, L.E. and Green, G.P. (2013) 'The social architecture of local food tourism: challenges and opportunities for community economic development', *Journal of Rural Social Sciences*, 28 (2): 1–27.

Douglas, N., Douglas, N. and Derrett, R. (2001) *Special Interest Tourism.* Milton, Queensland: John Wiley and Sons Australia, Ltd.

Du Rand, G. and Heath, E. (2006) 'Towards a framework for food tourism as an element of destination marketing', *Current Issues in Tourism*, 9 (3): 206–34.

Duram, L. and Cawley, M. (2012) 'Irish chefs and restaurants in the geography of "local" food value chains', *The Open Geography Journal*, 5 (1): 16–25.

Dwyer, L. and Wickens, E. (eds) (2014) *Event Tourism and Cultural Tourism: Issues and Debates.* London: Routledge.

Eaton, E. (2008) 'From feeding the locals to selling the locale: adapting local sustainable food projects in Niagara to neocommunitarianism and neoliberalism', *Geoforum*, 39 (2): 994–1006.

Echols, M.A. (2008) *Geographical Indications for Food Products: International Legal and Regulatory Perspectives.* New York: Kluwer Law International.

Echtner, C.M. and Prasad, P. (2003) 'The context of third world tourism marketing', *Annals of Tourism Research*, 30 (3): 660–82.

Echtner, C.M. and Ritchie, J.B. (2003) 'The meaning and measurement of destination image', *Journal of Tourism Studies*, 14 (1): 37–48.

Edensor, T. (2001) 'Performing tourism, staging tourism: (re)producing tourist space and practice', *Tourist Studies*, 1 (1): 59–81.

Edwards, A. and Llurdés, J. (1996) 'Mines and quarries: industrial heritage tourism', *Annals of Tourism Research*, 23 (2): 341–63.

Ekins, P., Simon, S., Deutsch, L., Folke, C. and De Groot, R. (2003) 'A framework for the practical application of the concepts of critical natural capital and strong sustainability', *Ecological Economics*, 44 (2): 165–85.

Ells, H. (2015) 'The impact of future food supply on food and drink tourism', in I. Yeoman, U. McMahon-Beattie, K. Fields, J. Albrecht and K. Meethan (eds), *The Future of Food Tourism. Foodies, Experiences, Exclusivity, Visions and Political Capital.* Bristol: Channel View Publications, Chapter 5, pp .62–74.

eMarketer (2004) *Global Ad Spending Growth to Double This Year*. Available at: www.emarketer.com/Article/Global-Ad-Spending-Growth-Double-This-Year/1010997. [Accessed 06/11/14.]

Enright, M.J. and Newton, J. (2005) 'Determinants of tourism destination competitiveness in Asia Pacific: comprehensiveness and universality', *Journal of Travel Research*, 43 (4): 339–50.

Enteleca Research and Consultancy Ltd. (2001) *Tourists Attitudes Towards Regional and Local Foods.* London: MAFF and the Countryside Agency.

Eriksen, S.N. (2013) 'Defining local food: constructing a new taxonomy – three domains of proximity', *Acta Agriculturae Scandinavica, Section B–Soil & Plant Science*, 63 (1): 47–55.

European Commission (2013) *Overview of CAP Reform 2014–2020*. European Commission.

Everett, S. (2007) *Food Tourism in the 'Celtic' Periphery: Spatial, Social and Cultural Resistance.* Unpublished doctoral thesis. Bristol: University of the West of England.

Everett, S. (2008) 'Beyond the visual gaze? The pursuit of an embodied experience through food tourism', *Tourist Studies*, 8 (3): 337–58.

Everett, S. (2012) 'Production places or consumption spaces? The place-making agency of food tourism in Ireland and Scotland', *Tourism Geographies*, 14 (4): 535–54.

Everett, S. (2015) 'Iconic cuisines, marketing and place promotion' in D.J. Timothy (ed.), *Heritage Cuisines: Traditions, Identities and Tourism*. Abingdon: Routledge pp. 119–31.

Everett, S. and Aitchison, C. (2008) 'The role of food tourism in sustaining regional identity: a case study of Cornwall, South West England', *Journal of Sustainable Tourism*, 16 (2): 150–67.

Everett, S. and Slocum, S.L. (2013) 'Food and tourism: an effective partnership? A UK-based review', *Journal of Sustainable Tourism*, 21 (6): 789–809.

Ewick, P. and Silbey, S. (2002) *Making Resistance Thinkable: Desired Disturbances of Everyday Legal Transactions*. Unpublished manuscript.

Fair Trade Advocacy Office (2015) *About Fair Trade*. Available at: www.fairtrade-advocacy.org/about-fair-trade/the-fair-trade-movement/113-about-fair-trade. [Accessed 12/12/15.]

Farley, D. (2009) 'New York develops a taste for gastropub', *The Washington Post* May 24, pp. 6–9.

Faulkner, B. (1997) 'A model for the evaluation of national tourism destination marketing programs', *Journal of Travel Research*, 35 (3): 23–32.

Feagan, R. (2007) 'The place of food: mapping out the "local" in local food systems', *Progress in Human Geography*, 31 (1): 23–42.

Featherstone, M. (1991) *Global Culture*. London: Sage.

Feifer, M. (1985) *Going Places*. London: Macmillan.

Fernandez Arnesto, F. (2001) *Food. A History*. London: Macmillan.

Fernandez, T. (2010) *More than Sun, Beach and Heritage: Innovating Mediterranean Tourism through Creative Tourism. Interactions, Co-operation, Competitiveness and Economic Development*. In 2010 RESER Conference papers. Gothenburg, Sweden (Vol. 30).

Fields, K. (2002) 'Demand for the gastronomy tourism product: motivational factors', in A.M. Hjalager and G. Richards (eds), *Tourism and Gastronomy*. London: Routledge, pp. 36–50.

Fischler, C. (1988) 'Food, self and identity', *Social Science Information*, 27 (2): 275–92.

Flandrin, J (1999) 'From industrial revolution to industrial food', in J. Flandrin and M. Montanari (eds), *Food: A Culinary History from Antiquity to the Present*. New York: Columbia University Press, pp. 435–41.

Fleischer, A. and Tchetchik, A. (2005) 'Does rural tourism benefit from agriculture?', *Tourism Management*, 26 (4): 493–501.

Font, X., Tapper, R., Schwartz, K. and Kornilaki, M. (2008) 'Sustainable supply chain management in tourism', *Business Strategy and the Environment*, 17 (4): 260–71.

Food and Agriculture Organization of the United Nations (2015), *Food Balance Sheets* 2015). Available from: http://faostat.fao.org/site/354/default.aspx. [Accessed 21/02/16]

Fossati, A., and Panella, G.. (2000) *Tourism and Sustainable Economic Development*. Norwell: Kluwer Academic Publishers.

Foxall, G.R. and Yani-de-Soriano, M.M. (2005) 'Situational influences on consumers' attitudes and behavior', *Journal of Business Research*, 58 (4): 518–25.

Franklin, A. (2001) 'The tourist gaze and beyond: an interview with John Urry', *Tourist Studies*, 1 (2): 115–31.

Franklin, A. (2003) *Tourism: An Introduction*. London: Sage.

Fraser, R.A. and Alonso, A. (2006) 'Do tourism and wine always fit together? A consideration of business motivations', in J. Carlsen and S. Charters (eds), *Global Wine Tourism: Research, Management and Marketing*. Wallingford, Oxford: CABI, pp.19–26.

Freud, S. (1995 [1914]) *On Narcissism. The Standard Edition of the Complete Psychological Works of Sigmund Freud*. London: Vintage Classics. 14, pp. 1914–16.

Friedland, W.H. (2002) 'Agriculture and rurality: beginning the "final separation"?' *Rural Sociology*, 67 (3): 350–71.

Friedrich, T., Kienzle, J. and Kassam, A. (eds) (2009) *Conservation Agrilculture in Developing Countries. The Role of Mechanisation*. Club of Bologna meeting on Innovation for Sustinable Mechanisation, Hanover, Germany, 2 November. Available at: www.clubofbologna.org/ew/documents/Friedrich_MF.pdf [Accessed 03/11/14.]

Friends of the Earth (2000) *The Economic Benefits of Farmers' Markets*. London: Friends of the Earth.

Frochot, I. (2000), 'Wine Tourism in France: a paradox', in C.M. Hall, L. Sharples, B. Cambourne and N. Macionis (eds) *Wine Tourism Around the World: Development, Management and Markets*. Oxford: Butterworth-Heinemann, pp. 67–80.

Fromer, J.E. (2008) *A Necessary Luxury: Tea in Victorian England*. Athens, OH: Ohio University Press.

Fullager, S., Markwell, K. and Wilson, E. (eds) (2012) *Slow Tourism. Experiences and Mobilities*. Bristol: Channel View Publications.

Gale, T. (2005) 'Modernism, post-modernism and the decline of British seaside resorts as long holiday destinations: a case study of Rhyl, North Wales', *Tourism Geographies*, 7 (1): 86–112.

Gammon, S. and Robinson, T. (2003) 'Sport and tourism: a conceptual framework', *Journal of Sport Tourism*, 8 (1): 21–6. Reproduced from original (1997).

Garrod, B., Wornell, R. and Youell, R. (2006) 'Re-conceptualising rural resources as countryside capital: the case of rural tourism', *Journal of Rural Studies*, 22 (1): 117–28.

Gazulla, C., Raugei, M. and Fullana-i-Palmer, P. (2010) 'Taking a life cycle look at crianza wine production in Spain: where are the bottlenecks?' *The International Journal of Life Cycle Assessment*, 15 (4): 330–7.

Geißler, R. (2007) *Weininteressierte und ihr Reiseverhalten*. Unpublished doctoral thesis. PhD.Austria: University of Innsbruck.

Gellynck, X., Banterle, A., Kühne, B., Carraresi, L. and Stranieri, S. (2012) 'Market orientation and marketing management of traditional food producers in the EU', *British Food Journal*, 114 (4): 481–99.

Gertner, D. and Kotler, P. (2002) 'Country as brand, product, and beyond: a place marketing and brand management perspective', *Journal of Brand Management*, 9 (4/5): 249–61.

Getz, D. (1991) *Festivals, Special Events, and Tourism*. Wallingford, Oxford: CABI.

Getz, D. (1993) 'Corporate culture in not-for-profit festival organizations: concepts and potential applications', *Festival Management & Event Tourism*, 1 (1): 11–17.

Getz, D. (1997) *Event Management and Event Tourism*. New York: Cognizant Communication Corporation.

Getz, D. (ed.) (1998) *Wine Tourism: Perfect Partners*. The First Australian Wine Tourism Conference, Margaret River, Australia, Bureau of Tourism Research.

Getz, D. (2000) *Explore Wine Tourism: Management, Development and Destinations*. Wallingford, Oxford: CABI.

Getz, D. (2007) *Event Studies: Theory, Research and Policy for Planned Events*. Oxford: Elsevier.

Getz, D. (2014) *Event Tourism*. New York: Cognizant.

Getz, D. and Brown, G. (2006) 'Critical success factors for wine tourism regions: a demand analysis', *Tourism Management*, 27 (1): 146–58.

Getz, D., Robinson, R.N., Andersson, T.D. and Vujicic, S. (2014) *Foodies and Food Tourism*. Oxford: Goodfellows.

Gibson, E. (1995) 'Selling to restaurants', *Direct Farm Marketing and Tourism Handbook*. Arizona: University of Arizona College of Agriculture, Cooperative Extension.

Gil, J.M. and Sánchez, M. (1997) 'Consumer preferences for wine attributes: a conjoint approach', *British Food Journal*, 99 (1): 3–11.

Gillmore, L. (2012) 'Europe on a plate: the tastiest food festivals', *The Independent*, 20 September.

Goddard, T. (2015) 'The economics of craft beer', *Smart Assets*, 23 January.

Godfrey, K. and Clarke, J. (2000) *The Tourism Development Handbook: A Practical Approach to Planning and Marketing*. London: Thomson.

Goeldner, C.R. and Ritchie, J.B. (2006) *Tourism: Principles, Practices, Philosophies*. New York: John Wiley & Sons.

Goffman, E. (1959) *The Presentation of Self in Everyday Life*. New York: Doubleday.

Goffman, E. (1961) *Asylum*. New York: Doubleday.

Gold, J.R. and Gold, M.M. (1995) *Imagining Scotland: Tradition, Representation and Promotion in Scottish Tourism Since 1750*. Aldershot: Scolar Press.

Goldstein, D. (2010) *The Gastronomica Reader*. California: The University of California Press.

Gómez, M. and Molina, A. (2012) 'Wine tourism in Spain: denomination of origin effects on brand equity', *International journal of tourism research*, 14 (4): 353–68.

Goodman, A. (2000) 'Implementing sustainability in service operations at Scandic hotels', *Interfaces*, 30 (3): 202–14.

Goodman, D. and DuPuis, E.M. (2002) 'Knowing food and growing food: beyond the production–consumption debate in the sociology of agriculture', *Sociologia Ruralis*, 42 (1): 5–22.

Goodman, D., DuPuis, E.M. and Goodman, M.K. (2012) *Alternative Food Networks: Knowledge, Practice, and Politics*. London: Routledge.

Goodman, M.K. (2004) 'Reading fair trade: political ecological imaginary and the moral economy of fair trade foods', *Political Geography*, 23 (7): 891–915.

Goodwin, H., and Boekhold, H. (2010) 'Beyond fair trade: enhancing the livelihoods of coffee farmers in Tanzania', in L. Jolliffe (ed.), *Coffee Culture, Destinations and Tourism*. Bristol: Channel View Publications, Chapter 12, pp. 181–96.

Goss, J., Cartier, C. and Lew, A. (2005) 'The souvenir and sacrifice in the tourist mode of consumption', in C. Cartier and A. Lew (eds), *Seductions of Place: Geographical Perspectives on Globalization and Touristed Landscapes*. London: Psychology Press, pp. 56–71.

Gössling, S. and Hall, M. (2013) 'Sustainable culinary system: an introduction', in C.M. Hall and S. Gössling (eds), *Sustainable Culinary Systems*. Oxford: Routledge, pp. 3–44.

Gössling, S., Garrod, B., Aall, C., Hille, J. and Peeters, P. (2011) 'Food management in tourism: reducing tourism's carbon "foodprin"', *Tourism Management*, 32 (3): 534–43.

Graburn, N.H. (2006) 'Arts of the fourth world', in M. Perkins and H. Morphy (eds), *The Anthropology of Art: A Reader*. Oxford: Blackwell Publishers, pp. 412–430.

Gramsci, A. (1934) Americanism and Fordism. In Hoare, Q. and Nowell Smith, G. (1971) *Prison Notebooks of Antonio Gramsci*. pp. 558–620. London: Lawrence & Wishart.

Grant, D. (2004) *The SAGE Handbook of Organizational Discourse*. London: Sage.

Gray, H.P. (1979) *International Travel: International Trade*. Heath Lexigton Books: Lexigton.

Green, G.P. and Dougherty, M.L. (2008) 'Localizing linkages for food and tourism: culinary tourism as a community development strategy', *Community Development*, 39 (3): 148–58.

Greenwood, D. J., and Smith, V. L. (1989) 'Culture by the pound: an anthropological perspective on tourism as cultural commoditization', in V. Smith (ed.), *Hosts and Guests: The Anthropology of Tourism*. Philadelphia: University of Pennsylvania, pp. 171–185.

Gretzel, U., Yuan, Y. and Fesenmaier, D.R. (2000) 'Preparing for the new economy: advertising strategies and change in destination marketing organizations', *Journal of Travel Research*, 39 (2): 146–56.

Griffin, M.R. and Frongillo, E.A. (2003) 'Experiences and perspectives of farmers from Upstate New York farmers' markets', *Agriculture and Human Values*, 20 (2): 189–203.

Gunasekara, R.B. and Momsen, J.H. (2007) 'Amidst the misty mountains: the role of tea tourism in Sri Lanka's turbulent tourist industry', in J. Jolliffe (ed.), *Tea and Tourism: Tourists, Traditions and Transformations*. Bristol: Channel View Publications, pp. 84–97.

Gunn, C. (1988) *Vacationscapes: Designing Tourist Regions*. New York. Van Nostrand Reinhold.

Guttentag, D.A. (2009) 'The possible negative impacts of volunteer tourism', *International Journal of Tourism Research*, 11 (6): 537–51.

Gyimóthy, S. and Mykletun, R.J. (2009) 'Scary food: commodifying culinary heritage as meal adventures in tourism', *Journal of Vacation Marketing*, 15 (3): 259–73.

Ha, J. and Jang, S.S. (2010) 'Effects of service quality and food quality: the moderating role of atmospherics in an ethnic restaurant segment', *International Journal of Hospitality Management*, 29 (3): 520–9.

Habermas, J. (1984 [1981]) *The Theory of Communicative Action, Volume One: Reason and the Rationalization of Society*. Cambridge: Polity.

Habermas, J. (1987 [1981]) *The Theory of Communicative Action, Volume Two: The Critique of Functionalist Reason*. Cambridge: Polity.

Haldrup, M. and Larsen, J. (2006) 'Material cultures of tourism', *Leisure Studies*, 25 (3): 275–89.

Hall, C.M. (2003) 'Health and spa tourism', in S. Hudson (ed.), *International Sports & Adventure Tourism*. London: Haworth Hospitality Press, pp. 273–292.

Hall, C.M. (2005) 'Rural wine and food tourism cluster and network development', in D. Hall, I. Kirkpatrick and M. Mitchell (eds), *Rural Tourism and Sustainable Business*. Bristol: Channel View Publications, pp. 149–64.

Hall, C.M. (2010a) 'Crisis events in tourism: subjects of crisis in tourism', *Current Issues in Tourism*, 13 (5): 401–17.

Hall, C.M. (2010b) 'Blending coffee and Fair Trade hospitality', in L. Jolliffe (ed.), *Coffee Culture, Destinations and Tourism*. Bristol: Channel View Publications, pp. 159–71.

Hall, C.M. and Gössling, S. (eds) (2013) *Sustainable Culinary Systems: Local Foods, Innovation, and Tourism & Hospitality*. London: Routledge.

Hall, C.M. and Macionis, N. (1998) 'Wine tourism in Australia and New Zealand', in R. Roberts and D. Hall (eds), *Tourism and Recreation in Rural Areas*, Wallingford, Oxford: CABI, pp.197–224.

Hall, C.M. and Mitchell, R. (2001) 'Wine and food tourism', in N. Douglas, N. Douglas and R. Derrett (eds), *Special Interest Tourism*. London: Wiley, pp. 307–29.

Hall, C.M. and Mitchell, R. (2008) *Wine Marketing: A Practical Approach*. Oxford: Butterworth Heinemann.

Hall, C.M. and Page, S. (2005) *The Geography of Tourism and Recreation*. Abingdon: Routledge.

Hall, C.M. and Sharples, L. (2008) *Food and Wine Festivals and Events Around the World: Development, Management and Markets*. Oxford: Butterworth Heinemann.

Hall, C.M. and Weiler, B. (1992) *Special Interest Tourism*. London: Belhaven Press.

Hall, C.M. and Wilson, S. (2008) 'Scoping paper: local food, tourism and sustainability'. An 'issues paper' developed for the Sustainable Norwegian Tourism Project, Centre for Sustainable Tourism and Geotourism, Western Norway Research Institute, Sogndal, Norway. Available at: www.academia.edu/151775/Scoping_Paper_Local_food_Tourism_and_Sustainability. [Accessed: 04/12/15.]

Hall, C.M., Mitchell, R., Hjalager, A. and Richards, G. (2002) 'Tourism as a force for gastronomic globalization and localization', in A. Hjalager and G. Richards (eds), *Tourism and Gastronomy*, London: Routledge, pp. 71–90.

Hall, C.M., Sharples, L., Cambourne, B. and Macionis, N. (2000) *Wine Tourism around the World: Development, Management and Markets*. Oxford: Butterworth Heinemann.

Hall, C.M., Cambourne, B., Sharples, L., Macionis, N. and Mitchell, R. (2003) *Food Tourism Around the World: Development, Management and Markets*. Oxford: Butterworth Heinemann.

Hall, D. and Boyne, S. (2007) 'Teapot trails in the UK: just a handle or something worth spouting about?' in L. Jolliffe (ed.), *Tea and Tourism: Tourists, Traditions and Transformations*. Bristol: Channel View Publications, pp. 206–23.

Hall, S. (1996) 'Politics of identity', in T. Ranger, Y. Samad and O. Stuart (eds), *Culture, Identity and Politics*. Aldershot: Avebury, pp. 129–35.

Halonen-Knight, E. and Hurmerinta, L. (2010) 'Who endorses whom? Meanings transfer in celebrity endorsement', *Journal of Product & Brand Management*, 19 (6): 452–60.

Hamid, A. and Raihan, N. (eds) (2011) 'Farmers' participation and supply chain issues: a case study of farmers' market in Kuala Lumpur vicinity', Las Vegas, October 6–8, Proceedings of the Academic and Business Research Institute Conference.

Hansen, C. (2015) 'The future fault lines of food', in I. Yeoman, U. McMahon-Beattie, K. Fields, J. Albrecht and K. Meethan (eds), *The Future of Food Tourism: Foodies, Experiences, Exclusivity, Visions and Political Capital.* Bristol: Channel View Publications, Chapter 4, pp. 49–61.

Harland, C., Nassimbeni, G. and Schneller, E. (2013) *The SAGE Handbook of Strategic Supply Management.* London: SAGE.

Harpham, T., Grant, E. and Thomas, E. (2002) 'Measuring social capital within health surveys: key issues', *Health Policy and Planning,* 17 (1): 106–11.

Harré, R. (1993) *The Discursive Mind.* Oxford: Blackwell.

Harris, D.R. (1996) *Origins and Spread of Agriculture and Pastoralism in Eurasia.* London: UCL Press, Smithsonian Institution Press.

Harvey, D. (1989) *The Condition of Postmodernity.* Oxford: Blackwell.

Harvey, M., White, L. and Frost, W. (2014) *Wine and Identity: Branding, Heritage, Terroir.* London: Routledge.

Hashimoto, A. and Telfer, D.J. (2006) 'Selling Canadian culinary tourism: branding the global and the regional product', *Tourism Geographies,* 8 (1): 31–55.

Haukeland, J.V. and Jacobsen, J.K.S. (eds) (2001) *Gastronomy in the Periphery: Food and Cuisine as Tourism Attractions at the Top of Europe.* Paper presented at the 10th Nordic Tourism Research Conference, Vasa, Finland.

Haven-Tang, C. and Jones, E. (2006) 'Using local food and drink to differentiate tourism destinations through a sense of place: a story from Wales – dining at Monmouthshire's great table', *Journal of Culinary Science & Technology,* 4 (4): 69–86.

Hays, S., Page, S.J. and Buhalis, D. (2013) 'Social media as a destination marketing tool: its use by national tourism organisations', *Current Issues in Tourism,* 16 (3): 211–39.

Heath, E. and Wall, G. (1992) *Marketing Tourism Destinations: A Strategic Planning Approach.* New York: Wiley.

Hede, A. (2008) 'The Airey's Inlet Farmers' Market: where the coast meets the ranges', in C.M. Hall and L. Sharples (eds), *Food and Wine Festivals and Events Around the World: Development, Managment and Markets.* Oxford: Butterworth Heinemann, pp. 279–85.

Held, D., McGrew, A., Goldblatt, D. and Perraton, J. (1999) *Global Transformations: Politics, Economics and Culture?* Cambridge: Polity Press.

Henderson, J.C. (2011) 'Celebrity chefs: expanding empires', *British Food Journal,* 113 (5): 613–24.

Henderson, J.C. (2014) 'Food and culture: in search of a Singapore cuisine', *British Food Journal,* 116 (6): 904–17.

Hendrickson, M.K. and Heffernan, W.D. (2002) 'Opening spaces through relocalization: locating potential resistance in the weaknesses of the global food system', *Sociologia Ruralis,* 42 (4): 347–69.

Hess, C. (2012) 'Constructing a new research agenda for cultural commons', in E.E. Bertacchini (ed.), *Cultural Commons: A New Perspective on the Production and Evolution of Cultures.* Cheltenham: Edward Elgar Publishing, pp. 19–35.

Higham, J. (1999) 'Commentary-sport as an avenue of tourism development: an analysis of the positive and negative impacts of sport tourism', *Current Issues in Tourism,* 2 (1): 82–90.

Higham, J. (2005) 'Sport tourism as an attraction for managing seasonality', *Sport in Society,* 8 (2): 238–62.

Hilchey, D., Lyson, T. and Gillespie, G.W. (1995) 'Farmers' markets and rural economic development: entrepreneurship, business incubation, and job creation in the Northeast', *Community Agriculture Development Series (USA)* Farming Alternatives Program, Dept. of Rural Sociology, Cornell University.

Hillel, D., Belhassen, Y. and Shani, A. (2013) 'What makes a gastronomic destination attractive? Evidence from the Israeli Negev', *Tourism Management*, 36: 200–9.

Hines, C. (2000) *Localization: A Global Manifesto.* London: Earthscan Publications.

Hinrichs, C.C. (2003) 'The practice and politics of food system localization', *Journal of Rural Studies*, 19 (1): 33–45.

Hjalager, A. and Corigliano, M.A. (2000) 'Food for tourists – determinants of an image', *The International Journal of Tourism Research*, 2 (4): 281–293.

Hjalager, A. and Johansen, P.H. (2013) 'Food tourism in protected areas – sustainability for producers, the environment and tourism?', *Journal of Sustainable Tourism*, 21 (3): 417–33.

Hjalager, A. and Richards, G. (2002) *Tourism and Gastronomy.* London: Routledge.

Ho, D.C., Au, K. and Newton, E. (2002) 'Empirical research on supply chain management: a critical review and recommendations', *International Journal of Production Research*, 40 (17): 4415–30.

Hobsbawm, E. and Ranger, T. (2012) *The Invention of Tradition.* Cambridge: Cambridge University Press.

Holloway, L. and Kneafsey, M. (2000) 'Reading the space of the farmers' market: a preliminary investigation from the UK', *Sociologia Ruralis*, 40 (3): 285–99.

Holloway, L., Kneafsey, M., Venn, L., Cox, R., Dowler, E. and Tuomainen, H. (2007) 'Possible food economies: a methodological framework for exploring food production – consumption relationships', *Sociologia Ruralis*, 47 (1): 1–19.

Hooper-Greenhill, E. (2013) *Museums and Their Visitors.* London: Routledge.

Horng, J. and Tsai, C.T.S. (2010) 'Government websites for promoting East Asian culinary tourism: a cross-national analysis', *Tourism Management*, 31 (1): 74–85.

Howes, D. (ed.) (1996) *Cross-cultural Consumption. Global Markets, Local Realities.* London: Routledge.

Hu, W. and Wall, G. (2005) 'Environmental management, environmental image and the competitive tourist attraction', *Journal of Sustainable Tourism*, 13 (6): 617–35.

Hu, Y. and Ritchie, J.B. (1993) 'Measuring destination attractiveness: a contextual approach', *Journal of Travel Research*, 32 (2): 25–34.

Hudson, S. and Miller, G.A. (2005) 'The responsible marketing of tourism: the case of Canadian Mountain Holidays', *Tourism Management*, 26 (2): 133–42.

Huh, C. and Singh, A. (2007) 'Families travelling with a disabled member: analysing the potential of an emerging niche market segment', *Tourism and Hospitality Research*, 7 (3–4): 212–29.

Hurley, K. (2015) 'Envisioning AgriTourism 2115: organic food, convivial meals, hands in the soil and no flying cars', in I. Yeoman, U. McMahon-Beattie, K. Fields, J. Albrecht, and K. Meethan (eds), *The Future of Food Tourism. Foodies, Experiences, Exclusivity, Visions and Political Capital.* Bristol: Channel View Publications, pp. 101–13.

Ignatov, E. and Smith, S. (2006) 'Segmenting Canadian culinary tourists', *Current Issues in Tourism*, 9 (3): 235–255.

Ilbery, B. and Bowler, I. (1998) *From Agricultural Productivism to Post-productivism*, in B. Ilbery (ed.), *The Geography of Rural Change.* Wallingford, Oxford: CABI, pp. 57–84.

Ilbery, B. and Kneafsey, M. (1998) 'Product and place: promoting quality products and services in the lagging rural regions of the European Union', *European Urban and Regional Studies*, 5: 329–41.

Ilbery, B. and Maye, D. (2005) 'Alternative (shorter) food supply chains and specialist livestock products in the Scottish-English borders', *Environment and Planning A*, 37 (5): 823–44.

Ilbery, B., Morris, C., Buller, H., Maye, D. and Kneafsey, M. (2005) 'Product, process and place an examination of food marketing and labelling schemes in Europe and north America', *European Urban and Regional Studies*, 12 (2): 116–32.

Inter-American Institute for Cooperation on Agriculture (IICA) (2015) Available from: www.iica.int/en/countries/barbados [Accessed 06/12/15.]

International Coffee Organisation (ICO) (2015) *Historical Data on the Global Coffee Trade*. Available from: www.ico.org [Accessed 03/11/15.]

International Culinary Tourism Association, (2012) *Culinary Tourism* [online]. Was available from: www.culinarytourism.org. [Accessed 30 June 2013], now see WFTA (2015).

Iso-Ahola, S. E. (1983) 'Towards a social psychology of recreational travel', *Leisure Studies*, 2(1): 45–56.

Jackson, L.A. and Singh, D. (2015) 'Environmental rankings and financial performance: An analysis of firms in the US food and beverage supply chain', *Tourism Management Perspectives*, 14 (1): 25–33.

Jackson, P. (2002) 'Commercial cultures: transcending the cultural and the economic', *Progress in Human Geography*, 26 (1): 3–18.

Jackson, P. and Holbrook, B. (1995) 'Multiple meanings: shopping and the cultural politics of identity', *Environment and Planning A*, 27 (12): 1913–30.

Jaffe, E. and Pasternak, H. (2004) 'Developing wine trails as a tourist attraction in Israel', *International Journal of Tourism Research*, 6 (4): 237–49.

Jamaica Observer (2014) 'Sandals seeks deeper agro linkages locally', *Jamaica Observer*, 24/01/2014.

Jamaica Observer (2009) 'Nothing to fear, Sandals reassures fretful farmers', *Jamaica Observer*, 19/4/2009.

Jamal, T. and Kim, H. (2005) 'Bridging the interdisciplinary divide: towards an integrated framework for heritage tourism research', *Tourist Studies*, 5 (1): 55–83.

Jefferies, J. (2002) *Cheese Rolling In Gloucestershire*. Stroud: The History Press.

Jochnowitz, E. (2004) 'Flavors of Memory: Jewish Food as Culinary Tourism in Poland', in L. Long (ed.), *Culinary Tourism*. Lexington, KY: The University Press Kentucky, pp. 97–113.

Jóhannesson, G.Þ., Skaptadóttir, U.D. and Benediktsson, K. (2003) 'Coping with social capital? The cultural economy of tourism in the North', *Sociologia Ruralis*, 43 (1): 3–16.

Johnson, H. (1989) *Vintage: The Story of Wine*. New York: Simon and Schuster.

Johnson, M. and Whang, S. (2002) 'E-business and supply chain management: an overview and framework', *Production and Operations Management*, 11 (4): 413–23.

Johnston, C. (2010) 'Coffee and coffee tourism in Kona, Hawai'i: surviving in the niche.

Johnston, G. and Percy-Smith, J. (2003) 'In search of social capital', *Policy & Politics*, 31 (3): 321–34.

Jolliffe, L. (2003) 'The lure of tea: history, traditions and attractions', in C.M. Hall, L. Sharples, R. Mitchell, N. Macionis and B. Cambourne (eds), *Food Tourism Around the World: Development, Management and Markets*. Oxford: Butterworth Heinemann, pp. 121–36.

Jolliffe, L. (2008) 'Connecting farmers' markets and tourists in New Brunswick, Canada', in C.M. Hall and L. Sharples (eds), *Food and Wine Festivals and Events Around the World.* Oxford: Butterworth Heinemann, pp. 232–49.

Jolliffe, L. (2007) (ed.) *Tea and Tourism: Tourists, Traditions and Transformations.* Bristol: Channel View Publications.

Jolliffe, L. (2010) *Coffee Culture, Destinations and Tourism* (Vol. 24). Bristol: Channel View Publications.

Jolliffe, L. (2012) (ed.) *Sugar Heritage and Tourism in Transition.* Bristol: Channel View Publications.

Jolliffe, L. and Aslam, M.S. (2009) 'Tea heritage tourism: evidence from Sri Lanka', *Journal of Heritage Tourism*, 4 (4): 331–44.

Jolliffe, L., Bui, H.T. and Nguyen, H.T. (2008) 'The Buon Ma Thuot Coffee Festival, Vietnam: opportunity for tourism?', in K.J. Ali, M. Robertson, A. Fyall and A. Ladkin (eds), *International Perspectives of Festivals and Events.* Oxford: Elsevier, pp.125–37.

Jolliffe, L., Kwan, K. and Yen, G.K. (2010) 'Coffee in Vietnam: international tourist experiences', *Coffee Culture, Destinations and Tourism*, Bristol: Channel View Publications, pp. 89–98.

Jones, A. and Jenkins, I. (2002) 'A taste of Wales—Blas Ar Gymru: Institutional malaise in promoting Welsh food tourism products', in A.M. Hjalager and G. Richards (eds), *Tourism and Gastronomy.* London: Routledge, pp. 115–32.

Jones, M.T. (2009) 'A celebrity chef goes global: the business of eating', *Journal of Business Strategy*, 30 (5): 14–23.

Jones, R. and Rowley, J. (2012) 'Food marketing: the public house sector', *Worldwide Hospitality and Tourism*, 4 (3): 255–70.

Jones, S. (2005) 'Community-based ecotourism: the significance of social capital', *Annals of Tourism Research*, 32 (2): 303–24.

Jurinčič, I. and Bojnec, Š. (2006) 'The role of wine consortiums in wine marketing and wine tourism development in Slovenia', in *STIQE 2006: Proceedings of the 8th International Conference on Linking Systems Thinking, Innovation, Quality, Entrepreneurship, and Environment, Maribor, Slovenia*, pp. 81–6.

Kalisch, A. (2002) *Corporate Futures: Consultation on Good Practice.* London: Tourism Concern.

Karim, M.S.A., Chua, B. and Salleh, H. (2009) 'Malaysia as a culinary tourism destination: international tourists' perspective', *Journal of Tourism, Hospitality & Culinary Arts*, 1 (33): 63–78.

Karlsson, H. and Karlsson, J. (2009) *Coffee Tourism: A Community Development Tool.* Kalmar: Handelshögskolan BBS, vid Högskolan i Kalmar. Available at: www.diva-portal.org/smash/get/diva2:220789/FULLTEXT02 [Accessed: 27/09/15.]

Kasim, A. and Ismail, A. (2012) 'Environmentally friendly practices among restaurants: drivers and barriers to change', *Journal of Sustainable Tourism*, 20 (4): 551–70.

Keefe, C. (2002) *Travelers Who Love History and Culture Spend More and Stay Longer than Average Tourists.* Washington, DC: Travel Industry Association of America.

Kelly, I. (2005) *Cooking for Kings: The Life of Antonin Carême, the First Celebrity Chef.* New York: Bloomsbury.

Kelly, John R. (1983) *Leisure Identities and Interactions.* London: George Allen and Unwin.

Kim, H. and Jamal, T. (2007) 'Touristic quest for existential authenticity', *Annals of Tourism Research*, 34 (1): 181–201.

Kim, S. (2012) 'Audience involvement and film tourism experiences: emotional places, emotional experiences', *Tourism Management*, 33 (2): 387–96.

Kim, Y.G. and Eves, A. (2012) 'Construction and validation of a scale to measure tourist motivation to consume local food', *Tourism Management*, 33 (6): 1458–67.

Kim, Y.G., Eves, A. and Scarles, C. (2009a) 'Building a model of local food consumption on trips and holidays: a grounded theory approach', *International Journal of Hospitality Management*, 28 (3): 423–31.

Kim, Y.H., Yuan, J., Goh, B.K. and Antun, J.M. (2009b) 'Web marketing in food tourism: a content analysis of web sites in West Texas', *Journal of Culinary Science & Technology*, 7 (1): 52–64.

Kivela, J. (1997) 'Restaurant marketing: selection and segmentation in Hong Kong', *International Journal of Contemporary Hospitality Management*, 9 (3): 116–23.

Kivela, J. and Crotts, J.C. (2006) 'Tourism and gastronomy: gastronomy's influence on how tourists experience a destination', *Journal of Hospitality & Tourism Research*, 30 (3): 354–77.

Kneafsey, M. (1998) 'Tourism and place identity: a case-study in rural Ireland', *Irish Geography*, 31 (2): 111–23.

Knowd, I. (2006) 'Tourism as a mechanism for farm survival', *Journal of Sustainable Tourism*, 14 (1): 24–42.

Korpela, M. (2010) 'A postcolonial imagination? Westerners searching for authenticity in India', *Journal of Ethnic and Migration Studies*, 36 (8):1299–315.

Kotler, P. (1989) 'From mass marketing to mass customization', *Planning Review*, 17 (5): 10–47.

Kotler, P., Bowen, J.T., Makens, J.C., Kotler, P. and Kotler, P. (2006) *Marketing for Hospitality and Tourism*. Upper Saddle River, NJ: Prentice Hall.

Kozinets, R.V. (2010) *Netnography*. London: Wiley Online Library.

Krippendorf, J. (1986) 'The new tourist: turning point for leisure and travel', *Tourism Management*, 7 (2): 131–5.

Kuisel, R.F. (1993) *Seducing the French: The Dilemma of Americanization*. California: University of California Press.

Lacy, J.A. and Douglass, W.A. (2002) 'Beyond authenticity. the meanings and uses of cultural tourism', *Tourist Studies*, 2 (1): 5–21.

Laing, J. and Frost, W. (2014) *Rituals and Traditional Events in the Modern World*. London: Routledge.

Lane, B. (1994) 'What is rural tourism?', *Journal of Sustainable Tourism*, 2 (1–2): 7–21.

Lang, T. (2003) 'Food industrialisation and food power: implications for food governance', *Development Policy Review*, 21 (5–6): 555–68.

Lang, T. (2010) 'Crisis? What crisis? The normality of the current food crisis', *Journal of Agrarian Change*, 10 (1): 87–97.

Laudan, R. (2010) 'In praise of fast food', in D, Goldstein (ed.), *Gastronmica Reader*. Oakland, CA: University of California Press.

Leask, A. (2010) 'Progress in visitor attraction research: towards more effective management', *Tourism Management*, 31 (2): 155–66.

Lee, C., Lee, Y. and Wicks, B.E. (2004) 'Segmentation of festival motivation by nationality and satisfaction', *Tourism Management*, 25 (1): 61–70.

Lee, I. and Arcodia, C. (2011) 'The role of regional food festivals for destination branding', *International Journal of Tourism Research*, 13 (4): 355–67.

Lees, L., Slater, T. and Wyly, E. (2013) *Gentrification*. London: Routledge.

Lefebvre, H. (1991) *The Production of Space*. Oxford: Blackwell.

Leslie, D. (ed.) (1995) *Tourism and Leisure: Towards the Millennium. Volume 1: Tourism and Leisure-culture, Heritage and Participation*. Eastbourne: Leisure Studies Association.

Lévi-Strauss, C. (1966) 'The culinary triangle', *Partisan Review*, 33 (4): 586–95.

Lévi-Strauss, C. (1970 [1964]) *The Raw and the Cooked: Introduction to a Science of Mythology*, trans. John and Doreen Weightman. London: Jonathan Cape.

Lew, A.A. (1987) 'A framework of tourist attraction research', *Annals of Tourism Research*, 14 (4): 553–75.

Lew, A.A. (2008) 'Long tail tourism: new geographies for marketing niche tourism products', *Journal of Travel & Tourism Marketing*, 25 (3–4): 409–19.

Lewis, S. (2003) 'The integration of paid work and the rest of life. Is post-industrial work the new leisure?', *Leisure Studies*, 22 (4): 343–5.

Li, M., Huang, Z. and Cai, L.A. (2009) 'Benefit segmentation of visitors to a rural community-based festival', *Journal of Travel & Tourism Marketing*, 26 (5–6): 585–98.

Lia, C.B., Othman, M., Chern, B.H., Karim, M.S.A. and Ramachandran, S. (2009) 'Customers' reactions to servicescape failure and associated recovered strategy: an exploratory study in the food service industry', *Journal of Tourism, Hospitality & Culinary Arts*, 1,.23–47.

Light, D. (1995) 'Heritage as informal education', in D.T. Herbert (ed.), *Heritage, Tourism and Society*. London: Mansell, pp. 117–45.

Lin, I.Y. and Mattila, A.S. (2010) 'Restaurant servicescape, service encounter, and perceived congruency on customers' emotions and satisfaction', *Journal of Hospitality Marketing & Management*, 19 (8): 819–41.

Lin, Y. and Huang, J. (2006) 'Internet blogs as a tourism marketing medium: a case study', *Journal of Business Research*, 59 (10): 1201–5.

Lin, Y., Pearson, T.E. and Cai, L.A. (2011) 'Food as a form of destination identity: a tourism destination brand perspective', *Tourism and Hospitality Research*, 11 (1): 30–48.

Litvin, S.W., Goldsmith, R.E. and Pan, B. (2008) 'Electronic word-of-mouth in hospitality and tourism management', *Tourism Management*, 29 (3): 458–68.

Liu, Z. (2003) 'Sustainable tourism development: a critique', *Journal of Sustainable Tourism*, 11 (6): 459–75.

Lockie, S. and Kitto, S. (2000) 'Beyond the farm gate: production-consumption networks and agri-food research', *Sociologia Ruralis*, 40 (1): 3–19.

Lockshin, L., Quester, P. and Spawton, T. (2001) 'Segmentation by involvement or nationality for global retailing: a cross-national comparative study of wine shopping behaviours', *Journal of Wine Research*,12 (3): 223–36.

Löfgren, O. (1999) *On Holiday: A History of Vacationing* (Vol. 6). California: University of California Press.

Lonely Planet (2013) *Peru*. 8th edn. London: Lonely Planet.

Long, L.M. (ed.) (2004) *Culinary Tourism*. Lexington, KY: University Press of Kentucky.

Long, M. (2011) *Global Appeal of Irish Pubs – World Invasion One Pint at a Time*. Available at: http://landlopers.com/2011/03/10/global-appeal-irish-pubs-world-invasion-pint-time [Accessed 07/12/15.]

Loudoun County (2014) *2014 Virginia Craft Beer Visitor Profile Report*. Available at: www.visitloudoun.org [Accessed 04/05/15.]

Lowenthal, D. (1985) *The Past is a Foreign Country*. Cambridge: Cambridge University Press.

Lu, P. and Jun Yi, L. (2014) 'The impact of electronic word-of-mouth on the online page view of restaurants', *Tourism Tribune*, 29 (1): 111–18.

Lucarelli, A. and Berg, P. O. (2011) 'City branding: a state-of-the-art review of the research domain', *Journal of Place Management and Development*, 4 (1): 9–27.

Lumsdon, L. and McGrath, P. (2011) 'Developing a conceptual framework for slow travel: a grounded theory approach', *Journal of Sustainable Tourism*, 19 (3): 265–79.

Lupoli, C.A., Morse, W.C., Bailey, C. and Schelhas, J. (2014) 'Assessing the impacts of international volunteer tourism in host communities: a new approach to organizing and prioritizing indicators', *Journal of Sustainable Tourism*, 22 (6): 898–921.

MacCannell, D. (1976) *The Tourist: A New Theory of the Leisure Class*. Oakland, CA: University of California Press.

MacClancy, J. (1992) *Consuming Culture*. London: Chapmans.

Macionis, N. (ed.) (1996) *Wine Tourism in Australia*, in J. Higham (ed.), *Proceedings of Tourism Down Under II – a Tourism Research Conference*. Dunedin: University of Dunedin.

Macionis, N. (1998) 'Wine and food tourism in the Australian capital territory: exploring the links', *International Journal of Wine Marketing*, 10 (3): 5–22.

Macionis, N. and Cambourne, B. (1998) 'Wine tourism: just what is it all about?', *Wine Industry Journal*, 13 (1):41–47.

Macleod, D. (2009) 'Scottish theme towns: have new identities enhanced development?', *Journal of Tourism and Cultural Change*, 7 (2): 133–45.

Magliocco, S. (1998) 'Playing with food: the negotiation of identity in the ethnic display event by Italian Americans in Clinton, Indiana', in J. Shortridge (ed.), *The Taste of American Place: A Reader on Regional and Ethnic Foods*. Lanham, MD: Rowman & Littlefield, pp. 145–61.

Mail Online (2013) 'Muddled American and Japanese tourists are cancelling trips to Britain in tens of thousands because they mistakenly believe they could catch mad cow disease from the foot-and-mouth epidemic, travel chiefs said today', *Daily Mail, UK,* 20 August.

Mak, A.H., Lumbers, M. and Eves, A. (2012) 'Globalisation and food consumption in tourism', *Annals of Tourism Research*, 39 (1): 171–96.

Malthus, T.R. (1959 [1798]) *Population: the First Essay*. Michigan: University of Michigan Press.

Manning, L., Baines, R. and Chadd, S. (2005) 'Deliberate contamination of the food supply chain', *British Food Journal*, 107 (4): 225–45.

Marinagi, C., Trivellas, P. and Sakas, D.P. (2014) 'The impact of Information Technology on the development of Supply Chain Competitive Advantage', *Procedia – Social and Behavioral Sciences*,147: 586–91.

Marsden, T., Banks, J. and Bristow, G. (2000) 'Food supply chain approaches: exploring their role in rural development', *Sociologia Ruralis*, 40 (4): 424–38.

Martin, A. and McBoyle, G. (2006) 'Scotland's Malt Whisky Trail: management issues in a public-private tourism marketing partnership', *International Journal of Wine Marketing*,18 (2): 98–111.

Martin, E. (2005) 'Food, literature, art, and the demise of dualistic thought', *Consumption Markets & Culture*, 8 (1): 27–48.

Marzo-Navarro, M. and Pedraja-Iglesias, M. (2012) 'Critical factors of wine tourism: incentives and barriers from the potential tourist's perspective', *International Journal of Contemporary Hospitality Management*, 24 (2): 312–34.

Masci, D. (2005). *An uncertain road: Muslims and the future of Europe*. Pew Forum on Religion & Public Life. Available at: www.pewforum.org/files/2005/10/muslims-europe-2005.pdf [Accessed 09/12/14.]

Mason, P. (2005) 'Visitor management in protected areas: From "hard" to "soft" approaches?' *Current Issues in Tourism*, 8 (2–3): 181–94.

Mason, R.J. (2010) 'Critical Factors in the Development and Performance of Food and Wine Trails in Australia'. Doctoral dissertation. Victoria University, Australia.

Mason, R. and O'Mahony, B. (2007) 'On the trail of food and wine: the tourist search for meaningful experience', *Annals of Leisure Research*, 10 (3–4): 498–517.

Matijaško, N. (2008) 'Muzej Alimentarium u Veveyu u Švicarskoj (Museum Alimentarium in the Town of Vevey, Switzerland)', *Etnološka istraživanja*, 12 (13): 341–5.

Maxey, L. (2007) 'From "alternative" to "sustainable" food', in D. Maye, L. Holloway and M. Kneafsey (eds), *Alternative Food Geographies: Representation and Practice.* Bingley, UK: Emerald, pp. 55–76.

Mbaiwa, J.E. and Stronza, A.L. (2010) 'The effects of tourism development on rural livelihoods in the Okavango Delta, Botswana', *Journal of Sustainable Tourism*, 18 (5): 635–56.

McBain, H. (2007) *Caribbean Tourism and Agriculture: Linking to Enhance Development and Competitiveness.* ECLAC. Available at: http://repositorio.cepal.org/bitstream/handle/11362/5056/S0700131_en.pdf?sequence=1 [Accessed: 13/12/14.]

McBoyle, G. and McBoyle, E. (2008) 'Distillery marketing and the visitor experience: a case study of Scottish malt whisky distilleries', *International Journal of Tourism Research*, 10 (1): 71–80.

McDonnell, A. and Hall, C.M. (2008) 'A framework for the evaluation of winery servicescapes: a New Zealand case', *Special Issue-Número Especial Turismo grastronómico y enoturismo Gastronomic and wine tourisme*, 6: 231.

McGehee, N.G. (2014) 'Volunteer tourism: evolution, issues and futures', *Journal of Sustainable Tourism*, 22 (6): 847–54.

McGehee, N.G. and Kim, K. (2004) 'Motivation for agri-tourism entrepreneurship', *Journal of Travel Research*, 43 (2): 161–70.

McGehee, N.G. and Santos, C.A. (2005) 'Social change, discourse and volunteer tourism', *Annals of Tourism Research*, 32 (3): 760–79.

McGovern, M. (2003) 'The cracked pint glass and the servant: the Irish pub, Irish identity and the tourist eye', in M. Cronin and B. O'Connor (eds), *Irish Tourism: Image, Culture and Identity.* Clevedon: Channel View, pp. 83–103.

McIntosh, A.J. and Bonnemann, S.M. (2006) 'Willing workers on organic farms (WWOOF): the alternative farm stay experience?', *Journal of Sustainable Tourism*, 14 (1): 82–99.

McKenna, J. and McKenna, S. (2010) *The Bridgestone Irish Food Guide (The Bridgestone Guides).* County Cork: Estragon Press.

McKercher, B., Ho, P. S., Cros, H.D., & So-Ming, B.C. (2002) 'Activities-based segmentation of the cultural tourism market', *Journal of Travel & Tourism Marketing*, 12(1): 23–46.

McKercher, B., Okumus, F. and Okumus, B. (2008) 'Food tourism as a viable market segment: it's all how you cook the numbers!', *Journal of Travel & Tourism Marketing*, 25 (2): 137–48.

Meethan, K. (2015) 'Making the difference: the experience economy and the future of regional food tourism', in I.Yeoman, U. McMahon-Beattie, K. Fields, J. Albrecht, and K. Meethan, K. (eds), *The Future of Food Tourism. Foodies, Experiences, Exclusivity, Visions and Political Capital.* Bristol: Channel View Publications, pp. 114–26.

Meler, M. and Cerović, Z. (2003) 'Food marketing in the function of tourist product development', *British Food Journal*, 105 (3): 175–92.

Meuter, M.L., Ostrom, A.L., Roundtree, R.I. and Bitner, M.J. (2000) 'Self-service technologies: understanding customer satisfaction with technology-based service encounters', *Journal of Marketing*, 64 (3): 50–64.

Meyer-Cech, K. (2003) 'Food trails in Austria', in C.M. Hall, L. Sharples, R. Mitchell, N. Macionis and B. Cambourne (eds), *Food Tourism Around the World: Development, Management, and Markets.* Oxford: Butterworth Heinemann, pp. 149–57.

Meyer-Cech, K. (2005) Regional Cooperation in Regional Theme Trails, in D. Hall, I. Kirkpatrick and M. Mitchell (eds), *Rural Tourism and Sustainable Business.* Bristol: Channel View Publications, pp. 137–148.

Michaelidou, N. and Hassan, L.M. (2010) 'Modeling the factors affecting rural consumers' purchase of organic and free-range produce: A case study of consumers from the Island of Arran in Scotland, UK', *Food Policy*, 35 (2): 130–9.

Middleton, V.T. and Clarke, J.R. (2001) *Marketing in Travel and Tourism*. Oxford: Butterworth-Heinemann.

Miguéns, J., Baggio, R. and Costa, C. (2008) 'Social media and tourism destinations: TripAdvisor case study', *Advances in Tourism Research*, 26 (28): 26–8.

Ministry of Tourism, Arts and Culture Republic of Maldives (2013) *Tourism Yearbook 2013*. Male: Ministry of Tourism, Arts and Culture.

Mintel (2009) *Gastronomic Tourism – International – May 2009*. Mintel.

Mintz, S. (1996) *Tasting Food, Tasting Freedom: Excursions into Eating, Culture and the Past*. Boston: Beacon Press.

Mitchell, M.A. and Mitchell, S.J. (2001) 'Consumer experience tourism: a powerful tool for food and beverage producers', *Journal of Food Products Marketing*, 6 (3): 1–16.

Mitchell, R. and Hall, C.M. (2001) 'Lifestyle behaviours of New Zealand winery visitors: wine club activities, wine cellars and place of purchase', *International Journal of Wine Marketing*, 13 (3): 82–93.

Mitchell, R. and Hall, C.M. (2003) 'Consuming tourists', in C.M. Hall, L. Sharples, R. Mitchell, N. Macionis and B. Cambourne (eds), *Food Tourism Around the World: Development, Management and Markets*. Oxford: Butterworth-Heinemann, pp. 60–80.

Mitchell, R. and Scott, D. (2008) 'Farmers' markets as events for local cultural consumption: The Otago Farmers' Market (Dunedin, New Zealand) explored', in C.M. Hall and L. Sharples (eds), *Food and Wine Festivals and Events Around the World: Development, Management and Markets*. Oxford: Butterworth-Heinemann, pp. 286–99.

Mitchell, R., Hall, C. M. and McIntosh, A. (2000) 'Wine tourism and consumer behaviour', in C.M. Hall, L. Sharples, B. Cambourne and N. Macionis (eds) *Wine Tourism Around the World: Development, Management and Markets*. Oxford: Butterworth-Heinemann, pp. 115–135.

Mkono, M. (2012a) 'A netnographic examination of constructive authenticity in Victoria Falls tourist (restaurant) experiences', *International Journal of Hospitality Management*, 31 (2): 387–94.

Mkono, M. (2012b) 'Slow food versus fast food: a Zimbabwean case study of hotelier perspectives', *Tourism and Hospitality Research*, 12 (3): 147–54.

Molz, J.G. (2004) 'Tasting an imagined Thailand: authenticity and culinary tourism in Thai restaurants', in L. Long (ed.), *Culinary Tourism*. Lexington, KY: University Press of Kentucky, pp. 53–75.

Momsen, J.H. (1998) *Caribbean Tourism and Agriculture: New Linkages in the Global Era*. Lanham, MD: Rowman & Littlefield.

Montanari, A. and Staniscia, B. (2009) 'Culinary tourism as a tool for regional re-equilibrium', *European Planning Studies*, 17 (10): 1463–83.

Mooney, G. (2004) 'Cultural policy as urban transformation? Critical reflections on Glasgow, European City of Culture 1990', *Local Economy*, 19 (4): 327–40.

Morgan, K. (2000) *Slavery, Atlantic trade and the British economy, 1660–1800*. Cambridge: Cambridge University Press.

Morgan, N. and Pritchard, A. (2005) 'On souvenirs and metonymy: narratives of memory, metaphor and materiality', *Tourist Studies*, 5 (1): 29–53.

Morgan, N., Pritchard, A. and Pride, R. (2002) *Destination Branding: Creating the Unique Destination Proposition*. Oxford: Butterworth-Heinemann.

Morgan, W. (2006) *Why Sports Morally Matter*. London: Routledge.

Morpeth, N. (2001) 'The renaissance of cycle tourism'. In N. Douglas, N. Douglas & R. Derrett (eds), *Special Interest Tourism*. Sydney: John Wiley, pp. 212–229.

Morris, C. and Buller, H. (2003) 'The local food sector: a preliminary assessment of its form and impact in Gloucestershire', *British Food Journal*, 105 (8): 559–66.

Moscardo, G., Minihan, C. and O'Leary, J. (2015) 'Dimensions of the food tourism experience: building future scenarios', in I. Yeoman, U. McMahon-Beattie, K. Fields, J. Albrecht and K. Meethan (eds), *The Future of Food Tourism. Foodies, Experiences, Exclusivity, Visions and Political Capital*. Bristol: Channel View Publications, pp. 208–22.

Moscardo, G., Konovalov, E., Murphy, L. and McGehee, N. (2013) 'Mobilities, community well-being and sustainable tourism', *Journal of Sustainable Tourism*, 21 (4): 532–56.

Moskwa, E., Higgins-Desbiolles, F. and Gifford, S. (2015) 'Sustainability through food and conversation: the role of an entrepreneurial restaurateur in fostering engagement with sustainable development issues', *Journal of Sustainable Tourism*, 23 (1): 126–45.

Mossot, G. and Duvat, V. (2013) 'The establishment of a sustainable management policy for coastal foraging (Oléron, France)', in F. Pineda (ed.), *Tourism and the Environment*. Southampton: WIT Press, pp. 1–12.

Mulcahy, J.D. (2015) 'Future consumption: gastronomy and public policy', in I. Yeoman, U. McMahon-Beattie, K. Fields, J. Albrecht and K. Meethan (eds), *The Future of Food Tourism: Foodies, Experiences, Exclusivity, Visions and Political Capital*. Bristol: Channel View Publications, pp. 71–87.

Muñoz de Escalona, F. (2011) 'Asturian "cider culture" as an incentive for tourism', *Turismo y Desarrollo: Revista de Investigación en Turisme y Desarrollo Local*, 4 (11).

Munt, I. (1994) 'Eco-tourism or ego-tourism', *Race and Class*, 36 (1): 49–60.

Murdoch, J. and Miele, M. (1999) '"Back to nature": Changing "worlds of production" in the food sector', *Sociologia Ruralis*, 39 (4): 465–83.

Mustonen, P. (2006) 'Volunteer tourism: postmodern pilgrimage?' *Journal of Tourism and Cultural Change*, 3 (3): 160–77.

Nabhan, G.P. (2014) *Cumin, Camels, and Caravans: A Spice Odyssey*. Berkeley, CA: University of California Press.

Nabhan, G.P. (2009) *Coming Home to Eat: The Pleasures and Politics of Local Foods*. New York: W.W. Norton & Company.

Najovits, S. (2003) *Egypt, the Trunk of the Tree, Vol. II: A Modern Survey of and Ancient Land*. New York: Algora Publishing.

National Farmers' Retail and Markets Association (FARMA) (2006) *Sector Briefing: Farmers' Markets in the UK*, FARMA.

Neumayer, E. (2003) *Weak Versus Strong Sustainability: Exploring the Limits of Two Opposing Paradigms*. Cheltenham: Edward Elgar.

Nexus, C. and Urban, E. (2003) *Twin Rivers Farm-food and Wine Trail: A Success Story*. Bairnsdale, Victoria, Australia: East Gippsland Shire Council.

NFP (2002) *The National Fisheries Policy*. Kampala, Uganda: Uganda Ministry of Agriculture, Animal Husbandry and Fisheries.

Nielsen, B. and Green Restaurant Association (2004) *Dining Green: A Guide to Creating Environmentally Sustainable Restaurants and Kitchens*. Green Restaurant Association.

Nielsen, J. and Martin, R. (1996) Creation of a new fisheries policy in South Africa: the development process and achievements. Available at: http://citeseerx.ist.psu.edu/viewdoc/download?doi=10.1.1.198.2410&rep=rep1&type=pdf [Accessed: 20/09/15.]

Northern Ireland Tourist Board (2012) *Northern Ireland Tourism Statistics 2012*. Available from: www.detini.gov.uk/northern_ireland_tourism_statistics_2012-3.pdf [Accessed: 15/09/15.]

Novelli, M. (2005) *Niche Tourism: Contemporary Issues, Trends and Cases*. London: Routledge.

Nunkoo, R. and Ramkissoon, H. (2011) 'Developing a community support model for tourism', *Annals of Tourism Research*, 38 (3): 964–88.

Nützenadel, A. and Trentmann, F. (2008) *Food and Globalization: Consumption, Markets and Politics in the Modern World*. London: Berg.

Oakes, T. (1999) 'Eating the food of the ancestors: place, tradition, and tourism in a Chinese frontier river town', *Cultural Geographies*, 6 (2): 123–45.

Ohe, Y. (ed.) (2002) 'Evaluating household leisure behaviour of rural tourism in Japan', *International Congress, August 28–31, 2002, Zaragoza, Spain*. European Association of Agricultural Economists.

Ohe, Y. (2010) 'Evaluating integrated on-farm tourism activity after rural road inauguration: the case of pick-your-own fruit farming in Gunma, Japan', *Tourism Economics*, 16 (3): 731–53.

Okazaki, E. (2008) 'A community-based tourism model: its conception and use', *Journal of Sustainable Tourism*, 16 (5): 511–29.

Okumus, B., Okumus, F. and McKercher, B. (2007) 'Incorporating local and international cuisines in the marketing of tourism destinations: the cases of Hong Kong and Turkey', *Tourism Management*, 28 (1): 253–61.

Opio-Odongo, J. (2003) *Sustainable Development and the Millennium Development Goals – Obligation*. Nairobi: UNDP.

Organ, K., Koenig-Lewis, N., Palmer, A. and Probert, J. (2015) 'Festivals as agents for behaviour change: a study of food festival engagement and subsequent food choices', *Tourism Management*, 48 (1): 84–99.

Otnes, C.C. and Maclaren, P. (2007) 'The consumption of cultural heritage among a British royal family brand tribe', in R. Kozinets, B. Cova and A. Shanker (eds), *Consumer Tribes: Theory, Practice, and Prospects*. London: Elsevier/Butterworth-Heinemann.

Oxfam (2015) *Farmers, Shoppers and Businesses – who wins and who loses in the world's food market?* Available from: www.oxfam.org.uk/~/media/Files/Education/Resources/Explore%20Fairtrade/Fairtrade_presentation.ashx. [Accessed 21/02/16]

Pan, B., MacLaurin, T. and Crotts, J.C. (2007) 'Travel blogs and the implications for destination marketing', *Journal of Travel Research*, 46 (1): 35–45.

Pantzar, M. and Shove, E. (2005) 'Consumers, producers and practices: understanding the invention and reinvention of Nordic Walking', *Journal of Consumer Culture*, 5 (1): 43–64.

Payne, T. (2002) *US Farmers Markets – 2000. A Study of Emerging Trends*. United States Department of Agriculture, Washington DC: Agricultural Marketing Service.

Pearce, D.G. and Butler, R.W. (1993) *Tourism Research: Critiques and Challenges*. London: Routledge.

Pearce, P. (1998) 'Marketing and management trends in tourist attractions', *Asia Pacific Journal of Tourism Research*, 3 (1): 1–8.

Pearce, P.L. (1991) 'Analysing tourist attractions', *Journal of Tourism Studies*, 2 (1): 46–55.

People 1st (2011) *State of the Nation Report 2011*. London: People 1st. Available at: www.people1st.co.uk/research/state-of-the-nation-2011 [Accessed: 20/04/13.]

Peters, G.L. (1997) *American Winescapes: The Cultural Landscapes of America's Wine Country*. Boulder, CO: Westview Press/HarperCollins.

Petrini, C. (2007) 'Slow food', *The Architect, the Cook and Good Taste*. New York: Springer.

Pillay, M. and Rogerson, C.M. (2013) 'Agriculture-tourism linkages and pro-poor impacts: the accommodation sector of urban coastal KwaZulu-Natal, South Africa', *Applied Geography*, 1 (36): 49–58.

Pine, B.J. and Gilmore, J.H. (1998) 'Welcome to the experience economy', *Harvard Business Review*, 76: 97–105.

Pine, B.J. and Gilmore, J.H. (1999) *The Experience Economy: Work is Theatre & Every Business a Stage*. Cambridge, MA: Harvard Business Press.

Pizam, A. and Sussmann, S. (1995) 'Does nationality affect tourist behavior?' *Annals of Tourism Research*, 22 (4): 901–17.

Pliner, P. and Hobden, K. (1992) 'Development of a scale to measure the trait of food neophobia in humans', *Appetite*, 19 (2): 105–20.

Plog, S. (1974) 'Why destination areas rise and fall in popularity', *The Cornell Hotel and Restaurant Administration Quarterly* 14(4):55–58.

Plummer, R., Telfer, D. and Hashimoto, A. (2006) 'The rise and fall of the Waterloo–Wellington Ale Trail: a study of collaboration within the tourism industry', *Current Issues in Tourism*, 9 (3): 191.

Plummer, R., Telfer, D., Hashimoto, A. and Summers, R. (2005) 'Beer tourism in Canada along the Waterloo–Wellington ale trail', *Tourism Management*, 26 (3): 447–58.

Poon, A. (1993) *Tourism, Technology and Competitive Strategies*. Wallingford, Oxford: CABI international.

Porter, M.E.(2011 [1985]) *The Competitive Advantage of Nations*. New York: Simon and Schuster.

Porter, M.E. and Kramer, M.R. (2006) 'The link between competitive advantage and corporate social responsibility', *Harvard Business Review*, 84 (12): 78–92.

Powell, H. and Prasad, S. (2010) '"As Seen on TV." The celebrity expert: how taste is shaped by lifestyle media', *Cultural Politics*, 6 (1): 111–24.

Prahalad, C.K. and Ramaswamy, V. (2004) 'Co-creating unique value with customers', *Strategy & Leadership*, 32 (3): 4–9.

Pratt, J. (2002) *Pilgrimage to the Holy Land of Tea, Imperial Tea Court/China Tea Tour Essay*. Online essay available at: www.imperialtea.com/tea/tours [Accessed 03/12/13.]

Pratt, M. (2011) *Profiling Wine Tourists, More Than Just Demographics*. 6th AWBR International Conference, Bordeaux Management School 9–10 June 2011.

Prebensen, N.K. and Foss, L. (2011) 'Coping and co-creating in tourist experiences', *International Journal of Tourism Research*, 13 (1): 54–67.

Presenza, A., Minguzzi, A. and Petrillo, C. (2010) 'Managing wine tourism in Italy', *Journal of Tourism Consumption and Practice Volume,2* (1): 46–61.

Preston-Whyte, R. (2000) 'Wine routes in South Africa', in C.M. Hall, L. Sharples, B. Cambourne and N. Macionis (eds), *Wine Tourism Around the World: Development, Management and Markets*. Oxford: Butterworth-Heinemann, pp. 103–14.

Pretty J. (2002). Agri-Culture: *Reconnecting People, Land and Nature*. London: Earthscan.

Pretty, J.N., Ball, A.S., Lang, T. and Morison, J.I. (2005) 'Farm costs and food miles: an assessment of the full cost of the UK weekly food basket', *Food Policy*, 30 (1): 1–19.

Pretty, J., Sutherland, W.J., Ashby, J., Auburn, J., Baulcombe, D., Bell, M., Bentley, J., Bickersteth, S., Brown, K. and Burke, J. (2010) 'The top 100 questions of importance to the future of global agriculture', *International Journal of Agricultural Sustainability*, 8 (4): 219–36.

Pringle, H. (1998) 'The slow birth of agriculture', *Science*, 282 (5393): 1446.

Pritchard, A. (ed.) (2007) *Tourism and Gender: Embodiment, Sensuality and Experience*. Wallingford, Oxford: CABI.

Putnam, R.D. (1995) 'Bowling alone: America's declining social capital', *Journal of Democracy*, 6 (1): 65–78.

Qazi, J.A. and Selfa, T.L. (2005) 'The politics of building alternative agro-food networks in the belly of agro-industry', *Food, Culture & Society: An International Journal of Multidisciplinary Research*, 8 (1): 45–72.

Quan, S. and Wang, N. (2004) 'Towards a structural model of the tourist experience: an illustration from food experiences in tourism', *Tourism Management*, 25 (3): 297–305.

Raymond, C. (2007) 'Creative tourism New Zealand: the practical challenges of developing creative tourism', in G. Richards and J. Wilson (eds), *Tourism, Creativity and Development*. London: Routledge, pp. 145–57.

Red Tractor (2015) *Red Tractor Assurance*. Available at: www.redtractor.org.uk. [Accessed 13/12/15.]

Reinsch, N. L., and Lynn, M. L. (1990) 'Diversification patterns among small businesses', *Journal of Small Business Management*, 28 (4): 60–70.

Renko, S., Renko, N. and Polonijo, T. (2010) 'Understanding the role of food in rural tourism development in a recovering economy', *Journal of Food Products Marketing*, 16 (3): 309–24.

Renting, H., Marsden, T.K. and Banks, J. (2003) 'Understanding alternative food networks: exploring the role of short food supply chains in rural development', *Environment and Planning A*, 35 (3): 393–412.

Reynolds, P.C. (1993) 'Food and tourism: towards an understanding of sustainable culture', *Journal of Sustainable Tourism*, 1 (1): 48–54.

Richards, G. (ed.) (1996) *Cultural tourism in Europe*. Wallingford: Cabi.

Richards, G. (2002) 'Gastronomy: an essential ingredient in tourism production and consumption', in A. Hjalager and G. Richards (eds), *Tourism and Gastronomy*. London: Routledge, pp. 2–20.

Richards, G. (2007) *Cultural Tourism: Global and Local Perspectives*. London: Routledge.

Richards, G. (2011a) 'Creativity and tourism: the state of the art', *Annals of Tourism Research*, 38 (4): 1225–53.

Richards, G. (2011b) 'Tourism development trajectories: from culture to creativity?' *Tourism & Management Studies*, (6): 9–15.

Richards, G., and Hall, D. (2003). *Tourism and Sustainable Community Development* (Vol. 7). London: Psychology Press.

Richards, G. and Wilson, J. (2006) 'Developing creativity in tourist experiences: a solution to the serial reproduction of culture?', *Tourism Management*, 27 (6): 1209–23.

Richards, G. and Wilson, J. (2007) 'The creative turn in regeneration: creative spaces, spectacles and tourism in cities', *Tourism, Culture and Regeneration*. Wallingford, Oxford: *CABI*, pp. 12–24.

Ritzer, G. (1993) *The McDonaldisation of Society: An Investigation into the Changing Character of Contemporary Social Life*. Thousand Oaks, CA: Pine Forge Press.

Ritzer, G. (2009) *McDonaldization: The Reader*. Thousand Oaks, CA: Pine Forge Press.

Robertson, R. (1994) 'Globalisation or glocalisation?' *Journal of International Communication*, 1 (1): 33–52.

Robertson, R. (2001) 'Globalization theory 2000+: major problematics', in G. Ritzer and B. Smart (eds), *Handbook of Social Theory*. London: SAGE, pp. 458–71.

Robinson, J. (1994) 'Tourism', in J. Robinson (ed.), *The Oxford Companion to Wine*. Oxford: Oxford University Press, pp. 980–1.

Roininen, K., Arvola, A. and Lähteenmäki, L. (2006) 'Exploring consumers' perceptions of local food with two different qualitative techniques: laddering and word association', *Food Quality and Preference*, 17 (1): 20–30.

Rojek, C. (1995) *Decentring Leisure*. London: SAGE.

Rojek, C. and Urry, J. (1997) *Touring Cultures*. London: Taylor & Francis (Routledge).

Ron, A. S. and Timothy, D. J. (2013) 'The land of milk and honey: biblical foods, heritage and Holy Land tourism', *Journal of Heritage Tourism*, 8(2–3): 234–247.

Rong-Da Liang, A., Chen, S. C., Tung, W., and Hu, C. C. (2013) 'The iInfluence of food expenditure on tourist response to festival tourism: expenditure perspective', *International Journal of Hospitality & Tourism Administration*, 14(4): 377–397.

Rosen, D.E. and Purinton, E. (2004) 'Website design: viewing the web as a cognitive landscape', *Journal of Business Research*, 57 (7): 787–94.

Rosenfeld, S.A. (1997) 'Bringing business clusters into the mainstream of economic development', *European Planning Studies*, 5 (1): 3–23.

Roth, M. (ed.) (1999) *Overview of Farm Direct Marketing Industry Trends*. Agricultural Outlook Forum 1999. Presented: Monday, 22 February. Available at: http://ageconsearch.umn.edu/bitstream/32905/1/fo99ro01.pdf [Accessed: 04/03/14.]

Rotherham, I.D., Hall, C. and Sharples, L. (2008) 'From haggis to high table: a selective history of festivals and feasts as mirrors of British landscapes and culture', *Food and Wine Festivals and Events around the World*, pp. 47–62.

Rusher, K. (2003) 'The Bluff Oyster Festival and regional economic development: festivals as culture commodified', in C.M. Hall, L. Sharples, R. Mitchell, N. Macionis, and B. Cambourne (eds), *Food Tourism Around the World: Development, Management and Markets*. Oxford: Butterworth Heinemann, pp. 192–205.

Russell, J.A. and Ward, L.M. (1982) 'Environmental psychology', *Annual Review of Psychology*, 33 (1): 651–89.

Ryan, C. (2003) *Recreational Tourism: Demand and Impacts*. Bristol: Channel View Publications.

Sage, C. (2003) 'Social embeddedness and relations of regard: alternative 'good food' networks in south-west Ireland', *Journal of Rural Studies*, 19 (1): 47–60.

Said, E. (1978) *Orientalism: Western Representations of the Orient*. New York: Pantheon.

Sandbrook, C. (2010) 'Local economic impact of different forms of nature-based tourism', *Conservation Letters*, 3 (1): 21–8.

Sassatelli, R. and Davolio, F. (2010) 'Consumption, pleasure and politics: Slow Food and the politico-aesthetic problematization of food', *Journal of Consumer Culture*, 10 (2): 202–32.

Saunders, C., Barber, A. and Taylor, G. (2006) *Food Miles – Comparative Energy/Emissions Performance of New Zealand's Agriculture Industry*. Lincoln University: Agribusiness and Economics Research Unit.

Sayer, A. (1992) *Method in Social Science: A Realist Approach*. Abingdon: Routledge.

Scalza, R. (2012) *Tours and festivals Showcase Canada's Delicious Wild edibles*. Available at: http://en.destinationcanada.com/content/travel_story_ideas/adventures-foraging [Accessed 11/12/15.]

Scambler, G. (2005) *Sport and Society: History, Power and Culture*. New York: McGraw-Hill Education.

Scandic Hotels (2015). Available at: www.scandichotelsgroup.com/en/sustainability. [Accessed 03/12/15.]

Scarpato, R. (2002) 'Sustainable gastronomy as a tourist product', in A.M. Hjalager. and G. Richards (eds), *Tourism and Gastronomy*. London: Routledge, pp. 132–52.

Schärer, M.R. (1996) 'Museology: the exhibited man/thing relationship: a new museological experiment', *Museum Management and Curatorship*, 15 (1): 9–20.

Schärer, M. (1987) 'A museum exhibition on food. a new alimentarium in Vevey, Switzerland', *Museum* 155: 145–51.

Schegg, R. and Fux, M. (2010) 'A comparative analysis of content in traditional survey versus hotel review websites', *Information and Communication Technologies in Tourism 2010*, pp. 429–40.

Scheyvens, R. (2011) 'The challenge of sustainable tourism development in the Maldives: understanding the social and political dimensions of sustainability', *Asia Pacific Viewpoint*, 52 (2): 148–64.

Schlecht, N.E. (2013) *Frommer's Peru*. New York: John Wiley & Sons.

Schlosser, E. (2012) *Fast Food Nation: The Dark Side of the All-American Meal*. London: Penguin.

Schultz, H., and Jones Yang, D. (1997). *Pour your Heart into it: How Starbucks Built a Company One Cup at a Time*. New York: Hyperion.

Scotch Whisky Association (2011) *Whisky Tourism Gives Economy Massive Boost*. Available at: http://www.scotchmaltwhisky.co.uk/scotchwhiskytourism.htm [Accessed 11/11/14.]

Scott, D. (2013) 'Food foraging the next travel trend in Australia, says gastronomic tourism expert David Scott', *Daily Telegraph (Australia)* 24 October 2013.

Seaman, C., Quinn, B., Björk, P. and Kauppinen-Räisänen, H. (2014) 'Culinary-gastronomic tourism – a search for local food experiences', *Nutrition & Food Science,* 44 (4): 294–309.

Seo, S., Yun, N. and Kim, O.Y. (2014) 'Destination food image and intention to eat destination foods: a view from Korea', *Current Issues in Tourism*(in press), 1–22. DOI: 10.1080/13683500.2014.934210.

Shalleck, J. (1972). *Tea*. London: Viking.

Sharples, A.E. (2003) 'Cider and the marketing of the tourism experience in Somerset, England: Three case studies', *Journal of Travel & Tourism Marketing,* 14 (3–4): 49–60.

Sharples, L. (2002) 'Wine tourism in Chile. A brave new step for a brave new worlds', *International Journal of Wine Marketing*, 14 (2): 43–53.

Sharples, L. (2003a) 'The world of cookery-school holidays', in C.M. Hall, L. Sharples, R. Mitchell, N. Macionis and B. Cambourne (eds), *Food Tourism Around the World: Development, Management and Markets*. Oxford: Butterworth-Heinemann, pp. 102–20.

Sharples, L. (2003b) 'Food tourism in the Peak District National Park, England', in C.M. Hall, L. Sharples, R. Mitchell, N. Macionis and B. Cambourne (eds), *Food Tourism Around the World: Development, Management and Markets*. Oxford: Butterworth-Heinemann, pp. 206–227.

Sharpley, R. and Vass, A. (2006) 'Tourism, farming and diversification: an attitudinal study', *Tourism Management*, 27 (5): 1040–52.

Shaw, G. and Williams, A.M. (2004) *Tourism and Tourism Spaces*. London: SAGE.

Shaw, G.B. (2000 [1903]) *Man and Superman*. London: Penguin.

Shaw, K. (2008) 'Gentrification: what it is, why it is, and what can be done about it', *Geography Compass*, 2 (5): 1–32.

Sheller, M. (2003) *Consuming the Caribbean: From Arawaks to Zombies*. London: Psychology Press.

Sheller, M. and Urry, J. (2004) *Tourism Mobilities: Places to Play, Places in Play*. London: Routledge.

Shelton, A. (1990) 'A theater for eating, looking, and thinking: the restaurant as symbolic space', *Sociological Spectrum*, 10 (4): 507–26.

Shultz, C. J., Burkink, T. J., Grbac, B., and Renko, N. (2005) 'When policies and marketing systems explode: an assessment of food marketing in the war-ravaged Balkans and implications for recovery, sustainable peace, and prosperity', *Journal of Public Policy & Marketing*, 24(1): 24–37.

Sidali, K.L., Kastenholz, E. and Bianchi, R. (2013) 'Food tourism, niche markets and products in rural tourism: combining the intimacy model and the experience economy as a rural development strategy', *Journal of Sustainable Tourism* , 23 (8–9): pp. 1179–1197.

Sigala, M., Christou, E. and Gretzel, U. (eds) (2012) *Social Media in Travel, Tourism and Hospitality: Theory, Practice and Cases*. Farnham: Ashgate Publishing.

Silkes, C.A. (2012) 'Farmers' markets: a case for culinary tourism', *Journal of Culinary Science & Technology*, 10 (4): 326–36.

Simchi-Levi, D., Kaminsky, P. and Simchi-Levi, E. (2004a) *Managing the Supply Chain: The Definitive Guide for the Business Professional*. London: McGraw-Hill.

Simchi-Levi, D., Simchi-Levi, E. and Watson, M. (2004b) 'Tactical planning for reinventing the supply chain', in T.P. Harrison, H.L. Lee and J.J. Neale (eds), *The Practice of Supply Chain Management: Where Theory and Application Converge*. Boston, MA: Kluwer Academic Publishers, pp. 13–30.

Sims, R. (2009) 'Food, place and authenticity: local food and the sustainable tourism experience', *Journal of Sustainable Tourism*, 17 (3): 321–36.

Sims, R. (2010) 'Putting place on the menu: the negotiation of locality in UK food tourism, from production to consumption', *Journal of Rural Studies*, 26 (2): 105–15.

Site Remarkables du Gout (2015) *Les Chemins du Goût*. Available at: www.sites remarquablesdugout.com/tourisme-gout/pages/fr/carte-produit_5.htm [Accessed 15/12/15.]

Slocum, S. and Everett, S. (2014) 'Industry, government, and community: power and leadership in a resource constrained DMO', *Tourism Review*, 69 (1): 47–58.

Smith, A. and Hall, C.M. (2003) 'Restaurants and local food in New Zealand', in C.M. Hall, L. Sharples, R. Mitchell, N. Macionis and B. Cambourne (eds), *Food Tourism Around The World: Development, Management and Markets*. Oxford: Butterworth-Heinemann, pp. 248–68.

Smith, N. and Williams, P. (2013) *Gentrification of the City*. London: Routledge.

Smith, S. and Costello, C. (2009) 'Segmenting visitors to a culinary event: motivations, travel behavior, and expenditures', *Journal of Hospitality Marketing & Management*, 18 (1): 44–67.

Smith, S.L. and Xiao, H. (2008) 'Culinary tourism supply chains: a preliminary examination', *Journal of Travel Research*, 46 (3): 289–99.

Son, A. and Xu, H. (2013) 'Religious food as a tourism attraction: the roles of Buddhist temple food in Western tourist experience', *Journal of Heritage Tourism*, 8 (2–3): 248–58.

Spielmann, N., Laroche, M. and Borges, A. (2012) 'How service seasons the experience: measuring hospitality servicescapes', *International Journal of Hospitality Management*, 31 (2): 360–8.

Spilková, J. and Fialová, D. (2013) 'Culinary tourism packages and regional brands in Czechia', *Tourism Geographies*, 15 (2): 177–97.

Spracklen, K. (2009) *The Meaning and Purpose of Leisure*. Basingstoke: Palgrave Macmillan.

Spracklen, K. (2011) 'Dreaming of drams: authenticity in Scottish whisky tourism as an expression of unresolved Habermasian rationalities', *Leisure Studies*, 30 (1): 99–116.

Spracklen, K. (2013) 'Respectable drinkers, sensible drinking, serious leisure: single-malt whisky enthusiasts and the moral panic of irresponsible Others', *Contemporary Social Science*, 8 (1): 46–57.

Spracklen, K., Laurencic, J. and Kenyon, A. (2013) ' "Mine's a Pint of Bitter": performativity, gender, class and representations of authenticity in real-ale tourism', *Tourist Studies*, 13 (3): 304–21.

Sri Lanka Ecotourism Foundation (SLEF) (2015) *Vision, Mission and Goals of Sri Lanka Ecotourism Foundsation 1998–2012*. Available at: www.ecotourismsrilanka.net [Accessed 06/12/15.]

Standing, C., & Vasudavan, T. (2000) 'The impact of Internet on travel industry in Australia', *Tourism Recreation Research*, 25(3): 45–54.

Statista (2014) Advertising spending of the prepared foods industry in the United States in 2013, by medium (in thousand U.S. dollars). Available at: www.statista.com/statistics/317663/prepared-foods-ad-spend-medium [Accessed 11/11/14.]

Stanley, J. and Stanley, L. (2015) *Food Tourism: A Practical Marketing Guide*. Oxford: CABI.

Standing, C. and Vasudavan, T. (2000) 'The impact of Internet on travel industry in Australia', *Tourism Recreation Research*, 25 (3): 45–54.

Stebbins, R.A. (1982) 'Serious leisure: A conceptual statement', *Sociological Perspectives*, 25 (2): 251–72.

Stebbins, R.A. (2007) *Serious Leisure: A Perspective For Our Time*. Piscataway, NJ: Transaction Publishers.

Stebbins, R.A. and Graham, M. (2004) *Volunteering as Leisure/Leisure as Volunteering: An International Assessment*. Wallingford, Oxford: CABI.

Stephenson, G.O., Lev, L. and Brewer, L.J. (2006) *When Things Don't Work: Some Insights into Why Farmers' Markets Close*. Special Report 1073. Oregon Small Farms Technical Report No. 25. Oregon: Oregon State University.

Stoddart, H. and Rogerson, C.M. (2004) 'Volunteer tourism: the case of habitat for humanity South Africa', *GeoJournal*, 60 (3): 311–18.

Stuart, D. (2008) 'The illusion of control: industrialized agriculture, nature, and food safety', *Agriculture and Human Values*, 25 (2): 177–81.

Swarbrooke, J. (2002) *The Development and Management of Visitor Attractions*. London: Routledge.

Swarbrooke, J. (2012) *Development and Management of Visitor Attractions*, 2nd edn. London: Routledge.

Swarbrooke, J., and Horner, S., (1999) *Consumer Behaviour in Tourism*. Oxford: Butterworth-Heinemann.

Tannahill, R. (1988) *Food in History*. New, fully revised and updated edition. London: Penguin.

Tapper, R. and Font, X. (2004) *Tourism Supply Chains*. Report of a desk research project for The Travel Foundation. Leeds Metropolitan University and Environment Business & Development Group, Leeds, UK.

Tarlow, P. (2003) 'Ideas for niche marketing', *e-Review of Tourism Research*, 1 (4).

Taylor, C. (1988) 'Various approaches to and definitions of creativity', in R.J. Sternberg (ed.), *The Nature of Creativity: Contemporary Psychological Perspectives*. Cambridge: Cambridge University Press, pp. 99–121.

Taylor, D.H. and Fearne, A. (2006) 'Towards a framework for improvement in the management of demand in agri-food supply chains', *Supply Chain Management: An International Journal*, 11 (5): 379–84.

Telegraph (2011) World's hottest chilli contest leaves two in hospital, 5 October. Available from: www.telegraph.co.uk/foodanddrink/foodanddrinknews/8808120/Worlds-hottest-chilli-contest-leaves-two-in-hospital.html. [Accessed 04/06/14].

Telegraph (2015) *The top 50 gastropubs in Great Britain 2015*. Available from: www.telegraph.co.uk/food-and-drink/pubs-and-bars/the-top-50-gastropubs-in-great-britain. / [Accessed 13/11/15]

Telfer, E. (1996) *Food for Thought: Philosophy and Food*. London: Routledge.

Telfer, D.J. (2000) 'Tastes of Niagara: building strategic alliances between tourism and agriculture', *International Journal of Hospitality & Tourism Administration*, 1 (1): 71–88.

Telfer, D.J. (2001) 'Strategic alliances along the Niagara wine route', *Tourism Management*, 22 (1): 21–30.

Telfer, D.J. and Wall, G. (1996) 'Linkages between tourism and food production', *Annals of Tourism Research*, 23 (3): 635–53.

Telfer, D.J. and Wall, G. (2000) 'Strengthening backward economic linkages: local food purchasing by three Indonesian hotels', *Tourism Geographies*, 2 (4): 421–47.

Terry, W. (2014) 'Solving labor problems and building capacity in sustainable agriculture through volunteer tourism', *Annals of Tourism Research*, 49: 94–107.

Thach, L. (2007) Trends in Wine Tourism. Discover the motivations of wine tourists and the challenges, benefits and trends in wine tourism. In *Wine Business Monthly* (August 2007). Available at: www.winebusiness.com/wbm/?go=getArticleSignIn&dataId=50125 [Accessed 12/04/14.]

Thicknesse, P. (1777) A year's journey through France, and part of Spain. Bath: R. Cruttwell. Available at: www.gutenberg.org/ebooks/16485?msg=welcome_stranger. [Accessed 20/02/16].

Thomas, H. (1997) *The Slave Trade: The Story of the Atlantic Slave Trade: 1440–1870.* New York: Simon and Schuster.

Thorn, J. and Segal, M. (2006) *The Coffee Companion: A Conoisseur's Guide.* Philadelphia, PA: Running Press.

Thornton, J. (1998) *Africa and Africans in the Making of the Atlantic World, 1400–1800.* Cambridge: Cambridge University Press.

Thrift, N. (1997) 'The still point: resistance, expressive embodiment and dance', in S. Pile and M. Keith (eds), *Geographies of Resistance.* London: Routledge, pp. 125–51.

Tikkanen, I. (2007) 'Maslow's hierarchy and food tourism in Finland: five cases', *British Food Journal*, 109 (9): 721–34.

Tilden, F. (1957) *Interpreting Our Heritage: Principles and Practices for Visitor Services in Parks, Museums, and Historic Places.* Chapel Hill, NC: University of North Carolina Press.

Timothy, D.J. (ed.) *Heritage Cuisines: Traditions, Identities and Tourism.* Abingdon: Routledge.

Timothy, D.J. and Boyd, S.W. (2015) *Tourism and Trails: Cultural, Ecological and Management Issues.* Bristol, UK: Channel View Publications.

Timothy, D.J. and Ron, A.S. (2013a) 'Heritage cuisines, regional identity and sustainable tourism', in C.M. Hall and S. Gossling (eds.), *Sustainable Culinary Systems: Local Foods, Innovation, and Tourism & Hospitality,* London: Routledge, pp. 275–90.

Timothy, D.J. and Ron, A.S. (2013b) 'Understanding heritage cuisines and tourism: identity, image, authenticity, and change', *Journal of Heritage Tourism*, 8 (2–3): 99–104.

Toffler, A. (1980) *The Third Wave.* New York: Bantam Books.

Tolkach, D. and King, B. (2015) 'Strengthening community-based tourism in a new resource-based island nation: Why and how?', *Tourism Management*, 48: 386–98.

Tomljenović, R. and Razović, M. (2009) 'Wine and sun and sea tourism: Fruitful relationship or impossible dream?' *Tourism*, 57 (4): 449–61.

Torres, R. (2002) 'Toward a better understanding of tourism and agriculture linkages in the Yucatan: tourist food consumption and preferences', *Tourism Geographies*, 4 (3): 282–306.

Torres, R. (2003) 'Linkages between tourism and agriculture in Mexico', *Annals of Tourism Research*, 30 (3): 546–66.

Torres, R. and Momsen, J.H. (2004) 'Challenges and potential for linking tourism and agriculture to achieve pro-poor tourism objectives', *Progress in Development Studies*, 4 (4): 294–318.

Tourism Concern (2014) *Working conditions in tourism*. Available at: www.tourismcon cern.org.uk/working-conditions-in-tourism/ [Accessed 12/02/15].

Tourism Concern (2015) *Volunteering*. Available at: http://tourismconcern.org.uk/volun-teer. [Accessed 03/06/15].

Trauer, B. (2006) 'Conceptualizing special interest tourism: frameworks for analysis', *Tourism Management*, 27 (2):183–200.

Trauer, B. and Ryan, C. (2005) 'Destination image, romance and place experience: an application of intimacy theory in tourism', *Tourism Management*, 26 (4): 481–91.

Tregear, A. (2003) 'From Stilton to Vimto: using food history to re-think typical products in rural development', *Sociologia Ruralis*, 43 (2): 91–107.

Tribe, J. (2010) *Strategy for Tourism.* Oxford: Goodfellow Publishers Limited.

Tseng, C., Wu, B., Morrison, A.M., Zhang, J. and Chen, Y. (2015) 'Travel blogs on China as a destination image formation agent: a qualitative analysis using Leximancer', *Tourism Management*, 46 (1): 347–58.

Turner, J. (2008) *Spice: The History of a Temptation.* London: Vintage.

Turner, R. (1993) 'Sustainability principles and practice', in R.K. Turner (ed.), *Sustainable Environmental Economics and Management.* London: Belhaven Press.

UK Government (2006) *The Food Hygiene (England) Regulations 2006.* London: The Stationery Office.

UNESCO (2006) *Towards Sustainable Strategies for Creative Tourism Discussion* Santa Fe, New Mexico, USA, 25–27 October 2006: Report of the Planning Meeting for 2008 International Conference on Creative Tourism.

UNESCO (2015) *Creative Cities network*. Available from: http://en.unesco.org/creative-cities/home. [Accessed 02/12/15].

United Nations (2015) *World Population Prospects The 2015 Revision Key Findings and Advance Tables (Department of Economic and Social Affairs of the United Nations Secretariat)*. Available from: http://esa.un.org/unpd/wpp/publications/files/key_find-ings_wpp_2015.pdf. [Accessed 21/02/16]

Urde, M., Greyser, S.A. and Balmer, J.M. (2007) 'Corporate brands with a heritage', *Journal of Brand Management*, 15 (1): 4–19.

United States Department of Agriculture (2015) *Promoting Local Food and Building Community*. Available at: www.usda.gov/wps/portal/usda/usdahome?navid=farmers market. [Accessed 05/06/15].

Urry, J. (1990a) 'The consumption of tourism', *Sociology*, 24 (1): 23–35.

Urry, J. (1990b) *The Tourist Gaze: Leisure and Travel in Contemporary Societies, Theory, Culture & Society*. London: SAGE.

Urry, J. (1995) *Consuming Places.* London: Psychology Press.

US Department of Agriculture (2008) *2008 Organic Production Survey.* Washington, DC: National Agricultural Statistics Service.

Uysal, M., Gahan, L. and Martin, B. (1993) 'An examination of event motivations: a case study', *Festival Management & Event Tourism*, 1 (1): 5–10.

Uzzell, D.L. (1989) *Heritage Interpretation.* London: Belhaven Press.

Van der Ploeg, J.D. and Renting, H. (2004) 'Behind the redux: a rejoinder to David Goodman', *Sociologia Ruralis*, 44(2): 233–242.

Van der Vorst, J. and Beulens, A.J. (2002) 'Identifying sources of uncertainty to gener-ate supply chain redesign strategies', *International Journal of Physical Distribution & Logistics Management*, 32 (6): 409–30.

Van Der Zee, D. and Van Der Vorst, J. (2005) 'A modeling framework for supply chain simulation: opportunities for improved decision making', *Decision Sciences*, 36 (1): 65–95.

Van Westering, J. (1999) 'Heritage and gastronomy: the pursuits of the "new tourist"', *International Journal of Heritage Studies*, 5 (2): 75–81.

Virginia Craft Brewers Guild (2015) Virginia Craft Brewers Guild. Available at: http://virginiacraftbrewers.org/default.aspx (Accessed 7/2/2015.)

Visit England (2015) *Afternoon Tea in England*. Available at: www.visitengland.com/things-to-do/afternoon-tea. [Accessed 21/02/16].

Visit Scotland (2011) *Scotland Visitor Survey 2011 and 2012*. Available at: www.visitscotland.org/pdf/External%20Visitor%20Survey.pdf [Accessed 03/05/13.]

Wakefield, K.L. and Blodgett, J.G. (1996) 'The effect of the servicescape on customers' behavioral intentions in leisure service settings', *Journal of Services Marketing*, 10 (6): 45–61.

Waldo, D. (1978) 'Organization theory: revisiting the elephant', *Public Administration Review*, 38 (6): 589–597.

Wan Hassan, W.M. and Awang, K.W. (2009) 'Halal food in New Zealand restaurants: an exploratory study', *International Journal of Economics and Management*, 3 (2): 385–402.

Wang, N. (1999) 'Rethinking authenticity in tourism experience', *Annals of Tourism Research*, 26 (2): 349–70.

Wang, Y. (2007) 'Customized authenticity begins at home', *Annals of Tourism Research*, 34 (3): 789–804.

Wang, Y. F. (2015) 'Development and validation of the green food and beverage literacy scale', *Asia Pacific Journal of Tourism Research*, 21 (1): 20–56.

Waters, M. (1995) *Globalization: Key Ideas.* London and New York: Routledge.

Watts, D.C., Ilbery, B. and Maye, D. (2005) 'Making reconnections in agro-food geography: alternative systems of food provision', *Progress in Human Geography*, 29 (1): 22–40.

Wearing, S. (2002) *Volunteer Tourism: Experiences That Make a Difference.* Wallingford, Oxford: CABI.

Wearing, S. (2004) 'Examining best practice in volunteer tourism', in R.A. Stebbins, and M. Graham (eds), *Volunteering as Leisure/Leisure as Volunteering: An International Assessment.* Wallingford: CABI, pp. 209–24.

Weaver, D. (2007) 'Towards sustainable mass tourism: paradigm shift or paradigm nudge?' *Tourism Recreation Research*, 32 (3): 65–9.

Weber, M. (1969/1919) 'Science as a vocation', in H. H. Gerth, and M. C. Wright (eds), *From Max Weber: Essays in Sociology.* London: Routledge, pp. 129–58.

Webb, D. (2002) 'Investigating the structure of visitor experiences in the Little Sandy Desert, Western Australia', *Journal of Ecotourism*, 1 (2–3): 149–61.

Wedel, M. and Kamakura, W.A. (2002) 'Introduction to the special issue on market segmentation', *International Journal of Research in Marketing*, 19 (1): 181–3.

Weiler, B. and Hall, C.M. (1992) *Special Interest Tourism.* London: Belhaven Press.

Wheeller, B. (1994) 'Egotourism, sustainable tourism and the environment: A symbiotic, symbolic or shambolic relationship?' in A.V. Seaton (ed.), *Tourism: The State of The Art.* Chichester: Wiley, pp. 647–54.

Whittlesea, E.R. and Owen, A. (2012) 'Towards a low carbon future–the development and application of REAP Tourism, a destination footprint and scenario tool', *Journal of Sustainable Tourism*, 20 (6): 845–65.

Williams, C. and Ferguson, M. (2005) 'Biting the hand that feeds: the marginalisation of tourism and leisure industry providers in times of agricultural crisis', *Current Issues in Tourism*, 8 (2–3): 155–64.

Williams, E. (1994) *Capitalism and Slavery.* Chapel Hill, NC: University of North Carolina Press.

Williams, E. (2013) 'Food museums', in K. Albala (ed.), *Routledge International Handbook of Food Studies.* Abingdon: Routledge.

Williams, H.A., Williams Jr, R.L. and Omar, M. (2014) 'Experiencing the experience: an examination of the significance of infrastructure, co-creation and co-branding within the transnational gastronomic tourism industry', *Transnational Marketing Journal*, 2 (1): 21–37.

Williams, P. (2001) 'Positioning wine tourism destinations: an image analysis', *International Journal of Wine Marketing*, 13 (3): 42–58.

Wilson, T.L. (2003) 'Tasty selections: an evaluation of gourmet food magazines', *Journal of Agricultural & Food Information*, 5 (2): 49–66.

Wilson, T.M. (2006) *Drinking Cultures.* New York: Berg.

Wolf, E. (2006) *Culinary Tourism: The Hidden Harvest.* Dubuque, IA: Kendall/Hunt Publishing Company.

Wolf, M.M., Spittler, A. and Ahern, J. (2005) 'A profile of farmers' market consumers and the perceived advantages of produce sold at farmers' markets', *Journal of Food Distribution Research*, 36 (1): 192–201.

Wood, N. T., and Muñoz, C. L. (2007). 'No rules, just right'or is it? The role of themed restaurants as cultural ambassadors'. *Tourism and Hospitality Research*, 7(3–4): 242–255.

World Commission on Environment and Development (WCED) (1987) *Our Common Future, Report of the World Commission on Environment and Development.* Available at: www.un-documents.net/our-common-future.pdf. [Accessed: 20/09/15.]

World Food Travel Association (WFTA) (2015) (previously known as the International Culinary Tourism Association) *Uniting Food and Tourism.* Available at: http://world foodtravel.org. [Accessed 09/04/15].

World Tourism Organisation (UNWTO) (2001) *World Tourism Vision 2020.* Madrid: World Tourist Organisation.

World Tourism Organisation (UNWTO) (2015) *UNWTO Annual Report 2014.* Available at: http://www2.unwto.org [Accessed 09/09/15.]

World Travel Market (2008) *Fiona Jeffery, Group Exhibition Director of World Travel Market.* Available at: www.wtmlondon.com/World Travel & Tourism [Accessed 05/03/10.]

World Travel & Tourism Council (WTTC) (2014) *Economic Impact Maldives 2014.* London: WTC. Available at: www.wttc.org/-/media/files/reports/economic%20impact%20research/country%20reports/maldives2014.pdf [Accessed: 14/09/15.]

World Travel & Tourism Council (WTTC) (2015), *Economic Impact Analysis.* Available at: www.wttc.org/research/economic-research/economic-impact-analysis/regional-reports [Accessed: 05/12/15.]

Worldtravelguide (2005) *Does voluntourism do more harm than good?* Available at: www.worldtravelguide.net/holidays/editorial-feature/voluntourism-should-i-volunteer-abroad. [Accessed 03/06/15].

Wu, D. and Cheung, S. (2002) *The Globalization of Chinese Food.* London: Routledge.

Xiang, Z. and Gretzel, U. (2010) 'Role of social media in online travel information search', *Tourism Management*, 31 (2): 179–88.

Xie, P.F., Osumare, H. and Ibrahim, A. (2007) 'Gazing the hood: hip-hop as tourism attraction', *Tourism Management*, 28 (2): 452–60.

Yeoh, D., 12 March (2013). 'A guide to Ipoh''s best food', *New Straits Times,* 12 March.

Yeoman, I. and McMahon-Beattie, U. (2015) 'The future of food tourism: the Star Trek replicator and exclusivity', in I. Yeoman, U. McMahon-Beattie, K. Fields, J. Albrecht and K. Meethan (eds), *The Future of Food Tourism. Foodies, Experiences, Exclusivity,*

Visions and Political Capital. Bristol: Channel View Publications, Chapter 3, pp. 23–45.

Yeoman, I., McMahon-Beattie, U., Fields, K., Albrecht, J. and Meethan, K. (eds) (2015) *The Future of Food Tourism. Foodies, Experiences, Exclusivity, Visions and Political Capital.* Bristol: Channel View Publications.

Yuan, Z. (2013) 'Dynamic effects and development tendency of coupling between rural tourism industry and big agriculture (English)', *Tourism Tribune*, 28 (5): 80–8.

Yurtseven, H.R. (2011) 'Sustainable gastronomic tourism in Gokceada (Imbros): local and authentic perspectives', *International Journal of Humanities and Social Science*, 1(18): 27–36.

Yurtseven, H.R. and Karakas, N. (2013) 'Creating a sustainable gastronomic destination: the case of Cittaslow Gokceada – Turkey', *American International Journal of Contemporary Research*, 3 (3): 91–100.

Zhang, X., Song, H. and Huang, G.Q. (2009) 'Tourism supply chain management: a new research agenda', *Tourism Management*, 30 (3): 345–58.

Zhao, W., Ritchie, J.B. and Echtner, C.M. (2011) 'Social capital and tourism entrepreneurship', *Annals of Tourism Research*, 38 (4): 1570–93.

Zhu, Y. (2012) 'Performing heritage: rethinking authenticity in tourism', *Annals of Tourism Research*, 39 (3): 1495–513.

Zukin, S. (2010) *Landscapes of Power: From Detroit to Disney World.* Berkeley: University of California Press.

INDEX

Page numbers in italics indicate images.